Life in and against
the Odds

Heidi Hoechst

Life in and against the Odds

Debts of Freedom and the Speculative Roots of U.S. Culture

TEMPLE UNIVERSITY PRESS
Philadelphia • Rome • Tokyo

TEMPLE UNIVERSITY PRESS
Philadelphia, Pennsylvania 19122
www.temple.edu/tempress

Front cover: May Day 2005, "Where Do We Go from Here?" In the Heart of the
Beast Puppet and Mask Theatre, Powderhorn Park, Minneapolis, Minnesota
(May 8, 2005)

> Enacting the process of disarmament, Uncle Sam's suit cracked open, leaving
> a naked man fallen to the earth listening to the pain of the casualties caused
> by the U.S. war in Iraq. Shedding weapons and skin into the earth, the nation's
> bones washed away into the oneness of all beings, re-membered through an
> enactment of a new pledge of interdependence: "*I pledge allegiance to the body
> of the earth; and all the beings who dwell together. As one, In diversity, With
> liberty and justice for all.*"

—CEREMONY ARTISTS: SANDY SPIELER,
JULIE BOADA, JIM KOPLIN, CHRIS LUTTER, AND ESTHER OURAY

Library of Congress Cataloging-in-Publication Data

Hoechst, Heidi, 1977–
   Life in and against the odds : debts of freedom and the speculative roots of U.S.
culture / Heidi Hoechst.
      pages cm
   Includes bibliographical references and index.
   ISBN 978-1-4399-1217-1 (hardback) — ISBN 978-1-4399-1218-8 (paper) —
ISBN 978-1-4399-1219-5 (e-book)   1. Equality—United States—History.
2. Nationalism—United States—History.   3. Speculation—United States—
History.   4. Capitalism—Moral and ethical aspects—United States.
5. Democracy—United States.   6. United States—Economic conditions.
7. United States—Social conditions.   I. Title.
   HN90.S6H64 2015
   305.50973—dc23

                                                                    2015013700

♾ The paper used in this publication meets the requirements of the American
National Standard for Information Sciences—Permanence of Paper for Printed
Library Materials, ANSI Z39.48-1992

Printed in the United States of America

9 8 7 6 5 4 3 2 1

Contents

Recognitions and Gratitude

An unanticipated fortune of having been circulated and displaced through various sites of intellectual exchange over the past decade and a half has been learning and thinking with a number of creative and dedicated groups and people who are committed to antiracist critical transformation. The gifts of collective wisdom run much deeper than the acronyms can adequately relay. My hopes for justice and present-tense freedom have been informed by NOW FREE: New Orleans Writers' Fierce Research Engendering Emancipation, Critical Resistance Oakland, Critical Resistance New Orleans, and a broad movement of anti–prison industrial complex activists and intersectional antiracist solidarity movements that are dedicated to the principled struggle of working in coalitions. I have learned so much about life, freedom, justice, and collective transformation from the Greater New Orleans Organizers' Roundtable (GNOORT); the Orleans Parish Prison Reform Coalition (OPPRC); Californians for a Responsible Budget (CURB); Starfish and Coffee; Asylum, the School of Unlimited Learning (SOUL) of the University of California, Santa Barbara; the Futures of American Studies Institute; my students in classrooms of various sorts who have collaborated in creative visionary dialogue; and artists like those at In the Heart of the Beast Puppet and Mask Theatre who create opportunities for poetically reenvisioning the world every day. For the way that all of these formations have expanded my horizons and called on me to think, act, and dream vividly in ways that intentionally stretch the boundaries of what we imagine is politically and economically possible, I am deeply honored and grateful.

So long as the predatory form of financialized capitalism remains at the helm of the global economy and so long as the nonprofit industrial complex overdetermines the terms under which culture is produced, cultural workers count on generous support in order to continue creating. Love of art, parades, puppets, protest, and theater is a fulfilling aspect of cultural backing, but love alone does not pay the rent. *Spirit House*, which is discussed in Chapter 5, remains in the holdings of the Greater New Orleans Fair Housing Action Center; it could be commissioned by contacting the writers. In 2014, In the Heart of the Beast Puppet and Mask Theatre faced financial distress that they continue to work through. Readers of this text might consider helping to prolong the life of the theater's work, which is discussed in Chapter 6, by making a monetary donation at www.hobt.org. In an experiment to disentangle activism from the nonprofit sector, Critical Resistance depends primarily on a donor base to support the grassroots activism of its national volunteer membership. Donations to www.criticalresistance.org can be a form of dreaming wildly in support of campaigns that aspire to build a world beyond cages, policing, and the (in)security state. The content of this book is of my own creation and has not been endorsed by any of these artists or groups. It is simply because my thinking has been shaped largely by my encounters and engagement with these cultural and visionary workers that I encourage others to lend them support.

This project has been sustained as well by collectivities and institutions that are still purely imaginary, but that have nevertheless marked my horizon for envisioning future life and freedom beyond the entrapments of racialized national capitalism. Although emancipatory spaces like the Center for Historical Accountability and Just Futures, the Inside Outside School for a Critical Commons, and the Institute for Post-institutionalized American Studies are only ideas that have not yet been realized in physical space, these institutional imaginings have been important resource hubs out of and toward which this project has been developed. Institutions that currently do exist in material form also created opportunities for pursuing this work. I am thankful for the library support, collections, and archival assistance of the Minnesota Historical Society, the Beinecke Rare Book and Manuscript Library, the Bancroft Library, and the Amistad Research Center. An Andrew W. Mellon Postdoctoral Fellowship in "History across the Disciplines," a California Cultures in Comparative Perspective research grant from the University of California, and a Bancroft Library research grant empowered me with funding to access the invaluable resources retained in these spaces.

People matter, too. The list is partial and the links are incomplete, yet in the denouement of unintentional forgetting and dreaming wildly, special gratitude is owed to Micah Kleit, editor-in-chief, and Temple University Press for taking a chance on this book. I am also thankful for the careful attention given to the work by anonymous readers whose insightful suggestions helped to transform an unwieldy journey across time and space into an organized engagement with the high-stakes intersection of cultural formation and speculative capitalism. It is a profound privilege to work with a press with the conscientious foresight to hold space for research that is guided by hopes that scholarship can contribute in some small way toward healing and transforming the divisions and cumulative injustices caused by centuries of racialized speculative capitalism.

And, of course, my appreciation for the widely dispersed cadre of writing crews, creative co-conspirators, colleagues, and comrades with whom I have been lucky to coordinate runs through and between multiple geographic axes.

In the South: Catherine Michna, Kate Kokontis, Gahiji Barrow, Geryll Robinson, Moon Charania, Red Tremmel, T. R. Johnson, Nancy Maveety, Isa Murdock-Hinrichs, Samuel Mark Anderson, Rachel Carrico, Rachel Lee, Helen Regis, Davina Allen, Pam Nath, Wendi O'Neal, Danny Ashby, Tara Echo, Micah Conkling, Mary Ellen Stitt, Margaret Tully, Jessica Wheeler, Desiree Evans, Monique Harden, and many, many others.

In the East: Alan Nadal, Elena Glasberg, Kate McCullough, Shelley Feldman, Jane Juffers, Sherry Martin, Tamar Carroll, Breawna Eaton, and participants in the Andrew W. Mellon seminar "History across the Disciplines" at Cornell University.

In the West: Clyde Woods, Eileen Boris, Barbara Tomlinson, Cedric Robinson, Eve Darian-Smith, James Kyung-Jin Lee, Julie Carlson, Jordan Camp, Tomás Carrasco, Damien Snyder, William Calvo, Felice Blake, Paula Ionide, Kathy Murray, Neda Atanasoski, Chris Guzaitis, Emily Cheng, to name a few.

In the North: Jeannie Piekos, Sandy Spieler, Susan Bernardin, Paula O'Loughlin, and my stalwart companions in revelry, Linda, Roger, Stacy, Kirsten, and Bailey Hoechst; Karin, Karlan, and Kiliahna Scruggs; and Alia Roca Lezra.

The original seeds for this project were planted as a dissertation under the cultivation of George Lipsitz, Nicole Tonkovich, Shelley Streeby, Michael Davidson, Camille Forbes, Benetta Jules-Rosette, and Jack Halberstam in the very early stages. I cannot understate how honored and continually inspired I have been to work under the mentorship, scholarly guidance, and activist intellectual examples of George Lipsitz and Nicole Tonkovich. George's ethical dedication to bridging scholarship with action and his principled demonstration of rigorous political and theoretical grounded engagement in antiracist world remaking has been critical for this work and its author. George encouraged me early on to live according to the principle that political analysis cannot and should not end on the written page, but rather begins as only one part of any political project that cannot be carried forward without engagement in collective action; analysis is simply a path to action, and action also encompasses how we live and negotiate and create pathways to freedom in the encounters that shape every single day. That George opened the field of American Studies up to me as a foundation from which to understand how the past is structured into present circumstances—both in the injuries it carries and in the possibilities of freedom it has yet to release—has been an incredible gift. Without this inherited wisdom, it is not clear whether I would have found the courage that it takes to break conventions in order to focus this life on work and struggles that are beholden to collective liberation, oppressed people's self-determination, and striving to meet people's still unfulfilled needs. Collective struggle, of course, happens regardless of what any piece of research can offer, but I am grateful for the opportunity to contribute what little I can in the spirit of honoring and learning how to live from the freedom dreams of the many.

This book, therefore, is dedicated to the idea and action of living freedom now. To the noncompliant daily radicals who exercise liberation, compassion, and generosity despite too many constraints and injustices, to the Bartlebys and the Mutineers, to the dreamers and the world remakers who walk beside us every day, to those who tread lightly and others who shout loudly in unpredictable and unseen ways, to the wisdom of those who refuse to accept that our possibilities for the future are limited to the horizon set by neoliberal racialized capitalism, I extend my deepest appreciation.

Life in and against the Odds

Introduction

Life in and against the Odds:
Racialized Risk, Debts of Freedom, and the
Speculative Roots of U.S. Culture

Speculative Nationalism

The situation is acute. And the odds can seem insurmountable. Ours is an historical phase defined by the power of economic adulation to effectuate human devastation. In this era, markets operate such that the benefits of speculation land in the bank accounts of the few while risk is collectivized and endured by the many. Under these conditions of severe economic and social inequality, the hands of the majority will never directly enter the major financial markets that now more than ever give shape to the world. When life is punctuated by repeated crises, people who pay a disproportionate price for investments that are designed against them become broken down and down and out. Many are left without a hope, and things fall apart. Not taking care of what holds people together has long-term consequences for collective liberation.

Freedom, the human capacity to reconfigure social relations and resources into life-affirming justice, is plagued by the incommensurable contradictions of a so-called democratic nation that operates in stealth in accordance with the economic protocols of racialized capitalism. The current era of relentless crisis after perpetual crisis is an expression of a long historical pattern of speculative nationalism: a cultural-economic arrangement through which fantastical promises of future political-economic rewards become a means of broad social dispossession. Speculative nationalism is the co-constitutive relationship between liberal nationalism and racialized capitalism that is expressed as a cultural promise of the nation-state form.

Speculative nationalism describes the way that national culture is systematically mobilized as a vehicle for racializing risk in volatile bubble economies.

Speculative nationalism is the process through which promises of plural democracy in the United States become economic instruments for capitalist predation. In this process, people's lived struggles to enact and demand diverse forms of freedom are appropriated into nationalist figurations, transmogrified through myth and optimism, brought into alignment with nationalist fictions, and then deferred as promises of freedoms yet to come. Speculative nationalism is the name for a form of cultural deferral that constitutes democracy as an anticipatory event. It is a mechanism of socioeconomic reproduction that answers people's insistent needs for freedom and justice now with future promises of liberal rights later.

Speculative nationalism thus describes a deeply historical chain of cultural-economic transactions through which people's lived struggles to demand present-tense freedom are systematically deferred to a nationalist culture of liberal futurity. In the exchange, future freedom becomes a placeholder for prolonging and preserving severely unequal racializing economic structures. Speculative nationalism suggests that the legal-political-cultural container that we often assume was created with the express intention of guaranteeing human emancipation—the United States nation-state form—serves as a fundamental racializing instrument for capitalist market expansion. The challenge to democracy that speculative nationalism implies is not simply the failure of the U.S. nation-state to live up to its ideals and potential; it is that nationalist promises themselves create and contribute to the problems of inequality and injustice that they purport to resolve.

U.S. nationalist promises of freedom—universalist assurances of life, liberty, and the right to seek happiness and fulfillment—are belied when their guarantor leads the world in human incarceration, charges the most for the lowest-quality health care among Western nations, bails out banks while evicting home owners, fails schools by privatizing cities, and exacts its authority as a global leader in a state of amnesia about its own ongoing state of colonial occupation. The sellout of public well-being in each of these cases is underwritten by investment opportunities in speculative markets. When financial investors deliberate risk in precarious markets that contribute to prison expansion, predatory home loans, the turnover of public schools to charters, for-profit hospitals, and other predatory economies, they focus primarily on potential monetary gains and losses.[1] When systematically racialized people are forced into untenable social conditions because they are disproportionately positioned by history and ongoing economic injustice to absorb this same risk, private investments become matters of life and death; when economic risk is leveraged on social inequality, poor people's ability to live generatively through life-affirming relations is too often wagered away by weak infrastructures that embolden financiers to accumulate profits.

Financial investors do not always recognize that, when the losses of speculative investments are compensated through social divestment, life for many becomes an act of death defiance. An affective result of this situation is that financial investors proudly claim rights to a bounty while equality and freedom come to look improbable and otherworldly for millions of others. The forces of history and everyday violence make ascendancy into new power relations urgently necessary while seemingly unlikely. Probability in practice is stacked in the interest of profits and power, but for everyone else the promise of freedom seems to smolder into nothing more than a collective pipe dream. And yet the odds are shattered daily by people's dedication to transformative action.

Against the odds, 30,000 people who are confined in California state cages—whose chief organizers are held in long-term solitary confinement—somehow coordinate a hunger strike demanding humane standards of living. These imprisoned peaceful resisters broaden the potential of human solidarity by leveraging five basic demands on a pact to end interracial hostilities both inside and outside the prison regime.[2]

Against the odds, hundreds of home owners in sorted-out cities fight foreclosures with petitions, occupation, eviction brigades, and self-organized collective cleanups of forcefully abandoned houses, and through their actions somehow intervene against bank-organized community asset stripping. Foreclosure resisters point to the neighborhood value of inhabiting houses and refuse to let bank evictions and property desertion infuse their communities with compounded distress and increased instability.[3]

Against the odds, indigenous people engaged in a land struggle unite across borders in a movement for coexistence and mutual respect and somehow divert a corporate campaign for extreme energy extraction that is slated to push pipelines through sacred tribal land. Activists unite around a global understanding of interdependence and somehow create conditions in which oil companies are scrambling to locate sites and legitimacy for their destructive proposals. Indigenous activists wage their struggle on reminders that sovereign land rights predate nation-states, that national boundaries are a fiction of history and circumstance, and that obscure neoliberal contracts are designed around promises that will, like those of the past, become future touchstones on a much longer trail of broken treaties.[4]

Against the odds, people who live in crisis-struck cities fight against shock doctrine economics and somehow challenge the privatizing movement to sell out every last bit of the public good to the "benevolent" predation of charter schools, nonprofit entrepreneurs, and charity capitalism.[5] Dominant modes of misrepresentation suggest that the city that was once New Orleans is now fully destroyed, yet people claim rights to memory and history by recognizing in their daily encounters that, although the future has changed, the past still remains. They congregate in streets named Desire and Music while reaching for redemption in playful processions. Against the odds of being systematically sold out, folks pound the pavement with their diasporic feet and somehow relocalize the terms of shared struggle in every beat.[6]

Against the odds, people everywhere refuse the fallacy of ineffectuality and trust in their creative ability to reshape the odds and somehow, in so doing against all likelihood, claim the right to fulfillment. They invest in affirmative relationships, and they gamble on the collective will to insist on infrastructures that are conducive to those hard to define *somethings* we call freedom and life.

Somehow people live on in the face of speculative contradictions. Somehow people continue to imagine a world of justice against the odds of a deck that has been stacked against them. This is a book about that somehow. It is an homage and a hunt for creative acts of noncompliance. It is a search for the ties, needs, dreams, and ingenuity that empower people to live in and against the odds of speculative nationalism. This book asks *how* the will to create and enact freedom against the imperial and captivating force of liberal promises is buried in speculative exchange networks. And it investigates *where* people's determination to defy the logic of anticipation erupts along the long chain of history that binds U.S. nationalism to speculative capitalism.

Revolutionizing the Odds

That people somehow insist on freedom in a nation that is fixated on pursuing economic growth at the expense of common existence is a telling indicator of the particularity of the odds that we are currently up against. The odds we now face are a new configuration of a much older pattern, the contours of which are defined by a deeply embedded national system of disproportionate risk and rewards. In the advanced phase of capital's deep imbrication with the nation-state form, extreme financialization readily tends toward predatory speculation.[7] This period of crisis, however, is in large part an elaboration of a much deeper historical condition: a patterned propagation of imaginative and material optimistic circumstances through which national culture emerged as an economic vehicle for capital's spatial expansion.

The long historical view offered in this book is intended to serve as a reminder that the fiction of inevitability is a recurring theme of acquisitive growth. Ineffectuality, as it responds to this trope, is a sentiment of crisis. It is an emotive reaction to untenable conditions, a subtle modality for breaking the collective will of oppressed people to resist unjust distributions of resources and power. The idea that beating the odds is an unlikely possibility is the negotiating strategy of capital's arrangement with nationalism. It is not a story that people have accepted without creative noncompliance and collective oppositional struggle.

The social risk of economic panics is that in periods of recovery the pressure to buy into myths and promises comes to seem like the only resource some people have for dealing with highly caustic life and death circumstances. The collateral damage of survivalist myopia is that, when people buy into the idea that there is no alternative, the revolutionary capacity of their shared and yet to be fostered dreams are subsumed into the distortions of market extremes. The U.S. nationalist reaction to contemporary crises has been a prolonged commitment to austerity and failed imagination. Having cut institutions, resources, and the public will for a better life from the body politic, the continued call to invest in the promise of the nation-state form also slashes from debate political visions for alternative freedoms. Rather than banking on social well-being, people tend to live in and against the daily consequences of an economy that speculates against the common good. At an abstract remove from the social consequences, financiers transform and corrupt basic social institutions by turning prisons, homes, hospitals, and schools into calculated opportunities for financial investment. Under the logic of too big to jail, the state redefines itself as "Lender of Last Resort," persuading the citizenry that people's only hope is to absorb Wall Street's losses. Backed by the dollars and authority of neoclassical economism, politicians suggest that there is no recourse against banks that are too big to fail and too powerful to punish. They draw on the fierce call of nationalism to make promises that public participation in this injustice will one day be compensated with economic recovery in an undisclosed future. They imply that with this recovery the nation's emancipatory potential will one day rise again. These familiar nationalist stories are powerful enablers of economic repression. Promises are agents of pecuniary punishment against people who neither anticipated nor participated in creating the financial hazard they now absorb.

The everyday actions of people whose lives are made, destroyed, and reconfigured under the systemic violence of a nation that is rooted in the fantastical futurity of speculative capitalism reveal the vulnerabilities of a nation-state that perpetually sacrifices the freedoms of the many to the profits of a few. Inevitability, improbability, and the idea of no choice are racializing abstractions of a speculative scheme. During the nineteenth century, White investors were legally endowed with the capacity to racialize risk through relations of force. At that time, it was possible for White businessmen to mitigate risk through abuse of enslaved people and incredible thefts of occupied land. In the present era, these relations of force have been reconfigured as risk and transformed into contracts as debt obligations.

The differential construction of human life embedded in the notion of debt creates the conditions under which investors are able to profit from prisons, plunder properties, pillage health, and loot from the future. The idea that people who are systematically oppressed somehow owe something to those who wield power and privilege has been the foundation of centuries of speculative bubbles and panics. It is the cultural foundation that enables the nation-state to maintain a progressive approach to democracy in which the universalism of freedom is systematically deferred and denied. The concept of "not yet" freedom is more than what makes U.S. democracy an incomplete project—it *is* the cultural trope that binds nationalism to the optimistic futurity of speculative capitalism. From the intrusion of nineteenth-century markets into the North American commons through the Wall Street–created twenty-first-century housing bubble, economic growth in the United States has fundamentally depended on culture to racialize and repudiate U.S. liberal nationalism's grounding on speculative risk.

The affective drive of speculative structures—*optimism, panic, aspiration, and longing*—is forged through interpersonal relationships in which distributions of power and profits are made in bargains related to time and space. The nation-state's capacity for speculative expansion has depended on its ability to hierarchically bind diverse people's hope for love and freedom to a fantasy of economic uplift. We may think of this fantasy as the American Dream, but we do not always consider how this dream has been balanced on a national promise of "not yet" freedom. People positioned to absorb the damages and destruction of capitalism in the United States often live under a contingent cultural contract of future freedom that is both political and personal. It is a mode of filtering desire into hegemonic expectations that comes through misappropriation of aggrieved people's struggles. National culture transforms people's struggles for democratic participation into anticipatory promises of equality and inclusion that are rarely realized in the present tense.

This book will take a journey across centuries of struggle to ask questions about how to revolutionize these odds. It will document why the descendants of people who were enslaved and colonized often end up at the tail end of many bad deals when they invest in national promises of egalitarian democracy. Inheritors of social injustice rarely enter speculative systems with the timing and resources of nationalism's historical benefactors. In the day-to-day operations of capitalist economies in the United States, people do not always recognize that the opportunity to benefit from the unfortunate timing of others is an outcome of the material processes of conquest and enslavement. But in tracing this privilege back through the unwieldy circulatory system of capitalism's imbrication with nationalism, the dustbin of history produces a wide array of outlets for disordering grassroots relationships with the potential to undo nationalism's bondage to speculative capitalism. To make good on bad histories it is important to recognize and register people's will to live in and against the odds of speculative capitalism. Creative acts of noncompliance and life-affirming social alternatives to nationalist exclusion are also useful resources for discovering how to pick and break neoliberal economism's seemingly impenetrable locks.

The contemporary era of rapid-fire economic crises intensifies the urgency for mobilizing responses to speculative capitalism that refuse to capitulate to the challenge of improbability. *Life in and against the Odds* offers a cultural map into the history of speculative capitalism in the United States, paying careful attention to how culture mitigates potentially radical disruptions of oppressive political-economic systems that rob people of lived democracy and meaningful justice. Life in the United States is and has been lived within and beyond the creative reach and cultural pull of affluent nationalism's speculative lust. People's ability to live in and against the odds of speculative predation—

their consistent efforts to dream and live freedom despite nationalism's systematic deferral of justice and equality to an undisclosed future—point to a radical indigestion in the belly of the beast. Most speculative exchanges, be they economic or political, are underwritten by subtle acts of defiance. Speculative futures are shaped in practice through competing claims on economic and social justice that call on us to live in the present with an insistence that freedom is something we need to live now.

Refusable Pasts

Speculation is more than the economic driver that has advanced and upset the notion of American progress since the nineteenth century; it is also the root and origin of nationalist visions of universal democracy. The vehicles of identification and appropriation that U.S. Americans are taught to relate to as national culture—literature, national parks, performances, parades—were often imagined and produced in speculative contexts where they functioned to negotiate shifting social relations. Familiar stories about what it means to be and belong in U.S. culture have been inscribed both figuratively and literally into the landscape of history through speculative processes. It can be no coincidence that many of the most revered and mundane traditions, images, icons, and precepts of U.S. nationalist culture emerged during periods of heightened economic speculation. The disorienting effects of bubbles and panics create contexts that leave people struggling to make sense of how the world works and where they fit in. A cultural impact of speculation is thus the tendency to create occasions in which seemingly coherent narratives of U.S. nationalism are clarified and solidified. However, U.S. culture is both a result of speculative disordering and an economic instrument because the narrative impulse to create stability out of volatility is fundamentally tied to the distribution and withholding of resources and justice. As a consequence, the collective cultural subconscious and proprioceptive experience of life on the national stage are largely oriented around speculative logics.

Speculative risk is how the very ideas of place, personhood, and power have been shaped and reconfigured in the United States. Under the speculative proposition of "not yet" freedom, the presumed lines between persons and things, objects and subjects, becomes even more blurry. Lives are made and unmade in the exchange. People win and people lose. These economic claims about the volatility of speculative markets are also rhetorical and cultural artifacts of the legacies that continue to stack the economic and social deck in the interest of people who inherit the material and cultural rewards of well-positioned sellers. Rewards of privileged inheritance do not come cheap. They extend from a pattern of cultural collusion—a nationalist script of "not yet" freedom—that has empowered speculative nationalists to offset challenges to their privileged positions.

This book reads U.S. history through the intimate webs that tie the inheritance of privilege to the cumulative racializing consequences of speculative economic exchange. In so doing, it disentangles fraught transactions between U.S. culture and economy in which alienated subjects become intimately enmeshed, antagonistic actors become interdependent, people become objects, objects become subjects, and things are never as clear as a single sale might suggest.

The economic structure of speculation is defined by the networked interconnection of highly intimate exchanges. Every speculative purchase is a double sale that takes place via a three-party transaction. One of these sales takes shape as an immediate exchange of money. A buyer pays a seller an agreed on price for a particular object. Simultaneously, however, a second sale takes place at the point of purchase in the mind of the speculative buyer. This secondary sale occurs in the imaginary realm of the future, where the buyer hopes the purchase can be resold elsewhere or later for a profit. Both sales are made through a minimum three-party negotiation. Part and parcel of every double negotiation between buyers and sellers is the life of the object at the center of the exchange.

Certainly buyers and sellers win and lose, but what of the object or commodity that is being exchanged? How does it figure in both the physical and imaginative transactions of a speculative trade? This book aims to investigate these questions. Each chapter presents a case study of a particular phase in nationalism's speculative adjustment. As a whole, these episodes reveal a pattern in capitalism's cultural history of leveraging unequal expansion on an elaborate race-making system of social disadvantage. In opposition to this historically interconnected process, the chapters look to the human lives that are subsumed in the production of commodities. The dialectical interchange between buyers and objects demonstrates that when "objects" are configured as the refusal of humanity, they do and must resist.

The abstraction that makes interconnected human relations seem separate and antagonistic in general economic relations are radically rearticulated under speculative circumstances. Historical materialism argues that social stratification is the cause of alienation in part because the commodity form makes relations between people look like relations between people and things. In the Marxian tradition, alienation is an estrangement from humanity that results from living in a classed society. Rather than associate with our material interdependence, the commodity form obscures the human actions and social organizations that contribute to the making of a commodity. We see the food that sustains us in a supermarket, for example, but not the millions of hands, ideas, and exchanges leading to the point of purchase.

Speculative commodities do not simply mask and obscure underlying human relations; they contain lives that have been taken and traded directly, often against the will of those lives. Because speculative nationalism originated in economies where land was stolen from people and people were traded as objects, every speculative exchange carries in it the human consequences of transforming life and livelihoods into tradable objects.

In the United States, most speculative investments are joined in a long chain of exchanges that can be traced to acts of human violation. Every speculative exchange that extends from this legacy, which, as this book argues, is most of the transactions that contribute to crises, assumes the risk of "objects" that invariably can and do resist. Lives traded as values unpredictably live on even after they have been denied and delayed. Through revolutionary resistance or subtle acts of noncompliance, people caught in the middle of trade insert third-party potential into every scene of exchange. In the tripartite negotiation of a single double sale, some people sell, some buy, and others change the terms of the exchange through poetic acts of life-affirming freedom by living toward justice and claiming freedom not in a far off future but in the playful art of living right now.

It can be no coincidence that we speak about people who have been socially and politically excluded from the rights and privileges of U.S. citizenship using the language of devaluation. The tenuous status between object and subject that this term implies is a carryover of speculative economies predicated on the power to mark people and their livelihoods with the violence of a price. The "values" through which an object became exchangeable, in this regard, were a weapon of mass dehumanization. We now often refer to people whose ancestry is haunted by lives and livelihoods marked as commodities for economic exchange as socially devalued. It is no surprise that the concept of valuation and human worth carries with it the specter of market categorization and implies a not yet full personhood that remains integral to speculative economies in the present. Although the descendants of slavery and conquest have been politically reclassified into a subjective status in the United States, with every speculative recurrence this ancestry carries over as a cumulative consequence of historical inheritance. In the present era, the ongoing forces of slavery and genocide are hidden in the concept of individual risk.

Cultural promissory notes of "not yet" freedom turn racialized risks into speculative advantages. Speculative nationalism promises an egalitarian transformation in which those who may have once been exchanged as resistant objects are asked to become explicit buyers and sellers. In this regard, nationalist promises of future freedom are race-making transactions in which lives once seen as objects by speculative investors are released from the status of commodity via anticipatory promises. The expectation of this contractual freedom is that subjects who were once objects will become buyers who might one day become sellers in an expanding marketplace. This could mean buying into the fantasies of a progressively expanding liberal democracy as well as buying into the trap of perpetual capitalist growth. In either case, the unsustainable imperative to expand benefits from the gradual "not yet" freedom of the national promise.

Deferral creates and prolongs asymmetrical distribution of opportunities and resources. It produces the necessary inequalities in time and location as preconditions for speculative predation and exchange. Systemic violence, unfulfilled promises, and foreclosed alternative freedoms are part and parcel of speculative nationalism, which balances on the idea that the consequences of a nation built on slavery and conquest, the residual effects we now call race, can one day be rectified and eventually overcome through the very system that created these conditions. Speculative nationalism also balances on the material expectation that racialized inequality will never disappear.

Life in and against the Odds seeks to make sense of the long historical system of interlocking power and denial through which freedoms deferred in one context become the fodder for crisis in another. It does so by locating *refusable pasts* in the speculative logics of racialized liberal capitalism. Refuse is an object and an action. It is both a noun and a verb. It might coalesce as a thing that acts against all probability. The noun *refuse* suggests actors, acts, and actions tossed into the dustbin of history. It indicates the stories and knowledge of disproportionate racial impact that liberal universality cannot afford to acknowledge. Refuse is thus the waste of devalued actions and dehumanized people whose stories have been systematically considered dispensable in nationalist systems of knowledge. Yet refusable pasts do not disappear. To refuse in the verb sense is to resist. Refused lives painfully, playfully, and persistently erupt against the grain of U.S. mythology. People's everyday efforts to negotiate capital's lived inequalities refuse sublimation. Refusals shape generative systems of struggle and knowledge. By highlighting the micropolitics of desire and uncertainty on which speculative nationalism emerges and circulates, *Life in and against the Odds* looks to refusable pasts for their potential in the reimagination of an antiracist world.

Gambling on Inequality

Periods of crisis make evident that individualized freedom and self-interest produce structural inequalities. In the euphoria of a bubble, needs and desires become atomized through economic activity. Social life, in the market view of the world, becomes an abstract realm of disconnected relations that mask how societies are susceptible to suffering caused by volatile economic interactions. Speculative fever seems to transform citizenship into market democratization, suggesting (per the logic of Adam Smith) that social accountability can be replaced by personal responsibility. Speculative economies are inherently divisive and atomistic because they balance on the notion that every buyer and seller is an equal party to be rewarded or punished for how they hedge their bets. The assumption that speculators act alone in the markets they make quickly disappears when options to cash in on investments run out.

We see during panics that speculative economies are vast networks of human interdependence. They are created through the acute dependence of buyers and sellers on differences of time, resources, and location to make profits. In speculative markets, every purchase, trade, sale, and investment has consequences for millions of others. But the risk of exchange is never spread evenly. Crises expose the collateral damage of routine economic behavior. They reveal the economic, social, and imaginative consequences of balancing economic growth on historical patterns of severe exploitation. In social life, we often recognize these difference as racial formations.

Taking economic advantage of historically aggrieved people's unfulfilled needs is costly for everyone in the long haul. Periods of crisis demonstrate the damage. Panics expose what can happen when people buy into the idea that economic activity is an individual liberty with no accountability to social relations. Economic collapses expose the violence of postured individualism. They show us that looking out only for "mine and ours" not only creates collateral damage for "them and theirs" but also returns as injuries to the self. Speculative thinking produces the conditions for collective undoing. Volatility and optimism are two sides of a single coin.

Speculative markets operate on optimism, and they deliver through predation. At the point of investment, speculation may look like throwing a wish into a purchase. It is both an economic exchange and an emotional yearning. Undergirding a buyers' confident acquisition is the speculative hope that, with limited labor and little foresight, a purchase will spin through an unpredictable series of exchanges, returning to the buyer as monetary wish fulfillment. What speculative buyers want is for their bets to pay off.

Speculation is not simply a desire to conjecture positive futures; it is also predicated on obscure dreams for inequality and injustice. This is because, at the heart of the gamble, what buyers need for their hopes to be realized are countless opportunities to procure wealth directly from other people. In the so-called normal operations of capitalist markets, this capacity is often regarded as an investor's aptitude for profiting without production. Lenders who profit from speculative circulation and exchange make their money from systemic differences in the organization of social power, information, and resources.

Investors do not refer to their exploitation of differences in time, location, and socioeconomic opportunity as the structural dynamics through which race is produced. Instead, they use the abstract language of economic parity to name these differences "interest" and "capital gains." In the abstract economic sense, interest is the income one earns from lending a sum of money. In practice, earning is not the outcome of labor and production; it is the result of a systemically produced opportunity for investors to advance "idle capital" to people without capital. A capital gain is imagined as the benefit of good timing, an investor's ability to earn money because of rising prices. Social stratification is interesting to investors because it creates the circumstances in which extending money into capital flows becomes possible. Investors expect that putting money into circulation will result in the return of more money. The face value of "more" is the result of rising prices and imposed costs such as fees and commissions. These costs are paid directly to the investor by people with less. In essence, this mode of earning is a form of direct appropriation. The investor assumes the money and dreams of people who enter economic relations without the same inherited privilege and opportunities of prior market entrants.

Class division makes this financial form of exploitation possible. An investment is never simply grounded in one person's desire for and pursuit of economic advancement. It is always part of a chain of relations within a broader economic system. In the case of speculative relations, exchange systems build confidence on the hopeful belief that successive buyers will pay higher prices to realize the initial buyer's dreams for dividends. Every buyer who makes a speculative bet gambles on the hope that somewhere across a network of exchanges another buyer will emerge who is willing (through desire or desperation) to pay more later for the very same object. Class division creates the conditions for this optimism because class inequality in capitalist systems often conditions how people who have been systematically exploited and oppressed participate in market exchange.

The constantly changing sameness of speculation marks different cycles of speculative capitalism with maddening repetitions of injustice. Racialized capitalism's endless return on the past disproportionately and cumulatively decreases the life chances of people who are the direct inheritors of the violence of enslavement, conquest, and nativism. Class violence is in part racialized in the United States because racialized groups continue to pay the economic and political debt of having been subjected to contracts of force and violence.

National culture often regards people who have been disadvantaged by capital's myriad expressions as unfortunate. It is not explicit about the ways in which misfortune, when shaped by group-differentiated vulnerability to structured inequality, has been historically constructed. The structural burden of history positions the descendants of violence to pay more for present purchases because their "late" entry into economic relations comes with the greater cost of price inflations and higher interest. Ongoing inequality often makes participation in "normal" economic relations more expensive for people who are born into little fortune. This is a burden that privileged investors often need and depend on as an unearned competitive advantage. In a speculative economy, class privilege expresses itself as the simple virtue of better timing. In historical terms, the good fortune of becoming buyers early on in a chain of exchange is the outcome of inheritance. The foundations of this inheritance are the speculative processes through which land, lives, and labor were stolen directly from millions of underprivileged others.

Speculative markets depend on the movement of what Marx called fictitious capital. Marx regarded as fiction the ownership of a value that does not exist. He theorized nonexistent value as shareholders' possession of the monetary equivalent of future returns. In the fictitious mode of ownership, the commodity, or object, is less important for its use and productive value than for its function as a carrier of expectant exchange value. At the point of future sale, in the best circumstances for the shareholder, this fiction is transformed into actual capital: another buyer pays out the fictional price that the shareholder expected as value. But at the point of sale—at the very instant when the fiction is materialized for the seller—capital is transferred once again as the fictitious possession of the new buyer. In this instance, the subsequent buyer takes ownership. When the driving purpose of this possession is to stake a claim on optimism, to take ownership of a value that does not yet exist, the exchange is a speculative one.

In Marx's formulation, fiction relates first and foremost to the anticipatory value linked to an object of exchange, which can be traced to the price an owner expects from its future sale. But the flow of fictitious capital also depends on another type of imagination—confidence, the invention of an optimistic fantasy that future sales will be possible. In bubble economies, this possibility balances tentatively on forward-looking faith in an endless chain of future buyers. The mechanism for realizing this fiction is not class division per se. Rather, as played out in the history of U.S. capitalism, speculative bubbles need to invent new buyers and invite them into the chain to maintain growth. In the United States, the creation of new buyers has consistently been tied to a racializing promise of national equality.

Racialized Risk

Risk, as it relates to the most affective articulation of capitalism in the United States, has been from the outset a racializing nationalist formation. Economic speculation, a shared social aspiration to gain monetary advantage from structural abstraction and market appreciation, has located both its source and its release valve in the cultural politics of human differentiation. Without a doubt, speculative markets are historically contingent economic practices that constantly transmogrify. In the United States, however, repeated episodes of speculative development are tied together by consistent race-making processes that are carried across diverse expressions of national culture.

Speculative nationalism is a system of racializing returns. When political and cultural beliefs in egalitarian democracy are not fortified with remedies for unjust economic conditions, they quickly become vehicles for prolonging inequality. This has been the case particularly during economic booms, when speculative fever often creates a climate of high spirits and high returns. The proliferation of excess resources and opportunities can make it seem as if general abundance will resolve class divisions. When that possibility is presented in the form of a promise to people who have been systematically excluded from full socioeconomic participation, however, it often comes with an ulterior motive. In the Ponzi view of speculative maintenance, for example, sustaining a bubble requires building the pyramid. Promises that link political possibilities with economic participation also turn people who have been excluded from society into a steady pool of potential buyers. When nationalist promises of future equality are effective in bringing new buyers into exchange economies, they create new opportunities for markets to grow. However, because formerly excluded buyers enter markets with delayed timing and from an out-sider position, their participation is hampered by differences in knowledge and resources. Ultimately, abstract promises of "equal" economic and political par-ticipation turn differences of inheritance and power into routine opportunities for earlier investors to exploit inequality as the normative practice of specula-tive exchange.

U.S. national culture encourages citizens to think of democracy not as a vehicle for speculative predation but as antithetical to economic exploitation. Nationalist histories of genocide and enslavement in the United States are a case in point. Imperial occupation and the theft of human life, nationalist culture explains, were the incredibly unfortunate outcomes of severely violent precapitalist economic pursuits. Primitive accumulation, some suggest, is a precursor to capitalist development that either has been or can eventually be outgrown through the progress of liberal democracy. Because nationalism is thus figured as a way to resolve the contradictions of capitalism, many well-intentioned democratic thinkers and social activists embrace liberal democ-racy as an antidote to severe marketization.

According to many of the staple progress narratives of U.S. national culture, multicultural democracy is the most practical and powerful political tool citizens have for rectifying the nation's grounding in violence. National progress narratives encourage citizens to assume that people whose viola-tion laid the groundwork of nation building can seek solace in the protective embrace of the liberal nation-state. This, too, is an affective economy, built on hopes of being regarded with the dignity of full personhood. Liberal rights and economic opportunities have been important resources for meeting unfulfilled human needs. However, they have not been sufficient for transforming the underlying contradictions that create and reproduce unfulfilled needs in the first place. Returning to the "source" is important for registering how history is transferred from the past to the future, for resisting recovery with transforma-tive remaking.

Speculative economies certainly expose the importance of regulation in capitalist societies. The basic capitalist growth imperative to expand and reproduce tends to become egregiously exploitative without rules and systems of containment. Abstract liberal equality, the notion that all people are equal under the law, does not always square up with day-to-day experiences of lived inequality. This is because U.S. national culture is not an alternative to capital-ist development but a functional corollary of capitalist economies.

Markets and politics work in tandem in the United States to propagate inequalities for economic expansion. This collaboration makes U.S. national-ism a speculative trope. In fact, U.S. nationalism aids and abets exploitation and capitalist innovation with its conceptual frameworks for human differenti-ation. Speculative markets depend on cultural legitimacy, which is created and reproduced via economic exchanges. Because expressive culture does not seem to have the same binding qualities as loan agreements or futures contracts, for example, we do not often think about the representational and affective dimensions of culture as economic formations. When scholars think about the relationship between culture and the economy, they tend to think about cultural objects as commodities.[8] Culture is registered as the products of creativity or perhaps as objects that we consume and exchange in webs of abstract values and meanings.

Markets are also made on myths of culture. Speculative economies are built on cultural formations that differentiate human value and valuelessness. These categories become the basis for making lethal patience a mechanism of deferral when there are constraints in capital flows. Thus, national culture is a representative system of conceptual exchanges through which people are given and denied personhood and value, and in this modality national cultural is an economic force.

Speculative contracts codify culture, hiding the way that profiting through exchange depends on variances in human valuation. Differences in personhood register economically as exploitable opportunities. Speculative bets prey on inequalities that are framed as mere differences in time and space. In the abstract sense, investors argue that markets proliferate on the basis of systemic dissimilarities in how resources and knowledge are organized, and that profitable disparities between seller and buyers are simply par for the course. The goal of a speculative exchange is to take advantage of these differences by finding a buyer who will pay more tomorrow for a purchase the seller has made today. Thus a speculative purchase, in its most basic form, is both the fulfillment of a seller's desire and the activation of a buyer's hope for a future exploitable opportunity. In this exchange, there is a perversely castigating aspect to any desire for redemption. At the point of purchase, a buyer may be aware of being exploited, but this awareness is contained by the buyer's hope to pay inequality forward. That is, speculative buyers hope for the chance to do to others what has been done to them, to directly appropriate the money and dreams of a future buyer who will pay higher prices. This makes speculation a system of contradictory fluctuation in which the remedy for inequality is to perpetuate future inequality.

The exploitation of speculative exchange does not look like exploitation in a productive economy. In productive arenas, exploitation can be measured in things like land expropriation, life appropriation, and labor exploitation. These direct, material forms of exploitation create lived inequalities. In the arena of exchange, however, these preexisting material imbalances create opportunities for secondary modes of exploitation: material inequalities caused by direct exploitation roll over into exchange relations as opportunities for a different kind of exploitation. In practice, this results in costs for those who enter the exchange system late in the game and function as the outlets through which previous buyers hedge bets for selling higher.

Through analysis of how racial ideas are reconfigured in relationship to speculative transitions, *Life in and against the Odds* argues that national culture fuels speculative economies by realigning oppressed people's freedom dreams with promises that prolong injustice and inequality. Anticipatory nationalist culture incorporates the heirs of racial injustice into a false democratic potential under expectant terms of eventual freedom, terms that are predicated on lived contingencies of subjugation and subordination. This uneven integration into abstract nationalist freedom is fundamentally an imbalanced contract of covert force. When U.S. national culture appropriates, mishears, and strategically misapprehends grassroots struggles to create egalitarian relationships, humane social conditions, and just economic systems, it rewrites freedom movements as debts of racial inheritance for aggrieved people to pay back. Culture thereby performs a central function in speculative regeneration because it normalizes and rationalizes freedom's deferral.

Much of U.S. national culture came into being as a patchwork of speculative recovery. The racial discourse of "not yet" freedom is speculative nationalism's reordering logic, a doctrine of not yet fulfilled promises and expectations that is circulated across time and place as a systematic telling and retelling of stories of national becoming and belonging. The nation's imbrication of racializing capitalism will not end with the fulfillment of promises because liberal abstraction maintains inequality. These unfulfilled promises are red flags of nationalism's intimate involvement in racializing economies.

The general assumption is that a market is speculative when prices and profits are untethered from the productive values of commodities during exchange. But this is only part of the equation. Economic bubbles and panics are emotional events. Bubbles are conditioned by interconnected hopes and fears. The pain of a crisis is felt in the present, but the roots of its injuries are held deeply in the past. At their heart, speculative panics are eruptions of the failed capacity to imagine and enact justice under the capitalist pursuit of self-interest. They are economic events, but they are also socially consequential moments of heightened cultural recovery. Although speculation is defined by future focus, speculative nationalism refuses social visions. Instead, it regenerates confidence in market practices that are built on dynamics of faith and fear.

In the United States, confidence, in both essence and practice, is a belief in supremacy expressed as a shared feeling, a hopeful conviction that people who have less will always want more or at least be convinced that they *should* want more. There is always a risk, however, that those with less will not want more or at least not in the way that speculators hope they will. People do enact and imagine life-affirming freedom and alternative economies in ways that do not align with the interests of capital. Yet speculative nationalism asks people who structurally inherit the imbalances caused by nativism, genocide, slavery, and exploitation to misrecognize the roots of nationalist freedom. Confidence, in this regard, is a race-making transaction. It is a belief carried by the benefactors of the nation's speculative origins that people who have inherited the violence of nationalist development can be convinced to buy into the nation's unrealized promises of democratic freedom. Economically, this is not a belief that comes from a political ethos for justice and equality; it is an advantageous temporal construction that investors depend on to hedge bets. The delayed script of national incorporation generates race as an economic category to absorb risk with exploitable human differentials.

Promises and principles of universal human equality, liberation, freedom, sustainability, happiness, and dignity are not in and of themselves mechanisms of economic exploitation. Hope is a potent political tool. It can empower people who have been caught in the cross hairs of capital and collusion to dismantle oppressive hierarchies. It can mobilize people to engage in long and beautiful struggles to fulfill fundamental needs for sustenance, shelter, sociality, and freedom. But hope can also work against collective liberation. National ideals for a democratic society often provide a meaningful outlet for organizing and broadening the strength of hope into a shared commitment and objective. Liberal promises of universal freedom are a widely accepted practical resource for materializing collective dreams for justice and equality. However, when democratic freedom is promised as a distant never realized possibility, hope functions materially as a roadblock to liberation. "Not yet" freedom is a social caesura in which injustices are reproduced as an impasse. Racialized risk, a speculative formation, is the chronic condition of U.S. nationalism.

Organization of the Book

Life in and against the Odds is written in and about the tradition of American Studies. It explores the narratives of speculative nationalism that the field has absorbed and how speculative principles were the foundation for its emergence. As much as the book concertedly engages the field of American Studies as an object of criticism, however, it is also committed to thinking through tensions in the past in honor of the field's grounding imperative to bring justice and social movement epistemologies to the center of intellectual work. In and against the American Studies tradition, this book addresses the symbiotic relationship of U.S. national culture and speculative economic violence. It explores the cultural-economic exchanges that have made "profound and bitter panic"—what James Baldwin calls the defining feature of White America's ongoing investment in "safety instead of life"—a daily condition of life under liberal nationalism's involvement with capital.[9] It challenges the patterned organization of society around a desire for speculative security and calls for historical accountability to the lives of people that have been leveraged to speculative predation through dispossession, enslavement, exploitation, and ancestry.

The three parts of *Life in and against the Odds* focus on the particular circumstances and conditions of different phases of speculative expansion in the United States. Part I begins in the nineteenth century in an era of industrial capitalist expansion when land markets and slave exchanges became a foundation for solidifying the notion of the nation-state form. Part II highlights the period of corporate capitalism during the 1920s and 1930s, when the expansion of the U.S. stock market brought speculation into the day-to-day lives of the nation's emergent managerial middle class. Part III focuses on the present era of financialized capitalism, engaging the crisis of 2008 with an eye on how the fallout from it shows that we continue to live in the aftermath of unresolved slavery and conquest.

Although each section of the book strives to account for the particularity of the constantly changing sameness of speculative economies, the goal is not to describe the economic intricacies of the historical phases of speculative capitalism. The book does not attempt to explain in great detail how and why bubbles collapsed into panic during different periods in the history of nationalism. Instead, it aims to make theoretical sense of the racializing structures and consequences of bubbles and panics with a focus on why and how racialized risk threatens actually lived participatory democracy. It investigates the cumulative consequences of speculative nationalism by questioning how and why race returns time and again as an outlet for absorbing economic risk. Thus, each part broadly outlines the historical processes through which speculative racial logics have been implanted in U.S. national culture in response and in relation to speculative economic climates. In this way, the book treats speculative episodes and events as touchstones for a historical materialist understanding of the conditions under which race is perpetually made and remade in the United States. It accounts for the particularity of different manifestations of speculative economies to the degree that differences within particular stages of speculative capitalism intersect and unfold, through complex cultural processes, as differences in the ways race is imagined and lived through U.S. national culture.

The purpose of this emphasis is to identify where and how speculative nationalism creates roadblocks to freedom, if and when people live in and against the odds, and what can be learned from past struggles and complex negotiations for bringing about new possibilities and enactments for human liberation in the present. How do people claim life in and against the odds, and why do their struggles show up as the cumulative consequences of a nation that remains committed to speculative expansion each time a speculative bubble erupts? The answer to this question is embedded in the history of the objects that have served as the promissory notes for the nation's "not yet" freedom—the objects through which refusable pasts are carried are as inconsistent and broad as the creativity it takes to claim and live life against the odds. Like the unpredictable predictability of market exchanges, the objects that circulate throughout the analysis in this book are partly coincidental and largely consequential.

Although the individual chapters focus on a discrete set of objects, they engage different objects as sites of cultural and economic investment. The particular objects at the foreground of each chapter have been selected for the ways in which they have come into being as "national" culture. The movement of each object in this process of becoming makes tangible the systematic circulation of nationalist fantasies of "not yet" freedom across time and space and how this circulation constructs race to absorb risk. More urgently, however, tracking the exchange of cultural objects, stories, and meanings through different sites of transfer brings into relief pathways where freedom dreams and self-activity are deferred and refused. Beginning with different scenes of speculative exchange, each chapter documents a tripartite speculative negotiation through a particular form of transfer. It maps not only forms of nationalist culture that are circulated to generate buy-in to "not yet" freedom but also disruptions to those forms that refuse the terms of the promise. The long historical arc of the book calls attention to the cumulative racializing consequences of a national culture that sustains economic booms and busts. The book considers the possibility of history across three levels of thought, action, and experience: how speculation constitutes and gives shape to nationalist conceptions of land, personhood, and collectivity.

Part I, "Land," strategically begins with studies of land and slave markets in which nationalist conceptions of space are written. Speculation has been inscribed in the nation-state both through stories and in physical landscapes, making speculative nationalism a cornerstone of many of the nation's most celebrated environments. The two chapters in this part speak to the ways in which the conceptualization of U.S. American space takes form through speculative endeavors.

Chapter 1, "Panicked Landscapes," begins with early nationalists' visions of staking a claim on the U.S. landscape. It opens during the 1830s in the context of speculative federal land markets, focusing on the role historical amnesia played in creating a space for national emergence. The chapter highlights a three-part transaction between federal land speculation, indigenous resistance to dispossession, and international freedom movements for a social democracy, as described by Nathaniel Hawthorne. The focal object of this convergence is the construction of a hetero-familial liberal model of national freedom that is carried throughout Hawthorne's fiction. The chapter's principal focus is the 1835 short story "The May-Pole of Merry Mount," which serves as an illustrative example of nationalism's response to complex demands for plural democracy. Hawthorne's vision of the nation normalized speculative land acquisitions with legitimating narratives for racially selective protections and institutions that ultimately protected the controlling interest of bourgeois nationalism.

Chapter 2, "Racial Returns," explores how the physical landscape in the U.S. West was redesigned to carry speculative nationalism. The chapter investigates the intersection of the speculative slave economy, the Reconstruction-era development of national parks, and the long deferral of abolition democracy. Yosemite National Park, this chapter argues, became an iconic example of how the national consolidation of industrial capitalism was organized around desires for profits that could keep up with slave speculation. Through a close reading of the career of Frederick Law Olmsted, the chapter argues that Yosemite was in part constructed as a speculative endeavor to introduce slave management tactics into the heart of industrial nationalism.

Part II, "Persons," examines how the early field of American Studies transfigured the racializing logics on which the United States was founded into its conceptions of American identity. It investigates the booms and busts of the early twentieth century with a focus on how the participatory democracy of the Cultural Front and New Deal eras was undermined by the speculative cultural constructions of race and gender. Both chapters in this part deal with the social movement and scholarly engagement with the meaning and particularity of American identity from which American Studies developed. The field took shape in contests over the meaning of personhood that worked in tandem with corporate campaigns to individualize risk in a shareholder's democracy. Chapters 3 and 4 explore the speculative returns of nineteenth-century racializing economies to the racializing impacts of New Deal cultural economies. In this era, return was both an economic and a cultural principle through which racializing cultural formations were inscribed and disavowed as the foundation of a uniquely "American" culture. The focus is on the American Studies tradition because it was, in part, through the establishment of this field of inquiry that speculative nationalism was "democratized" and institutionalized as a uniquely "American" identity.

Chapter 3, "Masks and Manipulations of Personhood," addresses the corporate era of speculative development in the United States, when populist scholars such as Constance Rourke, around whose work this chapter is organized, committed themselves to the construction of a new Lincoln Republic for national unity through vibrant critiques of capitalist exploitation, global fascism, and southern violence. However, the movement's ideas about pluralism and justice were balanced on aspirational, temporal assumptions that replicated in culture the economic takeover of personhood in U.S. law. The field of American Studies grew from proletarian populism into a nationalist adaptation to capitalist transformation, replicating the corporate takeover of legal personhood. Against the odds, descendants of slavery and conquest reinvented musical and dance forms as counter-epistemologies to reenslavement and the U.S. nation-state's settler contract.

Chapter 4, "Sacred Spaces of Structural Adjustment," examines what happened to the Cultural Front democracy when it was instituted in the curricula of U.S. universities. It offers a contrapuntal comparison of speculative longings and refusals through the lives of F. O. Matthiessen and W.E.B. DuBois. The divergent institutional and educational ideals of these thinkers highlight a battle of racial wills that played out through intimate desires and fraternal relationships. Matthiessen's political melancholia evidences a speculative struggle with ongoing segregation in the sacred White spaces of U.S. universities. Scholars such as W.E.B. DuBois, who like Matthiessen developed ideas about education at Harvard and in the fraternal atmosphere of New Haven, challenged the fraternal detachment of Matthiessen's American Studies. For DuBois the study of U.S. history was not a means to escape reality but a mechanism for dismantling capitalist race relations that undermined abolition democracy.

Part III, "Collectivities," grapples with the democratic implications and long-term consequences of shared yet plural understandings of U.S. national culture and identity. The chapters here engage continuities and discontinuities in U.S. culture as they emerge in the tensions between neoliberal individualization and collective cultural formations. Notions of land and personhood continue to circulate as the organizing principles of the contemporary era of speculative nationalism. Chapters 5 and 6 explore this dynamic with a focus on the U.S. housing crisis and its aftermath. Together, they shed light on why the disproportionate racializing impact of the twenty-first-century housing crisis is a cumulative effect of speculative nationalism. The odds against people of color were not simply created by new financial instruments; they were an outcome of long deferred freedoms rooted in the culture of liberal democracy.

The economic collapse of 2008 is a reminder that we continue to live under the shadows of slavery and conquest. Chapter 5, "Home Ownership Hope and the Sellout of the State," explains financialized capitalism's dependence on racialized risk. It considers roadblocks to freedom in the present era by asking what it means to reside in a nation in which people's homes, educational opportunities, health, and well-being are tied to speculative economies. The chapter pays particular attention to the work of culture in the age of mortgage expansion with an eye to the representation of housing as a national responsibility. The legacies of "not yet" freedom exposed by the foreclosure crisis are counteracted by housing, shelter, and neighborhoods that resist.

Chapter 6, "Revelry in the Multicultural Finance State," looks to the collective activities of one urban neighborhood that annually refuses the past. May Day festivals in Minneapolis's Powderhorn Park illustrate the ritual disruption of speculative nationalism. Speculative arrangements bring unlikely actors into intimate and particular scenes of exchange. When the rules of exchange are broken by revelry, alliances are forged on oppositional imaginaries. In the case of Minneapolis, members of the Powderhorn neighborhood actively respond to the social abandonment created by the speculative redistribution of state resources by building new vocabularies for an annual renewal.

As a whole, the chapters in the book showcase the interconnected patterns of negotiation that go into every speculative occurrence. There are sellers and buyers who are brought in by nationalism, but there are also objects and actors at the center of the exchange who resist in and against the odds. In this regard, actions not taken and struggles unheard are often as significant as agreements made and futures promised. Speculation functions on the pseudo-determinism of expectant returns. Because they are predicated on unknown futures, speculative economies are illogical, unpredictable, and unwieldy. Speculation is a condition in which fantasy and physicality become enmeshed. It is a mode of engagement in which desire and the harsh reality of actually lived existence often become convoluted at countless nodal points of interconnection.

In the context of an exchange, for example, buyers and sellers are tied into a complex web of material transactions, but they generally have little sense of where an object has been and where it will go as it moves throughout a speculative network. The irrationality of speculative systems can thus make it difficult to pin down a clear form that evidences and expresses a broader structure of interaction. It is no surprise that speculation balances on fantasy; this is true because speculation is a form of expectation forged of nonsense. To confront this challenge, *Life in and against the Odds* strategically deals with the objects at the center of the transaction showcased in each chapter as threads and connective tissues—nodal touchstones of different moments of exchange that can never tell the complete story of how the entire system operates. Each chapter follows an object through a series of economic and cultural exchanges, tracking the consequences of strategic and often capricious decisions and interactions as they circulate and take form as materializations of racialized capitalism.

The objective of each chapter is to elucidate how speculative capitalism is reliant on and constitutive of the racializing cartographies of U.S. nationalism. Different chapters map the discrete ways that economic returns in speculative markets are overwhelmingly engendered by cultural promises that racialize, displace, and discriminate through the deferral of "not yet" freedom. In sum, the book outlines the repeated minting and transforming of race in the United States as an economic formula for capitalist expansion. From this angle, each chapter explains how power and privilege in the United States take form via intimate exchanges and unlikely alliances. The social structure of U.S. racialization is built on systems of affective affinity that depend on collective confidence and mass complicity. Although often ideologically represented as inevitable, culturally reproduced structures of speculative feeling are vulnerable to everyday acts of noncompliance and noncooperation.

The Stakes of Freedom

Life in and against the Odds is predicated on the axiom that, despite the odds that have been stacked against them, people who live under the oppression of false promises have always claimed life by living as if they are already free. The central contention of this book is that, if we aim to move beyond the panic disorder of U.S. nationalism's imbrication in racialized capitalism, we must account for and attend to the pasts that have been denied and foreclosed in the steady sweep of speculative predation. Our debt to democracy cannot be paid back through symbolic inclusion and forestalled incorporation. Rather, it must be enacted through a careful and concerted accounting for the past in a commitment to settling unjust imbalances with creative transformation.

A tremendous amount of hegemonic fantasy work is required to make fundamental injustices look like freedoms that people desire. This book asks readers to contemplate the contribution of speculative fantasies to injustice and to the fate of freedom dreams when they are appropriated and aligned with speculative nationalism. How does submission to oppression come to seem like a valid social necessity and a sign of a person's moral worth? What allegiances and ideas about freedom and justice, debt and independence, fairness and recovery keep U.S. culture bound to the racializing violence of speculative thinking? What does it take to disregard acts of defiance and noncompliance that push up against the illogic of freedom's deferral?

Conditions of "legitimate" daily violence can make the mere act of survival, simply getting by, seem unimaginable for people who are targeted by history to become subjects of speculative predation. Claiming life in and against the odds indicates more than simply defying death by acting in compliance with the scripts that speculative nationalism expects people to internalize and follow. Life involves something that reaches beyond the daily art of prolonging existence, something more than negotiating unjust human relationships. Life lived in and against imbalanced odds suggests that *how* people faced with seemingly impossible chances manage to will continuation, navigate relationships, and claim a place in the world even when they are cornered into disempowering and dehumanizing situations is as important as the fact that people *do somehow* endure.

Somehow matters. People who are denied basic dignity, people who are positioned with little or no negotiating power, somehow intercede against all probability. The archive available for understanding the force of objectified people who do resist is limited at best. We cannot know in certain and universal terms how people whose lives are unwillingly caught up in speculative fury might have thought and felt about the internal contradictions and daily struggles of living on against the odds. Nevertheless, *that* the interjections of people dispossessed by the deadly coupling of economic optimism and cultural expectation refuse to disappear from the national culture indicates that people's self-determined and collective actions to transform, challenge, push against and break the constraints of racialized capitalism continue to matter. Refusable pasts communicate to the present the disruptive world-reshaping power of people's will to imagine, define, and claim freedom in and against incredible odds. Traces of disruptive noncompliance are meaningful reminders that when it comes to the possibilities of an antiracist democracy, learning how to enact and claim justice and freedoms capable of rearranging our planetary imagination and social organization is the *somehow* that matters most of all.

PART I LAND

In the field of American Studies, the landscape of the United States has been a foundational textbook of U.S. culture and history. The interdiscipline's project to link history and culture is often articulated in geographic terms, with historical epochs delineated by land-based transformation. The plantation, for example, becomes a metonymy for antebellum society. The urban factory stands in for the Industrial Revolution. The railroad becomes a metaphor of imperial expansion. The outward movement of domestic home buyers turns the land of suburbs into national signs of liberal prosperity.

There are many reasons that the cultural meanings and social terms of freedom in the United States have developed predominantly around land struggles and landscape iconography. First, because the nationalist phase of capitalist expansion is rooted in forces of spatial dispossession, enclosure, and dislocation, the differentiated right to human existence in the United States has been organized around when and how people occupy space. Human survival, in the colonizing equation of U.S. nationalism, is subject to unequally distributed permission to reside. Second, seventeenth-century U.S. nationalism grounded its notion of democracy on an idealized assumption that geography itself made North America a unique site of freedom. David Noble's masterful analysis of exceptionalist Enlightenment liberalism elucidates how bourgeois nationalists translated America's "sacred landscapes" into figurations of providential democracy to disavow the nation's structural ties to European capitalism.[1] Cover stories about a virtuous and timeless American landscape provided early nationalists fuel and fodder for inhabiting occupied territory as if land itself was a rightful inheritance. By imagining the U.S. landscape as timeless and boundless, early nationalists envisioned it as promising citizens harmony and unity. The land itself, many argued, endowed the U.S. nation-state with democratic potential and was thereby envisioned as the principle defense against encroachment by the destructive forces of European capital. U.S. national culture proliferated this formation with depictions of the nation-state as an island of democratic virtue, a bounteous scene of refuge protected and isolated from European capitalist corruption. When painting the picture of the United States as a lush democracy unified by nature, early nationalists intentionally wiped indigenous claims on the land from the palette of history.

Speculative politics and practices are also a central reason that land remains a dominant feature of both the organization and the understanding of U.S. culture. Figurations of a uniquely American landscape are rich repositories of historical dislocation caused by speculative deferrals. Land is a marker of speculative nationalism because the nation-state established its cultural footing during the nineteenth century, at a time when federal land markets and agricultural booms ballooned into intricately enmeshed speculative markets. These markets imaginatively dislodged land from its rootedness in place to circulate it conceptually as an exchangeable good. Land grabs turned land into a commodity and created space for slave markets, where people were uprooted as a circulating pool of exchangeable property and sentenced to work the land against their will. Because U.S. land was transformed into a speculative object, it was very rarely situated where it seemed to be fixed. In the abstract inversion of speculative exchange, the realm of trade where fantasy begets materiality, location becomes the product of multiple dislocations: any given plot of land carries within it someplace else. Speculation makes land a feature of resources and culture. Land is always at once material and figurative.

Economic speculation in the United States did not first appear in the nineteenth century; rather, it was always, in part, a driving force of conquest of the land base on which the nation was established. Even so, it was during the early nineteenth century that the history of speculative nationalism was directly written through U.S. land. We are accustomed to thinking about speculation in terms of time and futurity, but liberal nationalism turns this time into a matter of space. Thomas Jefferson, for example, set the grounds for refusing the speculative roots of the U.S. nation-state when he reframed territorial takeover as a stadialist theory of history. "Where this progress will stop, nobody knows," he declared, but the American experience was for him a long journey over a developing landscape. The course of history, in Jefferson's imagining, was a geographic expedition across laws of nature through the barbarous West into an orderly state of land-based democracy, for which the future was visible in the American East.[2]

The construction of democracy as a protective reserve of American progress has not disappeared from U.S. culture. It remains in the hoarding mentality that George Lipsitz calls the White spatial imaginary.[3] Lipsitz brilliantly maps how race materializes as a spatial formation because White America values pure and homogenous spaces. The possessive investment in White identity is tied to spatial ideas about property and values that have been created and secured through racial discrimination. White America's forcefully imposed belief that land can be owned teaches people to see resources as finite and other people as competition. When they fearfully come to see common goods and dynamically inhabited spaces through the lens of personal scarcity, they cling to individual interest and assume that others are threats to personal property. This logic manifests in time and space through land enclosures and private possession, gated communities, and personal security.

Thus land—how it has been written about, written on, imagined, and manipulated to match representations—remains one of the most important archives of social struggle available to scholars of American Studies. The chapters in this part redirect the American Studies tradition of reading the landscape as a textbook of U.S. history toward a critical land analysis that disinters how speculation is the bedrock of the nation's social and economic life. They draw on the field's tradition of analyzing land as an archive of deep historical and cultural meanings by reading land *in* texts and *as* texts. Chapter 1 explores representations of land in literary visions of the American Renaissance to ask where freedom struggles go when they are deferred and refused. Chapter 2 reads land as a text through the design and history of Yosemite National Park. It questions where and in what ways the racial geographies of economic speculation return when race-based economies are outlawed and overturned.

Each chapter experiments with a cultural-spatial analysis of history with the intention of challenging the limitations of Jeffersonian-influenced stadialist propositions of U.S. national history. Nationalist narrations map history as a progressive development in which the past disappears by the force of momentum. This way of thinking tends to assume that time unfolds as a long sequence of events that are held together by a single line of causation. History thus becomes a surface of change over time, but this perspective refuses much of what landscapes contain: struggles over meanings, contradictions, and simultaneous, overlapping forces; convergences of past and present that collapse in discrete locations; disparate desires for freedom and fulfillment; and acts of living toward freedom that have yet to be recognized and fulfilled.

It is no coincidence that the disproportionate racial impact of the 2008 housing crash maps with near geographic precision onto racialized spaces that were produced historically by segregation, credit redlining, and discriminatory housing policies.[4] Certainly the recent crisis highlights how race is made and repeatedly minted in the United States as the space-based recurrence of locally concentrated discrimination. The propensity of the past to fold into the present makes it necessary to think about time as a marker that repeatedly collapses into itself. History, when told through markers of land, does not unfold along a horizontal axis. Rather, time is compressed into conjunctural webs and meaning takes form through vertical depths. Stuart Hall's notion of historical conjuncture captures the ways in which divergent historical forces converge in particular time and space, carrying precedents of the past into new relational contexts where meanings undergo reconfiguration. A vertical spatial analysis of the past is also a way to think of space as a depth of historical conjunctures.

Beneath the surface of a single plot of land, multiple forces are compressed into relation by geography and cultural formation. The past is like geological pressure in landed temporality. When geologists analyze land, they consider how different elements overlap in particular spaces, but they also investigate how materials change in space when they are bound together under the pressure of the earth's surface. The weight of depth is transformative. It could be, for example, that carbon's subterranean change has an impact on social relationships. When unearthed, a mineral allotrope could become a tool for brilliance, a graphite resource with which to write a radical rumination. Or the altered form could take shape as a mineral symbol of luminescent adornment that is introduced into capitalist circulation on the back end of violent mining extraction.[5] Like geology, a vertical analysis of how land carries overlapping histories of speculative negotiation is a way to engage American Studies as a practice that can unleash transformative possibilities.

Any given depth of land in the United States contains within it centuries of aggrieved people's struggles to retain, make, and claim life before, beyond, and in negotiation with speculative nationalism. Bringing compressed struggles to the surface is one way to dismantle the nation's most captivating mythologies. A consistent theme of the so-called American Dream is that every era in the nation's past was freer than the one that preceded it. This story of nationalist progress sublimates deep histories of material contradiction. When revolutionary movements call for radical equality, they often base their demands on insights gained from lived solidarities and the common understanding that predatory structures must be dismantled. Yet national culture is often deployed to realign this knowledge with the compromises of abstract citizenship and liberal promises of "not yet" freedom. What happens to dreams of freedom when they are buried beneath the nationalist myths of futurity? The landscape of U.S. culture suggests that they circulate alongside other denied acts of justice in a patterned repetition of human repression by dislocation.

Panicked Landscapes

Dispossession, Liberal Nationalism, Allegorical Disposals

This council can make a law for giving to every head of family a separate parcel of land, which, when he has built upon and improved, it shall belong to him and his descendents forever, and which the nation itself shall have not right to sell from under his feet.

—THOMAS JEFFERSON, 1809

The mother of the nation has left you, because all her bones are being broken through the milling. She will return, however, if you get the White people out of the country and return to your former way of life. You yourselves can see that the White people are completely different from us. We are made from red earth, but they are made from White sand. You may always be good neighbors with them, but see to it that you get your old "beloved Towns" back from them.

—CHIEF KOYCHEZETEL, 1811

[The United States] maintain, as all others maintained, that discovery gave an exclusive right to extinguish the Indian title of occupancy, either by purchase or by conquest; and gave also a right to such a degree of sovereignty, as the circumstances of the people would allow them to exercise. The power now possessed by the government of the United States to grant lands, resided, while we were colonies, in the crown or its grantees. The validity of the titles given by either has never been questioned in our courts.

—CHIEF JUSTICE JOHN MARSHALL, 1823

The Scene of Exchange

In the speculative equation that turns land into money, debt is everything, and everything about debt in the United States is carried in the racializing legal fiction of an agrarian landholder's democracy. The promise of freedom in the United States was delayed by debt from the nation's very inception. Colonists waged a revolution in part against George III's prohibition against colonial script, a ban that kept the continent under the monetary thumb of international bankers. However, to fund the war early nationalists drew on domestic and foreign credit from France, Spain, and Holland. They later serviced these debts with additional credit, binding them deeper into economic relations of dependence. National autonomy would have to wait until payback was somehow made possible. From this economic perspective, the independence of 1776 was an anticipatory projection of democratic self-governance forestalled after the Revolutionary War by outstanding debt obligations. Self-determination during the early years of nationhood was pushed to a distant horizon. By 1786 the U.S. financial system was leveraged and delinquent to such a degree that few lenders would risk extending it further credit.[1] The overwhelming debt burden not only kept the nation under the economic thumb of creditor nations but limited the emerging government's capacity to invest in democratic infrastructure to realize its revolutionary optimism.

From the outset, U.S. nationalists drew on the liberal nation-state form to shore up and settle its accounts in ways that worked to the advantage of economic speculators. Contrary to the idea that national democracy could save the colonies from economic dependence, it was the nation-state that introduced and universalized speculation as the uneven path to national liberation. During the nation's infancy, of course, nationalist and speculator were often indistinguishable. A majority of the men who led the revolution and stood as the first two generations of U.S. government were shareholders in speculative land companies. Although the constitutional limiting of citizenship to property holders spoke in the Jeffersonian language of agrarian improvement, it also reserved a privileged trading position for landholders that would later prove profitable. Before the Constitution was signed, legislators had determined that the only escape from the federal debt would be to open a market in federal land sales.

Emancipation, nationalists argued, required the nation to create an incontrovertible source of revenue for eradicating the national debt. In response to this economistic line of political reasoning, the Land Ordinance of 1785 set the terms for selling public land in public auctions, "disposing" of it in competitive arenas to the highest bidders. It also outlined procedural terms for transforming public land into a commodity for circulation—surveying and dividing it into plots to be sold at a minimum price of one dollar per tract. Once land was released for exchange, it would be sold by the government with neither limits on the amount of land an individual or company could purchase nor requirements for buyers to settle or "improve" the land after purchase.

The 1785 ordinance differed significantly in tone from discussions of land at the constitutional convention. There, as the grounds for a political debate, land was framed as a root of rational citizenship, an anchor for long-term individual political investment in the future fate of a shared national democracy. The ordinance took an economic approach, mobilizing land for a short-sale trade-off of broader democratic ideals, and wagered an optimistic bet on an expedient transfer of private equity into the national budget. The hope behind it was that competition would result in high prices and quick sales so that the nation would be able to buy itself out of international debt. The ordinance did not incentivize or even create opportunities for non-landholders to take ownership of land and, in turn, increase people's chances for becoming full citizens under the prospective terms of the Constitution. Rather, it encouraged speculators and companies to dominate the buying field by dividing land into 5,760-acre allotments, which would be accessible predominantly to those with the buying power of large land companies.

The constitutional conceit that made property holding a precondition of the rights of national liberty was forged against this speculative backdrop. Of course, the idea of land on which citizenship was predicated emphasized democratic investment as the rationale for liberal restraint. Nevertheless, the landholders' pretense of democratic virtue also indirectly secured a favored economic trading position for men who were endowed with the rights and protections of full citizenship. The time to cash in on this citizenship arrived within a decade through another land law that provoked speculation.

The Land Act of 1796 solidified the 1785 ordinance with a plan to bank post-revolutionary independence on upping the ante on federal land sales.[2] In this instance, Congress was faced with the challenge of negotiating the agrarian ethos that had been the ideological backbone of the national Constitution. It did so with a provision that half of all available land would be sold in small plots of 640 acres. Ostensibly, auctioning off smaller parcels would make it easier for individuals to participate in the market. Further, the law offered purchasers a year of credit, so those without prior purchasing power might be able to afford property. The 1796 law was set up not only to individualize risk by redistributing debt to potential independent citizens but also to invite further speculation. It increased the minimum plot price to two dollars, which meant that the federal land market would continue to favor investors with established wealth and property.[3]

Democracy, or the path to it, was fundamentally renegotiated in the 1796 Land Act. On the one hand, the law demanded, as a matter of democratic necessity, that the nation become the arbiter of capitalist transformation. To free itself from its bondage to creditors, the national commonwealth would have to be converted into a sellable object. In this regard, the nation-state was rescripted as a vehicle for economic trade. As a result, the promise of democratic national futurity became an economic instrument because it was framed as contingent on converting land into a commodity that could be circulated and exchanged.

On the other hand, the act seemed to suggest superficially that servicing the demands of capitalist expansion was a temporary deviation that would later be resolved with the return of the agrarian vision. The implication was that after the debts were paid the independent nation would flourish through individual landholders' improvement of their claims. In this equation, the foundational vision of an agrarian democracy became a functional projection for legitimating the nation's a priori investment in capitalism. But the law, in the very terms of the trade-off it made, in effect undermined the promise that the Jeffersonian ideal could be restored and renewed after payment of all debts. In the open market, corporate speculators with surplus capital held a competitive advantage because they could purchase multiple tracts at a time and pay higher prices when competitive bidding led to inflation. In this context, the legal collapse of divergent approaches to democratic futurity entailed a stealth repurposing of the agrarian dream. To fuel the entire enterprise, speculators needed potential buyers. The law's appeal to individuals who aspired to propertied citizenship served double duty. It hailed non-landholders as potential future indebted citizens and, in so doing, increased the field of potential buyers upon whom land speculators could later prey.

Leveraging democracy on these imbalanced economic terms made for some contentious negotiation. The land up for grabs was already occupied, by both indigenous societies and optimistic settlers. Settlers and squatters schooled in the free land ideals of Jeffersonian republicanism had inhabited the land before it was sellable to enact their buy-in on the promise of agrarian citizenship. They argued against the plot of sellers, that their preexisting occupancy of "vacant" federal land should give them preemptive rights to purchase land titles.[4] In the historical transaction, however, even agrarians like Jefferson fell under the spell of the seller's advantage and advocated the sale of western land to restore the possibility of a self-governed nation. Jefferson promoted quick sales with no caps on the size of purchase on the heels of the Land Act of 1800, which had reduced the minimum purchase requirement to 320 acres and extended credit to four-year terms that could be paid back in installments. The act struck a balance between the promise of democracy and opportunities for occupiers to enter nationhood as citizen-debtors. Many farmers who purchased land on credit before this system was dismantled in 1820 did so with the optimism of speculative buyers. Credit was attractive to the degree that they could imagine paying off their debts with future yields. When land prices skyrocketed, however, so did loan defaults. In response to the crisis, the government set a precedent for a history of bailouts beginning with relief efforts in 1806.[5]

Like every speculative transaction, this two-party arrangement between nationalism and capitalism was threatened by the potential of objects to resist. Land, for many, is not a thing but a relationship that fixes social formations to particular geographic and ecological locations. From this orientation, circulating land is logically impossible. As a case in point, in 1811 Cherokee Chief Koychezetel delivered a cautionary prophecy to the Cherokee Council in which he called attention to the dubious proposals of nationalists like Thomas Jefferson, whose 1809 speech to the Cherokee Nation attempted to ensnare the tribe into distributing sovereign land as private property with the promise that this would secure its future. Chief Koychezetel saw the U.S. promise as social destruction intent on crushing culture and history through utter defiance of the land. Like the gristmill he referenced in the body of his address, the prophecy registered liberal nationalism as an instrument of environmental rearrangement, a tool for recomposing ecological elements and a violation of the meaning and purpose of land.

In Chief Koychezetel's prophecy, the land resists objectification. According to Tiya Miles, prior to the late eighteenth century Cherokee people treated possessions primarily for their use.[6] Thus the idea of inheritance was a contradiction. Because possessions had no use beyond the life of the possessor, they were burned and destroyed when the possessor died. During the late eighteenth century, however, encounters with White landholders gradually introduced private property into Cherokee societies such that some Cherokee people began to inherit properties that included land and enslaved humans. The first laws enacted by the Cherokee Nation in 1808 realigned matrilineal customs and culture with a western legal language of paternal households. They articulated the nuclear family as the locus of a new set of rules for protecting property. Jefferson's 1809 address did not introduce ideas that were foreign to Cherokee deputies. Rather, it heralded an expansionist pressure to be put on the Cherokee people to further adapt to the capitalist economy. Jefferson's promise played on the tension between Cherokee reformers and tribal conservationists by suggesting that fundamental change could be the answer to conservation. Chief Koychezetel's prophecy exposed the lie and mobilized an intertribal solidarity through which the land resisted.

Seven months after the prophecy was delivered, Cherokee, Shawnee, Choctaw, and Creek people entered into diplomatic conversations about protecting the land from U.S. nationalist encroachment.[7] Although the pan-Indian movement did not take root, the prophecy remained an important record of speculative nationalism's attempts to internalize all that it uprooted. The land, the prophecy declared, was being broken by sand, a reference to the crushing agent of the corn mills that were a tangible regional elaboration of a capitalist political economy. Just as the mills had subsumed indigenous agriculture, Jefferson's proposal was yet another sign of White people's relentless hunger to incorporate everything into their economic entrails. The prophecy carried a reminder of the Cherokee tradition in which the land—the corn goddess—spoke to and guided human action and movement. In this relationship, the Cherokee held the land as stewards and protectors in a mutually sustaining relationship. Land did not circulate in this relationship; rather, *people* circulated, in response to the ecological conditions that the land communicated to them.

Jefferson's verbal guarantee that turning land into private property would enable indigenous people to protect this relationship turned the world inside out. The colonial construction of an autonomous individual organized social existence around the abstract proposition that humans could effect the movement of *land*. In so doing, it inverted the order of human subsistence by presuming that authority over nature could be secured by the abstraction of ownership. As I discuss in greater detail later, the legal fiction that solidified this idea in the United States, *Johnson v. M'Intosh* (1823), arose directly from a case of misbegotten speculative investment.

The Form of Transfer

In the speculative saga of capitalism by conquest, land is everything and everything about land is carried in stories. This chapter disentangles the tripartite transaction between national democracy, the early nineteenth-century specu-lative economy, and oppositional expressions of land through stories written by Nathaniel Hawthorne.

Because Hawthorne wrote through a complex web of history, myth, and moral desire, his fiction has been a touchstone in the field of American Stud-ies. In Hawthorne's quest to make sense of the nationalist enigma—the ways that moral intentions devolved into historical tragedy—early American Stud-ies scholars found a method for reading myth as a social and cultural force. Scholars like Vernon Lewis Parrington and F. O. Matthiessen read Hawthorne's literary approach to the past as a fraught effort to rescue humanity and politi-cal ideals from the social conflicts and contradictions carried in the nation's economic foundations.[8] To this effect, they broadened scholarly analysis of myth beyond mere aesthetics of form to consider fantasy as a mechanism of escapism and political retreat. Although their assessments of Hawthorne's personal attachment to a privatized Puritan fantasy have been variously chal-lenged, what remains important in this early framing of literature as a socially reactive political strategy is that it made Hawthorne's work a foundation for thinking about how culture interacts with history.

Hawthorne's work was picked up more recently by scholars working toward an antiracist postnationalist form of American Studies. The tendency from this line of analysis has been to look to Hawthorne's fiction as a registry of nineteenth-century racial and class anxieties. His work has become for many a record of nationalist insecurity about empire building, a representation of North American panic about territorial and racial permeability. In the annals of Hawthorne, American Studies thinkers have found racial bewilderment caused by the market system, crises of language created by racial compromise, egali-tarian ideals disrupted by working-class culture, property compromised by colonizing swindling, and American innocence upset by western war and expansion.[9] Hawthorne has been a steady backdrop in the critical American Studies turn toward empire because his stories consistently point to links between nationalism and differential racialization, in particular as that racial-ization relates to the figuring of land and property into the construction of White liberal U.S. American identities.

Michael Colacurcio's identification of Hawthorne as a moral historian is perhaps most instructive for explaining why Hawthorne's work has long stood as a cornerstone case study of U.S. national literature. Colacurcio understands Hawthorne's storytelling as an interpretative mining of the ways in which the past arrives to us in the form of always already mythologized representations of the affective and moral elements of humanity that might indicate how the past was lived. Hawthorne's use of fiction as a deconstructive device involved a deeply intellectual effort to reconstruct the past through an honest and sym-pathetic treatment of moral contradictions. His stories productively work through the tensions of historical transmission—material inheritance, narra-tive misrepresentations, and mythic expectations—to recuperate a moral sensibility of the way that choices are made under fraught circumstances. As the many anachronisms and omissions in Hawthorne's stories suggest, his intention was not to recover the past as it was lived but rather to engage the allusions and myths through which the past would later be received. He found in the raw materials of representational tropes and historical travesties a means of learning about the roots of national shame, and he sought in the process to locate human experiences in which he could invest his hope for the future. Through fictional form, he investigated moral failures, reaching through the shortcomings of history toward stories of moral intentions and misdirected choices that could be reoriented and mobilized toward national salvation.

In the pitfalls and moral failures of the past, moral historians draw on fiction to reach beneath the prevarication of heroic myth in search of possibilities for national salvation. What they exhume is an approximation of the moral intention to learn about how choices lead to failure. Through stories, moral historians glean insight from tragedy to reorient the U.S. American predisposition toward fresh choices befitting the ideals of a democratic society. Thus, Hawthorne's sympathetic approach to historical figures accounts for violence while looking toward the affective intention that goes awry when humans are faced with the limits of their expectations. His painstaking effort to narrate and work through these contradictions was a means of staking an anticipatory claim on the unique space of the United States within the grand arc of world history. Hawthorne's feeling that the future is enmeshed in the past, his sense that hope is embroiled in destruction, and his method of repeatedly returning to the archives make him an exemplary author of speculative nationalism.

I take a slightly different approach to Hawthorne's stories, regarding them as a medium of cultural-economic exchange. I am interested not only in how the author engaged in speculative narration but also in how his stories circulated within a complex web of economic and cultural speculative transactions that defined the early nineteenth-century U.S. American landscape. Like legal tender, Hawthorne's stories carry abstract economic, cultural, and social values that, when exchanged by different hands and minds, compel the circulation of an additional object. In this case, the narrative transactions recorded in Hawthorne's literary ledger document at a distance the circulation of land. Hawthorne's stories were entangled affectively, aesthetically, and economically in speculative exchange. Through them, he wagered a bet on a contained democratic future. He hedged his expectations on his literary craft, using fiction to normalize and moralize liberal propertied citizenship as the most secure option for national freedom and salvation.

In naming his early stories *Twice-Told Tales*, Hawthorne called attention to the objective of his storytelling as narrative circulation. If the first telling implies an assumed familiarity with the tale being told, the second telling indicates Hawthorne's intention to use recirculation to endow a story with a realist fantasy as a method for generating new values. When Hawthorne broached the veneer of historical mythology in the stories he retold, he did so with an optimistic hope of imagining the human morality underlying historical processes. In an act of transhistorical mythical exchange, his second tellings produced a set of liberal principles through which to absorb a contested landscape into a nationalist future. In the transaction between past and present, the unsettled relationship between fantasy and reality functioned as an imaginative modality for disposing of risk.

In this regard, Hawthorne's stories did not act alone nor were they solely engaged with the narrative dynamics of the past. Rather, his fiction interacted with other stories in his contemporary environment as part of a broader climate of speculative negotiation. Hawthorne's literary investment in a nationalist futurity was only one form of textual trade among many others shaping a nineteenth-century cultural-economic bubble in which myths materialized as democratic futures and material violence was displaced into a series of myths. That is, Hawthorne's stories circulated within an intricate system of speculative narrative negotiations whereby panicked landscapes became the premise of national legitimacy.

Legal fictions were just as generative of speculative arrangements that endowed nationalists with an unjust political advantage by beating others out of noncapitalist relationships and inheritance of land. Hawthorne himself documented this tension in *The House of the Seven Gables*, in which a guilt-ridden exploration of deeds and commerce calls attention to the territorial delusions and legal ambiguities underlying the Jeffersonian proposition. It is no surprise that Hawthorne was perplexed about the validity of the nation's land titles. Like his own early efforts to fix the future, the legal declaration of the nation's right to occupancy was an effect of speculative fictions.

Playing the Odds of Legal Fictions

In the nation's manufacturing of a right to occupied territory, it defined land as property, and everything about property *took* place through duplicitous stories told by speculative land companies. The first U.S. legal case to engage the issue of indigenous rights began as a conflict over a speculative land trade. *Johnson v. M'Intosh* (1823) is remembered in legal history as the case in which Justice John Marshall fabricated a right of conquest out of the doctrine of discovery. However, the case began as a strategy of the United Illinois and Wabash Land Company to secure legal title to a fraudulent Revolutionary War land deal. The conflict and forgeries that defined the case began before the war. To understand how a private land purchase in 1773 could become the legal foundation for declaring the United States the rightful inheritors of North America, some legal history is in order.

The British Royal Proclamation of 1763 protected land west of the Allegheny Mountains for Native Americans. It forbade individual colonists from purchasing, settling, or taking possession of the land without license as legal representatives of King George III. As the grievance against the king in the Declaration of Independence for "raising the conditions of new appro-priations of lands" makes evident, this constraint did not sit well with the American colonists.

Sparked by an optimistic revolutionary spirit, one settler, William Murray, who acted on behalf of the aforementioned land company, purchased land in defiance of the Royal Proclamation. The hope of the company's speculators, it seems, was that, should the crown be overturned, the independent nation would honor the purchase, so Murray forged a document to present him-self as a rightful representative of the king to buy land located between the Mississippi and Illinois Rivers. To make the purchase in 1773, Murray con-vinced a commanding officer of a British military outpost that a 1772 British legal opinion that allowed British citizens to purchase land directly from Indi-ans in India overruled the Royal Proclamation. Through an act of forgery, he purchased approximately 23,000 square miles of coveted land, which contained the primary transportation channels of the international fur trade. Although this land was most likely held by the Iroquois Confederacy, Murray fraudulent-ly purchased it from Kaskaskias people.[10] They, too, were wagering that after the Revolution the transaction would be honored. However, the 1790 Com-merce and Intercourse Act prohibited anyone other than the federal govern-ment from making purchases from tribes, and it made the private deal messy.

Banking on its impression that nearly every key player in the U.S. govern-ment had some stake in honoring speculative land purchases, the United Illi-nois and Wabash Land Company optimistically spent five decades in court attempting to validate its title.[11] It failed in Virginia and in Congress. However, when Justice John Marshall, a well-known land speculator, took control of the Supreme Court, the company gambled on taking its claim to the courts, hiring a lawyer named Robert Harper, the son-in-law of one of the company's inves-tors who stood to gain a share of the holdings from legal recognition of the 1773 land title.[12] Harper told a good story about a nonexistent land dispute to create a legal premise for the company's property rights. Because the company paid the plaintiff, the defense, and all of the lawyers, Harper was able to handpick Nathaniel Pope, of the U.S. District Court of Illinois, to preside over the lower-court hearing. The judge agreed to honor a legal loophole that if both parties agreed to the facts of the case, those facts would not be subject to court review. Thus, Harper entered court with a case about an occupancy dispute with the defendant's tenant, a person who did not actually exist. Because the company had paid both parties in the case to agree that the facts of the tenancy were not in dispute, Harper was able to use those facts to question whether the Royal Proclamation invalidated the plaintiff's title to the land. Pope's decision was formulaic: the defendant had not trespassed, and the plaintiff was granted the option to take the case to the Supreme Court.

As it turned out, when the story got to the Supreme Court, Chief Justice Marshall did not buy into the land company's plan to use the courts as a busi-ness plan for land appropriation. He had a personal stake in rejecting direct sales between private parties and tribal representatives. Robert Lindsay argues that Marshall negotiated this case to solve a different case, which concerned a federalist promise to provide land grants to Virginia's Revolutionary War veterans. Marshall was looking for a way to honor this promise, but the problem was that the land the government had promised was held and occupied by the Cherokee people. Marshall spun the speculator's story into an *obiter dicta*, a juridical side commentary in which he established the nation's preemptive right to the land.[13] Following this spin, the decision declared, "The proceeds of all sales of land in the Western country, 'belonging to the United States,' are appropriated towards the discharge of public debt."[14]

The Marshall decision was in part an act of narrative recirculation. He drew the language for his argument directly from a dubious history he had previously written about George Washington. In doing so, he used a story he had told about the nation's forefather to assert that indigenous people's use of the land was at the pleasure of the nation. Because no tribes had ever questioned the validity of lands granted to the United States, Marshall duplicitously argued that the colonial governments that "discovered" the land should be granted title. This argument balanced on a technicality. Indigenous people had not disputed lands granted by the United States because at the time no such grants had officially been made. No indigenous people were represented in the 1823 Supreme Court case, even though the future of indigenous sovereignty was wrapped up in the Court's decision.[15]

Stories That Resist against the Odds

In the racializing removals of Jacksonian speculation, land claims influenced everything about life and everything about life was shaped by how land circulated. The transformation of colonial occupation into national possession meant moving land from one type of authority—indigenous stewardship—to another—national ownership. National removal policies presumed that coerced and forced displacement of Native people would free the land for market exchange. What nationalists did not anticipate was that the land would move with the people who were relocated. The resistance of the land to national ownership in this way is recounted in indigenous oral tradition.

Indigenous people have lived in and against the odds of conquest through stories that redirect risk onto liberal nationalism. The notion of private property balances on the idea that land can be treated as an abstract object, sold and circulated as an equivalent value in market systems of commodity exchange. Against the odds of such ideas, indigenous people claimed land and continued occupancy in both stories and ritual. Because they saw land not as a thing but as a relationship, when they were displaced they took the land with them. The risk to nationalism this posed was that, precisely when the land was "cleared" for ownership, it was, from the indigenous perspective, likely to slip away into a new location in defiance of the capitalist mode of circulation.

Selu is the first woman and spirit of the corn in the Cherokee oral tradition. She is the center of sacred rituals that have given Cherokee people life again and again in their long struggle to retain sovereignty in and against the odds of dispossession. Her story points to origins, but it is much more than a metaphor. Her life-enabling capacity is not fully explained by secular conceptions of theology. Secular thinking tends to sublimate the sacred as an aspect or belief of an individual or group. In such a framework, religious principles are often abstracted into symbolic narratives of personal belief and individual empowerment. Selu is much more than a narrative figuration that affirms the value of Cherokee people with her spiritual encouragement to reproduce tribal futures; she is a sacred relationship, a social force, and a cognitive structure that provides the Cherokee with a life-enabling epistemology. The theological, Selu suggests, is inextricable from the social, the ecological, the historical, and the economic. Thus her story conditions how life is lived and understood as a spiritual practice.

According to oral tradition, the Cherokee people have regenerated and cultivated longevity for many eras by honoring Selu at the Green Corn Ceremony. During the summer, the people mark the New Year as when corn is first edible, placing a ritual claim on land and space as an ongoing social relationship. The Green Corn Ceremony ritualizes women's agricultural knowledge as a central aspect of this relationship. Prior to the seventeenth century, corn was the primary means of Cherokee subsistence. Because it could be stored and preserved, many Eastern Woodland tribes are said to have depended on it when game and harvests were scarce. Theda Purdue argues that this dependence elevated women's status and power in Cherokee life because, as the principal farmers of corn, they carried ecological knowledge that held history and sustained the people.

Green Corn Ceremonies also suggest that women's intimate relationship to the land created the organizing wisdom of Cherokee society. Bringing in the sustaining corn harvest without endangering future yields was an ongoing process of maximizing harmony that required delicate negotiation and intimate knowledge of interrelated environmental elements—water, climate, soil fertility, storage reserves, seed. Perdue suggests that Green Corn rituals were similarly organized around a delicate manipulation of diverse social elements to maximize the health of the entire community. Spiritual and social purification rituals restored equilibrium to the social body as learned from the balancing relationship between people and land. The story of Selu stands in fundamental opposition to the violent fictions of debt and subordinating legal contracts on which liberal nationalism was predicated.

Oral tradition suggests that, pre–nineteenth-century Green Corn Ceremonies provided contexts for forgiving all debts, grudges, and crimes and were occasions when unhappy couples were released from marital bonds. Their rituals were a means of reconciling social disruptions and resolving all wrongs, with the exception of murder, in order to renew and restore social and economic balance. Women's presentation of the new crop was the focal point of many Green Corn Ceremonies. Following festivals, women engaged in informal practices of redistribution—planning for the year ahead by setting aside crops for visitors, feasts, and others facing hardships.[16]

A Green Corn Ceremony called *Poskita* in the Muskogee-Creek tradition began with the ritual burning of all worn-out possessions.[17] As with most Eastern Woodland tribes, Creek knowledge, resources, preexisting trade routes, and labor were forcibly integrated into the commodity circuits of colonial mercantilism. Yet, as Claudio Saunt argues, the continuation of purification rituals into the early capitalist era is evidence of the Creek people's deliberate decisions to live against the logic of private property and to prevent individual concentrations of wealth and resources within the tribe.[18] In 1835 John Howard Payne described a Green Corn ritual that he witnessed while conducting a federal investigation into widespread fraudulent speculation in Creek land. His account not only affirms the relationship between honoring the corn harvest and exonerating social injuries in Creek purification rituals but also shows how sacred practice was designed to bring order and equilibrium to the entire social system.

As speculators vied to stake a claim on the continent during the early nineteenth century, revivals of Green Corn Ceremonies among indigenous people became acts of living against the odds of colonial imposition because they sustained the sacred social ecologies that were a foundation of tribal sustenance. The *Springplace Moravian Mission Diary* recorded Cherokee prophecies of 1811 and 1812 that directed tribe members to use Green Corn rituals to purify the Cherokee Nation of White influence. Gregory Dowd reads this revival as a "revolt expressed in religious rhetoric," a spiritual rejection of land cession.[19] In the wake of the removal crisis of 1808–1809, these militant prophecies were used to stake Cherokee claims on the land by calling on the people to release Selu's broken bones from the gristmills of White colonizers.

Creek stories suggest that Green Corn Ceremonies remained an integral practice for living against the odds of dispossession and dislocation well after the nineteenth century. In contexts where soil, unfamiliar environmental elements, and contentious relationships among newly proximate tribes introduced agricultural and social challenges, the first communal act of some western Creek settlements was to establish the ceremonial grounds for the Green Corn purifications.[20] Theda Purdue quotes the oral history of a dislocated Creek woman:

When a tribal town (Tulwa) decides to move to another location, the chief, Heneha, medicine man, and Tustanagee sleep one night with the boundary of the ceremonial grounds. These four are responsible for the move of the tribal town. Only ashes under the top layer of the ashes of the old ceremonial fireplace to be moved are taken and placed in the place where the new location is to be established.[21]

The presumption of eastern speculators that they could lay claims on land is disrupted in these stories in two fundamental ways. First, the stories suggest that the land to be traded was often no longer situated where speculators expected. Second, as an adaptive technology for negotiating new relationships out of old attachments, Selu's story is a reminder that the past is an ongoing struggle despite nationalist efforts to resolve and refuse it. From the spiritual understanding of land as a relationship, the Creek woman's account suggests that land circulates with the people who must protect it and is likewise displaced in the process. In some oral traditions, for example, the Green Corn tradition of lighting new fires from the ashes of the old was a way to transplant ancestral relationships from ancestral locations into sites of relocation.[22] To this effect, western land became, through ritual, the living embodiment of an eastern antecedent.

National Allegory

In the racializing context of Jacksonian speculation, land was racialized and everything about race was disposed through fiction into the nation's panicked cultural landscapes. Aesthetic constructions of national democracy often worked in tandem with economic expansion as a repressive force against the insubordinate claims to life, dignity, and alternative economies of populations whose imagined extinction and status as property carried risk for Jacksonian democracy. When U.S. visions of an agrarian society were retooled within the private-property system of a speculative economy, nationalist ideals of liberal freedom bore much of the burden of reproducing land as an exchangeable commodity. The subordinating properties and sensory alienation of aesthetic experience served the land/slavery convergence by resisting the future refuse of the past.

The exchange in history for national allegory in the fiction of Nathaniel Hawthorne is a case in point. Hawthorne's concern to represent the contradictory and contentious legacies of the nation's past unfolds in much of his fiction as a teleological development that crosses the longitude of the nation's surface. Yet his texts often intersect with ideas, contexts, and direct passages carried from one story into another. They are also infused with the cumulative refuse of historical struggle from the pasts he points to as over and gone, which nevertheless remain pertinent to ongoing economic challenges. A vertical, spatial analysis of temporal overlapping in Hawthorne's various depictions of a national landscape unearths his anxieties about the ways that speculative futures balance nationalist inheritance on repeated acts of violence that racialize risk.

"The May-Pole of Merry Mount" allegorizes the intrusion of myth into the historical record through a Puritan invasion of the Mount Wollaston (now Quincy, Massachusetts) trading post in the seventeenth century. It is also a speculative object that mediates the climate in which it was written. Hawthorne wrote the tale in 1835 and published it in his first collection of stories, *Twice Told Tales*, on the eve of the Panic of 1837. These dates encompass the height of the Jacksonian land boom. In 1835 alone, land sales jumped to $15 million from $5 million in the previous year. In 1836, sales rose to $25 million.[23] The boom prompted states to invest in infrastructure, issuing as a whole more than $60 million in debt for the development of waterways and roadways. Nationalists imagined that this debt could be repaid with tolls rather than taxes.[24]

The land boom heightened the administration's interest in forcing removal. It was in this context that Marshall's decision in *Johnson v. M'Intosh* was recirculated politically as a speculative proposition. Even though Marshall himself attempted to reverse his decision in *Worchester v. Georgia* (1832) by arguing that discovery created only a preemptive right to land purchase, the Jackson administration continued to draw on the logic of the *Johnson* decision to coerce Eastern Woodland tribes into "voluntary" treaties to turn land over to the government, which led to U.S. officials negotiating the Treaty of New Echota in which 20 men—against the wishes of 16,000 signed Cherokee dissenters— agreed to cede eastern Cherokee land. Elsewhere, pressure on the Seminoles to forfeit land in Florida erupted into the Second Seminole War.

In response to the influx of speculators attempting to take advantage of preemption rights on Creek territory, the Creek people developed survival tactics of appropriating the resources of speculators who infringed on and sought to take their land. These intensified patterns of resistance brought indigenous people's lived resistance against speculative encroachment to just beneath the surface of every land sale.

At the same time, the land boom conscripted White working-class men into the imbalanced relations of the speculative marketplace.[25] Capital's surplus demand for exploitable labor, land, and bodies left the lower classes with limited capacity to negotiate for more favorable political, economic, and social rights and resources, and it introduced a daily risk of rebellion, violence, and resistance into the land economy. Between 1806 and 1832, the federal government assumed the burden of private debt, offering twenty-four different relief acts to individuals who had drawn on credit to purchase public land.[26]

In a broader eruption of the consolidated power of the disenfranchised and previously poor, the international freedom movements by women, abolitionists, labor, and anti-imperialists, that Michael Denning refers to as "the democracy," became a growing force during the mid-1830s.[27] This expansive international network of social movements sought to radically reorganize existing relationships of material inequality through its diverse demands for social protections, democratic institutions, education, and enfranchisement.[28] Hawthorne's representation of the motley interactions at Merry Mount suggests the ways that economic and political elites responded to the demands of these movements with selective promises of gradual national expansion along a temporal grid of differential social classification. Extending promises of private property and universal suffrage exclusively to White workingmen reinforced the hegemony of bourgeois nationalism both by breaking up the potential for broad class solidarity for a social democracy and by seeming to reflect Jacksonian ideals for a classless democracy.

"The May-Pole of Merry Mount" opens on the wedding day of a young couple, Edith and Edgar, in a festive celebration of communal liberation. The narrative centers on the destruction of the settlement's boundless freedom by Puritan invaders who wield their swords against the colony, level its foundations, and murder the majority of the community. Edith and Edgar are the only survivors. The story speaks to the class and racial anxieties of the mid-nineteenth-century speculative build-up of the U.S. nation-state, but it bases its concerns for the present in a mythical depiction of the seventeenth-century Ma-re Mount plantation run by Thomas Morton. The layering of history in the form of allegory mediates the risk of rebellion and resistance through economic amnesia about its historical referent.

Morton's Ma-re Mount, as he unapologetically described it in his 1637 *New English Canaan*, was expressly established as a center of trade for colonial expropriation. Like Hawthorne's stories, Morton's account was a twice-told tale. It was both a legal grievance against the Massachusetts Bay Company for the destruction of his plantation and a testimony to the exploitable natural resources that the crown had been denied with his exile from the colonies.[29] It also expropriated indigenous epistemologies to offer a detailed proposal for extracting raw materials from the "rich, hopeful, and very beautiful [North American] Country." Morton justified his venture on a feudal conception of debt: his obligation as King Charles's "humble vassaile" to re-create North America's "tractable nature" through colonial violence and the labor power of indentured and constrained trans-Atlantic workers.[30] He designed this venture on intergroup differences, endeavoring to extort the differential knowledge and work of Eastern Algonquian–speaking people and motley members of the small group of English proletarian workers he had brought with him. A maypole at the center of the plantation marked the colony as a port for sending plants, pelts, minerals, and fish to Europe and bringing "drums, guns, pistols, and other fitting objects" into the Americas. It also came to symbolize Morton's unconventional strategy for forcing connection and collaboration between European and indigenous men through intimate exchanges of Native women's bodies. And, of course, it set the scene for the contentious rivalry with Puritan New England that is notoriously associated with May Day 1627.

Book I of *New English Canaan* showcased Morton's copious design for spatial imposition, suggestively detailing indigenous geographies and trade routes, alliances, enmities, and cultural practices that he prefigured as future British assets. It offered a plan for superimposing a global mercantilist economic system on preexisting North American networks and knowledges. Morton's phallic vision of colonial authority was haunted, however, by the various ways that this landscape was created and made through the counter-meanings and modes of inhabiting space that he sought to control. He described indigenous people who were both suffering from plague and confronted by competing European colonial interests as "covetously desiring" trade with England. The text, in combination with Morton's arrest for selling arms to Native people, *also* revealed, as it concealed, the struggles of indigenous people to retain group autonomy, practices of commoners, and understandings of nature that defied the colonists' market vision.

New English Canaan did not dismiss these counter-meanings, but rather "artfully and industriously" shifted the desire for alliance and trade onto Native people. Morton also expropriated and resignified reflections of noncapitalist indigenous economies through the idea of a North American "commons." This act of re-creation provided him with a strategy for conscripting European labor through consent. As Peter Linebaugh and Marcus Rediker have argued, the seventeenth-century enclosure movement at the center of Europe's capitalist transformation produced new legal regimes of unfreedom and dispossession that balanced on privatizing subsistence land and broadly criminalizing vagrancy, beggars, rouges, and common people's land uses as "not working." The record is unclear as to whether the thirty-seven men who performed the physical work of constructing Ma-re Mount under Morton's watch landed in the Americas by choice—out of limited recourse to food, resources, and work—or by force—out of the need to pay back debts or to serve criminal sentences. Morton's orchestration of their relationship with the indigenous people through pagan rituals, however, appealed to and endeavored to realign their likely desires and memories for shared rights, collectivity, and freedom from tyranny with a subtle extension of a colonial "commons" that he presented as the unique promise of his capitalist "Canaan."

Land-identified ceremonies like the Green Corn festivals practiced by Eastern Woodland tribes suggest that indigenous women's relationship to the land might have been the seed of a sacred ecology from which life-affirming egalitarian social, economic, and cultural values sprouted. Morton's use of the maypole certainly replicated a British trope of the "Gaelic" as a framework in which he constituted his sense of racial superiority to a primitive "other." He drew on a legacy of colonial supremacy to assert, "I know this falls out infallibly where two nations meet: one must rule, and the other be ruled, before a peace can be hoped for. And for a Christian to submit to the rule of the salvage [*sic*], you will say, is both shame and dishonor."[31] Yet Morton's manipulation of preexisting social systems made it likely that something of the gendered epistemologies, the cornerstones of similar indigenous ceremonies, was part of the cultural exchange that Morton negotiated around the maypole.

The complexity of what this land might have become to the indigenous women through whom Morton sought to mediate the contact and competing interests of indigenous and European men, however, remained in the shadows of a colonial imagination that was forged on a vision of necessary rape. An opening poem in Morton's volume collapses indigenous women's fate with his hopes for the land (italics mine):

If art and industry should do as much
As Nature hath for Canaan, no such
Another place for benefit and rest
In all the universe can be possessed.
The more we delight it by discovery.
The more delight each object to the eye
Procures, as if the elements had here
Been reconciled, and pleased it should appear
Like a fair virgin, longing to be sped
And meet her lover in a Nuptial bed,
Decked in rich ornaments to advance her state
And excellence, being most fortunate
When most enjoyed. So would our Canaan be,
If well-employed by art and industry,
Whose offspring now shows that her fruitful womb,
Not being enjoyed, is like a glorious tomb,
Admired things produced which there die,
And lie fast bound in dark obscurity—
The worth of which in each particular,
Who list to know, this abstract will declare.

Morton's poem staged market integration as nature's salvation through his displacement of colonial desire onto land and women. It also constituted marriage as a violent wager on women's lives by metaphorically making it the binding force for bridging incompatible articulations of land and freedom. It accounted for a colonial optimism that registered nonviolence as a lost opportunity and land as a potential commodity. It responded to a European struggle for subsistence, independence, and community with an understanding of land as a shared and common good. And it attempted to override indigenous claims of autonomy and strategies for self-preservation that balanced on recognitions of land as an interrelationship defined by the indigenous people's responsibility, endowed by the creator, to act as the stewards of nature, a relationship in which land cannot be bought and sold.

Morton's poem and his trade practice prefigured a pattern in which the intimate event of heterosexual marriage became one way that White settlers undermined indigenous people's common title to nonfungible land. In John Howard Payne's account of a Creek Green Corn Ceremony in 1835 (concurrent with the period in which Hawthorne wrote), he told of dining with a White couple and noted that the husband "is continually marrying Indian wives—probably to entitle himself to their lands."[32] The practice of dispossession through domestic familial contract was codified during the late nineteenth-century period of assimilation as a form of "race suicide" that entailed indigenous women's loss of tribal identity as the cost of marrying into the White national body.[33]

When Hawthorne rewrites the complex negotiations and conflicting historical meanings that contributed to the development of the Ma-re Mount plantation as a utopian expression of populist unity, he injects intergroup difference and opportunistic colonial antagonisms deep into the heart of national identity. His resignification of the relationships and categories that were essential to Morton's economic imaginary operates in tandem with the speculative climate of the 1830s. Hawthorne was a proud gambler in his youth and wrote during a period of intense economic speculation with long-lasting implications for race mapping through national intimacy.[34] Although he did not directly address economic speculation in his writing, stories like "The May-Pole of Merry Mount" draw on the marital contract in a way that instrumentally mediates the social tensions that can be expected when groups with conflicting ideas about the economy are forced into relationships of economic exchange. Like Morton's use of intimacy, the narrative benefits from the marriage contract used as a resource for securing future returns on national expansion for White elites.

The seventeenth-century marriage contract in Hawthorne's story mediates nineteenth-century economic insecurity by filtering specters of diverse crossclass, antiracist, feminist, and sovereignty struggles into a singular expression of unfulfilled desires for nationalist belonging. Through Edith and Edgar's union, the text reclaims the North American landscape for White nationalist becoming. It offers propertied domesticity as a salve that not only presents the nation with a palatable past of colonial amnesia but also ameliorates the panic of the nation's investment in White security at the expense of others' lives.

The story grounds national memory in a colonial vision of the world. It begins with a mise-en-scène that limits history to contrasting stakes in spatial expansion: "Men [had] voyaged by thousands to the West; some to barter glass beads, and such like jewels, for the furs of the Indian hunter; some to conquer virgin empires; and one stern band to pray."[35] The dislocation of workers, women, and indigenous people from this privileged view of the colonies results in a retrospective reassurance of the land as a White racial inheritance. The allegorical conflict does not pivot on a primary concern over *who* will ultimately possess the North American landscape; rather, the story is organized around dual teleologies of White "overcoming" that work to draw up and negotiate a contract for settling the terms upon which White nationalism would imaginatively take ownership of the land. Would the nation inhabit the landscape on risky economic expansions that depended on differential conscriptions of potentially noncompliant groups into a unified market system? Or would it inherit North America under an ideal of geographic isolation and exclusion that would make violence and eradication of all difference a precondition for White preservation?

Edith and Edgar's marriage allows the nation to have it both ways— performing a narrative closure that projects unity as both a promise of abstract democratic inclusion and the source of social and economic stability. The allegory invests in both of these legacies, skimming from each a productive return on national identity before imaginatively shedding the risks of difference and instability as irrelevant national prehistories. More concisely, we can read the formation of national identity here as building from a speculative system of cultural exchange: The national future that the narrative envisions reaps the rewards of both the democratic spirit of the revels at Merry Mount and the regulatory social ordering of the Puritans, but it does not maintain possession of either of these "objects of exchange."

In the case of Merry Mount, like Morton's economic manipulation, the story extracts the benefits of a sense of democratic freedom as it seeks to "secure" the landscape for nationalist futures through manipulation and transplantation of oppressed people's counter-meanings and practices of inhabiting space. By rhetorically claiming time and space as instruments of national progress, the allegory surreptitiously reconfigures the indigenous people and English workers who negotiated the problems, displacements, and denials caused by violation, dispossession, and exploitation *as* the problems creating nineteenth-century social and economic instability.

The title of the story initiates this removal policy with a name change that helps to reconstruct the nation as a scene of democracy through the rejection of its participation in market economies. The name "Ma-re Mount," from the Latin *mare*, may have indicated the sea, emphasizing the transatlantic trade that was the purpose of Morton's settlement. The root *mas maris* may have suggested the "erect phallus" around which Morton attempted to organize this trade. Hawthorne's respelling of the plantation as "Merry Mount," however, points to the land as a site of excess and jollity. In his revision, the mount itself subtly becomes the productive source fueling this merriment.

The subtle change in nomenclature defers the necessity of reckoning with the ongoing contentious and intersecting legacies of colonial occupation by making acts of resistance appear both as antithetical to the definition of the particular space and as cautionary memories of prenational social instability that are better traded off into the dark shadows of memory. At the nuptial scene, for example, the wedding couple preemptively mourn that "nothing of futurity will be brighter than the mere remembrance of what is now passing."[36] This declaration takes for granted an identity based on the memory of emancipatory freedoms that releases the couple from their connection to the ongoing politics of social transformation.

The association of freedom with the landscape and the depictions of the crowd at Merry Mount replicate the exceptionalist organization of republican democracy that, according to David W. Noble, was operating through nationalist constructions of a virtuous democracy that idealized a wide and available nature as the source of individual freedom. In the mid-nineteenth century, pervasive cultural portrayals of a vast and available wilderness symbolically separated the timeless space of a virtuous U.S. nation from the corrupt and boundless time of European capitalism. It cannot be an accident that many of the most iconic images and celebrated histories of a virtuous U.S. landscape—

like those of scholars such as George Bancroft, the artists of the Hudson River School, and American Renaissance authors like Hawthorne—were produced during the speculative boom of the 1830s. Certainly, the Jacksonian democracy of 1828 renewed and expanded the nation's belief in a classless democracy. Bancroft, like many others, understood the official incorporation of working-class men into the national polity as a sign that the nation had finally overcome local differences and colonial hierarchies of the past.[37]

Landscape ideologies also preserved categories of racial difference that were integral to the nation's international adjustment to its speculative land hunger. Projections of an uncontaminated national landscape mystified the labor, lives, and losses that the nation incurred when it expanded its attachment to dispossession and enslavement to feed speculative desires. In this regard, as much as celebrations of a national landscape sustained the idea of a classless democracy isolated from global corruption, they also fundamentally helped to advance the differential racializing logics of savagery and human commodification that further entrenched the United States in international exchange.[38]

Through its representation of a virtuous and free national landscape, "The May-Pole at Merry Mount" ascribes the unpredictability and irrationality that structured the speculative economy of the 1830s to the behaviors and actions of individual inhabitants of the plantation, whom it configures as yet to free themselves from the irrationality and corruption of Europe capitalism. The revelers are described in a language that was broadly deployed in the nineteenth century to condemn speculators for monopolizing individual property and to accuse discrete economic actors of turning citizens into peons of debt—an unruly rabble of "minstrels," "mummers," and "mountebanks." This discourse exercises a dexterous cultural distancing that makes the speculative ventures through which the nation was materially expanding appear to be incompatible with national identity. The narrator asserts, "It *could not* be, that the Fauns and Nymphs, when driven from their classic groves, *had sought refuge* [italics mine], as all the persecuted did, in the fresh Woods of the West."[39] This negative declaration imparts to the Merry Mounters responsibility for class-stratifying and racializing violence, reconstituting the desiring subjects of deferred freedoms into alignment with the racializing logics of speculative conquest through promises of White national stability.

The figuration of Edith and Edgar as escapees from capitalist corruption is established through their recognition of the emancipatory spirit that takes *and makes* (the) place (of Merry Mount) on their wedding day a "counterfeit of happiness."[40] Through their foreboding insights about impending crisis, their nuptials become a tutorial for tempering euphoria. As the narrator explains, "No sooner had their hearts glowed with real passion, than they were sensible of something vague and unsubstantial in their former pleasures, and felt a dreary presentiment of inevitable change."[41] The couple commits a "high treason" of sadness about the "giddy tribe" at Merry Mount as they come to see the "shapes of [their] jovial friends [as] visionary, and their mirth unreal."[42] In scripting cross-class democratic struggle as an impossible social fantasy, this lament works to preempt any critique of and resistance to the organizing structures of liberal nationalism. The boundless joy at the revels might be read through an historical lens as a reflection of carnivalesque strategies for working-class resistance that temporarily sought to turn the capitalist world on its head.[43] Edith and Edgar survive the onslaught of the Puritans in part because they reject the power of everyday people to radically transform the world. Their doubt and resolve in combination with their rejection of the hedonistic sexuality and wild pursuit of "vanities" contributes to their survival because it leads their Puritan opposition to see them as pliable subjects for social realignment.

The Puritan invasion that marks the story's narrative intrigue serves this construction by making the violence of and contest over settler colonialism a symptom of zealotry among a particular group of religious fanatics. The story signals early American penal repression, terror, and colonization through the "stocks," "whipping posts," and "weapons [that] were always at hand to shoot down the struggling savage" as symbolically opposed to the unsustainable freedoms represented by Merry Mount's maypole.[44]

On the one hand, this legacy maps neatly onto a Jacksonian exaltation of the nation's expanded democracy through a representation of an overthrow of internal repressions and external violence that supplied the nation with a platform for reading diverse struggles for social democracy, dignity, autonomy, and land as signs of its ability to overcome differences and colonial hierarchies in moving toward gradual fulfillment of its destiny of universality. On the other hand, as it intersects with Edith and Edgar's memory of freedom, this legacy lays the groundwork for a disciplinary discourse of liberal citizenship that benefits from a memory of Puritan social regulation: "From the moment that they truly loved, they had *subjected themselves* to earth's doom of care, and sorrow and troubled joy [italics mine]."[45]

At the center of each of these trades, the fungibility of marriage serves as a transferable vehicle through which futures are negotiated. The circulation of marriage across texts and within this story bestows on the national identity an allegory that seeks to exchange an historical connection to a repressive regime for a liberal abstraction of governmental authority that depends on a disciplined citizenry. In other words, the Puritans are not rewarded with Edith and Edgar's allegiance. Likewise, the nationalist fantasy that the story maps does not stake a claim on the colonial legacy of Puritanism as an antecedent to the nation. Rather, the circulation of the marriage fantasy through this formation returns to nationalism the benefit of a gendered mode of social ordering on which to reinvest in a domestic construction of a "more democratic" ideal of social stability. The proceeds of having first circulated this construction through Merry Mount return in the allegorical formation as memories of freedom and liberation through which the narrative mediates class transformation in the broader nation. In the "tie that united" the couple, the narrator says, "were intertwined all of the purest and best of their early joys."[46] Marriage becomes in this instance a receptacle for living democracy as a feeling of unity through liberal identity that is protectively configured against social and economic chaos and crisis.

It does not seem coincidental that Hawthorne imagined this romantic contract at the conjuncture of Jacksonian democracy's expansion to incorporate working-class men *and* the nation's increased entrenchment in speculative land markets. This marriage contract is also a racial contract that exposes the liberal democracy that Hawthorne develops as at once emancipatory, disciplinary, divisive, repressive, and racializing. In both associating freedom with the land itself and sanitizing Merry Mount of its working-class rabble, the marriage stakes a claim to the North American landscape as a romantic promise for expanding a falsely egalitarian classless democracy. This formulation is especially powerful for preserving the racial categories undergirding the expansion of the cotton and land booms. Stories like Hawthorne's helped to produce confidence in the nation's capacity for sustaining these bubbles because they solidified ideas about racial difference, justified dispossession and enslavement as unavoidable economic necessities, and mitigated risk by framing conflict as a relic of the past. Thus such speculative narratives optimistically preordained a future in which the not yet stolen livelihoods and personhood of indigenous and African people were limitlessly available for future exploitation. In this regard, Hawthorne's story intimately interacted with the Jacksonian marketplace as a medium through which to dispose of the nation's political and economic debts by the execution of future sales.

Debt Disposal

In the speculative land economy of the early nineteenth century, risk was everywhere and everything related to it was wrapped up in nationalist abstractions that refused the past. Figures like Andrew Jackson publicly disparaged speculation so long as it burdened his White worker's democracy with the dangers of risk. Three days after the passage of the Indian Removal Act in 1830, Congress passed the Preemption Act, which promised to bring the nation closer to the propertied citizenship that Jefferson had imagined. It created the right of preauction land purchase at the minimum price of $1.25 to settlers who had occupied or improved surveyed lands.[47] The convergence of these acts is suggestive. The Preemption Act expanded opportunities for affordable land purchases by rewarding settlers for working the land. It also initiated Jackson's longer campaign to stabilize the land market by curbing speculation—an effort that erupted in the Panic of 1837 when he passed the Specie Circular requiring all land purchases be made in gold or silver.[48] Despite Jackson's democratic pretention of expanding workers' access to land, his advocacy of the Indian Removal Act showed that his worker's democracy was contingent on national policies that officially racialized risk.

Prior to assuming the presidency, Andrew Jackson was not averse to speculation; neither, despite his public stance, was he against the practice when he
was president. As a private citizen, he had acquired his fortune as a merchant
and land speculator. In 1795 he narrowly evaded bankruptcy when a credit
relationship from which he expected payment went awry. He absorbed his loss
by selling large quantities of his own land and property.[49] As a military official and public person, Jackson had acquired a surplus of public land that he
used to cushion White investors from similar losses. He forced the cession of
21 million acres of Creek land in the Creek War of 1813–1814. In 1819 he ille-
gally invaded Seminole territory in Spanish Florida and coerced the tribe into
the Adams-Onís treaty, which granted the United States the state of Florida.[50]
As president between 1829 and 1837, his removal policies dislocated the five
Southeastern tribes, allowing the confiscation—through force and treaty—of
25 million acres of rich land.

On the economic front, Jackson took a presidential stance against internal
improvements and the investment of federal funds in joint stock companies.
His states' rights platform gained him popularity in the South, but not as much
as his stance against protective tariffs did. In the American system, the duties
on cotton exports were between 33 and 50 percent.[51] The Compromise Tariff of 1833 negotiated by the Jackson administration gradually reduced this to
20 percent. In the same period in which land policy expanded the privileges
and protections of a White western frontier, southwestern land grabs and more
favorable economic terms for cotton exchange promoted a new speculative land
boom that balanced on producing race as a vulnerability to a credit economy
that was backed by confidence in the nation's capacity to expropriate sufficient
land to cover debts.[52]

By 1835 the slave/land conjuncture gained momentum when an increase
of five cents per pound in international cotton prices fueled a 9-million-acre
increase in public land sales. The land bubble inflated to sales of 20 million
acres in 1836.[53] Alasdair Roberts calls this period the "biggest exercise in privatization ever undertaken." Fueled by a massive democratization of credit from
banks and the injection of capital from the United Kingdom into northern
trade and financial centers, the speculative boom produced a 150 percent inflation of real estate values.[54] A concurrent slave bubble increased the population
of enslaved people by 215 percent in Alabama and 300 percent in Mississippi
between 1830 and 1840.[55]

Cultural narratives that affectively dislocated signs and memories of intergroup contact and resistance were of particular service to the land/slavery economic bubble. In breaking up the motley crowd at Merry Mount, Hawthorne's
story limits possibilities for living democracy through cross-class interethnic
relationships that give rise to alternative land and human economies. The story
conscripts White workers' aspirations for freedom to align with the deferred
promises of liberal nationalism. At the same time, it denies insubordinate

claims to life and dignity for people whose future exploitation and dispossession the nation counted on to fulfill its promises.

The trope of "disappearing Indians" appears twice in the story. The first is described as a noble "counterfeit"; in the second, a spectator is described through the actions of revelers who "striv[e] to communicate their mirth to him, as a *grave Indian* [italics mine]."[56] Whether by an attempt at wit or an inadvertent discursive doubling, these representations of an always already dubious counter-identity perform a narrative sleight of hand. In the movement from history to allegory, the text reconfigures a seventeenth-century system of colonial expropriation and exploitation into a speculative system of exchange at the same time that it fantasizes—either because of a failure to understand the promises of freedom or because of the author's lack of representation—that grave Indians were logically destined to become Indians relegated to graves.

The apologetic act of looking backward at an ongoing violent present was always already conditioned by the negated meanings and uneven interdependencies deflected in expressions of contrition. Yet the turn away from an imagined stable and uncomplicated past was also a turn toward the memories and violence that national culture worked to repress. The interdependence of speculative markets and U.S. nationalism, in this regard, was always also a project of racial negotiation—a struggle over diverse ideas about freedom and alternative social mappings. In contexts where the risk of resistance reemerged as a viable potential, Hawthorne returned to the story to recirculate nationalism as a site of economic security.

Hawthorne rewrote the scene at Merry Mount in 1859 as a "Sylvan Dance" in *The Marble Faun*. Through near replication of his descriptions of the New England settlement, he "returns" the dancing fauns and nymphs, who had provided legitimacy for his allegory of freedom, back to "their classic groves."[57] By the 1850s, the expansion of the nation's land markets and the peak in global cotton prices was paving the way for a speculative boom in southern slave markets, where the price of a person was cut loose from prices in the cotton economy.[58] When Hawthorne wrote his final novel, his investment in a virtuous and stable nation had left him belly up in the tragedy of history.[59] Imperialist war with Mexico, growing labor unrest, and a system of enslavement that—in defiance of his infamous optimism, refused to "vanish like a dream"—had left him doubting the promise that nationalism could salvage the future. *The Marble Faun* registers panic over the cultural investment that "Merry Mount" enacted as it seeks to re-create a memory of America as a place "where there is no shadow, no antiquity, no mystery, no picturesque and gloomy wrong, nor anything but a common-place prosperity, in broad and simple daylight, as is happily the case with [his] dear native land."[60]

The Marble Faun follows the development of two young American artists, Hilda and Kenyon, through a literary equivalent of a Roman Grand Tour. Rome becomes in the novel a spatial geography for containing temporal dissonance as the couple interacts with two mysterious European figures, Miriam and Donatello. Nancy Bentley compellingly argues that the novel's representation of an ancient Roman past as a decrepit and decaying site of corruption counters the romance of U.S. national progress, which heightens the fantasy of American virtue.[61] The differentiation of space as time—that is, Europe as past, North America as future—works to elevate the U.S. nation-state to the status of the "world's leading republic" with the expropriation of classical Roman art as an antecedent of a living democracy.

Miriam and Donatello could blend as easily into the crowd in the mythic forests of Merry Mount as they do with a motley rabble of "plebian damsels," "French soldiers," "German artists," "the Pope's Swiss guardsmen," and "English tourists" in the "grassy glades" of Europe.[62] Donatello emulates the faun of Praxiteles. Miriam is a nymph-like maiden whose strange retreat from a mysterious model leads her to clandestinely caper through secret pathways, forests, and caverns. Bentley argues that Hawthorne borrows tropes of U.S. racism to represent both of these figures. Donatello resonates as a noble savage; Miriam's secret ancestry shrouds her in a melodramatic tragedy that marks her with the semblance of a tragic Mullata.[63] Through these figures, Europe becomes the psychic repository into which the text dumps U.S. speculative anxieties about racializing violence. Once it has dislocated America's panicked socioeconomic landscape onto a fiction of European chaos, the novel tentatively reinvests in the abstract promise of stable progress that it reattaches to U.S. land.

The cultural work of national recovery in the novel takes place through yet another "marriage pageant," in which U.S. economic and racial anxieties are reconfigured and contained, in a near verbatim scene from Merry Mount, by the European proletariat. Miriam absorbs anxieties over expanded slavery by voluntarily asking to be "vanished from" the collective scene, while Donatello absorbs liability for expansionist violence by falling into a murderous rage. The novel creates a renewed opportunity for national reinvestment by recirculating and dislocating increasing U.S. economic and social instability onto a chaotic and immoral European past.

The young artists' anticipated return home is also a return to a cultural process of national recovery: "The years, after all, have a kind of emptiness, when we spend too many on a foreign shore. We defer the reality of life, in such cases, until a future moment, when we shall again breathe our native air."[64] However, reality is constantly faced with the specters of resistance that cannot be fully resolved through the narrative displacement of a memory-infused landscape. The novel tellingly reveals that the apologetic act of looking backward at an ongoing violent present is also a turn toward insubordinate histories, difficult negotiations of structurally produced differences and records of violence that cannot be fully deflected by expressions of contrition. Hawthorne's romantic lament is plagued by a liberal desire to resolve social conflict with an affective remorse. The Americans' return to the nation is a fictional reconciliation from which the sympathizer can take comfort without having to experience the material discomfort of dismantling systemic injustice.

The disorientation that is caused by the bandaging of social wounds with psychic compensation can fester until it reaches a point of panic. Before he returns to his "dear native land," the novel's American protagonist Kenyon becomes disoriented at Carnival. A heavy martial presence marks the carnivalesque scene as laden with potential risks of collective uprising, international tension, class conflict, and undisciplined manifestations of freedom. When confronted by "an absurd crowd" and shot with lime dust, Kenyon falls into a "feverish dream" and is poked and prodded by "orang-outangs" and clowns. His confused encounter with figures that symbolically demarcate radical alterity sends him into a state of "comic alarm and horrour [sic]."[65] Faced with a reminder of the critical resilience and persistence of the many whose lives, labors, and texts contributed to the making of his national fantasy, from Ma-re Mount to the U.S. South, he is filled with panic at the moment he seeks to return. As he struggles his way through the unruly crowd, he is filled with panic that his objective faith in national progress may only be an aesthetic fiction that has been stolen on debts of freedom to indigenous people, African Americans, ethnic immigrants, and objectified women.

As his counterpart Hilda, an adept "copyist" of classical art, prepares for her return to America's dear native land, she clings to a bracelet jeweled with stones "dug out of . . . sepulchers."[66] She clings to her wrist and is reminded of the death and destruction she has seen in Rome and hopes to leave behind. Her tears seem to suggest that she understands that the future she pursues is destined to become a copy of the past she seeks to refuse. Her sorrow reveals that the desire to return to a stable domestic future is also built on anxieties about identification with imagined freedoms that had "not yet" and could "not yet" manifest socially. Averting her gaze from the suggestive and diverse calls for economic, social, and racial reordering that erupt in imperfect cultural efforts to "secure" the national future, Hilda identifies with a dream of U.S. progress, looking confidently toward America with "a hopeful soul."[67] To justify her optimistic possession of her *native* land, Hilda tenaciously tries to transform tragedy with tears.

The differential racial categories that are repeatedly made and rewritten to sustain speculative bubbles may "disappear like a dream" as the cultural landscape is revised through circulation, but the distance and dislocation that are endlessly required to maintain the fantasy of universal democracy in the name of speculative dependency point also to the ways that insubordinate memories and aggrieved people's demands for alternative futures always leave a material trace. In the frantic exchange between speculative expansion and national fiction, the imagined landscape reproduces what it refuses: a nation whose investment in the future is balanced on the constantly changing sameness of reproducing racial geographies as the necessary precondition for arriving at a security that is always not yet. It is no small matter that Hawthorne gambled on this future by implicating Rome. In a pattern that we still see today, he attempted to make the lived injustices of speculative nationalism somebody else's problem.

Sublimating Refuse

In the speculative drive to uproot indigenous epistemologies and refuse the past, the imposition of hetero-patriarchal domestic property relationships is everything, and everything about private property is secured by sublimation under liberal governance. Hawthorne's fiction is a useful resource for understanding the working of aesthetic constructions as the social force through which individuals submit to the economic authority of bourgeois liberalism. His story "Main-Street" suggestively delineates the aesthetic as a social process. It explores the nature of art, representation, and visual pleasure beyond what is contained in the object of art, highlighting how culture's pleasing effect extends from social regulation. In Hawthorne's formulation, the aesthetic is a proprioceptive mode of social interaction that extends the external expectations of an abstract authority into the visual stimuli of viewing subjects. The feeling of pleasure that such an engagement creates subordinates the dissonance created by the sense of autonomy that an individual assumes through submission to governing forces. "Main-Street" elucidates the abstracted voice of liberal aesthetics in a performance in which authority becomes visible.

Elizabeth Peabody's introduction to the anthology *Aesthetic Papers*, in which "Main-Street" first appeared in 1849, presents the aesthetic as a democratic forum of artistic exchange in which "all may meet."[68] Her goal for the volume was to create a cultural space for objectively and impersonally sharing ideas about how to reach high ideals of universalism. Peabody saw aesthetic production as a "phase in human progress which subordinates the individual to the general, that he may reappear on a higher plane of individuality."[69] Favoring the "feeling expressed" in art over form and content, she presents aesthetics as a sensory technology whereby the subjective response of a viewer gradually unfolds into universal ideals of beauty and truth. She imagines that the collective exploration of the particular tastes of the nation manifests as a unified expression of national values. Yet the particularities that shape this type of universal become a privileging authority for subordination and exclusion. Paul Gilmore has theorized the romantic concept of the aesthetic as a feeling of universality that stems from the individual's failure to recognize self-interest and personal taste as shaping pleasurable responses. When observers do not register that the "feeling expressed" by art emerges through their particular reception of it, they can come to see universal truths as contained in the object. This feeling of universality thus alienates those whose particular values constitute, and so subsequently align with, presumed universalisms from the internal senses that secure their privileged position.

Hawthorne's story similarly elucidates a national objectivity as requiring subjects to shed their sense of personal perception. In particular, it is concerned with the way that identification with the nation depends on acts of sensory illusion to sustain citizens' attachment to universal history. In "Main-Street," a showman presents the history of the New England landscape in a mechanical puppet show. As he turns the crank of his contraption, he presents the nation's march of progress. Every turn brings a new set of puppets onto the stage of history where they represent key markers of different eras. Metonymically, the violence of colonial occupation is swept away by industrial innovation, becoming a mere backdrop to the mechanized narrative of progress. As streets replace forests, living Indians are displaced from "nature" and become stolen "artifacts" in the Peabody museum. Infamous civil dissenters such as Thomas Morton and Anne Hutchinson are introduced and excised by the public whippings of Puritan terror. Liberty in North America, the showman argues, was once an "iron-cage."[70] Yet in "telling the whole story of the vast growth and prosperity of one race, and the fated decay of another," the showman draws the viewer toward what he terms the "sunshine of the present."[71] Unfortunately, the puppet machine breaks down and the showman's presentation never arrives at the present. However, he assures the audience that "beauty would have beamed upon them" had his contraption not failed.[72] It is precisely this failure that produces the individual under the privileging authority of the aesthetic. Because the audience cannot see the abstract promise that the showman describes, they must imagine what it might be. When they then associate this internal vision with the shared themes the showman has provided, they incorporate a particular perception that favors their own senses into what they can then assume is a national universal.

Abstraction of this sort is a risky business. To achieve the "feeling" of objective universality, observers must first contend with dissonant representations. The showman warns his audience that they may encounter "for instance, the misplacing of a picture, whereby the people and events of one century might be thrust into the middle of another; or the breaking of a wire, which would bring the course of time to a sudden period."[73] Joel Pfister argues that, in refusing to aestheticize the nation's history, Hawthorne here recuperates an historical memory of the costs of colonization. Although the narrative certainly documents colonial violence, it also accounts for the tragedies of history as the cost of a liberal social contract.

Breaching the norms of audience silence, a noncompliant spectator dismisses the puppet show as a "manifest catch-penny."[74] Rather than see the beauty that the showman promises, he is disappointed by the cheap pasteboard puppets, the products of a mechanically reproduced commodity culture. So disturbed is he by the anachronisms in the showman's presentation that he eventually leaves and demands a refund. The autocratic showman intervenes: "Human art has its limits and we must now and then ask a little aid from the spectator's imagination."[75] When the spectator resists universal prescription, he is told that this is an outcome of his own failed perception: "'But, sir, you have not the proper point of view.'"[76] The showman's insistence ultimately reveals that the price we pay for national unity is the material dislocation of our will to dissent: "Sit further back" the viewer is ordered, and "the slips of pasteboard shall assume spiritual life."[77]

Two factors matter in making sense of the demands of this aesthetic relationship as a delineation of a liberal contract that balances universality on obligatory self-alienation. First, the house is full and only one viewer objects. Second, as the emphasis on mechanical representation and commodity culture suggests, the show takes place in an historical context in which workers and immigrants have become geographically and economically positioned to seek resources and representation as part of the nation. When bourgeois nationalism is faced with the threat of incorporating difference, it mobilizes aesthetic and political abstractions into regulatory requirements of individual subordination to "shared" ideals, the means through which citizens with privileged property maintain their universalizing authority.

In her reading of Walter Benjamin's classic essay "The Work of Art in the Age of Mechanical Reproduction," Susan Buck-Morss emphasizes the compensatory work of aesthetic production in ameliorating the shock of modern industrial life. Submission to the repetitive automation of rationalized labor desensitizes workers to the imagination. Art, Buck-Morss argues, appeals to the alienation of workers as a way to make reified life appear as if it were still human.[78] The daily shock of modern existence is numbed through identification with fantastical ideals of human experience that are presented to workers as objective truths. As Hawthorne's showman suggests, the incorporation of universalism under conditions of dissonance demands that the subject become insensate to proprioceptive experience. His elucidation of this aesthetic process intimately maps the enabling properties of speculative nationalism.

When the sublimating expectation of aesthetic production is grounded in universalisms that are erected from the privileged time, space, and access that endow bourgeois nationalists with speculative advantage, the rights and resources that the nation calls freedom easily become coercive terms for conscripting compliance with expectant denials. The broken machinery of national progress, Hawthorne suggests, is only repairable when discordant citizens sublimate feelings of inaccuracy and injustice to a fragmented perception.[79] His national script teaches us that the speculative contract of "not yet" freedom is a system of temporal stratification that reinforces the interests of universalizing authority on an aesthetic credit that desensitizes subordinated subjects from the shock of exploitation and injustice while making it feel as if their inegalitarian incorporation into national fictions is a fulfillment of their particular desires. When mid-nineteenth-century European immigrant workers claimed a right to enfranchisement on the grounds that they were owners of their personhood and labor, and when workers and farmers forced the nation to liberalize preemption laws with an 1862 Homestead Act that promised free land to the landless, they tactically accessed resources and opportunities that protective self-interested elites had previously denied to the majority. In so doing, however, they entered a contract of political speculation in which they gambled on the hope that accepting the contract of "not yet" freedom would one day result in equal opportunity. The economic construction of propertied citizenship can make it necessary for aggrieved people to make do under constrained conditions by accessing resources on economic terms that support power's authority. Under the capitalist commodification of virtually all means of subsistence, identification with the propertied freedom of liberal nationalism may seem to be the only means for regenerating life. In such conditions, the liberal freedom of speculative nationalism is defined by the will to defy death. Buying into this freedom as a promise of life or democracy, however, can be very dangerous.

The 1862 Homestead Law, for example, made some landless citizens property owners, but it did not undermine speculative power. Indeed, unsympathetic congressional landholders weakened the law with additional land laws favoring, times five, speculative monopolies. The land policies and acquisitions of the railroads, for example, were speculatively designed to profit from settlers who sought free land but encountered a West that had already been purchased. When we read this speculative transformation as a sign of democratization, we risk reinvesting in colonial reason and legacies of enslavement. One reason that an aesthetic understanding of economic relationships is so important is that it teaches us to pay attention to feelings about freedom that are not grounded in justice, to beware of promises that are not really gifts.

The cost of the colonizers' reasoning is evidenced in Thomas Jefferson's promise to the Cherokee people, to whom he offered the legal terms of liberal governance in exchange for a guarantee of Cherokee land and sovereignty. His advocacy of a system of private property that would follow the government's rules of preemption—by which the right to own came from the labor of "improvement"—drew on the norms of patriarchy to void an indigenous epistemology that was largely cultivated by women's agricultural labor. The masculinist construction of the individual in this case not only violated women's knowledge, lives, and autonomy but also eradicated indigenous sovereignty in the name of democratic progress. When Jefferson did not recognize how the Cherokee people had for centuries developed and cultivated intimate relationships with the land that he sublimated, he grounded sacred epistemologies, such as those carried in Green Corn Ceremonies, in a hetero-patriarchal economic construction. Jefferson instrumentally drew on a gendered construction of private property to undermine indigenous people's communal relationship with land that made it fundamentally not for sale. Like Hawthorne's stories, the romantic fiction of a masculine-centered family strove to sever collective understanding so that land could be separated and atomized. In this context, marriage became a racializing construct because it set the privatization of land into motion, laying the groundwork for the Cherokee's later forced expulsion.

Thinking about race and gender through the networked logics of speculative nationalism can give us a clearer view of the ways in which economies differentially position groups as competing and antagonistic and how atomization can regenerate volatile speculative systems. Tracing speculative systems of exchange through culture allows us to grapple with these differential positions and the often contradictory ideas about land, justice, and freedom that they create.

In the land/slave convergence of the nineteenth century, Native American and African American resistant adaptations of cultural meanings about land were constructed through and against, prior to and as a result of, the racializing processes of intersecting and mutually sustaining speculative markets. Autonomy and the right to self-government, for many tribes, was grounded in immemorial sacred sites entrusted by the creator to tribes to protect and occupy.[80] This bequest was not premised on ownership and dominion but on sustaining the land so that future generations might access life-sustaining freedom. As Claudio Saunt and others have argued, to negotiate uneven confrontations with imperial forces, indigenous groups often reframed myth and traditions using the conventions of Western historical narrative. During the eighteenth and nineteenth centuries, many indigenous leaders and activists mythologized their contact with earlier colonists to support indigenous rights to tribal autonomy. In the context of severe pressure on Native people's sovereignty, the fluid narrative boundaries between memory, history, and story both informed indigenous differences and articulated sovereign rights in legally recognizable terms based on them.[81] Paradoxically, the narrative tactics that enabled the limited recognition of indigenous people under the terms of nation-to-nation treaty making also lay the foundation on which the U.S. nation-state continues to justify conquest by equating land with money.[82]

Within the speculative economy of the slave market, on the other hand, land was configured as a commodity equivalent to the sublimation of personhood for a price. This relationship was defined through international exchange as a relational fluctuation of exchange values. What happened to land prices in the abstract could on the ground make a radical difference in whether or not enslaved people were forced into movement. The operative impossibility of viewing an enslaved person as an agential object instilled southern exchange networks with an organization of Blackness that Fred Moten has called an "extended movement of a specific upheaval, an on-going irruption that anarranges every line."[83] The predictable unpredictability of displacement under slavery that is not sensory in abstract value was lived and felt daily on the ground. Southern land was a marker of broken connections that created motherless children, partnerless lovers, and ancestorless descendants. When African American people reckon with land as a locus of rupture, they must engage the cultural contradictions of the commodity form—not just for the mystification of alienated labor, but also as a carrier of multiple negotiations, alternative meanings, and practices of resistance that speak past and through exchange value.

The liberal production of land as property, these differential racial outcomes suggest, is constantly disrupted by indigenous epistemologies that move land through dislocation, by the embodied exertions of humans objectified who continue to act, by the worker's claim to self as property, by the debtor's refusal to pay back, and by the commoner's assertion of collective holdings that may still be evidenced in resistance to work among the nonindustrious poor. Possibilities for remapping and rethinking the world abound beneath the layers of national mythology. But locating frameworks for making do with them can feel like an explosive project because it requires sifting through landmines of speculative adjustments that have benefited from pitting different groups against one another.

Exploring this dynamic is the objective of the next chapter. This chapter ends with a proposition. The aesthetic corollaries of economic systems should teach us to look gift horses directly in the mouth. When we do this, we are likely to find the possibility of the impossible. In the belly of the beast, or what Audra Simpson frames as living in Columbus's entrails, we cannot help but sense indigenous knowledge that survives against conquest.[84] In embracing the stance of the unruly spectator, we might better understand the challenges we face and the transformative possibilities that reemerge when we resourcefully and critically recall, rework, and redistribute creative capacities for mapping futures with no commitment to speculative structures that propagate violence. Andrea Smith draws on Manu Meyer's notion of a racial remembering of the future to call attention to the life-generating, future justice that this stance might enable. The objective of reckoning and remembering cannot be to recover and recreate the world as it once may have been. Rather, when we recall how Native nations "are and have always been nations that change and adapt to surrounding circumstances," we are backed by the knowledge that other freedoms are possible, that conditions that make life merely possible can be transformed by creative and resilient actions to live against the odds of death-defying freedom into conditions that make life meaningful and affirming.[85]

Racial Returns

Slave Speculation, Managerial Capitalism, the Spectacular Sites of Yosemite

This bill simply proposes to take possession of the property which is abandoned—left in such a condition, that, unless we do take care of it, it will be unimproved and fall into decay and ruin, and waste and desolation be spread over the country.

—SENATOR LAFAYETTE FOSTER, 1862

This bill proposes to make a grant of certain premises located in the Sierra Nevada mountains, in the state of California, that are for all public purposes worthless, but which constitute perhaps some of the greatest wonders of the world. The object and purpose is to make a grant to the State . . . that the property shall be inalienable forever, and preserved and improved as a place of public resort.

—SENATOR JOHN CONNESS, 1864

If I go wid you I be good as dead, so if I got to dead, I might's well dead here as anywhere. So I'll stay and wait for the Yankees.

—HARRY, 1862

The Scene of Exchange

Counter to what the progressive imaginary of liberal nationalism recalls about the abolition of slavery, for many nationalists during the 1860s the sound of freedom rang bells of panic. During the early years of the Civil War, enslaved people anticipated and prepared for a radical reorganization of society. Speculative nationalists planned ahead with disingenuous partial comprehension. While advocating for the moral urgency of abolition, nationalists fearfully set out to protract emancipation because they imagined Black freedom would result in total economic collapse. Abolition emerged as a very real possibility in the United States after decades of speculative bubbles and panics. Much of the volatility in the U.S. economy was directly connected to the cotton economy.

Cotton grew, moved, and returned to the South on credit. Southern bank ledgers, plantation records, and financial histories of the 1830s, 1840s, and

1850s suggest that the slave-backed cotton economy was built on annual cycles of optimism and anxiety.[1] Edward Baptist has found that during the 1830s, for example, half of the value of U.S. exports was tied to cotton. Many planters depended on "accommodation loans" to carry costs during the planting season. Cotton buyers drew on commercial credit to buy up and export bales. Credit crossed through the South to the North, through London and Liverpool, from New York to New Orleans, returning as payment to the planters, merchants, movers, insurers, marketers, and manufacturers who participated in making the global cotton market.

The New Orleans and Natchez branches of the U.S. Bank, according to Baptist, lent one-third of its capital to the cotton economy. Much of this financial capacity was coupled with loans from planters' banks for the purchase of thousands of enslaved people from the Old Southwest. The Consolidated Association of the Planters of Louisiana in New Orleans, Baptist argues, made it possible for speculators to securitize slaves as backing for stock. Borrowers bought stock in the association by mortgaging slaves and land. When borrowers traded these stocks with the London merchant bank Barron Brothers, they turned slave-backed securities into liquid capital. Because the social entrepreneurs who had devised this scheme had also convinced the state of Louisiana to back the association with $2.5 million in state bonds, stockholders traded on the invisible backs of the enslaved with the confidence that, should the global market fail, much of the risk would be absorbed by the state.

In the case of Barron Brothers, Baptist finds, "the sale of the bonds created a pool of high-quality credit to be lent back to the planters at a rate significantly lower than the rate of return that they could expect that money to produce. That pool could be used for all sorts of income-generating purposes: buying more slaves (to produce more income to serve as the collateral for still more borrowing) or lending to other enslavers."[2] Risk was rampant in this stock exchange because borrowers could use the same asset to back multiple stock purchases. Slave buyers could also use short-term bank loans to purchase human commodities and then back new loans on the persons they had purchased even though they still owed banks for those bodies.

Overleveraging during this era created system-wide vulnerability that came back to the price of cotton. The dangers of system risk were made apparent in 1836, when major European brokers collapsed because overconfidence and overproduction had caused cotton prices to fall so much that they could no longer cover companies' debts. Europe's financial ruin returned to the U.S. South, where the top ten cotton brokers in New Orleans also collapsed.

Nevertheless, by midcentury, confidence returned to the South when global cotton prices rose again. The renewed and restored cotton bubble of the 1850s contributed to ancillary bubbles in commercial agriculture, land, and human chattel. And this speculative web was not at all contained in the South. Foreign stockowners held an estimated 58 percent of southern stocks. Northern financiers, insurers, providers of goods, and doctors counted on slave bubbles for the estimated 13.5 percent of the price of a person that went back into north-ern businesses with every slave sale. Everyone, from brokers, manufacturers, shippers, and marketers to the workers whose unaccounted lives and labor sus-tained the global cotton economy, was intimately enmeshed in a speculative web.[3] At the center of this global economic entanglement was the fate of mil-lions of enslaved people.[4]

Kenneth Pomeranz calculates that in 1860 enslaved people in the South picked cotton at a rate four times faster than their ancestors had in 1800. By 1830, 80 percent of the cotton used in the British textile economy was imported from the southern United States. In 1859, the South sent 2.1 billion pounds of cotton across the sea, a sign of cotton's dominance as the most widely traded global commodity of the mid-nineteenth century.[5] The entire global economy, it seemed, hinged on the labor and lives of people held as slaves. Thus when the war showed signs that slavery might actually be eradicated, many worried that the entire transatlantic economy would fall with it.

On the basis of this economic concern, Senator Lafayette Foster in 1862 approached Congress with a proposal. To prevent a crisis, he argued, cotton production could not stop. But to guarantee labor that would work the fields, he rationalized, the nation would have to defer Black people's rights to freedom and justice. To prevent financial catastrophe the nation would take possession of abandoned property, by which he meant both land and people.

The economic anxiety that led Foster to advise Congress to act as tempo-rary slaveholders was both general and intimate. In 1862, the federal treasury was burdened with an exponential debt of 23.9 million unsettled state claims for war reimbursement. During the early years of the Civil War, the cost of reimbursement skyrocketed to $1 million per day, threatening to deplete funds for paying congressional salaries. The public was agitated, demanding that treasury secretary Salmon P. Chase overturn rules that would allow state governments twenty-five years to pay off war debts.[6] Looking for a means of paying off these debts, Foster found an opportunity in a convergence of events that had occurred months earlier. First, rising cotton prices on the European exchange during 1861 had created an enticing inducement for the government to get involved in cotton production.[7] Second, war confiscations in Port Royal, South Carolina, had tentatively placed 10,000 formerly enslaved human beings under the authority of the federal treasury. Pushed by urgency and the threat of "waste," Foster's plan was to sentence the human "contraband" who had been abandoned by plantation owners in the South Carolina Sea Islands to working their way toward full emancipation while the federal government held their lives in the balance until they could prove and pay their worth as potential citizens.

Foster justified his proposal with simplicity: if the federal government did not act as the overseer of the supposedly abandoned cotton fields, the annu-al crop would go to ruin. Thus he urgently called for officially writing "not yet" freedom into national policy so that federal agents would be authorized to systematize, penalize, and coercively "democratize" the labor of formerly enslaved people. The plan he submitted to Congress was delivered in the form of a twofold promise. First, he assured his colleagues that resignification of slavery as a benevolent and necessary temporary condition of forced indenture would protect the government from lost revenue from wasted crops. Second, he promised that people who peacefully agreed to delay their freedom might one day, in some undisclosed future, be allowed to buy their way into the limited emancipation of the general free-labor economy.

Foster's assurances sounded a curious alarm over agricultural and social devastation. His apprehension about the potential devastation that would spread across the "country" without national recovery was peculiar because it focused on potential federal financial losses, which only months earlier would have been private. Prior to southern planters' desertion of the land he discussed, the federal government had not held a direct stake in or expectations about the gains or losses of the annual crop. Rather, during the antebellum period this was a concern of planters who often hedged their bets on their ability to turn humans into liquid assets should a crop go belly up. That is, when a crop failed under private control, southern property holders often sold off enslaved property to cover their losses. Neither crop ruin nor the possession of people would register officially on the federal balance sheet. Yet Foster's rhetorical stance that he sought "simply" to "take care" that the land the government had only recently absorbed not be forsaken such that "ruin, and waste and desolation be spread over the country."

Foster's use of the term "country" speaks in two mixed moralistic and economistic registers. On the one hand, the term points to the particularity of Port Royal Sound, from which, in November of 1861, the entire White population had fled after a Union Army victory. Before leaving, many plantation owners set out to destroy their property. Some demolished farm equipment. Some burnt the cotton crop. Others murdered enslaved people. Some kidnapped "their" human chattel, and others attempted to convince the enslaved people to "escape" from the Yankees with them. Foster drew on a primitivist fantasy of Black developmental inferiority to insert federal intervention into this scene as a national obligation to protect the "not yet" freeable lives of people who purportedly depended on national paternalism for their survival.

Of course, his posture of aid was self-serving to the "country" in the nationalist meaning of the word. Certainly Foster was concerned about the national debt, as his own pay and future were on the line. The nearly 200 abandoned plantations constituting the "abandoned property" at stake had yielded one of the largest crops local planters could recall the year prior.[8] Given the spike in global cotton prices, Foster saw an enticing prospect for relieving national debts. In this regard, the loss that he presented to Congress as imminent was not so much a loss that would have detracted from what the government then held as it was the loss of an opportunity to profit from a system the government just so happened to have inherited out of war. Foster's panic, in other words, was a speculative one. His proposition wove threads of apprehension about debts that preceded the government's assumption of property into a global financial system that was overleveraged on human collateral. Racialized risk of this propertied variant, however, created limits on Foster's optimism. Because much of the financial risk in the notoriously volatile cotton market was securitized on the bodies of enslaved people, freedom presented a threat of financial collapse. Full emancipation would strip the underlying asset prices out of the heart of the cotton exchange, which was likely to leave any investor in the system under financial water.

Foster's guise of nationalist compassion is inextricable from his speculative interest in hedging a bet on global cotton to alleviate the national debt. Making money in the system he hoped to exploit required maintaining slavery. Thus his plan did everything to make slavery necessary. Federal appropriation of the means of subsistence that the people of Port Royal required for survival created the dependence on which Foster preyed. His "welfare" policy for the South took all resources and opportunities under federal ownership, giving formerly enslaved people few options but forced labor, which Foster called an experiment toward freedom.

Congress approved Foster's bill, but the policy it contained was never officially executed. Still, it remains an important event in the history of speculative nationalism because it officially entered a racializing formation of life as debt into the Congressional record. Foster's plan may have died in the place of Port Royal, but its legacy lives on in the nation's most revered and symbolic physical landscape, Yosemite National Park. Foster's diatribe against waste was an expression of a much broader structural adjustment. His proposal to defer Black emancipation is connected, through an eccentric web of coincidental successes and failures, to the development of Yosemite. Redesigning the physical landscape of the United States into a symbol of democracy may not have been directly proposed as a financial policy for alleviating fears of speculative collapse, but the panic in Foster's appeal ultimately found a sense of security through the construction of public parks.

This chapter argues that the creation of U.S. national parks emerged from a panic of national reconstruction. During Reconstruction, Foster's racializing fiscal formulation of life as debt returned again and again across the national scene. From the southern economy to northern industry, "not yet" freedom worked its way into the national consolidation of industrial capitalism through symbolic landscapes in the American West. From the cobbled pathways of the southern slave pens through the eastern trails of urban parks, the roads that the nation built to keep ahead of the financial ruin it feared emancipation would create spread across the entire country. Twisting through diverse labor regimes toward the California coast, the nation's reconfiguration of freedom as debt wound its way through the mountains and valleys of the Northwest and materialized as the winding roads and scenic vistas of Yosemite.

The Form of Transfer

This chapter tracks how the speculative hopes underlying the U.S. slave economy were transplanted into the managerial center of industrial capitalism through the form of U.S. national parks. To make its argument, the chapter follows the career of Frederick Law Olmsted through a series of coincidences and connections by which the southern plantocracy's speculative pattern of racializing risk on the labor and liquidity of Black lives supplied the logics and policies whereby differential racialization became the foundation of U.S. industrialism.

Prior to becoming the United State's most prominent and revered landscape designer, Frederick Law Olmsted was known as a prolific travel writer who reported on the conditions of southern slavery for northern readers. Olmsted's first book, *Walks and Talks of an American Farmer in England*, documented his engagement with European parks and recorded his reflections on the daily activity of what was then the world's central point in the global cotton exchange, the docks at Liverpool. On the basis of this book, Olmsted was hired by the *New York Times* in 1852 to write a series of articles reporting on the economic and social conditions of the South.[9] He spent a total of fourteen months in the South, drawing on his observations to publish sixty-five articles by 1854. In 1857 he published an additional ten letters for the *New York Daily Tribune*. Olmsted's journalism shifted in tone from ethnographic observation, narrative exposition, personal reflection, and economic evocation to abolitionist polemic for a free-labor economy. It ultimately became a thrice-told tale of financial misrecognitions that the author drew on as the basis for combining civic moral reform with managerial free-labor capitalism.

Olmsted reedited his Southern writing as a trilogy that purported to compare and evaluate regional modes of agricultural production: *A Journey in the Seaboard Slave States, with Remarks on the Economy* (1856), *A Journey through Texas, or a Saddle Trip in the Southwestern Frontier* (1857), and *A Journey in the Backcountry* (1860). These books highlighted both large- and small-scale cotton, tobacco, sugar, and rice production on plantations and farms with an eye to the social ideologies, values, and practices of people across the U.S. South. When Olmsted abridged them once again in 1861 as *The Cotton Kingdom*, he wrote not only for a British audience but also from within the burgeoning context of the Civil War. Subtle observations and momentary fascination with plantation efficiency give way in this ultimate articulation to what appears at first as an illogical political proposal for exacting freedom through "Subjugation!" but he explains: "This is a Republic, and the South must come under the yoke of freedom, not to work for us, but to work with us, on equal terms, as a free people. To work with us, for the security of a state of society . . . one system or the other is to thrive and extend, and eventually possess and govern the whole land."[10]

In this early work, Olmsted regarded enslaved people as potential recipients of the North's "sound and safe progress in knowledge, civilization and Christianity," but his abolitionist position was not premised on moral and political concern about emancipating human beings.[11] His writings did not treat the idea of subjugating the South into freedom as a contradiction because his argument was an economic rather than a social one. As an economic principle, freedom was for Olmsted a name for the abstract liberal universal though which the South could be incorporated into his utopian vision for a nationally secured productive capitalist economy. His descriptions of the South were as much records of his scorn for what he saw as the irrational unpredictability of southern markets as they were a reductive economic endorsement of a labor theory of value. Landscape reconstruction entered this equation in the aftermath of slavery as a technology for extracting profits akin to the inflations of speculation through new forms of managerial "ingenuity."

This chapter pursues the twists and turns through which moral projects to civilize so-called savage, backward, and underdeveloped people into free workers according to this labor theory of value also legitimized (in the minds of those whose privileged status as full citizens had been secured through inheriting ownership of the land, lives, and labor of the oppressed) the positioning of colonized, formerly enslaved, non-European immigrants and women to anticipate rather than participate in the life of the nation. Although Olmsted's movement through the South to the West is an integral part of the story, the objective of this analysis is neither to biography Olmsted nor to isolate him as the sole culprit and investor in the racializing scheme of speculative nationalism. He is but one figure who acted within a much broader fabric of radical social and economic transformation. His trajectory through different scenes and landscapes, however, elucidates a particularly potent example of racial meanings in one context—*southern slave markets*—returning elsewhere and later as a new expression—*wasted time in the Reconstruction Era.*

Racial returns on "not yet" freedom were twofold during Reconstruction. On one hand, the moral formula for constituting life as debt was broadly traded across diverse regional economies as a way to hedge speculative hopes. On another hand, the speculative formulation of "not yet" freedom made it possible to mask the speculative sentiments undergirding managerial industrialism's moralizing economy while enabling producers to offset losses through the continuation of racialized risk.

Olmsted's career points to the national landscape as a financial record of the deeply ingrained practices through which racialized capitalism systematically produces and reproduces race to absorb fiscal risk. This chapter reads this record with a focus on how the circulation of explicit ideas and practices for leveraging risk on the South's oppressive racism was transferred into subtle cultural processes of "not yet" freedom through which risk was racialized in the free-labor economy. As recorded in the material landscape, "wasted" southern time was moved into "worthless" western space and re-created as a national symbol of democratic freedom. Lafayette Foster's proposal, as I discuss, is one detail in the transfer: his plan came direct from Olmsted's studies of the South. As important in the web of interactions, however, were the lives ensnared at the center of each transaction. People claimed freedom in resistance to speculative policies like Foster's that made national futurity dependent on slavery's implicit return. The actions of people who refused to be objects on the Port Royal plantations coveted by Foster provide a striking case in point.

Life in the Odds

Prior to the Civil War, 83 percent of the population of Port Royal lived under enslavement. The retreat of plantation owners created a liminal space in which to occupy the status of former enslavement. Many people staked a claim to this status by rejecting the entreaties of their former owners, refusing to work in the cotton fields, disabling the means of cotton production, and possessing the land for subsistence agriculture. Foster's bill sought to treat such actions with a rhetorical sleight of hand that would shift the terms of slavery without requiring a change in the material practice of forced servitude. In May of 1861, Benjamin Butler set a precedent for claiming Black bodies as "confiscated property of war." The Union took advantage of this method of appropriation when it claimed possession of both the land and the remaining residents of Port Royal using the legal process of "condemnation." Formerly enslaved people were transformed into "contraband" state property through the transfer of private title for public use. In the legal sense, they were released from private ownership and "condemned" to the nation-state for the public's good.

The means through which this human form of contraband was "abandoned," however, was not as simple as Foster presented it. Many of the 10,000 inhabitants who remained when plantation owners fled had been left behind. Certainly, however, to suggest that all of the African American people who remained had been deserted unwillingly is a counterfeit of history. Walter Johnson brilliantly argues that contemporary scholarly efforts to understand enslavement are haunted by a fantasy of "agency" that leads many historians to overstress an imagined African American autonomy of resistance. The liberal confiscation of the meaning of freedom balances on an individualist romance of self-willed action. No such possibility of independent autonomy exists under any differentiating social structure, let alone under enslavement by which Black thought and activity were organized during the nineteenth century. The form of speculative nationalism that caught African American people at Port Royal in a matrix of transition made them simultaneously enslaved and formerly enslaved, property and potential persons, helplessly destitute and competent labor. Within such contradictions, freedom and repression, liberation and entrapment, action and subjugation operated synonymously. In his use of the category "abandoned property," Foster attempted to fix this status as an inherent aspect of African American people. The bill he proposed addressed cultivation as both an agricultural and social project. The primitivist fantasies of Black subjectivity in his bill created the economic possibility for deferring freedom so that Black labor would be available to government overseers.

Foster's depiction of uncared for property glossed over the diverse life-affirming strategies that formerly enslaved people innovated to produce what Johnson identifies as "insistently transcendent . . . new creative, vibrant and sustaining forms of human being."[12] Many of the thousands of people who remained in Port Royal were escapees of murder and kidnapping by their former owners. Some fled to coastal plantations from elsewhere as refugees of war and enslavement. Others likely came to Port Royal from places that had not yet been claimed by Union forces with the hope that the disorder of national transformation would create subtle opportunities for exercising self-determination and dignity. The confusion and disconnect between the chains of the South and the laws of the North certainly meant that people everywhere had a stake in determining what freedom might become. Many did not accept the terms of Foster's nationalist conscription. Like Harry in the chapter epigraph, many people remained when the plantation owners left because they refused to accept life under any form of enslavement.

Harry refused a freedom that was predicated on simple death defiance when he claimed that going with his former owner would be as "good as dead." He stayed in Port Royal hoping for a new organization of power, with the understanding that staying might also result in physical death. It is precisely in his rejection of the idea that life simply means breathing another day that Harry gambled on the possibility of dying in Port Royal to claim more out of life. His wager arrived on the printed page as a declaratory recollection within a chain of iterations. As his words circulated from an actual or perhaps only imagined act of spoken defiance through the pride of memory inscribed in the private journals of a listener's delight, they became an archive of subversive histories. When reframed as a text for public consumption, Harry's rebellion spread and surreptitiously usurped the transaction between nationalism and speculation under which he was then living, with a third-party reminder of millions of lives held in the balance. His attempt to beat the odds of a speculative dispute appeals to a long tradition of place-making improvisation that draws on religious hopes for an afterlife as a tool to withstand conditions on earth.

Charlotte Forten, a free African American who recorded Harry's words, had convinced the Philadelphia Port Royal Relief Society to support her as a volunteer teacher in October 1862. In her journals, she described a rhythmic epistemology of deathly spiritual transcendence as the defining aural landscape of the time she spent on the coast.[13] Forten recollected John Brown's revolutionary life marching on through musical refrains that she taught the children. As the song carried Brown's soul across the Port Royal landscape, it also remembered the materiality of a life that "mouldered in the grave." She also recorded traditional musical verses, many of which registered deep desires for death as a site of connection and emancipation—for example, "Lay my body in the graveyard" and "My mudder's gone to glory and I want to get dere too."[14] The way death signified as life affirmation in these spiritual rhythms suggests an insistence on solidarity and connection in the context of a cruel calculus of quantification that had forced separations remembered in lyrics like "Old edler . . . young sister . . . young bruder . . . young member where hab you been."[15] Under the structural limitations that Harry faced when asserting his will to stay and risk death at Port Royal, his understanding that he was as good as dead there as anywhere contradictorily registers as a means of undermining the mathematics through which his status would inevitably be shaped—by the battles of competing political economic interests.

In such a context, Harry's embrace of the possibility of death willfully contradicted its own presumption of futurity. His was not a declaration of his capacity to live on under conditions of duress. It was not a compensatory agreement to accept promises of future rewards—be they from an owner, from a nation, or from theology. Rather, by setting the terms on which he would face death, Harry affirmed himself in the present as a major stakeholder in global financial networks. His indifference to his own death indicates a strategy for undermining the economic confidence of the militant economic competition presuming to hold his life in the balance. His narration of laughter in the face of structural panic reverberates into the future desires of competing economic camps, insisting that neither had a chance of *ever* fully controlling the future of Black life. Harry's defiance was radically subversive because it did not look to the "Yankees" as saviors, but rather recognized the odds that northern freedom could also produce or prolong death.

In framing his chance for life through the specter of death, Harry cunningly called attention to his understanding that he lived in the cross hairs of competing ruling classes, neither of which had an interest in justice. What he may not have known explicitly, he suggested implicitly: the deck of the entire economy was stacked against him because all of its cards were invested in slavery. In such a context, Harry's manipulation of the terms of salvation showed the grounded epistemology of a person who was aware that his life was subject to third-party wagers in a zero-sum power struggle between competing financial interests. He demonstrated keen awareness that all of the choices presented to him were designed to use his life as an object toward the racialization of risk. In such a scenario, as Cedric Robinson has argued, the most plausible strategy available to subjects of economic racialization for achieving justice was to extort it from the ruling classes.[16]

Like many others, Harry lived in and against the odds. As volunteers of the American Missionary Association observed when they arrived at the "unimproved" land of Port Royal a month following Foster's plea, formerly enslaved people were using the land to grow corn, potatoes, and other staple crops as complements to family diets that were rich in fish and oysters.[17] Missionaries also discovered that formerly enslaved people were reluctant to relinquish the impromptu subsistence practices that they had begun to develop and that they were disinclined to return to the arduous and violently managed labor system that they associated with their enslavement in the cotton economy. Foster's worry over the spread of desolation in this regard was not so much relevant to the actual land and people the nation assumed to be contraband property. It was rather an expression of his understanding of systemic speculative risk and his fears that the nation's exponential debt could become the ruin of the White supremacist liberal nation.

The Plantation Fantasy Exchange

Foster did not author his bill for "not yet" freedom. He inherited it from Frederick Law Olmsted, who had devised the plan on the sidelines of a plantation as a popular spectator and reporter on the slave South. In Olmsted's writing on policy and public space, the managerial formation of industrial capitalism grew from the "waste" of slavery's speculative imagination. Across a long career in which he imaginatively and physically wrote and reconstructed the nation in various forms, Olmsted participated in a network of transactions through which the capitalist contradictions of a free-labor democracy would be inscribed in the nation as scenic vistas. Terming slavery "waste" created returns for free-labor reformers by instigating the relocation of financial confidence from systems of exchange (slave speculation) to modes of production (labor repression). Northern reformers drew on the category of waste both as a criticism of the ostensible inefficiency of plantation production and as a mechanism for regarding "free workers" as autonomous individuals who chose and designed their own subjection to repression. During the Civil War, the category of waste created a landscape for a national vision to bureaucratize plantation regimes as models for increasing free-labor productivity. The terms for organizing life under the sign of debt through which Foster proposed to forestall African American manumission did not officially materialize in Port Royal, but they were tested in labor camps as a managerial strategy for the racial division of labor on California's Gold Coast. This construction also infiltrated the landscape design and ideology of the nation's first public park and contributed to the gradual dispossession of the Yosemite Indians. It began as a reaction to economic frustration caused by a strategic misapprehension of the extent to which enslaved labor was tied to the circulatory system of the speculative global cotton economy.

Olmsted was not unique in how he abstractly differentiated southern plantations and speculation from northern industrialism. His early writing focused on the South with an ethnographic authority, distinguishing self from other for his northern readers. He appealed to northern audiences using familiar conventions of a moral geography: a narrative partitioning of slavery to the undeveloped South understood in contrast to the progress and liberation of a democratic North. Yet the partitioning device most prevalent in Olmsted's writing was less political and cultural than it was economic.

Olmsted's southern texts falsely rendered intersecting goods, labor, and financial markets as discrete and self-contained abstract economies: The free-labor North and the slave South. Because this abstraction made it possible for

Olmsted to regard labor as the primary indicator of all market behavior, he framed North and South as mutually exclusive systems of production.[18] From collapsing various aspects of economic production, distribution, consumption, and exchange into a singular focus on productive relations, Olmsted assumed a classical position that labor was the "only true generator" of value and capital accumulation.[19] Olmsted's abstraction diverted his attention from the movements of goods and financial resources that intimately tied the North to the South and created the possibility and need for labor markets in general. Given that industry and agriculture were dissimilar productive arenas, it is difficult to fully assess the validity of the mid-nineteenth-century reformer's claims that plantation slavery was as a whole more "wasteful" and inefficient than the free system of labor exploitation.[20] What is clear, however, is that Olmsted's myopic fixation on productive output distracted him from assessing the ways that both northern and southern labor markets were tied to the financial and speculative markets of slavery.

Karl Marx drew on Olmsted's assessment of the wastefulness of slavery in the first volume of *Capital* to account for valorization as the capitalist's struggle against productive inefficiency. Marx's reading of objectified labor followed Olmsted's contention that all wealth was the outcome of alienated labor. The objectification of labor power, according to Marx's well-known formulation, is the magical sleight of hand that creates surplus value. According to Marx, the price a capitalist pays for abstract labor on the open market realizes labor's exchange value and alienates its use value. In the daily work of production, however, capital consumes labor for its use value. "Valorization" is the name Marx gave to the cost differential between the purchase price of objectified labor and usefully expended, alienated labor power. He drew on Olmsted's discussion of slavery as an example of inefficiency and waste undermining the capitalist's effort to reduce the costs of production by eliminating inefficient tools and practices. Waste, in this understanding, was the name Marx borrowed from Olmsted for anything that impedes the capitalist's ability to maximize profits through the reduction of labor costs.[21]

The challenge of reading capital against the backdrop of slavery's inefficiency was not so much related to what were likely Olmsted's valid representations of cumbersome tools and unsympathetic working conditions. Rather, what requires further consideration is both writers' conclusion that "production based on slavery [is] more expensive."[22] In the case of the South that Olmsted observed, this argument held only so long as the financial infrastructure of capitalist production was abstracted from the labor process. From the vantage point of financial markets, most prices in the global economy were in some way tied to a financial system that carried risk on the slaveholder's capacity to liquidate human commodities.

Olmsted's argument that slavery was wasteful was marked by frustration over the failures of slaveholders to manage time and labor toward the maximization of labor power. "The constantly occurring delays, and the waste of time and labour that you encounter everywhere," he wrote, "are most annoying and provoking."[23] He repeatedly called enslaved people "wasteful" and "careless," attributing this perceived behavior to the character of the enslaved rather than to the conditions of captivity and coercion.[24] He referred to enslaved people as "stupid, indolent, wasteful, [and] treacherous," remarking often on the "rascality" that caused enslaved people to "sometimes refuse to labor."[25] The "loss of time" created by daily acts of noncompliance, he contended, caused "the marvelous neglect or waste of natural resources of the country."[26] From this critique, Olmsted began to stage a fabrication of the producer's injury that capitalists repeatedly performed in acts of naming their limited power to extract the *costs* of indolent workers from future profits. Olmsted played with the fantasy of inverse grievance when he argued that slaves "become less and less value as producers, and more and more expensive as consumers."[27] Olmsted backed his calculation of *costs* with estimated quantifications. For example, in comparison with immigrant Irish farmers, he argued, "the carelessness of negroes" caused crop "loss between three and four hundred *per cent* [italics in original]."[28] In another instance, he counted on a plantation owner to corroborate his calculus with the planter's own claim to measure labor that had not been exerted: "The truth is, that in general, a slave does not do half the work he easily might; and which, by being harsh enough with him, he can be made to do."[29] Neither Olmsted nor his informant showed their math because, like most of the estimates Olmsted offered as support for his free-labor campaign, their conclusions were based on observation and optimism and not on actual receipts or ledgers.

A false calculus of waste was nevertheless the foundation of Olmsted's argument that expendable workers under free-market capitalism were much more cost-effective than production premised on the labor power of enslaved people. Contracts, he argued, protected industry against loss when workers took ill, died, refused to work, or became disabled. The costs of feeding, clothing, and disposing of noncompliant workers that Olmsted assumed burdened the South were of no concern to free-labor employers. In addition, he contended that wage incentives encouraged northern workers to author their own exploitation. To this effect, he provided anecdotal evidence of a case during an English harvest of "labourers at work without leaving the field or taking any repose for sixty hours. . . . Such services men may give voluntarily, for their own regard to the value of property to be saved by it, or for the purpose of establishing their credit as worth good wages."[30] Above all, Olmsted promoted labor competition as the primary mechanism for disposing of the "waste" of the slave economy: "The man who cannot command the current rates[will be] the first to be dropped on a reduction [and] the last to be taken out at an increase of force."[31]

In general, Olmsted relied on observations of poverty—low earnings, poor diets, and "shabby" hovels, which he saw as the defining condition of the majority of southern citizens—as the primary evidence of slavery's "waste." Yet, especially in his earlier writing, he also revealed his fascination with the wealth and affluence of the slaveholding aristocracy. Indeed, even in *The Cotton Kingdom* he was at pains to explain "points where the forces of wealth seem to have concentrated,"[32] but he confessed, "There are apparent exceptions, and I have been at times a good deal puzzled by them."[33] Keeping to his conviction that slavery was inherently less profitable than free labor, he strangely conceded that "by unusually skillful and energetic management, under favourable circumstances, the labour of slaves, in certain instances, seems to accomplish as much for its course as that of free labourers at the North."[34] Actual financial records suggest that it is much more likely that the division of wealth Olmsted observed in the South was shaped by a system of speculative finance that concentrated wealth in the hands of a minority while making access to markets prohibitively unaffordable to the majority. Olmsted's misrecognition of speculative wealth was particularly pernicious because it set the stage for a long career in which he endeavored to procure profits that could compete with the inflation of speculative bubbles through repressive management of working people that he imagined as "unusually skillful."

Olmsted was certainly aware that the overall southern economy included markets in goods and finance along with labor. He was also intimately familiar with the commodities market in human chattel in which the value of a person was configured not only through labor power but also through the enslaved person's status as an embodied asset. "The sale and purchase of men, women and children, regarding them so distinctly as property, and property entirely is such an insult to the human race, that nothing else that disgraces the name of man more demands the shame and indignant protest of all men."[35] Olmsted's lament recognized, as Walter Johnson eloquently delineates, that in the South "enslaved people had a measurable monetary value whether or not they were ever sold."[36]

Olmsted traveled the South during a period of bank suspensions that caused a decentralization of global debt relations. Following the panic of 1837, the 1840s was a period when debtors liquidated assets, and credit and commerce were reorganized through exchange notes and systems of local investors.[37] During the 1840s, debtors who had wagered on slave-backed securities in planters associations and through merchant banks liquidated slave properties to pay back debts in an effort to recover from crisis; this made a slave nearly equivalent to cash. Although slavery may have been less efficient as a labor market, for many slaveholding was instrumental in avoiding bankruptcy. Enslaved people remained a valid security that some debtors drew on to extend the terms of their credit and avoid litigation.[38] Yet, as Michael Tadman argues, the bubble that propelled the interregional movement of over a quarter of a million human commodities during the 1850s was connected more than anything to rising global prices of staple crops. Tadman also calculates that the majority of sales from the upper to the lower South were made in private exchanges to take advantage of speculative prices. In this context, by selling surplus properties slaveholders benefited from profits that were higher and more immediately accessed than profits that would be accrued from the use value of enslaved labor.

What Olmsted configured as "waste" Johnson reveals as the central contradiction of slavery: "The abstract value that underwrote the southern economy could only be made material in human shape—frail, sentient and resistant."[39] In fact, Olmsted was privy to the daily discussions that filled southern streets where market participants attempted to negotiate and fix value in an unstable and unpredictable system of exchange made even more tenuous by the possibility of objects who might always resist. Indeed, some of the men with whom he spoke declared that slaves often were not profitable "except to raise for sale."[40] In another striking episode of speculative disavowal, while in New Orleans he crossed paths with a group of "twenty two negroes . . . standing in a row. Each wore a blue suit and a black hat, and each held a bundle of additional clothing and a pair of shoes in their hands."[41] He purported to misread the group of "fine manly figures" as free workers on a leisurely respite from a nearby plantation, but his fascination with the men waned when he was told that they had traveled from Virginia with a speculator and had recently been purchased by a local planter. Faced with the affluence of a single buyer who had paid $20,000 for this property purchase, Olmsted did not engage his own pretense of "puzzlement" but instead reverted to frustration over the high costs of slavery. He was certain that the enslaved people the buyer had purchased could never work off the price that had been paid for their labor.

As he crossed the South, Olmsted skillfully obfuscated the financial networks and exchange relationships through which southern elites accumulated and concentrated wealth. In so doing, he often recalibrated his observations of plantation agriculture into abstract visions for managerial practices that he fantasized would solidify and sustain lofty economic returns on free-labor cost reductions.

For example, he recounted the claims of a sugar planter near New Orleans that the majority of agriculture, "whether a sugar or cotton plantation, in this country, is usually essentially a gambling operation."[42] The planter clearly indicated that he, like most others, had accumulated his property—both land and slaves—by going "heavily in debt; frequently the purchase is made three quarters on credit."[43] He said that he had expanded his holdings in an economy that was structured on luck, describing his use of credit to plant crops for sale as similar to "betting on a throw of the dice."[44] Those who yielded sufficient crops to make payments on outstanding credit notes, he explained, were also rewarded with opportunities for credit expansion, which enabled them to purchase additional assets. But, as the planter also explained, farmers whose crops failed habitually borrowed additional local credit, "often at not less than 25 per cent per annum" to cover payment on earlier loans. It was the planter's opinion, according to Olmsted, that the entire southern economy balanced on speculative cycles of optimism and depression, citing a previous cycle of bad harvests that landed nearly every planter in Louisiana and Mississippi in "very embarrassed circumstances" of indenture to creditors. However, with the next breath he stated, "Everybody feels strong and cheerful" about the prospect of better returns in the present climate.[45]

In a curiously strategic display of economic naivety, Olmsted sidestepped the planter's financial assertions by focusing myopically on conditions of daily labor on southern plantations. He regularly reframed examples of plantation prosperity as outcomes of technological developments and innovative management. In redirecting his analysis away from the financial infrastructure of the South, Olmsted subtly reworked the speculating planter's articulation of debt as a free-labor vision for innovatively extracting labor power as the basis for healthy economic growth. He applauded the farmer's use of drainage systems while reluctantly commenting on the "great wealth" he saw as stemming from "the capital, labour, and especially human life, which have been and which continue to be spent in converting the swamps of Louisiana into sugar plantations."[46] Olmsted was especially intrigued by the planter's effort to "give the labourers a direct interest in the economical direction of their labour."[47] An annual Christmas dole was evidence to him of an additional value that the farmer extracted from furnishing his property with a figment of self-determination.[48] By rewarding productive workers and penalizing those who were "careless or lazy," Olmsted subtly implied, the planter inventively transformed forced workers into willing solicitors of their own subjugation.[49]

In a telling example, Olmsted stated that during the grinding season enslaved people "worked with greater cheerfulness than any other season" despite the "severity of the labour required of them."[50] For two or three months a year, he said, many of these workers were "on duty fully eighteen hours a day" and the planter kept them "constantly at work."[51] It is nearly impossible to test the validity of the outrageous claim that these conditions would make workers cheerful. Yet it is striking that Olmsted's premise for imagining conditions of indenture as if they were tentative scenes that some "envied" anticipated the arguments for leisure space that gave rise to Olmsted's lasting posterity.[52] His contention was that the slaves he observed had "a degree of freedom, and of social pleasure, and variety of occupation which brings recreation of the mind, and to a certain degree gives them strength for, and pleasure in, their labour."[53] The proposition that promises of leisure time—even if accessed only as a promise in the mind—could be instrumental in maximizing labor time became a central feature of Olmsted's free-labor advocacy.

Indeed, many of Olmsted's speculative ideas about the promise of managerial capitalism materialized on the sideline of this and similar large-scale plantations: "Men of sense have discovered that when they desire to get extraordinary exertions from their slaves, it is better to offer them rewards than to whip them; to encourage them, rather than to drive them."[54] Like these sensible men, Olmsted also "discover[ed]" on the plantation what he imagined was the profit potential of a brutal calculus of bodily differentiation. He assumed that speculative prices could be matched and superseded by the type of "practical talent for organization and administration" that he witnessed on some plantations.[55] He associated the "most favourable aspects" of plantation bureaucracy with the calibration of bodies—from "full" to "quarter-hands"—on the basis of which planters systematically divided labor by task:[56] "All of them were working by tasks and were overlooked by negro drivers. They all laboured with greater rapidity and cheerfulness than any slaves I had seen; and the women struck their hoes as if they were strong, and well able to engage in muscular labour."[57] The idea that forced workers might be organized to take pleasure in the constraints of deterministic bodily separations and socioeconomic subordination underlay Olmsted's misapprehended capitulation to labor repression as the principal source of southern wealth.[58] His analysis tentatively invested in what he reluctantly saw as the promise of labor repression—under "unusually skilful [sic] and energetic management, under favourable circumstances, the labour of slaves, in certain instances, seems to accomplish as much for its course as that of free labourers at the North"—through a vision of the health and happiness of enslaved workers.[59]

The psychic compensation that Olmsted began to associate with leisure space and "social pleasure" in this parallel recollateralized Black bodies in the interest of a northern vision of democratic labor. That is, Olmsted's descriptions of workers made happy and strong by the promise of time off set the stage for an interregional catachresis. His analysis reconfigured the bodies on whom southerners had previously backed speculative ventures as ingenious strategies that could later serve to organize and consolidate a free-labor economy. Debt did not disappear from Olmsted's fascination with the racial regime of southern labor, but the global economy's systemic vulnerability to investments leveraged on embodied assets was made invisible by the way he reallocated and particularized debt as the ontological condition that Black workers must overcome to be emancipated.

Olmsted regarded plantation practices that were likely intended to reap rewards from the survival strategies and surplus labor of enslaved people's "free" time as benevolent expressions of social and economic uplift that also protected enslaved people from market corruption. He documented how one planter, Mr. X., allotted land to his human holdings for cultivating vegetable and animal products that he "agreed" to purchase. This agreement was built on an imbalanced credit arrangement that enabled Mr. X. to borrow from his own property to "purchase from his own negroes" enough food to feed his family and support his holdings, while "allowing" Black captives to sell any excess in local markets.[60] Olmsted read enslaved people's ability to offer credit to their owner as a sign that they might become fit for freedom through education and adaptation to the rationalized logic of economic self-discipline. His optimism that people could be bound to a free-labor economy, as his interaction with a plantation owner he called Mr. R. suggested, balanced on developing moral frameworks for restricting workers' economic opportunities.

Mr. R., like other plantation owners, expressed frustration with the pervasive illicit trade between enslaved people and a "nuisance of petty traders."[61] Although he offered a moral apologia for what he saw as an irrevocable "curse of slavery" that had been "unfortunately fixed upon" the South, condemning it with a "duty" to "make the best of a bad thing," he described punishing enslaved people for engaging in commerce with "lazy vagabonds" as a detriment to the power of enslavement to enforce productivity. Poor whites, he insisted, "demoralized his negroes. Seeing them living in apparent comfort, without much property and without steady labour, the slaves could not help thinking that it was unnecessary for men to work so hard as they themselves were obliged to, and that if they were free they would not work."[62] As it turned out, Olmsted seems to have agreed that cleaning up the "waste" of slavery would require similar efforts to cultivate "good discipline."[63]

In his forty-eighth letter for the *New York Times*, Olmsted discussed a contradictory platform for overcoming slavery using practices of managerial discipline adapted from plantations: "The advantages which are to be obtained by the combination of the force of many hands, when efficiently controlled and judiciously directed by a central administration, cannot be doubted. Such advantages are obtained to a greater degree under the Southern system of labor than in the Free States."[64] In *The Cotton Kingdom*, he combined credit and discipline into a proposal for emancipation:

> The ascertained practicability of thus dealing with slaves [through an internal system of credit incentives], together with the obvious advantages of the method of working them by tasks, which I have described, seem to me to indicate that it is not so impracticable as it [is] generally supposed . . . to rapidly extinguish Slavery, and while doing so, to educate the negro to taking care of himself, in freedom. Let, for instance, any slave be provided with all things he will demand, as far as practicable, and charge him for them at certain prices—honest, market prices for his necessities, higher prices for harmless luxuries, and excessive, but not absolutely prohibitory prices for everything likely to do him harm. Credit him, at a fixed price, for every day's work he does, and for all above a certain easily accomplished task in a day, at an increased price, so that his reward will be in increasing ratio to his perseverance. . . . When he has no food and shelter due to him, let him be confined in solitude, or otherwise punished, until he asks for opportunity to earn exemption from punishment by labour.

It is no small matter that the centerpiece of this proposal came from Olmsted's observations of one of the 1,500 capital-intensive sugar estates on the Southern Mississippi, where planters used innovated strategies for synchronizing gang labor, racially pricing bodies on expectations of exertion, and using violence and incentives to prolong physically taxing work. According to Richard Follett, sugar planters lost "without compensation $100 million of private capital from [their] portfolios" when slavery was abolished.[65] When Olmsted extracted this system as an explanation of cotton, rice, and sugar wealth, however, he made a promise to the nation that it need not worry about debt. By constituting freedom as a buyable commodity that would compensate enslavers for legacies of injustice, his vision would relocate the liabilities of the national economy onto the formerly enslaved. The obviating promise of future freedom, in Olmsted's vision of emancipation, condemned the formerly enslaved to forced labor as the only means for building the credit he sought to establish as a precondition of emancipation.

Olmsted leveraged his nationalist speculation on presumptions of moral duty and fantasies of individuated familial fulfillment. Encouraging formerly enslaved people to marry, he suggested, could be highly useful for making "industry and providence fashionable":[66] "Oblige [indentured workers] to purchase food for their children, and let them have the benefit of their children's labour, and they will be careful to teach their children to avoid waste, and to honour labour."[67] His plan also banked on moral constructs and social approbation to disaggregate collectivities. "The beneficent function of gossip," he argued, was that those who refused to work under the death-defying contract of anticipatory freedom would "operate as cautions for the future."[68] Where example might not serve to create social condemnation of resistance, Olmsted proposed taxation: "Let those who have not gained credit . . . sufficient to support themselves in comfort when prevented by age or infirmity from future labour, be supported by a tax upon all the negroes of the plantation. . . . Improvidence, and pretense of inability to labour, will then be disgraceful."[69]

This proposal of a moral inventory as a mechanism for limiting freedom to a condition of credit prefigured a type of economic nationalism that first tactically misapprehended the racializing foundation of economic speculation and then re-created racial taxonomies as a means of absorbing risk. Olmsted's misguided notion that free labor by indirect force could marshal economic transformation, if not exceed the profits concentrated on plantations, reveals how integral cultural configurations are in upholding speculative economies. In this case, the moral cartography with which Olmsted proposed to map a free-labor future evidences a ruse of economic manipulation whereby speculative profits came to seem tenable via a downward spiral of "labor-saving" racial divisions.

In a letter written in 1853, Olmsted offered an example of the direction his plan would ultimately take. He advocated cutting the cost of labor: "By the introduction of coolies, laboring freely, as they may be had, accustomed to labor in their native rice fields at exceedingly low wages, the price of rice might be reduced greatly without diminishing the profit of its culture."[70] He repeated this proposal in 1854 in an analysis of plantation management: "I have always looked with confident expectation to a considerable competition with slave labor to arise out of the Chinese emigration to California. . . . A million laborers could probably be recruited in China under a contract for a series of years to be paid one-quarter the wages now paid for the slaves."[71]

When Olmsted was appointed codesigner and first supervisor of construction for New York's Central Park in 1857, he inadvertently planted the seeds of a managerial formation of free-labor capitalism that had germinated in slavery as racialized debt. Within the broader arc of his various roles as a cultural reformer, Central Park registers as the landscape for socially experimenting with re-creating the nation as an economic vehicle for redistributing speculative risk via regulatory oversight of national recreation. While building Central Park, to prove that free-labor management could compete with speculative fantasies, Olmsted tested his aptitude for cutting labor costs. His reinventions of the national landscape often took shape through ideas about social engineering, cost-saving labor practices, and moral cartographies of a disciplinary democracy. This is to say, his misguided constructions of labor-generated plantation prosperity remained a primary backdrop against which he built public environments to manage the leisure time of U.S. citizenship. He designed Central Park around a deliberate objective of sustaining social divisions and ameliorating conflict and social unrest. In this regard, the park provided the ground in which to plant the seeds of labor divisions in a national-capitalist reorganization that had sprouted from his figuration of racialized life as debt. The "waste" of slavery—a speculative disavowal transformed into a racializing system of "cost-saving" social division—lives on in the nation's most revered and celebrated democratic landscapes.

Leisure, Labor, and Dispossession

During the mid-nineteenth-century's drawn-out reconstruction of national freedom as mandatory labor, the antidote to speculative fictions of socioeconomic "waste" often came in struggles over place. Olmsted did not initiate plans for Central Park. The lobby for a landscaped public park emerged from private-property owners and real estate investors who sought to increase uptown property values by replacing workshops, asylums, and poor people's settlements with landscaped garden villages. Developers hoped that a public park would both increase the "actual or speculative value of lands in its vicinity" and encourage the displacement of people living in the areas that they degraded as "waste."[72] Yet by accepting the position of designer and developer of the park, Olmsted became a central participant in the historical process of displacing Blackness to discipline immigrants and poor workers for the benefit of White property owners on land whose name called up indigenous memories.

In 1857 roughly 5,000 people lived in the area that is now Central Park. Most were low-wage workers in service jobs who supplemented paltry wages with resourceful use of the city's "refuse." In the "wilderness" of Uptown, free African Americans, immigrants, and "outcast whites" gleaned fuel, food, and clothing from nature's commons and the city's streets. Seneca Village, a settlement that was the target of much middle-class disapprobation, recalled in its name antecedent land stewards, but it was no longer inhabited by Seneca people during the 1840s and 1850s. Rather, middle-class cultural producers couched racial anxieties about cross-racial amalgamation in representations of the village as a site of "plunder and devastation" created by sloth, scavengers, paupers, and criminals.[73] Depictions of the "savage" inhabitants of what many colloquially called "Nigger Village" concealed the importance of Seneca Village as one of the most established communities of free African Americans in the U.S. North. In 1855, half of the 260 residents in the four-block radius of the village were African American property owners with an average residency of twenty-two years. In a city where racial bias severely limited access to land, loans, and inheritance, Seneca Village—its stability, multiple religious and community centers, and rates of ownership—was a remarkable testimony to the African American struggle to sustain life against the odds of racialized capitalism.

Central Park generated speculative returns on racism for White property owners whose "splendid private residences" on average doubled in value when the park was completed. The "fancy prices" that White property owners accrued did not simply indicate the returns garnered from the forced eviction of African Americans; they also demarcated the force of culture as an economic engine in the destruction and co-optation of place and freedom. The profits that White people made on spatial entitlement reconstituted the subsistence freedoms established and enacted by Black and poor people in the park as "not yet" free subjects of moral reform displaced in the city's broader social fabric. In the context of the economic depression of 1857, this social fabric was patterned on overlapping technologies of retrenchment.

In addition to dispossessing African Americans through eviction, Central Park was constructed on a managerial lust for reducing expenditures, which contributed to cutbacks in the wages of White workers. At the peak of construction, between 1859 and 1860, the park was among the city's largest employers. As supervisor, Olmsted retrospectively figured his work as an episode of managerial moral heroism in which he conditioned "a mob of lazy, reckless, turbulent and violent loafers" into "a well organized, punctual, sober, industrious and disciplined body."[74] He did this, in part, under short-term contracts that allowed him to penalize less productive workers with wage reductions and to fire those who missed work. He also laid off workers en masse and later rehired them in task-based "gangs" for lower wages. Olmsted did not hire any Black workers in the park, but the combination of his self-aggrandizement for "revolutionizing the management of public works" and a public sentiment that "Central Park laborers [were] driven like niggers through the streets—paraded like a log of human livestock" suggests that his fantasies of plantation benevolence were not far from his organization of labor.[75] He was certainly accused of affronting White workers by hiring recent Italian, Scottish, and Irish immigrants and for using military-style role calls as a disciplinary strategy.

The management of bodies in space extended for Olmsted into the landscape he designed to unify the economically fragmented citizenship to which his own practices contributed. He plotted the park to collapse the "sights" of bourgeois luxury and the "scenes" of mass cultivation into a regulated social space.[76] During Central Park's first years, Olmsted hired police officers to patrol and "prevent disorderly & unseemly practices upon the park" and to instruct visitors in proper park use. Officers were hired on the condition that they demonstrate military precision toward cultural refinement, with meticulous grooming, regulated salutes, and orderly marches. They were to enforce rules that discouraged free association and resourceful use of nature's commons—such as grazing livestock, gathering fuel, and fishing. They worked as gatekeepers to ban military, target-company, and civic processions, as well as any vehicle showing signs of commercial use.

For Olmsted, Central Park was a site and sight of moral reform, an extension of his presumed revolutionary capacity to clean up social vice and blight through the careful orchestration and oversight of leisure space. This is to suggest that his aesthetic and cultural engineering was never simply about symbolic identification with an abstract notion of a national democracy. Rather, his strategic use of landscape development to coordinate human interactions with nature and others was also a social petri dish in which he experimented with environmental, citizen, and worker "cultivation" to reduce the market price of labor. Actualizing an aesthetic construction of free social space through the material reconstruction of place afforded Olmsted an opportunity to develop pragmatic categories for social reform that were instrumental in reconstituting a free-labor economy through practices inspired by slavery. In the project of controlling and dividing labor, aesthetic and social order were mutually interdependent.

Olmsted established elaborate taxonomies of botanical life in Central Park, in tandem with new social nomenclatures of idleness, dishonesty, and vice that weeded the nonindustrious and noncompliant out of civic and market participation. The political and economic crises sparked by the Civil War allowed him to expand his cultural experiment into a plan for codifying White patronage of racialized labor as the dominant articulation of a nationally consolidated economy. In this case, he entered a proposal to make capitalist estates and gang labor the cornerstone of national reconstruction into the official Congressional record.

From his post with the U.S. Sanitary Commission, Olmsted had authored a bill for dealing with "contraband" slaves in Port Royal. When Senator Lafayette Foster introduced it in Congress as an urgent measure, it sparked a fraught Congressional debate over how (not) to end slavery. The bill included a near verbatim recommendation of the managerial technologies Olmsted had observed and admired on sugar and cotton estates in his earlier writings. As Richard Follett shows, plantation owners at the time apprehensively struggled to maintain discipline by violence and incentive when faced with enslaved people who were often inspired by war to flee, disobey rules, and destroy and appropriate property.[77] In the chambers of Congress, nevertheless, White representatives debated terms that not only sought to keep slavery in place but also set a precedent for expanding a model of capital-intensive plantation production into new national spaces. When the bill that Olmsted authored passed the Senate on March 7, 1862, the federal government *nearly* became the central administrator of a national takeover and expansion of plantation slavery.

Slavery Returns in Life as Debt

In the strange circumstances of life as debt, freedom was a national fiction for death-defying emancipatory conscription. During the war, many entrepreneurial nationalists who callously institutionalized their moral guardianship of formerly enslaved people through the calculus of "contraband" found that the virtue of freedom came at a price. Formerly enslaved people often circumvented the nation's restrictive promises of death-defying liberation with life-affirming actions in defiance of a national culture of constraint. Because the Union assumed that enslaved people owed the nation for their lives, the notion of contraband—confiscated war property—smoothly transmogrified in legislative debate as a debt that enslaved people must pay through obligatory labor. The Trumbull amendment to the First Confiscation Act of 1861 drew on the official construct of condemnation to transfer titles regarding slaves as property into state entitlements to put Black people to public use.[78] Under confiscation, the nation did not claim ownership of the bodies of enslaved people, but retained possession of former slaves as "contraband" labor power. For formerly enslaved people, wasting time under the constraints of owing time was likely their principal time to claim time for freedom.

The Union capture of Port Royal, South Carolina, prompted a speculative frenzy of outside interests who saw the islands as a hotbed of economic opportunity. Joyce Hollyday describes the influx of missionaries, carpetbaggers, speculators, cotton agents, statisticians, and philanthropists to the islands almost immediately after the Union declared victory on November 7, 1861. When fleets of profiteers, planners, and volunteers arrived, they encountered a growing population of African American refugees and plantations that had been thoroughly pillaged by Union soldiers. In the turmoil of the moment, treasury secretary Salman P. Chase authorized figures like William R. Reynolds to collect contraband cotton. Reynolds paid African Americans a mere "dollar for every four hundred pounds of unginned cotton delivered at the steamboat landing, deduct[ed] the value of any salt, molasses, or other staples they used from the plantation stores [and] arranged to have all the cotton ginned in New York."[79]

Like others, Olmsted saw the sea islands as an opportunity to test his theories of social and economic discipline. In a letter to his father on February 24, 1862, he took credit for writing Foster's bill and expressed a hope that he would be appointed general manager of the policy: "I shall go to Port Royal, if I can, and work out practically every solution of the Slavery question—long ago advocated in my book."[80]

The solution Olmsted provided in Foster's Port Royal plan put all means of subsistence under government control, denied formerly enslaved people land and resources for self-determined survival, and authorized state agents to enforce Black labor requirements with moral instruments of social control. The bill charged supervisors with "induc[ing] those indigent persons to support themselves, and live in an industrious, orderly, and respectable manner; and when necessary, they [were] to be authorized and required to use decent and humane means of constraint against idleness, dishonesty, and vice."[81] Olmsted envisioned "clerks and guards" who would broker this contract as "simply members of the partnership of a community, appointed by their fellow-partners to transact, agreeably to their instructions, such business as they shall have agreed to in common."[82] Olmsted campaigned to convince the president, Congress, the treasury secretary, the secretary of war, and the public that the nation would work like a business collaboration by holding on to a credit that Black workers would accrue on the path toward purchasing full ownership of their own labor.[83]

In an appeal to President Lincoln dated March 8, 1862, Olmsted discussed how variants of gang labor and division of work by task would help the nation meet short-term urgencies and create long-term solutions for regulating future Black citizenship. He proposed that the central administration be provided the "means of entailing upon [resistant workers] a sure punishment for indolence and violence," such that formerly enslaved people would become "honest, prudent, industrious, and discreet."[84] This transitional system, he argued, would create opportunities for cultivating slaves as free-labor citizens by continuing to draw on their forced labor to absorb the threat of systemic risk.[85] Because Foster's bill was introduced toward the end of the planting season, many senators accepted Foster's claim to urgency with the logic that "nature may not wait."[86] For those in the know, however, the pressure of time was likely less about nature than it was about a state anxiety over losing profits rapidly pursued by the hoards of private interests who were swarming to the islands.

Skeptical senators brought up the danger that the bill would put the federal government in the business of slavery as a plantation owner.[87] Some expressed concerns about the bill's imprecise delineation of department jurisdiction, about the risks of government corruption, about the failure to offer the "contraband" just reparations, about the fine line between salvation and "devastation" the policy created, and about setting a precedent of federal bureaucracy in a managerial consolidation of agricultural capitalism. In spite of senatorial concerns, Foster's discourse of "waste" garnered a vote for a one-year trial of Olmsted's plan.

Charlotte Forten's descriptions of life in Port Royal a few months later suggested that the former slaves had wasted no time in claiming life and freedom in a form other than debt. Her journal instructively revealed alternatives to the "not yet" freedom Congress debated. She recalled participating in a discussion of the "noble truths told in the most beautiful language" by D. A. Wasson in his "grand article, 'The Law of Costs.'"[88] Wasson called out speculative efforts to mobilize the nation in the interest of class prosperity in an abolitionist reversal of the burden of debt. He contended that the nation's foundation on natural rights to freedom and order identified politics with universal "justice" and created a debt to virtue paid for by war. The cost of risk could best be covered with full emancipation of African Americans.

In classrooms and conversations, Forten offered strategic lessons in the histories of enslaved people who collected on promises with active resistance. She taught students the history of Toussaint L'Ouverture and the ballad of John Brown.[89] She attended gatherings with Black union soldiers where the stories of Robert Smalls and the revolts at Santa Cruz were the focus of conversation.[90] Her accounts of meetings with former slaves are most notable for breaking free of White abolitionists' economic and military logics.

Most of the escapes that Forten documented occurred during times that slaves were working. Some slaves laughed in the face of denigration by White soldiers. Others who were commanded to carry goods for transport or wait to load furniture for retreating slave masters described hiding away, deciding to stay behind with confidence that their owners would not return.[91] These narratives did not put faith in a national promise but staked claims on life against the odds through attachments that slavery denied: living connections to children and grandchildren, declaring the liminal moment of freedom when no one could whip or drive them as the "happiest year of [a] life," and maintaining an embittered separation from encroaching northerners out of skepticism based on the cruelty that they had lived and endured.[92] Embittered banishment of nonlocal people, it turned out, was perhaps one of the most incisive mechanisms for retaining self-defined freedom. The anxiety that likely undergirded congressional pleas of urgency played out in practice as White competition for mass plunder. During the later part of her stay in Port Royal, Forten's journals recorded "depredations" of soldiers who had "stolen poultry, and everything else they c'ld get on the plantations, cheated the Negroes, and in some instances even burned their houses."[93]

In the end, Olmsted was never authorized to take charge at Port Royal. While Forten traveled to South Carolina, he made a speculative gamble with Secretary Chase, who offered him Edward Pierce's post as Port Royal supervisor. However, Olmsted rejected the offer out of what seemed to be his concern that the capacities of the Treasury could not meet his aims and expectations for implementing and enforcing social regulation. Although his bill had passed the Senate, Olmsted's desire to enact the policy under the authority and resources of the War Department did not pan out. He asked that the bill be put to sleep while he contemplated Chase's job offer, and it was never officially awakened. However, the bill's managerial suggestion of a plantation-style capitalism lived on in industry—not in the South but in the West. When Olmsted's principles for gradual manumission crossed the nation, they paved the way for a racial return on slavery that planted speculative desire deep in the heart of industrial capitalism as well as in the U.S. landscape. "Practically every solution of the Slavery question" that Olmsted had developed in the South made its way into the winding roads of Yosemite in design plans that effectuated the slow dispossession of Native people.[94]

Let No Bad Bet Go Unwasted

Under speculative economic conditions, labor repression can never humanely make up for unfulfilled desire when luck dries up. When investors in speculative markets articulate deflation as loss, they often reassert their subjectivities as rational economic agents who have been wronged by misguided projections. The notion of loss demarcates little more than capital's desire for accumulating profits in a world of abstraction in which investors presume ownership of inheritance by virtue of off-putting risk onto oppression. Yet when risk is managed through the exploitation of others, the injuries to justice are far more capacious: the economic savings of dividing labor, punishing workers for moral offenses, and racially differentiating terms for the workplace often come at human costs of aggression and exhaustion.

When Olmsted lost his bid at Port Royal in the spring of 1862, he accepted a post as labor manager of California's Mariposa Gold Mining Estates. There he drew on his Port Royal proposal with an eye to restoring profits to a speculative peak through productivity practices that would make freedom just another word for wages left to lose. When he arrived at the 44,000-acre estates in October of 1863, Olmsted was prepared to manage a lucrative large-scale operation. After a month, however, he realized that the estates' gold was largely depleted. Olmsted's new bosses had purchased the property on the basis of a financial record inflated by a single $100,000 mineral extraction. They had not been fully aware at the time of purchase that these profits were the outcome of a gold vein that had dried up. In November 1862, Olmsted reported to his employers that the property was barely producing, its expenses were too high, and the company was in severe debt to workers whose wages had been deferred repeatedly to sustain boarding houses and company stores. He declared that "previous management was the worst possible & the luck had run out months before [he] got there."[95] Further, workers who felt cheated out of wages were "not merely discontented, but sometimes bitterly so."[96]

Fashioning himself a West Coast economic engineer of free-labor innovation on par with the ostensibly prudent slave managers he had observed on plantations, he argued that workers in the mines were being paid too much and were not efficiently organized. Because Olmsted could not make gold, he sought to produce profits by "improving" on management strategies he had outlined in his southern writing. In his own practice, he "threw" out the waste of slavery by cutting the pay of workers; doubling the company's profits by providing food, clothing, and shelter *but* making the cost of these resources the responsibility of workers; and drawing on culture as a strategy for worker regulation. He used moral categories resonant with his ideological underpinnings for Central Park to castigate workers for their inappropriate understanding of democratic community. Their detachment from "associations with a fixed community," he argued early in his employment, was "making it exceedingly difficult, at present, to exact industry & discipline."[97]

By March of 1864, Olmsted had imposed wage restrictions on more compliant workers by requiring superintendents to pay "at the lowest practical rates."[98] He argued that Mariposa paid its workers higher than did surrounding mines and those who disagreed with the reductions were free to quit. Olmsted also maintained, counterintuitively, that lower pay would make workers more inclined to work for longer periods at higher rates of efficiency in pursuit of increasing their meager paychecks. As in the plan he had developed for Port Royal, he fixed a wage scale on a divided labor force itemized around biological deterministic inscriptions of different bodies as suited to particular tasks and specialties. His strict adherence to maximum wage rates created wage reductions for many workers. He cut pay from a rough average of $4.50 per day to no more than $3.15 for the highest skill set. This reduction was the first of many proposed toward the final goal of $2.75 per day. To counterbalance pay cuts, Olmsted reduced room and board rates at company lodges but threatened to penalize those who opted out of company shelter and provisions on the grounds that self-care reduced workers' labor power by increasing their levels of exhaustion.

Olmsted seemed unconcerned with the week-long strikes for new "benefits" when he described workers' responses to his changes. Instead, he depicted strikes as an opportunity to release insubordinate workers from their contracts and further suppress wages by provoking racial competition. Chinese immigration to California was his opportunity to implement the international competition he had previously imagined as a solution to the "waste" of southern slavery. There was no need, as he saw it, to meet the demands of violent strikers when he could employ "Chinese at $1.75 to take the place of laborers at $2.75 and $3."[99] Thus when strikers came to him with a plan for compromise, he declined "to make any change to the rules [he] had given the Superintendents."[100] As administrator of one of the largest employers in central California, he knew that he had a near monopoly on the labor market and that cutting wages would "in the end help to a much larger gross reduction of expenses."[101] He assumed that Chinese workers would work for lower wages and demand fewer resources than any resistant employees who might resign.

This cost-saving potential of racial division seeped through the lines of Olmsted's western observations.[102] Before the strike, he called attention to the industry of the "Digger" Indians; he mentioned a series of robberies by a surplus labor pool of "Mexicans, Indians, Chinamen or blackleg Secessionists."[103] His writings were haunted by a legal structure of criminality in which people of color were punished with hangings and shootings for crimes that White people paid for only with jail time.

Discussions about race were also the core of the philosophy of American civilization that Olmsted began to espouse while working for Mariposa: "The History of Civilization in the United States in the Last Fifty Years." These unpublished volumes were organized by a Lamarckian taxonomy of racial differentiation of groups by proximity to various virtues of "civilization." Englishmen and Germans, he argued, were endowed with "industry . . . well-balanced supply and demand . . . sobriety and inoffensiveness."[104] Yet they did not possess the democratic virtue of community that ranked highest on his scale of values. "Mexicans, Chinese, and Negroes," he claimed, possessed this quality at a higher rate than Europeans, but they were not fully acclimated to the value of industriousness and proper modes of civil social exchange. Although his racialist propositions were organized around the idea of middle-class propriety, civic responsibility, and individual self-interest, his actual treatment of different groups promised pathways to democratic inclusion in which *some* individuals from various backgrounds could eventually become "civilized," but the economic constraints through which they had to pass ensured that *most* of them would not.

From the moment he became manager of the Mariposa estates, Olmsted despised the brazenness of White workers he perceived as exhausting company resources with their demands for fair wages and self-determination. He broke up collective organizing by firing workers found responsible for strikes and by targeting sites of collective association by blaming mob aggression on "a good deal of drunkenness and gambling houses."[105] Culture was the indispensable central technology of Olmsted's economic design for producing speculative-like returns via labor cost reductions. To mitigate group resistance, he purchased periodicals and literary volumes from Edwin Godkin to supply a reading room that he hoped would "draw off the considerable number of Cornish miners from the dram shops and gambling booths with the rest."[106] During the workday, Olmsted sought profits from manufacturing intergroup antagonisms. When the day was over, however, the tensions his policies created cast workers into a volatile social climate that was always at risk of erupting into either intergroup violence or collective mobilization. Like the organized collectivity of disaggregated democratic identification he encouraged in Central Park, the library appealed to workers as atomized thinkers whose identification he sought to filter through fiction as a distraction from the possibility for a radical democracy emerging from communication around lived associations.

Under the pretext of guaranteeing workers fair prices, Olmsted invested substantial amounts of company capital in the "Store, stock and good will of the business of Mariposa" in a culminating effort to oversee the entirety of workers' subsistence needs: food, shelter, leisure, and wages.[107] Although he neither advocated nor discouraged a credit system for binding workers to the company, his tight control of their existence certainly indebted many to his managerial strategies.[108]

In his plans for the gradual manumission of Port Royal Blacks, Olmsted had rearticulated various modes of regional production into a temporal formula of progression toward freedom—from slave property to indentured worker to freely contracting laborer. When he explored racializing divisions of industrial gang labor in the West, this formula worked to bring concurrent regional labor systems into a temporal vision of progress toward compliant civilization to subjugate all workers under the authority of middle-class managers. His cultural and economic practices subjected White workers who had made gains toward independence and good wages to a backward trajectory toward wage repression and potential debt. For racialized workers, he backed his offerings of unfair wages with cultural projections of future national belonging. The "not yet" freedom of national progress, in this formulation, contributed to various trajectories of subjection designed to make social stratification and racial competition the legitimating conditions for White middle-class managerial and cultural authority.

Olmsted was certainly aware that the repressive management of labor risked provoking social tensions and resistance. The forms of culture that he offered workers encouraged them to spend their "free" time and citizenship identifying as individuals whose entry into citizenship emerged in attenuated relationship to social bodies through representation. Like solitary reading, his ideas for managing leisure and landscapes encouraged one-to-one encounters with cultural formations while materially isolating cultural consumers from their objective positions within collective social bodies. That is, cultural individuation produced a structure for social atomization that worked to separate citizenship from lived human interactions.

For Olmsted, culture functioned as a social intermediary through which to dislocate contentious possibilities for social collectivity into illusive ideals of imaginative individualism. Moreover, he was variously concerned about the psychic fatigue and health costs of positioning laborers to work toward future freedoms that were made ever more distant by cutbacks and regulatory constraints. In this regard, he imagined leisure time as a curative for the increased physical exertion he envisioned as necessary for mitigating productive "losses." On May 17, 1864, a federal proposal to grant the land of the Yosemite Valley to the state of California produced an opportunity for Olmsted to plot a proposal that would serve both concerns. His plans for designing Yosemite's "natural" landscape leveraged his concerns about sustaining future profits on a cultural compensation of public space.[109]

Trading Manumission for Dispossession

When racialized risk is circulated across divergent geographic contexts, the economic returns on cultural differentiation can spread in unanticipated and elusive directions. Olmsted's design proposal for re-creating Yosemite as a site of national recreation focused heavily on building roads and trails that would produce intimate encounters between viewers and nature. He sought to offer citizens a series of disconnected scenic vistas at an aesthetic remove from external relations. As with his vision for the creation of and clashes with group-differentiated free-labor pools, Olmsted's design for national culture emphasized segregating and separating people using a divide-and-conquer strategy to invite groups to make gains or perceive losses at the expense of others.

Olmsted's propensity for exchanging bureaucratic strategies for managing risk within a broad national network of cultural and economic transactions indicates how disaggregated legacies of racialization are often intimately interconnected. At the intersection of economic anxiety over national reconstruction and cultural optimism over the democratic promise of national parks, racializing designs on speculative expansion became the cornerstone for managing the nation's labor and leisure. Olmsted's "visionary" appropriation of managerial strategies from the harsh conditions of gang-labor plantations moved across the nation in labor practices, through economic and social desire, and in verbatim reproductions of textual fragments. As they played out in discrete geographies, the effects and outcomes of parallel strategies were eerily resonant with severe exploitation and at the same time strikingly dissimilar in their historical particularity.

The climax of the Civil War certainly must have created substantial economic anxiety among overly leveraged southern slaveholders who faced the risk of losing their primary assets. During this same period, the creative efforts of national reformers to restructure and nationally consolidate a free-labor industrial capitalist economy suggested the broader nation's concern with problems of systemic risk that spread well beyond the regional terrain of the South. Indeed, reformers like Olmsted arbitrated slave-era financial permeation with labor policies and cultural practices that also extended from southern loci. Through a series of textual transactions, Olmsted laid a foundation for a new national contract whereby the organizing logics of social division and gradual manumission, with which the nation imagined salvaging the southern economy, were traded into the West, where they would later influence the gradual dispossession of Yosemite Indians.

Unlike Olmsted's proposals for the South, the targets for this transfer were not articulated as a single group with internally categorized differences who were to be temporarily excluded as a whole from the status of citizenship. Rather, the logics of race that Olmsted absorbed from the South returned to his thinking as abstract principles for managing the social interactions of diverse groups of workers through environmental cultural constraints. The establishment of Yosemite also generated economic returns on such abstract racial rearticulations. In Olmsted's plans for a national park, plantation patterns of racialization were reinscribed nationally as a racial division of labor that balanced on a series of cultural prohibitions that ultimately worked to dislocate Native American people from their homeland in what became Yosemite National Park.

When Senator John Conness introduced his bill proposing the preservation of Yosemite, he argued that the land to be preserved was "for all public purposes worthless."[110] This rhetorical transaction effectively transformed an occupied territory into a national commodity. Conness's declaration devalued the lived struggles of Yosemite Indians for whom the space was a site of cultural memory, language, and subsistence. For Olmsted, whose reputation in Central Park and geographic proximity led the shipping industrialists behind the bill to recommend him to Yosemite's board of commissioners, Conness's proposal created a context for returning once again to his speculative interests in cultural manipulation. The "worthless" space of Yosemite seems to have suggested a payback on the nationalist construction of freedom as debt with a national symbol of unity promising universality.

In his 1865 "Preliminary Report Upon the Yosemite and Big Tree Groves," Olmsted recycled many of the key strategies he had earlier proposed for Port Royal. Like his Port Royal proposal, Olmsted's plan for the development of Yosemite was never made official. Even so, it remains important in the lore of the National Park System as a document of the managerial logics underlying democratic promises of U.S. public space. The report prescripted the vision of the 1916 National Park Act in its framework, which was adapted for park regulation and evidences the conservationist logics of environmentalism that would later become instrumental in dispossessing indigenous people using disciplinary cultural procedures.[111]

The report reproduced the designer's attraction to the disciplinary procedures and social incentives he found so enticing in southern plantations, but it reformulated his earlier regard for social division and cultural regulation with an eye toward dividing citizens and managing leisure (as seen in his work on Central Park)—a shift that ultimately reworked culture as a mechanism for large-scale managerial capitalist reproduction. Olmsted envisioned Yosemite as a site that would serve multiple imperatives for industrial reproduction. As with the promise of time off after the sugar harvest, tourism would encourage the biological and social reproduction of a national labor pool that would "willingly" increase production on the incentive of future leisure and through the force of family regulation. In addition, Olmsted's design plans for manipulating pathways and vistas for individual spectatorship would enable the reproduction of labor divisions that were organized around gang-style practices of racialized hiring and firing by ameliorating social fatigue and limiting potentially tense social interaction.[112] By implication, the California land grant of Yosemite Park and the Mariposa Grove of Big Trees created a state-sponsored possibility for attending to the failures of lived democracy under a consolidation of capital that was dead set on repression and racial division through a promise of public land that replaced founding articulations of democratic freedom through land ownership with private encounters with land vistas through spectatorship.

The day after the federal government passed the Yosemite Land Grant bill, September 28, 1864, Olmsted was appointed manager of the Yosemite Valley and Mariposa Big Tree Grove by California governor Frederick F. Low. Almost a year later, on August 8, 1865, he presented his "Preliminary Report" to fellow commissioners and the California legislature. The text of the report seemed to transfer key objectives of the Port Royal Plan directly into a series of aesthetic designs and managerial proposals. It argued that central administrators and a board of commissioners were necessary for "rigidly enforcing" tourist behavior so that visitors could adequately appreciate the picturesque landscape. Olmsted imagined that construction would require the majority of the park's development budget, $25,000 of the total budget of $37,000, to be allotted to building one-way roads and isolated scenic vistas that would allow tourists to observe the sights without the burden of having to associate with others.

Like those for Central Park, the plans Olmsted outlined in the report provided, on a national scale, a restorative counter to the debilitating and alienating effects of capitalism. This project at once obfuscated and reproduced the economic relations and hierarchies through which social order was threatened and uncultivated abject classes were created. In his plans for Yosemite, Olmsted represented a middle-class imaginary that simultaneously reinforced the productive capacities of laborers. He intended spectators to look toward the nation together without actually having to see one another. The abstract citizenship Olmsted invoked for the future of Yosemite covertly proposed to manage in culture a universal "equality" around an undifferentiated viewing public that was stratified in society.

By regulating the possibilities for public association, Olmsted's park design presented private democracy as public experience through the social mediation of scenic pleasure. In this formulation, the "not yet" freedom of workers, who daily labored to attain social equality within a structure that depended on denying equality to secure profits, projected a new promise. According to Olmsted, the scenic liberty of his design "not only gives pleasure for the time being but increases the subsequent capacity for happiness and the means for securing happiness."[113] With freedom, property, and equality at stake, the park depended on the aesthetic preservation of "natural scenery" to mediate the "unnatural" antagonisms of daily life. Outside the park, the divisive practices of labor exploitation conditioned citizenship around market competition and inequality. Inside, Olmsted promised spectators an alternative to daily competition with an invitation into spectator equality. This cultural configuration of land-based democracy depended on preserving nature against constructions that would create "an unpleasant object to the eye in the midst of the scenery."[114] However, Olmsted's plan traded social equality for visual uniformity. Although he could manipulate the landscape so that all spectators would see the same sights, he could not guarantee that they would absorb these sights from the same perspective.

Richard Grusin reads Olmsted's 1865 report as a blueprint of landscape production that produces space both geologically and culturally. He tracks Olmsted's design objectives for Yosemite to produce both "natural scenery" and the representation of "natural scenery" simultaneously. For the "picturesque course" through which tourists would experience Yosemite as both nature and representation of nature, the signs of construction that would make such a course available were to be concealed even as their use would make them evident. Olmsted built his profession as a social reformer on the proposition that in producing nature as an aesthetic object the designer was in part obligated to relinquish his agency to nature.[115] He banked on the unlikely insinuation that the reproduction of nature as an aesthetic object would temporarily level social stratification by at once cultivating the masses and curing the nervous disorders of the elites.

Grusin argues that Olmsted's design revolved around a "psychological economy of recreation" to encourage economic prosperity against the emergent medical threats of neurology and exhaustion.[116] During his tenure as secretary of the U.S. Sanitary Commission, Olmsted connected to doctors Silas Weir Mitchell and William Alexander Hammond, from whom he adopted a theory of neurasthenia that imagined recreation as the antidote to the mental exertions of the marketplace. In his proposal for Yosemite, nonpurposeful activity suggested a counterbalance to the exertions and anxieties of daily capitalist competition. The scene of retreat, however, also visibly centralized the social stratifications that the park aimed to alleviate. To deflect class tensions, Olmsted's social agenda for Yosemite, as Grusin notes, "allow[ed] for irreducible private aesthetic experiences to take place within a system of social circulation and exchange."[117] Olmsted's report offers an alert to the ways in which capitalism banks on affective human responses. To protect a system that predicated economic growth on managing and exacerbating social inequality, he invested in national leisure as a mechanism for conserving optimism for the future. In his equation, controlling workers' minds was imperative for conserving workers' bodies:

> But there is a special reason why the reinvigoration of those parts which are stirred into conscious activity by natural scenery is more effective upon the general development and health than that of any other, which is this: The severe and excessive exercise of the mind which leads to the greatest fatigue and is the most wearing upon the whole constitution is almost entirely caused by application to the removal of something to be apprehended in the future, or to interests beyond those of the moment or of the individual; to the laying up of wealth, to the preparation of something, to accomplishing something in the mind of another and especially to small and petty details which are uninteresting in themselves and which engage the attention at all only because of the bearing they have on some general end of more importance which is seen ahead.[118]

By offering diligent workers the promise of relief from exhaustion, Olmsted created an investment strategy for social elites to withhold freedom as a promise that would be endlessly deferred to the petty tasks of daily labor under the obligatory mandates of managerial authorities. The productive respite from such obligations regenerated the dreams of middle-class belonging and a "subsequent capacity for happiness and the means of securing happiness" as a basis for securing exploitable labor.[119] In addition, through the park's "laws to prevent unjust use by individuals of that which is not individual but public property," he proposed regulatory standards to protect common interests, monitor public association, minimize cross-class contact, and criminalize behaviors deemed unrespectable. The tenuousness of his design was exposed by his insistence that park use be "rigidly enforced" and closely monitored.[120] As he had in Central Park and for leisure time around the Mariposa estates, Olmsted presented a plan for a progressive cultural binary through which the (idea of) national democracy could be preserved from the "artificial pleasures [of working people], such as theatres, parades, and promenades."[121] As he had previously, Olmsted explicitly proposed for Yosemite that park laws "must be made and rigidly enforced" using both a police force and a strategic manipulation of tourists' encounters with natural iconography.[122]

The returns on this disciplinary investment were not designed to bring about the compensation; economic stability; equalities of opportunity; resources; social power; or collective association that many workers struggled for in their daily lives. Rather, they offered select citizen-workers a feeling of fulfillment at a distance from daily labor so that when they returned to work they would have memories to ameliorate the stress of exploitation. Olmsted's report proposed management techniques for regulating park use that would guarantee tourists pleasant and peaceful encounters with nature. Vistas would be designed to create a feeling of freedom for people considered "not yet" capable of responsible democratic self-determination. He advocated disciplinary mandates against "indolence and vice" strikingly similar to those he had imposed in Central Park, proposed for Port Royal, and attempted to bring about with literary cultivation in Mariposa. In this context, he limited how land could be used by redefining Native people's common resources as public property to be protected with "laws to prevent unjust use by individuals." He particularly targeted "Indians and others [who] have set fires to the forests and herbage" as causing "wide-scale destruction" of the visual landscape.

Because Yosemite had been granted to the state of California, which did not have a reservation system, it was not possible for Olmsted to push for the official removal of Native people from the park. Although he did not have a lasting physical presence in Yosemite and his proposal was not implemented formally as park policy, his construction of indigenous ways of life—hunting, fishing, clearing undergrowth for forest regeneration—as "abuses" against the future viewing pleasures of unnamed citizens did inform the gradual dispossession of Yosemite's Indians. Backed by the nationalization of the park's visual iconography, the cultural logic that Native people remained in Yosemite on the basis of the nation's good will re-created their historical and political claims to the valley as conditional contracts in which they were indebted to the nation's future.

Because the Native people living there had never signed a treaty with the government, when the National Park Service took control of Yosemite half a century later in 1916, the national challenge of organizing and making sense of their continued residence in, and ancestral claims to, the valley fell to the administrative authority of the Park Service. The policies that the service progressively drew on to constrict Native lives, practices, and actions in the park recalled Olmsted's 1865 Preliminary Report: restrictions on "vices" such as gambling and drinking alcohol; conditions on how Indians could interact with tourists; resignifications of traditional modes of subsistence as grounds for eviction; *and, when these strategies were no longer effective*, mandates that made labor for the park service a requirement for Native people's continued residency in their homeland.

Olmsted did not write the official policies conditioning the later slow dispossession that would gradually remove the Yosemite Indians from the park. His report did, however, create a precedent for drawing on conservationist pretenses as a vehicle for criminalizing indigenous practices. "Indians and others [who] have set fires to the forests and herbage," he argued, had caused wide-scale destruction of native plants and species that had "almost wholly disappeared."[123] Thus what had been a long-standing method of cultivating plant and animal diversity in an indigenous mode of subsistence, designed around the control of consumable natural resources in Yosemite Valley, became an affront to the national posterity of the United States.[124] Olmsted transposed nineteenth-century "vanishing Indian" rhetoric into an accusation that indigenous people were a threat to the nation's environmental future.[125] In suggesting the indigenous people's relationship to the space as a habitual "abuse" of the nation's "principle of justice," Olmsted designed a precedent for registering indigenous survival as a crime against the nation.[126]

The methods that the Park Service eventually used to remove indigenous people from the valley resonate clearly with the disciplinary propositions that Olmsted presented to senators for the management of former slaves in Port Royal. Until the establishment of Yosemite, the relative isolation of the valley, according to Mark Spence, protected most of the people living there because they were beyond the radar of state bureaucrats. Thus when the National Park Service took charge in 1916, organizing and understanding Indians' continued residence in the valley—and their ancestral claims to it—became an administrative responsibility that park administrators met with labor and behavioral regulations. What paid off in this case were racializing fictions of romantic Indians that many promoters envisioned would enhance the "natural experiences" of tourists, whose desires for so-called authentic encounters became opportunities for many Yosemite Indians to sell crafts, services, and photographs. The park service also incorporated them into the tourist economy by making work in the park a requirement of continued residency. It balanced regulations against vice on idealized fantasies of noble and natural Indians, *and because* the majority of employment options for Native people were restricted to aesthetic and manual labor, performing as "nature" in the park's "scenic tableau" became for many an obligatory condition of retaining their claims to the valley.

By the 1930s, the mythic expectations of planners, administrators, and visitors had led to revision of a discourse that had been prefigured in the first design plans for the park—that modern Indians might become a scenic affront to the viewing interests of "millions of future visitors." With the development of a contained "Indian Village" in 1929, park administrators expanded regulatory adoptions that increasingly threatened Native people's peaceful residence in their ancestral lands. At this time, Superintendent Charles Thomas declared habitation within the park an official privilege that could be revoked if a resident was found guilty of moral infractions: "If anyone [who] was constantly breaking a regulation . . . did not want to work reasonably steady, [could not] get along with his neighbors, or in any way prove[d] to be a poor member of the Village . . . he would have to go away and give up his house."[127] The Park Service later added restrictions against hunting and park habitation by "non-Yosemite" tribes. Moreover, because it did not make exceptions for structural factors such as limited work opportunities that were beyond the control of vulnerable employees, it revoked the residency rights of park employees from the moment they retired.[128]

The racial return that came from reconfiguring Native people's ancestral attachments to the land as a borrowed privilege for which they were indebted to future visitors' encounters with "picturesque nature" was a gradual dispossession that never required an official policy of Native American removal. Indigenous people lived against the odds of this national project of environmental protection until 1996, when Jay Johnson, an indigenous park ranger, retired from the park service and was then required to leave his home in Yosemite.

Speculating in "Those Who Kill"

The nation's intersecting investments in deferring Black freedom as a condition of credit, relegating indigenous survival as a debt to national pleasure, and compensating low-paid labor with debits toward recreation congeal under the crustal pressure of the Yosemite's pristine wilderness. The spatial instantiation of the park created cultural conditions for a compression of historical verticality in which various managerial efforts to co-opt, undermine, and eradicate life-affirming political acts of freedom were transformed into a shared landscape of "not yet" freedom that made the inheritors of colonialism, enslavement, and repression responsible for abrogating the nation's debt to speculative desire. This convergence did not originate in the peaks and valleys where it ultimately played out. Rather, it developed in abstract exchanges of a national cultural imagination that was fixated on equating democracy with space.

Before Yosemite officially became a tourist destination, it was already both real and imagined. Congressmen did not need to travel to the West Coast, nor did they need to see images to know what Yosemite should look like. When Senator John Conness proposed a grant for claiming Yosemite as a national park, he drew on a preexisting mythical construction of the valley as a "wonder of the world."[129] Indeed, he grounded his argument in an obligation to respond to cynicism that had been raised about the exceptionalism of U.S. nature at the 1851 London World's Fair, where British spectators "declared [a cross-section of a giant sequoia] to be a Yankee invention."[130] The bluffs, falls, trees, rivers, cliffs, and meadows of the Sierra Nevadas were certainly breathtaking, but the visual iconography through which the park had been mediated conditioned the development of national parks as much as it shaped our ongoing interaction with a landscape that remains both lived and imagined. The vertical history of Yosemite, then, proceeded from images and expectations that could only be fulfilled when space collapsed into and conformed to broadly circulated figurations of a democratic U.S. landscape.

The political approval of the bill to create Yosemite stemmed from the cultural logic of U.S. imperialism that, according to David W. Noble, was cultivated in a false binary between the timeless and available landscape of the U.S. nation and the corrupt markets of Europe. The U.S. national formation of a White bourgeois male universalism, Noble argues, relied on this ideology of timeless nature to present a nation—one economically contingent on social inequality—as classless and unified.[131] In the first half of the nineteenth century, for example, artists like Thomas Cole, Frederic Church, and Asher B. Durand, of the Hudson River School, adapted the metaphor of two worlds in spectacular paintings of boundless landscapes free of human corruption. These artists depicted as uninhabited and benign environments that in reality were impacted by urban industrialism, rural poverty, and conflicted occupancy. Majestic landscape painting, says Noble, was a trope employed in the early nineteenth century to envision the United States as a protected reserve where liberal democracy could freely flourish. Thus, before Congress approved the Yosemite land grant and before Olmsted was charged with supervising park development, images of Yosemite as an exceptional example of the nation's open and available democratic frontier had already been fixed in the national imaginary. Olmsted planned to make the landscape match its image.

Albert Bierstadt's paintings of impressive Yosemite landscapes from the early 1860s were translations of scenes he had earlier imagined on the East Coast. They exposed viewers to Yosemite as an illustration of nationalist iconography. The scenes were familiar. They had been painted before, in another context, for the similar purpose of turning occupied territory into national fantasy. They have been reproduced endlessly, teaching us to see Yosemite without ever having to look at it. C. L. Weed's photographs from 1859 and Carlton Watkins's stereoviews for the California Geological Survey rearticulated a spectacular fantasy as actual landscape in images circulated in tourist promotions like Josiah Whitney's 1864 *Yosemite Book*. The roots of this legacy began in 1855 with J. M. Hutchings's *California Magazine*, Horace Greeley's 1859 *New York Tribune* reflections, and John Muir's nature writing from the 1870s, as well as National Parks legislation from 1864 and 1890. In 1864, William Henry Brewer reinscribed visual iconography as the scientific truth of the national landscape in his official survey of Yosemite for the California Geological Survey.

As William Alsup's recent photo tour of the original survey suggests, maps and numbers cannot fully contain what humans expect to see when they look for Yosemite. The landscape that has been endlessly circulated—through railroad advertisements, books, images, T-shirts, credit card backdrops, shot glasses, film, calendars, television, the photographs of Ansel Adams, snow globes, and memory—is available in reality only to the extent that paths, roads, and vistas have been manipulated to fulfill tourist expectations.

Indigenous struggles against colonial encroachment reveal strategic disruptions of speculative nationalism that resist the odds of racialized investments. The U.S. nation-state called on the landscape to promote a vision of freedom, but records of Native people fighting to retain sovereignty in the Sierra Nevadas stretch back through histories of U.S. nationalism, capitalist expansion, war, Mexican nationalism, and Spanish colonialism.[132] In his 1880 book *The Discovery of Yosemite*, the ex-soldier Lafayette Bunnell recorded the first Euro-American sighting of the valley in 1851. This "wonder of the world" was discovered while an Anglo militia was tracking a group of "disaffect[ed] and restless" "savages" during the "Indian war."[133] Bunnell's account of this war and his "discovery" is still received by many as the only remaining "firsthand" account of Americans "finding" Yosemite.

Bunnell's pretense of clearing the historical record of "mutilated [facts that had been] blended with fiction" is disrupted by his reiteration of the simultaneous annihilation and romanticizing of Yosemite's "disappearing" indigenous past.[134] His book was published thirty years after his failed military effort to expel Indians from the valley and fifteen years after Yosemite had been made a tourist site, at a time of continued indigenous presence in the park. It attempted unsuccessfully to represent continuing struggles as completed conquest. Like innumerable other historians of Yosemite, Bunnell ineffectively participated in the rhetorical colonization of the Sierra Nevadas by producing "document[s] of barbarism" as a "full statement of facts."[135] The struggles over cultural meaning that took place in historical records and accounts were troubled constantly by the dangerously resilient people who by 1880 had undergone multiple deaths and dislocations only to reappear again and again like the Cheshire cat, taunting the "victors" of history with its trickster-like persistence. Disappearance and erasure were the stories told about Native people in Yosemite, but they were not the stories the people lived by. Indigenous people's history in Yosemite was a persistent negotiation in the face of multiple efforts to exploit their labor and dispossess them of their land and history.

By all accounts, the coastal centers of Spanish mercantilism in the colonial period of Alta California (1769–1823) attracted more coastal Miwok Indians than inland Yosemite Indians into their exploitative missions, presidios, and pueblos. Nevertheless, present-day historical studies, like those of Yosemite historian Alfred Runte, reify spectacular fantasies of a protective national landscape. Runte and others argue that tribal autonomy was preserved by geographic barriers to White settlement, but this framework willfully denies the possibility that indigenous people in Yosemite very likely maintained indirect and unarticulated contacts and connections with others who experienced the coastal restructuring of Spanish colonialism. They may not have been incorporated into the Spanish colonial system, but tribes with whom they traded and interacted certainly were. Thus Spanish mercantilism, having changed the economic and cultural conditions of other Native peoples, most certainly influenced Yosemite patterns of trade and exchange in the valley.

Steven Hackel shows that indigenous labor shaped every aspect of Spanish colonialism. Franciscan profits were supported by indigenous labor in formal and informal networks, by contract and punishment, and by promises of social independence throughout missions, military presidios, and pueblos. Although scholars still debate whether this labor should be read as "slavery, genocide, or salvation," it is agreed that older Native American agricultural practices were incorporated into the restrictive and regimented system of mission agriculture that radically replaced indigenous patterns of social organization.[136]

Beginning in the mid-1820s, Mexican control of Alta California incited another reorganization of social and economic practices in Central California. The shift of economic control from missions to settlers, the expansion of foreign trade, and the establishment of private land titles meant changes in indigenous land and labor practices. Indians who abandoned the missions became landless and jobless. Mexican settlers exploited Native workers as a supplementary labor pool for large *rancherias*. Freedom from the missions often led to a form of peonage in which Native people were legally bound to work to pay back debts incurred for basic supplies, for daily food and resources for subsistence-level vegetable gardening and cattle raising.

The military campaign in which Bunnell participated came on the heels of the Mexican period. U.S. encroachment on the Sierra Nevadas threatened the land, sovereignty, and survival practices of Native people with yet another economic reorganization, one conditioned by speculative fever and militant imperialism. The people Bunnell and his fellow soldiers pursued into the Yosemite Valley in 1851 were a mixed Miwok-speaking group.[137] Bunnell and the volunteer battalion of former Mexican War soldiers had arrived in California to try their luck in the Gold Rush. In her history of the southern gold mines of Mariposa County, Susan Lee Johnson highlights the confluence of multiple modes of labor production brought into contact and conflict in the gold mines adjacent to Yosemite Valley. The shift from major economies of agricultural cultivation to raw mineral extraction again meant changing social conditions for the Miwok-speaking people. Johnson argues that the economic reorganization of the Sierra Nevadas "included independent prospecting and mining partnerships as well as altered Miwok gathering practices, Latin American peonage, North American slavery, and, later, Chinese indentured labor."[138] In fact, war against the Miwok in 1851 was a result of conflict in the mineral economy that exploded in 1848.

The rapid settlement of the Central Valley by European immigrants in the late 1840s radically decreased animal populations, farming opportunities, and traditional modes of subsistence for Miwoks. Immigrants directly harassed them, and intergroup tensions showed all signs of increasing as mining expanded and the mineral resources diminished. James Savage, a prominent trader, promised protection and subsistence to the Miwoks, employing them to gather gold in exchange for clothes, blankets, and food. For Miwok workers, this was an opportunity to retain autonomy and subsist in their radically reorganized homeland; for Savage, the Miwok workers were a docile labor force tied to colonial-style exploitation. Anxieties and inconsistencies in Bunnell's description of Savage revealed deep traces of Miwok efforts to retain autonomy. Bunnell was surely an unreliable narrator, hoping to profit from the romanticization of what was rapidly becoming a major tourist scene and to legitimate his participation in a private militia that used extralegal force to protect exploitative economic practices. Indeed, his renaming of the valley "those who kill" suggested his desire to profit from a story of national bravado.

Risk, threat, and bravery overwrite a narrative that is fundamentally about legitimating White appropriation of indigenous resources. A series of livestock raids and indirect threats purportedly motivated Savage's effort to maintain peaceful communication with the indigenous people he employed. In this description, Savage appeared as a friendly but unrelenting authority, passing "the friendly pipe" while warning Native people that cutting their ties, or rebelling against him, would be cause for no less than total war. Should his "friends" revolt, Savage assured them, "the white men will come and fight against the Indians. Their numbers will be so great, that every tribe will be destroyed that joins in a war against them."[139] It was some friend who incited a war by interpreting legitimate opposition to pillage as a just cause. In Bunnell's recollection, the military battalion was assembled because a Miwok leader encouraged his tribe to look at the numbers instead of the rhetoric, to see the weakness of Savage's claim. In speaking about deceit and calling attention to the limited support for Savage among other White settlers that he had witnessed when they traveled together to an urban center, this Miwok leader knew that White encroachment was not a foregone conclusion.

Bunnell knew that his actions were questionable. Only after he was certain that the victory had been won did he concede: "We had sufficient general intelligence and knowledge of their character to know that we were looked upon as trespassers on their territory, but were unwilling to abandon our search for gold, or submit to their frequent demands for an ever increasing tribute."[140] Bunnell's recollection dismissed too freely a past that was far from over in 1880 when he published his manuscript. The indigenous struggle he inscribed as defeated had, in fact, been far from over in 1851. Native disappearance was not a foregone conclusion when Senator John Conness introduced a bill to claim the area as a site for national recreation on May 17, 1864. The valley remained a bountiful site of home, subsistence, culture, memory, and stewardship for indigenous people who resisted European encroachment. Yet Conness associated the valley with ruin, decay, and desolation in his proposition that the land be granted to the nation under California's protection. As previously mentioned, he argued that the terrain was "for all public purposes worthless."[141]

It does not seem accidental that Yosemite was established on a discourse of waste. Conness's disingenuous conceit that Yosemite's value was purely aesthetic recodified the nation's development as a speculative investment that had been systematically purchased on racializing transactions. When read in the broader context of national reconstruction, Yosemite registers systemic panic about economic futures. In this instance, the future's contract of U.S. nationalism anticipated the "posts" of slavery and conquest with terms that positioned historically violated groups to submit their labor, land, and "not yet" free lives to a promise of future democracy. The legislative decision to invest in a plan to convert spatial imagination into a tourist location functioned like the double sales in a speculative market. Looking backward, the nation claimed space as a site of freedom on the premise that history and conflict could be eliminated from that space. Looking forward, Congress gambled on the promises of reformers that workers would pursue freedom in labor and cultural discipline when enticed with promises of national identification. On both counts, this bet depended on racializing constructions of freedom's deferral, which redefined a necessity to keep living injuries—forced labor, dispossession, repression, and exploitation—as pathways for accessing the rewards of the nation.

The public historical record inconsistently remembers who first advocated the creation of Yosemite Park. Private accounts from Olmsted's descendants intimate that he originated "the idea of making a reservation."[142] Yet the bill that John Conness introduced in the Senate in 1864 was presented to him by "gentlemen of fortune, of taste, and of refinement" and seems to have come directly from the pens of industrial shipping magnates.[143] Olmsted may not have been directly involved in the speculative interest that figures like Israel Ward Raymond, the California representative of the Central American Steamship Transit Company of New York, had in developing Yosemite. Yet much as Olmsted had buried the speculative economic variables beneath his fascination with southern wealth in a free-labor argument about "wasted time," national dialogues about the Sierra Nevadas as "worthless space" buried the speculative interests of the nation's economic elites.

In a letter dated February 20, 1864, Raymond represented the Yosemite Valley to Senator Conness as a nonmarketable geographic site, contending that "abrupt precipices ranging from 2500 to 5000 feet high" meant that there was "no access to it but by trails over the debris deposited by the crumbling of the walls."[144] He insisted that the arduous trek to usable resources would make it nearly impossible to extract raw materials from the "bare Granite Rock" that was "covered only by pine trees."[145] He believed that the landscape could "never be of much value" and thus it was not "worth while for the Government to survey these mountains."[146] Conness adapted this assumption for a congressional audience, effectively presenting an occupied territory as a vacant a priori capitalist wasteland.

In suggesting that a land survey would be a waste of time, Raymond established a means to draw on cultural categories as an investment strategy for developing new markets. As Stephen Germic has argued about Yosemite, surveying land in a private-property economy incorporates space into a system of value by producing it as an exchangeable commodity. The incorporation in geographic maps of what Lefebvre refers to as absolute space—uncharted territories outside capitalist networks—produces the abstract universality (value) through which space is made fungible.[147] This abstract value makes space intelligible within the networks of exchange at the core of capitalist modes of production. Until newly "acquired" lands were surveyed in the nineteenth century, they remained beyond the official networks of commodification, circulation, and exchange that characterized the national economy. U.S. law required the geographical mapping of lands for settlement and the distribution of private property with titles and specified plots. Although perhaps not stemming from a definition of labor in the classical sense, the work of mapping functioned in nineteenth-century territorial expansion to produce abstract spaces as commodities that could be bought and sold in the open market.[148] Embedded in Raymond's representation of valueless land, then, lies the possibility of postponing land surveys that would integrate Yosemite into resource-depleting market systems. In the immediate context of Gold Rush busts and abandoned mines in Mariposa County, Raymond developed a plan to preserve value in Yosemite by describing it geologically as already used up. In so doing, he protected the space from speculative expropriation.

Following trends of land speculation and market expansion in the 1830s, territorial expansion provided the mid-nineteenth-century solution to industrial capitalist overproduction. In a productive climate guided by the giddy optimism of speculative investment, it seemed logical to circulate products by developing peripheral consumer markets capable of absorbing surplus capital from productive centers. This move offered a spatial fix to some of the problems of industrial production.[149] In theory the creation of new markets not only forestalled the economic busts caused by capital oversaturation; it also impeded the growth of the surplus and the potentially disgruntled labor that such busts produced.

When Raymond postponed the land survey and represented the resources of Yosemite as fundamentally exhausted, he happened upon a strategy for "perfecting" history through the perpetuation of speculative regeneration. He presented this regeneration free from the corrupting effects of spatial expansion and the (apparent) necessity of drawing on existing capital and/or debt to enter new markets. The public space became a site where value could be extracted from land that was already assumed wasted and depleted. Similarly to Olmsted's misreading of slave exchange as labor value, here capitalists and policy makers deferred the inevitable busts of speculative fantasies by imagining space as infinitely renewable. As unsurveyed and valueless, the land itself remained absolute and not exchangeable. In this categorization lay the possibility for an alchemy of value without the dangerous capitalist contradictions of market instability, a speculative fantasy of endlessly reproducing and self-generating markets. This is to say that the production of Yosemite as public space allowed Raymond and other men of refinement to imagine a nationally regenerating site of circulation in which the nation's surplus could be absorbed endlessly, not by expanding markets but by mobile tourist citizen-consumers. In this plan, the elsewhere of tomorrow on which capitalist overproduction depended was relocated onto the leisure time of today.

Whereas capitalist space is often rendered through abstract sites of circulation and consumption, Raymond's proposal positioned Yosemite as circulating and consumable. By preserving Yosemite lands from private networks of circulation and exchange, he advocated a public policy for market regeneration based on a representational fallacy of nature's stasis. Raymond included a provision that "leases may be granted for portions not to exceed ten years" with the idea that nontransferable land would be "inalienable forever" yet regularly reinhabited for "market regeneration."[150] Between Raymond's proposal to Senator Conness and Conness's instruction to I. M. Edmund to "let the bill be inalienable" in the draft he produced, the industrialists' proposal for "forever" became "inalienable for all time" in U.S. Statute 184.[151]

The switch in language from "forever" to "all time" opened the policy to a double reading. The reference and circulation of a temporal metaphor incorporated various modes of production into the revised bill. The shift from an abstract "forever" to "all time" tenuously unified a national body through the absorption of various social relationships. The preservation of nature "forever" referenced an agrarian imaginary of a timeless landscape akin to the imaginary Noble delineates. The emphasis on "time," moreover, invited those whose daily lives were measured by the time clocks of the industrial workforce, the wasted time of slave production, the overtime of indigenous workers, and the borrowed time of immigrant contracts into the leisure time of public space. With this inclusion, the clause of "inalienability" called on the universal terms of the original Declaration of Independence to perform the difficult work of forging new meanings out of a fragmented society.[152] This strategy played out through a cultural bank note that had already shaped the nation's imaginary: visions of landscape as empty territory that nationalists exchanged to legitimate propertied notions of middle-class citizenship.

The story of Yosemite suggests that the nation's desires for racial returns are not simply economic but outcomes of cultural circulations that move across spaces and over time within a larger narrative arc of speculative nationalism. Techniques and cultural logics that deny freedoms in one context circulate and return elsewhere and later, to be reapplied similarly and particularly across recurring speculative bubbles and panics. Speculative nationalism draws on hope and prosperity to make the familiar and unacceptable appear emancipatory and necessary, making structural systems appear different and disconnected. The landscape recalls not yet resolved histories of slavery and conquest that fold into one another at the heart of the nation. It is thus no surprise that when later generations look to the land for national meaning, they find themselves faced with racial returns caused by the nation's still deferred freedom.

PART II PERSONS

The American Studies tradition came out of an early twentieth-century speculative reframing of liberal nationalism as market democracy. For people who had survived the speculative climate of the Gilded Age in a culture of nationalism that equated productive labor with democratic virtue, corporate appropriation of the language of democracy during the early twentieth century created a need for reimagining citizenship. In the years leading up to the Great Depression, corporate reformers followed the cues of state war bond campaigns to expand the market in common shareholders by marketing speculation to average people as a way to express patriotism.[1] As Wall Street encouraged citizens to envision investment as a pathway to democratic opportunity, scholars, activists, artists, and writers joined working people in proletarian movements. As corporations moved to extend speculative volatility into everyday households, American Studies emphasized productive virtue as the basis for a multiethnic celebration of workers' rights in the productive economy. This Popular Front solidarity acted to create stability in culture through the proletarianization of American art and identity.

It is no surprise that the economic collapse of 1929 generated support for a mass social movement. When the promises of a previous era of speculative growth and national reconstruction collapsed on a nationwide scale, people expressed frustration and anger with failure and inequality. The photographic and literary concentration on White people's suffering in Depression-era art suggests further that citizens who may have imagined their place in the nation secured by progress into Whiteness were upset by conditions of poverty, social exclusion, and injustice previously reserved for racialized people. The economic crisis created an opportunity for corporations to reorganize themselves through appeals to this disappointment. To realign the universe in the speculator's interest, companies set out to discipline citizens as potential shareholders and to organize workers as compliant producers. Proletarian movements recognized corporations' dependence on worker and shareholder buy-in. Activists used corporate reliance on the underclasses as leverage to write new social charters expanding democracy to all working people. They fought to achieve official recognition of the working class through legal protections of unions, demanded increased wages in exchange for increased productivity, and reorganized the state system of social support to protect most workers from hardship and poverty.

The wave of popular cultural intellection that gave rise to American Studies took place through negotiation of racial cartographies that lingered from previous eras of speculative expansion. Cultural Front successes created a situation in which workers and scholars could imagine and celebrate nationalist overcoming at the expense of people who still lived in the shadow lands of conquest and slavery. To resolve the contradictions of their own age, early scholars in the field returned to the culture of the early nineteenth century in search of redeemable national identities. In their quest for a usable past, they struggled to make sense of how people who had been excluded from nationalism under the violence of nineteenth-century objectification could fit in a nation that had yet to achieve lived universal democracy.

The field of American Studies was not initially organized to create material responses to the ongoing backlash against radical reconstruction, nor was it responsive to indigenous dissent against colonial containment. Rather, it began as a political search for a stable meaning and space for U.S. American democratic identity that would be open to changing demographics. Unfortunately, this aspiration often took the form of wish fulfillment in which scholars and activists prematurely imagined resolving the nation's racial foundations through the "not yet" freedom of gradual cultural incorporation. As populism filled the nation's cultural stages with hopeful images of collectivity and interethnic solidarity, corporations claimed the nation's legal stages with a spectacular inversion of the logic of personhood. With treaties signed and slavery outlawed, private companies during the corporate era of speculative realignment folded discriminatory legacies of direct human objectification into racializing legal abstractions. To protect private business, companies manipulated the hard fought for rights and protections codified for former slaves in the Fourteenth Amendment. Unintended and unanticipated corporate takeover of the concept of personhood gave companies rights with little responsibility while legal repression of radical reconstruction left people with responsibilities and few rights.

The chapters in this section investigate American Studies as a field that developed out of the uncertainty and contradictions of this early twentieth-century speculative reorganization. They focus on two founders of the field whose attempts to reconstitute the meaning and space of American democracy inadvertently reproduced a culture conducive to the theft of racialized people's rights to personhood. As illustrative examples of two predominant approaches to the study of the American past, Constance Rourke and F. O. Matthiessen's contributions to the establishment of American Studies demonstrate how the cultural transaction between U.S. democracy and speculative capitalism in the early twentieth century regenerated race as an outlet for risk. The two schools of cultural thought that these scholars represent made a coherent American identity a prerequisite of democratic participation; in the first case, as a proletarian celebration of folklore and performance; in the second, through aesthetic critique of literature and art. The field's inception on the basis of inadvertent assumptions that unity depended on racial uplift, however, suggests that much of U.S. culture functions like a form of credit—producing investments in legacies of enslavement and colonialism through a national payback system that makes the traumas and tragedies of history a cumulative liability that historically aggrieved people must abrogate as the criterion for accessing the privileges and rewards of the nation. Similar to the futures contracted in the speculative economies of the early twentieth century, the construction of "not yet" freedom as the basis of U.S. culture operated as a mode of transaction within a broader integrated network. It was deployed widely and differentially in particular exchanges, mutually and relationally producing imbalanced trading positions that resulted in disproportionate gains and losses. Thinking about race and gender through networked logics reveals culture as a central technology for how economies differentially position groups as competing and antagonistic.

What were promises and hopes of an ideal future and democracy for the founders of American Studies during the early twentieth century became the nostalgic past for many twenty-first-century pundits and economists during the crisis of 2008. The age of New Deal prosperity was built on a privileged subject position that occluded the cumulative and stratifying impacts of repeated speculative crises on people who were racialized to absorb speculative economic risks. So much of the response to the twenty-first-century global economic collapse has been based in longings for New Deal–style regulations and reforms, desires for policy measures that come attached to affective recollections of the 1940s as a period of unity and national prosperity.[2] There are legitimate economic and political reasons for renewed scholarly focus on the collective gains and social formations that came out of the New Deal. The danger that comes with looking to the Keynesian welfare-warfare state as the model for reclaiming economic prosperity and addressing inequality, however, is that celebrations of the New Deal often come with widespread forgetting of how the economy recovered on the back of stolen personhood. The New Deal was culturally orchestrated by containing freedom in a racializing colonial contract that reinforced the legitimacy of the White liberal state.

Legal and social measures that segregated society around unevenly allocated prosperity were only part of the story. The Wagner Act, the Social Security Act, and the Federal Housing Act included exclusions and restrictions that had a disproportionate impact on the descendants of slavery. The raw deal of New Deal racism was unfair distribution of social services, discriminatory lending, and housing segregation.[3] As Thomas Shapiro has shown, racialized people who patiently worked toward and invested in New Deal promises continue to face structurally impossible time delays that reduce the odds of overcoming inherited inequalities.[4] The symbolic gestures and cultural compensations of

American identity in the New Deal era were not enough to prevent the cumulative consequences of speculative deferral from erupting once again in the disproportionate racial impact of the recent housing collapse.

Life-affirming stories and songs, dances, and institutional ideas for structural transformation remain among the refuse of the Cultural Front's American recovery. Masks of American identity conceal enactments of freedom in which personhood figures more fully than anticipatory rights. The chapters in this section look beneath U.S. cultural identity to identify freedoms that react against the ascriptive violence of nationalist becoming.

Masks and Manipulations of Personhood

The National Popular, Corporate Minstrelsy,
Improvisation in the Offbeat

The Amendment sought to prevent discrimination against classes or races . . .
Yet, of the cases in this Court in which the Fourteenth Amendment was applied
during the first fifty years after its adoption, less than one-half of 1 percent invoked it in protection of the negro race, and more than 50 percent asked that its
benefits be extended to corporations.
—JUSTICE HUGO BLACK, 1938

Probably we are still a folk—an imperfectly formed folk—rather than a schooled
and civilized people. This fate is strange enough in a modern world, but from
the beginning we have also had another destiny. . . . Conflicting forces have thus
been set up, but we shall hardly be able to select another course at this late date.
—CONSTANCE ROURKE, 1942

On her right hand she had her two middle fingers between her forefingers cut
off, and she played with the three. So she played a blues like this all day long,
when she first would get up in the morning.
—JELLY ROLL MORTON, 1938

The Scene of Exchange

The historical context was ripe for an oppositional people's movement
against speculative capitalism. Between the Reconstruction era and 1930,
the U.S. labor pool grew from 12 million to 50 million workers. The U.S.
population increased from 40 million to more than 123 million.[1] Thirty million immigrants settled in the United States, 13 million of whom arrived from
non-Northern European countries between 1886 and 1925.[2] Meanwhile, Black
workers continued to fight against repressive campaigns to undermine abolition democracy in the South. The horror of southern pastimes—lynching and
Jim Crow violence—resonated across the nation as a shame on par with the rise
of European fascism. Ethnically concentrated hurdles and hardships were also
a part of everyday life in the United States. The interethnic, antifascist, and racially conscious worker's struggle to combat intersecting forms of exploitation

that emerged from this context called for fair conditions, life chances, and lived human equality.[3]

The Cultural Front, as Michael Denning scrupulously documents, galvanized the energy and insight of cross-class internationalist social struggle into an interethnic popular campaign to revive the broken promise of the Lincoln Republic.[4] In the context of a sweeping economic depression, populist demands for the type of "new birth" constitution that Lincoln delivered at Gettysburg rang through art, music, protests, and parades as a freedom call for economic justice. The Depression reanimated a popular consensus that money movers, corporate monopolies, and land-holding elites were the source of racial sectionalism, concentrated power, and nationwide poverty. In response to antiprogressive impulses, a vernacular democracy predicated on interclass solidarity became the foundation of a renewed national-popular culture. Popular-front Americanism permeated the nation with a proletarian vision of national promise—a people's movement to restore and expand ideals of freedom, justice, and interethnic social democracy. The conditions and affects out of which the Cultural Front emerged were perfectly in tune to revive Gilded Age populism's strategic attack on financial speculation. Yet the situation was different and the difference mattered.

The coalition of debt-ridden farmers, reformers, women's temperance groups, and churches that became a People's Party during the 1890s coordinated millions of people across the nation into a unified critique of speculation. From the cotton fields of the South to the wheat fields of the central plains, the populist alliance staged a pointed rhetorical attack on post–Civil War corporate rule and financial speculation.[5] Although the coalition was loose, ranging from farmers to religious zealots, it garnered strength from its identification of a clear political target: a disconnected plutocracy with no investment in the public interest. The populist call for a return to egalitarian principles resonated as a force that could ameliorate lived social schisms. Its mode of mass mobilization glossed over internal differences, combining a diverse array of denizens and detractors into a singular struggle with many accents. The force that bound the motley crowd together was a common enemy: the nonproductive money movers whose actions brought hardships to worksites, homes, businesses, and places of governance. The same vicious culprit loomed large during the Great Depression, but by the 1930s the economic situation that underwrote Gilded Age populism had been reorganized and seized by the investment economy.

Drawing on the momentum of war bond patriotism, stockbrokers during the early twentieth century effectively branded the private purchase of corporate stocks and bonds an expression of nationalist loyalty. Julia C. Ott describes the funding of World War I with private bonds as a nationalist campaign that struck a deliberate chord with the spirit of populist democracy. In a clear effort to absorb and realign the freedom dreams and struggles of diverse groups with the economic imperatives of speculative nationalism, the Treasury Department targeted private citizens as well as "ethnic societies, African American groups, women's clubs, churches, businesses, trade organizations and labor unions" to fund and support national liberation.[6] Wartime propaganda depicted private investment in federal securities as a national obligation, a symbol of citizens taking "stock" in the promise of U.S. democracy by holding a "share" in the nation-state. For ethnic immigrants, government advertisements suggested that the purchase of war bonds signaled dedication to the nation and a ticket to citizenship. Similarly, African Americans were pressured to purchase bonds against a backdrop of minstrelsy to prove their aptitude for racial progress. Mass investment retained its momentum after the war when private financial institutions appropriated the rhetoric of financial nationalism.

On the postwar domestic front, financial marketers advertised corporate stock ownership as a salve to the wounds of exploitation and inequality. Trust managers sold stock as a ticket to the nation's not yet realized democratic promise. Investment, they argued, created opportunity for individual liberty because "shareholder democracy" could emancipate exploited workers and indebted consumers from the constraints of economic inferiority. This reorganization of political aspiration exponentially increased mass investment in private financial markets during the early twentieth century. By the end of the 1920s, 3.5 million people had opened a brokerage account, and 2 million of those had purchased private shares. By 1930 the number of ordinary shareholders had skyrocketed to 10 million.[7] Because the financial industry had strategically transformed international fascism into a marketing opportunity, much of this stock was underregulated. As Ott explains, brokers on the New York Stock Exchange articulated investment as part of a global struggle in which democracy and investment were united against "deadening regulation, statist appropriation, and communist oppression."[8] Financial interests won the war of words, their prize a right to trade with no enforceable accounting rules and no requirements to make financial information available for audits. Thus participants in the corporate resignification of nationalist democracy were often uniformed of speculative bubbles and price inflation.

In a climate in which a broad majority had economically enmeshed their futures in corporate investments, the clear enemy of the populist movement was made to disappear by economic interdependence. Making matters more difficult, promoters of private investment actively wore a mask of democracy to dismantle populist accusations against Wall Street as a predatory den where the lives of real people were gambled away. Ott argues that financial marketers associated stock with protective insurance. Because majority holders in a financial exchange staked their fortunes on the future purchases of novice investors, financial promoters concentrated their response to potential class revolt on enticing working people to buy into speculative markets. Marketers distanced new trusts from critiques of speculation with claims that "their new product would resolve animosities based in class, disparities of wealth, and the endemic cyclicality of modern industrial capitalism."[9]

Like all speculative endeavors, Jazz Age financial ascendency balanced on people's imbalanced arrangements in time. During the war years, government promoters seeking to break people's habits of saving promoted federal securities as a form of meaningful deferral. By limiting purchases in the present to investments, government savings officials suggested, citizens would be compensated with returns that they could use later to reward themselves with more valuable goods. But even though anticipatory refrains compelled people to invest in both government and private securities, their rhythm did not match common people's timing. President Hoover, for example, built his "empire of fairness" on the promise that any person in America could become a millionaire. His particular assemblage of democracy and hopefulness provoked an intimate relationship between private desires for economic well-being and national assurances of future social belonging.[10] However, chimeras of economic egalitarianism in a class-stratified society obscured how wealthy people invested in speculative markets to reproduce their class status with the knowledge that they possessed adequate resources for hedging risk.

Branding financial speculation as democratization hid risk in promises of middle-class uplift.[11] Yet the stockholder's democracy could never be evenly balanced because a shareholder's vote was determined by the number of shares held and not on the basis of equal votes for everyone. Further, the secret world of majority shareholders was not much different from Ponzi-style swindling. Although the common folk bought stock in an open marketplace, profitable Jazz Age investments were made in invitation-only investment pools where inside traders were known to circulate rumors to "common shareholders" to drive up the prices of their own stocks. Once prices were elevated, the stocks were dumped on the general public when prices began to fall.[12] In this regard, legal protections that made inflated stock opportunities so attractive to middle-class investors during the early twentieth century also masked capital's continued dependence on impoverished workers and farmers to absorb the fallout of economic collapse.

In practice, promises of liberal equality reconstituted internal market hierarchies. When humble citizens with limited financial knowledge pooled their modest incomes and bought stock on credit for inflated prices, they increased their economic vulnerability. Common investors, who had neither time nor money on their side, were the source of returns for market insiders who profited from price increases and concentrated knowledge.[13] The wealth that common citizens lost when they gambled in stocks did not vanish. It was upwardly redistributed, through the failure of a promise, to banks and professional investors who had beaten the crash. Many pulled out of their investments before 1929, reentering the sweeps in the aftermath to buy up the debris of the economy on the cheap.[14]

On the surface, commodities markets in the early twentieth century appeared quite different from those that had shaped the early nineteenth century. After all, objects and lives that had circulated in exchange in the previous century had been converted into persons by the Fourteenth Amendment or into peoples by tribal sovereignty. Some of these persons were even marked as potential buyers in the burgeoning speculative economy in corporate stock. Yet the shared language and affect of market democratization behind the corporate structure of feeling anchored its ideological weight in residual legal and cultural politics that had undermined freedom in earlier centuries.[15]

The intimate transaction between capitalism and nationalism in this climate registered an uneven battle over the meaning and use of the concept of personhood that was at once cultural, economic, legal, and, for many, personal. After the passage of the Fourteenth Amendment, for example, White southerners assaulted the promise of universal human freedom using the clause of exception that was attached to abolition. That is, the Thirteenth Amendment provision that involuntary servitude could be used as penalty for crime enabled a reorganization of slavery under the penal code. Black codes against vagrancy, penalties for breaking labor contracts, and a system of debt peonage that often left Black farmers owing more to company stores for food, clothes, and subsistence goods than they had earned from their share of an annual crop created an excuse for White authorities to engage in the violence of mass incarceration.[16] This southern assault on Black personhood was aided and abetted by expansion of the convict labor system. Lethal combinations of harsher sentences and steep accruing fines for subsistence "crimes" enabled the penal state to embezzle the personhood of those it convicted despite Radical Reconstruction's legal guarantees of freedom and equality. Moreover, government subleases of incarcerated people made reenslavement a state business.[17] The reorganization of speculative practices as a standard aspect of corporate business re-created a sense of separation of the economy of the North from that of the South.

Popular front nationalism reinforced this distinction. The unifying force of populist attacks against economic injustice was lost when common people tied their futures to corporate speculation. Deflecting the imbrication of citizens with shareholders, the Cultural Front registered its economic critique in an adaptation of nationalism as a site of escape from regional and ethnic conflicts. The rhetoric of universal progress and individual opportunity was as much a part of proletarian culture as it was a cornerstone of financial propaganda. Cultural workers seeking to remake the Lincoln Republic relied on hopes that national unity and democracy would make racial injustice disappear. In this regard, nationalist culture worked with speculative economic reconversion in a collective harmony that masked structural racialized deferrals.

Taking class revolt to the streets, proletarian culture of the 1930s celebrated folklore, "common" people, and universal democracy as expressions of diverse groups. Similarly to the financial markets' hijacking of the rhetoric of national democracy, the Cultural Front rearticulated in an understated way people's self-actualized movement into nationalist expressions of collective aspiration. The post-Reconstruction era may be one of the most unrecognized periods of purposeful antiracist resistance in U.S. history. In contrast to the forced migrations that had shaped the landscape of the nineteenth century, people's mass movement from South to North and across oceans during the early twentieth century evinced their fight to free themselves from unconscionable social conditions. Black people's mass exodus from the South between 1910 and 1930 signaled willful life-affirming resistance against legal repression, erosion of political rights, social segregation, economic denigration, and mass violence and injury caused by Jim Crow suppression of Radical Reconstruction. For different reasons and in other economic circumstances, mass immigration indicated purposeful action to remake basic conditions of existence by people moving themselves to a new continent.

The Cultural Front created both a stage and a substitution for the radical potential overflow from mass migratory action. As capitalists marketed democracy through financial investment, proletarian artists and academics subtly realigned the complex reasons and aspirations behind frenetic migrations with a singular vision of national progress and unity. Through art, music, and literature, cultural workers incorporated racialized and ethnic people into the symbolic fold of an ostensibly expanding nationalist democracy. The desire for representational reconciliation, quite often, did not come from aggrieved people. Rather, nationalist cultural ascription incorporated difference into an unprecedented plurality, aligning freedom movements with proletarian Americanism. Culture, in this nationalist adaptation, was retooled as a weapon of collective dissent, as a unifying force to make good on the equality, rights, and personhood that had been conferred universally by the Fourteenth Amendment. In this case, also, however, the timing was off for people whom the law was designed to protect.

While democratic culture celebrated ethnic and racial progress on cultural stages, corporate minstrels actively seized the rights of personhood on legal stages. The guarantee of personhood and equal protection in the Constitution of 1868 had laid the groundwork for a total reconfiguration of U.S. democracy. When formerly enslaved people drew sanction from the Fourteenth Amendment's formal guarantee of equal citizenship, they participated in democratic governance, using enfranchisement to build public schools and re-creating legislation for egalitarian economic conditions. Abolition democracy gave life to the legal construction of personhood by actively reconfiguring shared governance and allocations of common resources to meet the collective needs of all.[18] Sadistic repression of Radical Reconstruction turned the South into a scene of failed national promise. Mass Black migration was a refusal to accept the life-destroying consequences of the elimination of due process of law.

The human protections of the Fourteenth Amendment did not fare much better in the nation's highest courts. In 1886, with an administrative sleight of hand, the hard fought for equal personhood that Black people had earned in the Fourteenth Amendment was extended to private corporations. The Supreme Court never actually decided that corporations were people in *Santa Clara County v. Southern Pacific Railroad*. Rather, C. Bancroft Davis, not incidentally a former president of a railroad company, wrote the assertion into the legal heading of an interpretation of a comment by Chief Justice Waite.[19] Nevertheless, the assertion has masqueraded ever since as a legal precedent for extending the rights of individuals to private companies.[20]

Corporate appropriation of the Fourteenth Amendment set the stage for a bizarre reversal of legal protection. Under the masquerade that corporations are a special type of legal person, following the Standard Oil Decision of 1889 they became the only people in the United States permitted to own other people. Of course, creating a holding company to invest in the stocks that sustain other "corporate persons" is not the same as the human slavery that is legal under the Thirteenth Amendment. Unlike humans, whom the law says can be subjected to servitude as a punishment for crime, corporations are special because limited liability guarantees that a corporation's holders will not be held accountable for corporate crimes. The charade of personhood gives artificial life to "artificial entities," empowering corporations to enter into contracts, sue, and be sued. Corporations are also special in that they are endowed with the possibility of perpetual life. If stockholders divest, the corporate person remains open to future investment. The ethical distance from corporate responsibility creates an economically attractive shelter from damages and debts for individual investors, but it is not always in the best interest of actual breathing humans.[21]

As Justice Hugo Black wrote in 1938, 288 of the cases heard by the court under the Fourteenth Amendment between 1890 and 1910 dealt with expanding the rights of private corporations; only 19 dealt with the lives and rights of slavery's direct descendants. The Cultural Front did not reconcile these contradictions. Rather, the radical revision of national democracy that took center stage in popular front culture often inadvertently reproduced the temporal distinctions and abstract logics of shareholder democracy. In making solidarity and a unified American identity the foundation of critiques of capitalist inequality, the internationalist, antifascist, antilynching cultural movement that gave rise to the field of American Studies also inadvertently undermined the personhood of racially marked people.

The concurrent late nineteenth-century unfolding of differentially rendered notions of personhood around corporate impermeability and Black vulnerability occurred in disparate institutional and regional conjunctures that were not quite causally connected or relationally determined.[22] Cultural Front artists, intellectuals, and activists tended not to directly address regional, historical, and economic differences when they celebrated the interethnic promise of universal citizenship. Yet the cultural redemption of democracy—a figuration of a united national culture—constituted a new national meaning in which these divergent developments were articulated as convergent cultural formations. At the intersection of speculative capitalism and U.S. nationalism, Cultural Front producers grappled with interregional cultural conjunctures. In their efforts to reconstitute an egalitarian nationalism, they often dismissed the hard facts of deeply ingrained interregional systems of human disparity as simple roadblocks to a not yet realized universal freedom. As a consequence, the national-popular

culture of the early twentieth century unintentionally sustained the racial
logics of speculative nationalism as the basis for multiethnic democracy.

The Form of Transfer

The approach to democracy taken by early twentieth-century financial interests
and that taken by cultural opponents of economic injustice were remarkably
similar. U.S. nationalism in both realms registered campaigns to incorporate
sundry members of a polyglot society into a coherent articulation of shared
identity and action. Democracy in both was constituted proleptically through
masquerade. To be American, stock market promoters suggested, meant
investing in the promise of future earnings, donning in the meantime a mask
of equality while waiting for windfalls to prove the charade true. Conversely,
the Cultural Front rehearsed a universal democracy that was uniquely configured to unite an evolving and expanding plural society. Although the culture of
democracy spoke in the language of national unity, it did not reflect an already
existing cross-class harmony. Rather, through the art of masquerade the movement presented an image of what could be, seeking to organize difference into
a shared mythology by enticing average people to perform in its vision. Put
another way, the expansive repertoire of American typology that constituted
the cultural backdrop of the early twentieth century created a stage that called
on common people to identify emergent expressions of popular nationalism
as aspects of the self. Becoming American in both cases entailed adapting to
political and economic transformation—or the changing configurations of
the economy and citizenship—based on faith that masks of unity and progress
would eventually grow into lived equality and freedom.

In the field of American Studies, Constance Rourke's detailed studies of
U.S. art, performance, and folklore are particularly illustrative of speculative nationalism's performative formation.[23] Rourke's underappreciated part
in creating American Studies is useful as a reminder of the field's fundamental commitment to reckoning with culture as a socioeconomic force. In her
pathbreaking reflections on the emancipatory role of art in common people's
democracy, Rourke was keenly attuned to the relationship between the material
conditions of U.S. society and the emergence of the nation's folk traditions.[24]
Her wide-ranging reflections on folk culture at once critically engaged the
relationship between folklore and national cultural development and served
as ledgers of the economic forces that informed the "still experimental" forging of an egalitarian nation with an artistic identity "distinctively [its] own."[25]
Rourke's assessment of the early republic, for example, is compellingly suggestive of the ways that differences between capitalist production and exchange
inform national ideas about artistic value. She saw fine arts patronage in the
post-revolutionary period as determined in part by the mercantile networks
that shaped the global economy of the eighteenth century. The measurement
of the value of high art among the global elite, in Rourke's estimation, was

premised on "detaching art from the ruck of common life" and configuring it as an object of exchange in global markets that circulated wealth.[26] Folk art, with its democratic impulses, she believed, derived value not from incorporation into systems of exchange but rather from a symbiosis of form and function that she saw as ostensibly grounded in the use value of art as a social artifact. According to Rourke, tools, fabrics, legal documents, music, and images supplied an emergent national collectivity with the material resources necessary for surviving new contexts and conditions. These objects also functioned as mediums of communication documenting the populace's "underlying patterns of thought, feeling or preoccupation."[27] Basically, Rourke saw folk forms as distinctive because they were connected to "common" people's quotidian survival.

As it pertained to the corporate transformation of speculative capitalism, Rourke's research highlighted speculation as a prominent socio-analytical category of the Depression era through which delicate battles for resources and representation were staged. In her studies of nineteenth-century comic humor, she identified the profit-driven self-interest of individual speculators as a major obstruction to the development of a lived national democracy.[28] She even called for a version of U.S. history that accounted for how "the issue of speculation with its attendant evils was a major issue [between 1830 and 1850] and must eventually be handled on a parity with nullification, slavery, and changes in the financial system, indeed as inextricably interwoven with these."[29] In this challenge, she implicated particular nineteenth-century economic actors as perpetrators of social violence: boosters of western development who manipulated and profited from government-sponsored indigenous land dispossession, settlers who took advantage of land grants and subsidies for rail road expansion, and traders who exchanged human commodities in southern slave markets.

In the context of a subsequent era of speculative crisis, Rourke's emphasis on the use value and human contributions necessary for the production of folk art pointed to a subtle materialist critique of the political and economic costs of speculative markets. Rourke's mapping of the social and formal characteristics of cultural production was largely motivated by her desire to recover the nation's folk legacies and rearticulate them as a refined national art that she hoped would retain the collective spirit of a people's democracy. She faced the "difficult cultural problem" of organizing major U.S. art around a "synthesis of certain deep lying qualities in American life."[30] If informed by the popular spirit of the nation, she suggested, national art could serve as a useful resource for upholding common people's stake in the privileges and protections of the nation.

Rourke analyzed a wide array of cultural objects, expressions, and themes over the course of her career. Her archive extended from comic almanacs, pamphlets, joke collections, sports weeklies, newspapers, and staged burlesques to plays and the literature of major U.S. writers, among them Hawthorne, Melville, Whitman, Poe, Twain, and Henry James. In her synthesis of common themes and developments that first appeared in the speculative climates of the nineteenth century, Rourke engaged "comic triumph" as a crucial building block of 1930s artistic culture.

Rourke was an exceptional proponent of some of the most radical visions of interethnic, cross-class democracy in the Cultural Front movement.[31] Her scholarship suggested a profound effort to reconfigure dominant systems of value as a way to mobilize folk forms against the "many economic, social, and cultural crossroads" of the early twentieth century.[32] Rourke's project was explicitly a tactical reaction to the devaluation of popular culture by U.S. literary and artistic critics.[33] Her call for expanding the cultural epistemologies and democratic interventions of common citizens also contributed to the Cultural Front's political stance against racial lynching, international fascism, and Depression-induced poverty. In making a case for the social and cultural importance of folk forms as carriers of particular regional and racial knowledge, Rourke dramatically challenged the boundaries between cultural analysis and political action. She hoped to emancipate U.S. culture from the "ancient snobberies" and exclusionary practices that regulated elite assessments of fine art, using "new inclusions" that were both artistic and material.[34] As editor of the Federal Art Project's *Index of American Design*, for example, she enacted a powerful precedent for creating institutional changes that matched her intellectual commitment to plural democracy.[35] She insisted on the value of popular expression, but also strongly supported employing struggling artists and opening up new spaces for egalitarian art.

Although Rourke implicitly recognized divergent value systems as the source of formal disagreements about what constituted worthy art, the context in which she wrote did not allow a complex treatment of the tensions and conflicts that overlapping and intersecting constructions of value often produce. In identifying folk strains from the nation's past, she hoped to uncover a national tradition capable of lifting democracy from the depths of a nationwide depression. Looking for forms of relief in the past is a common response to economic collapse. At the moment of crisis, the present plummets from its singular temporality into prolonged cumulative patterns of injustice. Progress narratives fall apart. The weight of a future that never arrives places past and present in an intimate embrace. Circumstances undoubtedly change, but the patterned regularity of "not yet" freedom acts as a reminder of permanent deferral arriving at the present from the unresolved past. Rourke was deeply invested in meeting ongoing demands for social justice, drawing on nineteenth-century folk forms to negotiate recurring economic and artistic ruptures. Yet the promises of collective freedom she found in expressive culture often worked against her because they enmeshed her in the politics and racial practices of speculative nationalism.

Rourke was not wrong to hope that cultural recovery could lead to justice and unity during her time. But her inferences regarding the connections between cultural production and economic developments, value systems and political formations, and cultural representation and democratic emancipation do provide an opportunity to assess how notions of national futurity often supply economic systems of value with a symbolic principle of deferral that enables the perpetuation of social injustices. Because Rourke's hopeful investment in the nation as a site of future emancipation evinces this dynamic, her work is an instructive example of a speculative economic and cultural interdependence that mediates material risk through temporal constructions of racial difference. The unintentional sacrifice of justice for unity in Rourke's work too quickly assumed that culture could heal the wounds caused by centuries of democratic deferral. Unfortunately, her faith in a nationalist futurity caused her to misread sustained inequalities and subtle resistances against nationalist imperatives as simple precursors to a "not yet" achieved national fate, as symptoms of the nation's prolonged "primitive" state.

Rourke first set out to discover the richness of the U.S. American past during the speculative boom of the 1920s. Her first book-length studies— *Trumpets of Jubilee* (1927), *Troupers of the Gold Coast* (1928), and *American Humor* (1931)—thus located culture at the intersection of social, economic, and legal rupture. Her studies of nineteenth-century masquerade and folklore typologies intervened in an intellectual and political environment that did not allow her to theorize how reconciling competing systems of value—between fine art and popular art as much as between cultural forms and economic patterns—might unwittingly contribute to processes of differentiation that enabled capitalist markets to sustain imbalances of profit and power. Rourke could not have been expected to question what it might have meant that she grounded her cultural reimagination of national democracy in a future equality that depended on "rais[ing] the level of popular taste."[36] In her historical context, it was likely unthinkable that this notion of futurity might run the risk of aligning emancipatory struggles with economic logics that necessitated exploitation. Nor did Rourke's intellectual and political environments make it possible for her to consider that her focus on national unity might participate in reproducing material conditions of uneven racializing exchange.

Rourke worked to dismantle elite standards of artistic taste that she saw as "chaining" U.S. artists to a set of external expectations of subject and technique.[37] It would not have been expedient for her to question the intricate connection between national culture and economic patterns in which her own criticism was enmeshed. Nevertheless, her studies of national folklore reveal the aesthetic and political culture of U.S. nationalism as a primary technology of crisis management. A diagnostic reading of Rourke's investment in the nationalist masquerade therefore reveals that the particular form of cultural exchange she saw as most "American" concealed a counter-archive of people's cultural struggles to beat the odds of the racializing residue in the nationalism she optimistically sought to recover.

On American Types and Nationalist Promise

Rourke's lasting influence is largely attributed to her identification of three archetypes at the core of U.S. American identity: the Yankee, the backwoodsman, and the minstrel. In *American Humor*, her most influential contribution to American Studies, she developed elaborate genealogies of each regional figure, registering cultural patterns of dialect and gesture as emerging out of speculative economies. The patriotic bravado and vigorous independence of the trope that would later become the Yankee, according to Rourke, was a comic adaptation of the habitual masquerade of pioneer peddlers whose early contributions to wealth redistribution are strikingly resonant with the conditions of exuberant exchange and volatile crashes in bubble economies. "The peddler moved relentlessly," Rourke wrote, showing his wares "where inhabitants had barred their doors and double-locked their money-tills in vain."[38] Through evasive speech and stories, he provoked awe among villagers in the objects he traded. "He made his way into their houses, and silver lept into his pockets" until he "left with most of the money in the settlement."[39]

Traces of nineteenth-century land grabs set a spectacular stage for the tall tales of the backwoodsman. Rourke read the hyperbolic narratives of western adventurers as inverted markers of the national inheritance of an expropriated indigenous past. In his celebrations of westward expansion, the backwoodsman adopted a "comic oblivious tone" that made it possible for him to trade fast and loose in national fantasy at a symbolic distance from the "horror, terror, [and] death [that] were written large in the life of the rivers and forests."[40]

The tension between speculative economies and popular culture also informed Rourke's larger body of research. In her first book, she argued that the national polity of the United States originally unified as an audience for influential leaders such as Horace Greeley, Harriet Beecher Stowe, and P. T. Barnum. The reformers, abolitionists, and entrepreneurs of a spectacular racial imposture that she identified as popular leaders reached their peak of fame during the 1850s. While they crossed the North "voicing the popular will" for an emergent national audience, speculative fever in the slave market was keeping questions of race at the center of the southern economy.[41] In her second book, Rourke found the origins of a U.S. theatrical tradition in the context of the Gold Rush. The excitement surrounding bawdy performances on the California coast emerged in the context of a euphoric drive to speculate in mineral extraction.

Rourke imagined American culture as emerging within the spatial conjunctures created by speculative expansions and in opposition to the exploitation on which speculation depended. Her sense of the popular arose from the idea that North Americans "have always gathered easily in crowds."[42] Yet the collective will of the populace that she found in cultural expression more often than not took form indirectly through representative figures who broadcast this spirit to audiences. In this configuration, U.S. democracy was revealed as an act of alignment into preconfigured expectations rather than the act of collective determination by the people whom nationalism purported to represent. This aspect of Rourke's work fit popular nationalism into a speculative cultural formula. It revealed a cultural transaction that purchased symbolic possibilities but rested on an imagined freedom relieved of the material weight of minoritarian points of view. Rourke's compromised vision of popular participation wagered a high-stakes bet on national culture that was burdened by the material risks of an economy that remained divided, racialized, and volatile. Her sense of mediated representation leveraged this risk by interpreting opposition and antagonism as blocked desires for cultural unity, depicting those who benefited from subordinating others as united through affect to those who resisted power. False unity also positioned the critic as a cultural manager endowed with the authority to speak for aggrieved populations without reckoning with their actual needs and aspirations.

For example, the intraregional rivalries and conflicts at the core of each of the three figures that Rourke most celebrated flattened into singular expressions of regional uplift when she engaged the challenge of cultural difference.[43] What tied the nation's most representative tropes and traditions together for Rourke was a collective will to overcome the economic disparities of a prenational past. Her rendering of national amalgamation took place first and foremost through humor: "Laughter produced the illusion of leveling of obstacles in a world which was full of unaccustomed obstacles. . . . [it] created ease, and even more, a sense of unity, among a people who were not yet a nation and who were seldom joined in stable communities."[44] The shared social enjoyment of a good joke as the basis of a national community balanced on a critical creation of a posteriori shared desires to construct the nation as the natural site for future egalitarian freedom. Rourke retroactively envisioned American types as outcroppings of repeated performance and collaborative imagination, as evidence of the collective storytelling of regional populaces whose situated regional resistances and aspirations for democracy provided the roots of U.S. American identity. She saw myths as expressions of a bottom-up nationalism made lively and diverse by historical development and regional idiosyncrasy. The Yankee symbolized for her the American Revolution. The backwoodsman symbolized a westward expansion in a bold rejection of European civilization, politics, and culture. In a recognizably compromised form, the minstrel stood for the promises of abolition democracy.[45]

For Rourke, broad multiregional national progression toward a lived democracy may have originated in opposition to the violent racial and regional economies of the nineteenth century but it grew into a voracious popular spirit for an egalitarian freedom as the basis of national culture. The absorption of this popular will in the common themes and aesthetics of the nation's major authors suggested to her that the nation remained committed to overcoming prolonged patterns of inequality.[46] Yet the grounding of these types in an uneven property system, colonialism, and enslavement worked in tandem with her lingering reverence for external categories of artistic value. Both teleologies tied her hopes for a plural nation to assimilation, normative sexuality, and Whiteness as preconditions of national unity and market integration.[47]

Rourke believed that "a consistent native tradition had been formed, surviving cleavages and dispersals," but that a "mature" American art had yet to be developed by the early twentieth century.[48] "The ellipses created by migration and change," she argued, made the past largely unknowable; however, artists who "consciously work[ed] toward a discovery of our traditions, [and] attempt[ed] to use them" to invest in "retrospect and the legendary approach" would be guaranteed an "inevitable place" as respected and representative U.S. Americans.[49] This symbolic construction translated into material and social processes on several levels. It negotiated the racial compromises of national unity with an aesthetic ideal for the future that incorporated ethnic and racial difference under the sign of Whiteness. And it deprived social "beings" of their right to demand justice in the present by redefining them in nationalist terms as "not yet" subjects bound to the trajectory of "becoming" free citizens of the future. Rourke's optimistic investment in legendary narratives as promises of flourishing national culture shared a particular rhythm with the confidence in market growth fueling the speculative markets she saw as antagonistic to democracy.

Speculative bubbles in both nineteenth- and twentieth-century markets inflated because of a socially disseminated faith in the future that economists label confidence. In both contexts, prices were often propelled to prohibitive heights, causing a concentration of wealth among investors who profited as much from their capacity to buy stocks as from their ability to entice increasingly vulnerable buyers into risky stock purchases with hopes of making profits.[50] The stock bubble of the early twentieth century produced massive returns for bankers, businessmen, and experienced investors largely because loose credit made it possible for average people to buy on margin at great risk to their limited assets.[51] Stock market expansion gave new shape to the intimate relationships conditioning speculative exchange in the early and mid-nineteenth century, between sellers, buyers, and human commodities that carried memories of and subtle actions for a world emancipated from capitalist objectification. The expansion of futures markets camouflaged the power imbalances of these tripartite transactions through the creation of centralized trading floors where commodities circulated only as abstractions.

By the early twentieth century, day-to-day transactions in futures markets seemed to escape the multidirectional dynamic of human movement that was a staple of nineteenth-century speculation. Corporate stock traders no longer faced the "constraints" created by the disruptive resistance of commodities in circulation—be they human lives, ancestral lands, or cumbersome materials extracted and produced by human labor. When Rourke began to mine the archives for a usable past, the economy was being restructured around distance, such that investors had no interaction with actual commodities. Any underlying uneven and contentious relationships of economic exchange were concealed by paper tokens, and commodities circulated through symbolic references to prices without actually changing hands. The stock exchange took hegemonic form as a natural function of corporate business in the United States. The symbolic dissonance that organized its everyday existence bled into daily life as a tone of optimism about economic progress and profits. Common people who invested in stock often had no idea of the underlying business practices and conditions of production their purchases supported.[52] Even though racial differentiation was removed through abstraction from scenes of exchange, capital continued to racialize risk. Rourke's vision of national culture did the same for popular democracy.

Rourke's outline of how humor operated during the nineteenth century through a patterned disavowal of the material conditions of economic appropriation and settler colonialism suggests the limits of her own contextualization of sentimental plantation fantasies that she understood as informing the tradition of minstrelsy by White players. In her estimation, White performers gleaned a veritable treasury of emancipatory aspirations from their observations of enslaved people, who were the inspiration for a cultural type that "became, in short, a dominant figure in spite of . . . conditions."[53] This notion of dominance indicates Rourke's own impressionability regarding a disavowed inversion of speculative circuits of exchange. She described the South as a region where "the negro was to be seen everywhere . . . on small farms and great plantations, on roads, and levees."[54] But this visual landscape of relative stasis failed to register how all of the types she read as distinctively U.S. American mapped economic exploitation, indigenous dispossession, and the forced movement of enslaved people.[55]

The differences that distinguish Rourke's comic types appear to be matters of style and manner, causing her to move too quickly past how each was informed by opposing and interconnected economic systems that depended on difference and separation. Rourke's reading of the Yankee as uniting various "racial strains" from Northern Europe that had become "well mixed" to shape a new nation was for her an historical lens for envisioning the United States as a nation among nations that was grounded on principles of ethnic inclusion.[56] The hyperbolic adventures of backwoods figures who faced an uncertain world full of "strange horizons, a totally unknown continent" with bold excitement suggested a precedent for the Cultural Front movement.[57] Similarly, the "sentimentalized" minstrelsy in which Rourke identified White people's "wish to prove that [the Negro] possessed moral worth, dignity, and capacity" indicates an aspiration to make racial inclusivity a cornerstone of twentieth-century American democracy.[58] In bringing together all three tropes, Rourke imagined a unified vision of national freedom as a quest for anticipatory emancipation. For example, she celebrated flatboats as sites where regional differences mixed "in a new national mythology, forming a striking composite, with a blank mask in common."[59]

Surely, nineteenth-century flatboats were places where people from various regions and class backgrounds came into contact. They most certainly were stages where various myths were rehearsed and performed. However, Rourke's cultural vision of unity is belied by the weight of antagonistic interregional economic forces. That is, Rourke assigned too little significance to the function of these vessels as mediums of economic exchange. The blank mask of entertainment that she attached to the nascent nation also concealed the economic circumstances that necessitated flatboats in the first place. These transitory social spaces moved minerals, animal skins, and alcohol from lands expropriated from Indians in the West, transported enslaved people and the products of their labor across the South, and carried raw materials and monetary returns to an industrial North that was conditioned by worker exploitation and capital circulation.[60] To approach an early twentieth-century society in the midst of change with adventure and promise was certainly a powerful alternative to the violently exclusionary nativism and anti-Black violence of the late nineteenth century.[61] However, as legacies for a new democracy these cultural symbols ran the risk of only "tolerating" difference so long as existing structural privileges and hierarchies remained undisturbed.

Speculative Nationalism's Masked Transcendence

The 1930s view of racial identity that Rourke drew on now seems passé, but the differential constructions of value, temporality, and personhood underlying her analysis offer insight into the dependence of speculative futures on the perpetual manipulation of symbolic and material values. Systems of cultural and economic exchange help to sustain the racially demarcated material conditions that enable capital to absorb crises by prolonging exploitation. Like some proponents of multiculturalism, diversity, or postethnicity in the late twentieth century, Rourke sought to bring about democratic closure prematurely by speaking *for* rather than *from* aggrieved groups. In her case, the problem of racial and class unevenness was an issue less of how she defined race than of how her understanding of national culture produced a racially contingent construction of liberation that enabled the reproduction of capitalist exploitation.

By the early 1940s, the rush to rediscover the nation's past that informed the wide circulation of art, literature, and music in the Cultural Front prompted Rourke to develop a broader theory about the significance of democratizing art. Her posthumous text *The Roots of American Culture* was bracketed by essays that grappled with the slippery meaning of culture as a concept: the first, to diagnose the nation's past; the last, to prescribe a future for U.S. art.[62] The essays built from a hybrid sense of culture as an intricate relationship between the manners and customs of a people and the aesthetic expressions of a civilized society. Rourke was a student of Ruth Benedict, a mentor who drew her attention to Franz Boas's "scientific" approach to culture in anthropology. Through a combination of approaches, Rourke regarded culture as the "whole configuration" of interrelated thought, action, and expression of a particular group, town, or region. In this view, the life of the community was recognizable in main tendencies that spanned a society's "special tenacities, currents of thought, contagions of feeling, [and] its dominant arts."[63]

Rourke was skeptical of configurations of fine art as defined by the standards of beauty, taste, and luxury among elites. Her alternative sense drew on Vico's notion of stages of civilization to map an artistic legacy that moved from primitive folk wisdom through the ostensibly more complex stages of thought in science and philosophy. These higher stages, she assumed, would be the basis for sophisticated artistic expression, for turning popular refrains into national ideals. Rourke also drew on Herder's literary understanding of folk cultures as fundamental expressions of the distinct histories of nations. Her aspirations for a democratically grounded artistic national culture did not escape the differentiation of owning culture (in the form of fine art) and being culture (in the anthropological sense) that she hoped to transgress when combining these theories. The emphasis on "assuming" the attitudes of common people in her remarks about culture resonate with an elevated stress on taking "possession" of the past that frequently showed up in her New Deal–era writing.[64]

Where the optimism of Rourke's early work gave way to urgent mandates to recover the past, the long legacy of deploying culture as a means of selectively differentiating populations crept into her analysis. She encouraged artists to take ownership of national culture by taking possession of the instincts of common people who, as objects of study, become objects of culture. The disciplinary division that is maintained in the discourses of possession and tradition approximated a form of dispossession when she explained that folk traditions "belonged to the mass of the people and . . . to the insurgent, the revolutionary class."[65] When Rourke called for the "discovery of the American past" to be "appropriated" as a "natural possession" that "belongs to us" as the basis of her theory of cultural development, she made folk art the inheritance of emerging fine artists whose work was considered fine precisely when critics and others determined it had developed beyond primitive expression.[66]

The racial undertones of this contradiction are striking in *The Roots of American Culture*, in which Rourke framed minstrelsy as a basis for developing a "negro literature."[67] She acknowledged the nineteenth-century critique of early minstrelsy as White parody, yet she continued to assume that the relationship between minstrel performers who "knew the Negro at first hand" and the Black people they observed and mimicked were signs of "primitive" aspects of Black culture.[68] She aspired to incorporate African Americans into an imagined future democracy based on cultural commonality, but she inadvertently legitimated a cultural hierarchy that gave artistic license to more "developed" segments of society to possess and take ownership of those whose lives were dismissed as primitive expressions *of* a cultural past. The imagined reconciliation that this possessive incorporation of cultural difference would produce depended on the perpetuation of the very inequalities it purported to resolve.

In a society that remained stratified by wealth and race, aesthetic and symbolic reconciliation was attractive precisely because it was premised on inequalities that made social transcendence seem appealing.[69]

The future national culture that Rourke pursued emerged out of intimate negotiations structured by competing affects of hope and aspiration, promises and deferrals. Yet her idealization of cultural transcendence concealed these tensions in a symbolic imaginary. In an instructive example, Rourke often described comic masquerade through reference to masks as physical objects. In a description of the Yankee type, for example, she concluded that the "mask was a portable heirloom handed down by the pioneer. In a primitive world crowded with pitfalls, the unchanging, unaverted countenance had been a safeguard."[70] A mask as a private inheritance and transferable commodity points to the inherent inequalities of liberal democracy. As a symbolic representation of abstract citizenship, the mask of sameness is a performative device that relegates difference and inequality to private life. The various stages that appeared in Rourke's work—physical spaces and temporal constructions—served metonymically as public universality. They provided platforms for putting abstract ideas of universal equality into cultural circulation. In the offstage realm of private life, "stages" protect hierarchies and injustice. That is, the expectation that historically aggrieved people must pass through "stages" of cultural development and assimilation to be recognized as full persons preserves White privileges of time and space under the "neutral values" of individual liberty.[71]

If the mask of Rourke's Yankee is taken as a symbol of the political state, it represents a universality in which an undifferentiated citizenry is promised equal access to liberty. Anything is available to anyone inasmuch as "the law is the same for all."[72] To wear the mask guarantees the individual alienated inside the Yankee an equal right to "own" it as a transferable commodity. In this case, donning the face of the social ideal of universality provided the Yankee the liberal freedom of property that allowed him to exchange "the mask" as fungible property. The universal mask of the backwoods trope bore a face of national interest that allowed individual buyers to cash in on land for private settlement and exchange. A White minstrel's appropriation of a Black mask suggested to Rourke a promising expanding configuration of universal national incorporation. Yet she did not see how this symbolic reconciliation was structured by speculative logics that undercut her desires for equality. In the economy, when bubbles inflate investors increase their reliance on the unwitting cooperation of exploited people. Vulnerable populations fulfill speculative dreams on three counts: as buyers of overpriced commodities, as labor whose future exploitation will mediate crises, and as lives that are made expendable through abstract transactions. This dependence also creates narrow and elusive opportunities for aggrieved people to force alternative visions of emancipation into material and cultural relations.

The form of national culture informing Rourke's scholarship similarly depended on the cooperation of aggrieved groups to sustain its vision of multicultural inclusion. Her vision for national unity was itself the product of a speculative formulation because it appropriated the struggles and will of aggrieved people who attempted to forge freedom beyond the constraints of objectification, and then reconfigured these movements as national fantasies balanced on unity and sameness as promises of a distant-future abstract equality. Contingent inclusion enables those who are invested in the privileged hierarchies of liberal nationalism to defer the desires for empowerment, autonomy, dignity, and community of those disproportionately positioned to absorb economic risk to some perpetually promised but never quite realized time of "not yet" freedom in the future. This type of cultural exchange is instrumental in material reproduction because it manipulates freedoms that have been earned and enacted as future rewards yet to be won through disciplined cultural uplift.

Ralph Ellison's reading of Rourke's study of masquerade reveals the ambivalence of her emancipatory vision.[73] On one hand, he argues, the legacy of slavery cut so deeply through the "moral heart of the American social drama" that White men donned blackface to symbolically escape "moral identification with their own acts."[74] Nathan Irvin Huggins argues that what made minstrelsy funny to nineteenth-century White audiences was that Black people were objectified as "naturally foolish in roles that White men imagined themselves playing in real life."[75] This comedic display of Blackness encouraged assimilation by ethnic White people only by teaching them to mock and exclude groups that were rendered non-normative.[76] On another hand, Ellison considered masquerade a technique for imagining "otherwise" in an unequal world. In this guise it can register hidden desires for social and national transformation. The joke of national identity, however, is that when those who stage projections of emancipatory desire confront the dangers and possibilities of becoming that which they perform, they also put the farce of power on display. In the case of minstrelsy, the racial authority that White men performed also revealed itself as inherently deluded because knowledge of the falseness of representation left them anxiously on guard against Black men who, they suspected, were "seeking to take [them] in" with their own manipulations of comic negotiations.[77] Cedric Robinson's reading of early minstrelsy gives credence to the intimate contest over representation and resources that such fears exposed. He argues that the context of slavery out of which the minstrel tradition emerged could make rebellion seem impossible because many assumed that Black people were permanently confined to a form of social nonexistence that separated them from the possibility of resistance.

The "joke" in Rourke's gradually inclusive national universality does not "slip the yoke," but instead depends on the distance of a prior temporality to contain the ways that African Americans pushed against and subverted the racial fantasies propping up White supremacy. Her faith in White minstrelsy as a primitive resource for Black artistic development sidestepped transformation as a criterion for social justice. It also caused her to miss an alternative genealogy of Black performance that grew from people's negotiation and critique of the racializing fantasies of White supremacy. In the antebellum era, White appropriation of minstrel resistances worked as humor because equal opportunities remained distant for Black people both on and off the stage. When Black performers did take the stage, they did so under constraints that called on them to perform familiar reflections of prevailing racial assumptions. In this period, audience anticipation stemmed largely from minstrel shows themselves. To meet expectations, Black performers layered imitations: they performed Blackness as a representation of Whiteness caricaturing Blackness.

Interregional Refusals

Historically what most united the regional cultural forms that Rourke and others celebrated were not similarities in how people in different regions imagined and strove for nationalist freedom. Rather, each form connected to a regional economy that was differentially enmeshed in a speculative system that balanced on mutually reinforcing patterns of racializing violence. Indian removal and western land grabs created new territories for the expansion of domestic slavery during the 1830s. Dispossession provided the precondition for a speculative land boom during the mid-1830s that also fueled a steady market for speculation in counterfeit bank notes that floated value on confidence and interregional exchange.[78] When the public imaginary could no longer sustain an assumed equivalence between confidence and the material backing of monetary notes, this bubble erupted in the Panic of 1837.

Panic did not result in national caution and a return to economic rationality in this period. Rather, land that had been "released" into the market through indigenous expulsion freed up territory to expand slavery. This created the conditions for a later bubble in the domestic slave trade. Walter Johnson argues that a region and a nation were built out of the multivalent negotiations that defined the speculative relations of U.S. slavery.[79] His research unmasks how slaveholders purchased a stake in the "commercial and social aspirations of the expanding southwest" through the forced migration of thousands of people.[80] When indigenous people were forced west, room was made to force Black people south. Many White people in northern industry and finance profited from these intersecting networks of speculative circulation. People who moved and were moved throughout the South traveled on capital circulation from the North through loans or factorage houses, insurance companies, and shipping. In the speculative bubble of the 1850s, an estimated 13.5 percent of the price of a person returned to the North in the form of interest, commissions, and fees.[81] Any private slave sale within this multiregional political economy of slavery took place through intimate relationships between sellers hoping to sell high, buyers hoping to buy low, and enslaved human properties who had very tenuous means of negotiating their futures at the point of sale. Yet these sales were also conditioned and enabled by regional, national, and global financial markets.

Although Rourke celebrated the Yankee as the "symbolic American" who eventually "turned into Uncle Sam," it cannot be forgotten that in nineteenth-century daily life the Yankee was better understood as a deceptive salesman whose fortune depended on tricks and trade, not as an emancipatory social subject.[82] In addition to participation in indigenous removal, the backwoodsman was just as likely a reflection of a trapper or other "agent of commerce" on the frontier as he was symbolic of a brave national persuasion toward democratic expansion.[83] Rourke's evasion of the speculative underpinnings of what she saw as the origins of the minstrel tradition are especially indicative of the compromises she made when locating freedom in national culture. She made a place for the South as a site of regional difference on par with the North and the West by interpreting the White minstrel's "happy-go-lucky" performances as manifestations of cultural appreciation that seemed "as if the Negro were assured of his own nationalistic position":[84] "The Negro minstrel was deeply grounded in reality, even though the impersonators were white, even though the figure was a myth."[85]

When Rourke located a place for Black people in the nation in a return to White minstrelsy from the 1830s through the 1850s, she rehearsed a call to objectification that was carried through national culture from the constricted performances and codes of contact in the slave jails, through White minstrelsy's mockery of freedom, into the South's Reconstruction-era backlash against emancipation that landed in the tyranny of lynching that was of major concern to Cultural Front activism. To envision a future in which a racially inclusive democracy would be possible, she repeatedly returned to the Jacksonian era, when such inclusion was unimaginable. Her project privileged a period prior to abolition with the aim of healing the broken promises of the Lincoln Republic, drawing on cultural affect to repair the "new birth" constitution that Lincoln promised at Gettysburg. Rourke was certainly not the only critic of this period to draw on a romantic idea of Black culture in her hope that she might make a place for honoring Black people's rights and dignity. Her reading of the minstrel tradition lay claim to Black struggles for freedom, suggesting an alliance with contemporaries like W.E.B. DuBois, who called attention to the "yearning and suffering" for emancipation heard in the "rhythmic cry" of enslaved people's songs.[86] To a greater degree than Rourke, DuBois understood the White minstrelsy of the early nineteenth century as an antipodal response to songs that "*forced* [italics mine] themselves upon popular attention."[87] In the sorrow sounds of Black folk, DuBois heard a spiritual heritage that arose "in the land of [Black] bondage" to become what was "the only American folk music."[88]

Rourke's allegiance to nationalist constructions of liberal progress, on the other hand, hindered her ability to see the White minstrel's use of racial caricature as a form of fraud, ridicule, and emancipatory repression.[89] Rourke certainly attempted to account for the material and human violence of enslavement. However, it is a telling indication of the racial limits of Cultural Front nationalism that the only resolution it saw for racial injury was to filter Black suffering through White appropriation.[90]

When Rourke accepted the "self-parody" of players like Emmett as rooted in a Black heritage, "which surely went back to a common dance of the Negro," she dropped a beat that resonated in DuBois as what Fred Moten calls the "objection to subjection"—that is, "the freedom drive that animates Black performance."[91] When DuBois argued that the emancipation of slaves produced the material conditions for the emancipation of all men, he was referring to the resilient resistance against southern campaigns to unite northern and southern economic interests around the returns on exploitation that were derived from pitting White and Black workers against one another.[92] The exhibition of force and hatred that southern elites required to repress Black people's hold on freedom during Reconstruction was evidence for DuBois of the nation's increased reliance on enfranchised and unionized poor White men to resist the transformative actions of people determined to live freedom outside of objectification. For DuBois, when White minstrels "made fun" of this drive they did not honor "the struggle for emancipation that gained in power through the '40s and 50s."[93] Rather, they actively elided the accounts of physical violence, forced separations, and roadside lynchings that the verses of Black music continued to record well into the early twentieth century.[94]

Saidiya Hartman's analysis of the seductive instrumentality of performance calls attention to the ways in which the slave system put the competing interests of property holders and commodified humans on display. This form of "entertainment," depending on where one stood in relation to the stage, at once suggested management and rebellion, social control and restricted identification, accumulation and community making, pleasure and subjection.[95] These were negotiations that also played out on a daily basis in the vast networks of intimate exchange that constituted the market in enslaved people. The imbalanced contracts made in the southern slave jails took on new significance in the 1850s, when slave prices diverged from international cotton prices. The decade that Rourke credited with a peak in the "popularity" of the minstrel tradition—which she optimistically registered as a sign of the future incorporation of Black people into national culture—was one in which Black people were circulated as objectified bodies in an economy that was premised on optimistic projections of returns on sales of their lives elsewhere and later.[96]

The antebellum seeds of democracy that Rourke attempted to recuperate from the minstrel tradition caused her to avoid expressions of Black self-activity that mapped a new freedom from the ruins of the nation after slavery. They also made Black national inclusion more about White desires than about African American freedom dreams. Her treatment of minstrelsy was symptomatic of a U.S. ideal of ascendancy in which people who had been violated by nationalist impositions were assumed to be aggrieved out of desire for national inclusion. When rights and resources are distributed through the nation-state, people strategically seek recognition and resources through forms that make survival more bearable. This does not necessarily mean that those who demand justice and accountability from their oppressors believe in the mythological freedoms of American dreams. The question that arises from Rourke's suggestion that minstrelsy was a route to Black incorporation is less about Black people's embrace of the popular-nationalism she imagined coming into being than it is about why White nationalism *needs* the people whose freedom it defers to identify with the nation at all.

In the case of speculative nationalism, promises of national inclusion are useful tools of social management. This is especially the case when promises of "not yet" freedom require aggrieved people to set aside their memories of struggle and counter-imaginary in exchange for a compromised unity. The act of becoming American, Rourke's analysis suggests, is an assimilationist mandate to act toward a future in which differences and disagreements are ultimately shed. The Whiteness of the Lincoln Republic's multiracial American ideal was masked by the Cultural Front's celebration of regional difference. However, the perpetuation of White supremacy in an era of multiethnic expansion was expressed in the way that culture preserved market inequalities as an expression of antebellum culture. Rourke's sense of cultural development overlooked the fact that Black people during Reconstruction fundamentally transformed the meaning of democracy by actively re-creating law, politics, and society in the South. The populist attachment to a selective antebellum democracy helps to explain how the mask of racially inclusive popular nationalism—the incorporating gesture to extend personhood to former slaves—could set a stage for the theft of democracy by corporate capitalism in the postbellum era.

Rourke's cultural pursuit of promises of future resolution kept her from opening up sites of tension and noncompliance. In this regard, her construction of past and future refused to recognize the nation's debt to Black people whose self-activity refused bonds of historical debt and legal indenture in movements for radical social transformation. Instead, it regarded Black freedom as an invitation into White liberty, a slow progression though which descendants of slaves must prove their worth as full citizens by shedding attachments to the past as a means of aligning themselves with the nation's purported progressive cultural destiny. Rourke's invocation of a mythic past inadvertently produced a masked reversal. It claimed the victories of Black struggle and resistance for investors in White national unity. Speculative nationalist incorporation is an ascriptive technique that rules through failed and deferred universality. Speaking in universals, national culture claims and invites an authority over those it includes, but people who seek meaningful justice and freedom are not often looking for empty promises and future possibilities. In and against the odds, they find subtle ways to improvise transformation to create conditions for lived freedom now.

Improvisation in the Offbeat

Even when the minstrel form was deployed to satiate public fantasies about Black inferiority, the accessibility of the form to Black performers throughout the late nineteenth and early twentieth centuries created occasions for them to subversively occupy and transform culture on different terms. Cedric Robinson shows that by the late nineteenth century Black actors covertly stretched the genre by deepening understandings of the hurts and hardships of slavery, rearticulating the terms of Black sexuality and beauty, and challenging the natural superiority of Whiteness. In addition, although still seeming to fulfill White representational desires, they used the genre to celebrate symbols and histories of Black liberation.[97] When Rourke looked past the delicate battle for freedom that encoded messages carried, she unintentionally devalued self-activity and alternative freedom as signs of democratic enactment. Her desires for a democratic society were substantially weakened by her failure to acknowledge the consistent efforts of Black artists in the early twentieth century to carry on a legacy of Black expression in the literary revival of Harlem, the tentative establishment of Black theater, and the establishment of Black cinema in the 1920s and 1930s. What scholars, artists, and activists like Rourke often missed when they constructed a coherent sense of postbellum U.S. American identity were memories of long histories of radical improvisation that rolled from the blues across minstrel stages and carried over into the break of the Jazz Age.

The great trickster philosopher Jelly Roll Morton hints at this legacy in the stories and piano accompaniments he recorded for the Library of Congress during the late 1930s. As he ruminates on the history of jazz through words and sounds, Morton calls attention to the ways that White desires for Black art opened up opportunities for collective transcultural improvisation. In particular he points to New Orleans in the early twentieth century as a city where the circulation of millionaires produced ancillary interest in cultural workers. For Morton, although the opera house influence set a melody from which to begin, the rise of jazz was a coming together of "every type of music" by artists who saw in White wealth opportunities for material survival: "They had every class. We had Spanish. We had colored. We had whites. We had Frenchmans. We had Americans. . . . We had 'em from every part of the world. New Orleans was a stomping ground for the greatest pianists in the country."[98] The story of jazz, he says, is impromptu "com[ing] down in order to go up" through which the dissonance of "blatant noises and discordant tones, something that would be even harmful to the ears" is transformed into "sweet, soft, plenty rhythm."[99]

The art of living against the odds, according to Morton, takes place through subtle adaptations, intermingled experiences of creatively making do with—and collectively making more from—whatever is available. Morton brought this sensibility to the minstrel stage in the scores he developed for blackface performers. In discussing Morton's "Frog-i-More," William Russell outlines the artist's emphasis on invention. The tune, an improvisation for a minstrel show, shows "unlimited imagination and mastery of motivational variation."[100] Russell's detailed analysis implies a sonic replication of masquerade, describing the way that Morton held a regular beat in the left hand, suggesting a steady veneer of musical compliance that is challenged and transformed in the under hand by the rhythmic variety of "shifted accents, slight delays, and anticipation."[101] Such improvisational disruption harkens to the polyglot alternatives and resourceful manipulations of freedom imaginaries carried in the offbeat. In this sense, improvisation is neither casual nor impulsive but a supple system of deeply historical knowledge strategically exercised in negotiation of constantly changing forms of constraint.

Jelly Roll Morton's sense of jazz is one such counter-archive of social struggle, an illustrative example of the form of structural critique and social movement that Clyde Woods calls the blues epistemology. The blues tradition, Woods brilliantly demonstrates, is a body of theory generated by people whose survival has been systematically compromised by the political economy of plantation slavery. The music is a shared archive of oppressed people's explanations and understandings of the causes and consequences of the history of slavery and its multiple extensions. As racialized people's critique of and desire for social development and change, the blues are organized around world-remaking longings to develop self-determining free communities.[102] The blues response to crisis and transformation is notably different from the reactionary investment in recovery and reaffirmation that Rourke looked for in the U.S. cultural tradition. For example, Morton's rendition of the Creole song "La Misère" critiques the nation's avoidant attitude toward the roots and consequences of the Depression: "They speak of the depression, but they don't know what it is."[103] Suggesting that prolonged conditions of racialized inequality are the baseline that runs through repeated episodes of temporary crisis, the tune disseminates survival wisdom for getting by: "If there's no sugar, my friend, serve salt instead."[104]

Morton credits Mamie Desdoumes for his education in blues knowledge. Beneath a steady rhythm of an opera house melody, he attributes her adaptation to disfigurement: missing two fingers, she played with three. As Morton speaks, he shifts tempo and key. Engaging in ventriloquism, he recounts in Desdoumes's voice a long and creative struggle to make beauty out of hardship.[105] As a foundational myth of the blues epistemology, the life-affirming upbeat of "Mamie's Blues" functions analogously with the severed promise of the Louisiana Convention of 1868. Alan Lomax documented the climatic shift from New Orleans' polyphonic ethnic hybridity to a stark Jim Crow racial division: "In the first years of reconstruction New Orleans led the fight for the ballot, free schools, equal rights for women and other democratic reforms in the South."[106] Jazz, Morton's story implies, was a logical adaptation of freedom struggles when White violence began to overthrow legal gains. As an archive of history, jazz contains the status and struggles of people who had fought for and created a plural democracy. As a theory of power, it suggests people's incredible capacity to adapt and live on even when the ligaments they depend on are violated and severed. As a form of collectivity, jazz resonates as a life-creating activity and form of power through which freedom is lived and felt in the present tense. Improvisation is a claim on justice that comes from "communities whose members have been compelled to look beyond surface appearances, to imagine how what 'can be' lies hidden inside 'what is'" and then teaches people to live in that possibility.[107] Freedom lies in the sound and spirit of Mamie's adaptation to bodily disfigurement and Morton's reclamation of her willed transgression of the limitations her missing fingers placed on her capacity for musical expression.

Speculative nationalism claims such emancipatory struggles as its own, turning freedoms imagined in and against liberal abstractions of anticipatory futures into the property of the nation. Jelly Roll Morton's controversial comments about copyright reflect his concerns about White appropriation. When he speaks of jazz, Morton readily acknowledges that the source is never contained in the individual. Rhythms and beats are always aspects of diverse influences and improvisations. The art of invention in every break is also a bridge connecting past, present, and future. According to Alan Lomax, Morton considered his songs "reflections of what a whole musical community had to say." Lomax ungenerously described Morton as a megalomaniac for wishing he had copyrighted jazz. It seems more likely, given Morton's accounts in the 1930s, that his desire to stake ownership of the tradition may have been more than an egotistical pursuit of recognition. Morton certainly received ample acknowledgement for his influence, skill, and brilliance as a composer. His frustration over not being able to sue White bandleaders who profited from appropriating jazz was very likely a broader critique of White people's ability to draw on Black culture to prop up their own power and privilege. The possessive language of ownership, in this regard, was an available resource Morton pointed to as a way to delegitimize White people's appropriation of Black freedom and culture as their own. By calling attention to the limitations of U.S. law, Morton tactically manipulated the notion of ownership. Cultural appropriation is less about turning art into a possession, he covertly indicates, than it is a form of group-differentiated dispossession, a theft of the opportunities that aggrieved people produce through collective and creative struggle.

When jazz was invented, Morton's history reminds us, both the cultural and legal stages of the nation were engaged in theft of Black personhood. Calling forth soul in the offbeat responds to dispossession with a cultural claim on life and meaning—an assertion of personhood and freedom—against the odds of legal-cultural appropriation.

Corporate Minstrelsy

The Fourteenth Amendment was the outcome of a long and bitter battle against a legal, economic, political, cultural, and social system that condoned the enslavement of human beings. As much as it represents a legal imperative to regard all humans as equal persons with equal rights under the law, it is historical evidence of Black people's self-actualized opportunities to live free of a system of violent objectification. In turning the amendment over to corporations, the nation's highest court sold people's chances for actualizing freedom to the force of capital. Early nationalists did not envision corporations as persons or citizens: they saw corporations as chartered to serve the public interest, and as such corporations were instrumental in building the nation's transportation, commerce, and educational infrastructures. The perpetual life granted to these artificial entities by the Fourteenth Amendment was at first limited to contracts and litigation. However, corporate misuse of the amendment to protect the individual rights of corporate bodies in the late nineteenth century gave rise to the masquerade that corporations are people. Because this fiction continued with the support of the courts, market share increasingly trumped human will because the overvaluation of shareholder interest created illegitimate cause for fixing the future for perpetuity. Jim Crow segregation and Lochner-era disregard for labor protections, a minimum wage, and economic regulation created conditions for absorbing the costs of corporate expansion, which rendered dispensable the lives and rights of people of color, immigrants, and the poor.

Constance Rourke's analysis of national-popular culture called attention to the performative tactics that were necessary for lending this ruse legitimacy. In documenting inequality as a condition of a prenationalist past, she called into being a nationalist future freed of the violence of capitalist imposition. Her studies of treaties are a telling indicator of the way that culture legitimates the norms of the colonizing state. In these studies, she returned to the site of transaction, narrating the conditions under which indigenous people signed treaties with the United States: "In spite of the fact that tribes were considered nations treating in equality with the United States, in spite of earnest diplomatic assurances, pressure upon the tribes continued. Their lands were continually being seized on flimsy pretexts by speculators."[108] In response to the perceived economic manipulations of speculators, she justified the role of the U.S. state as arbiter of justice and fair negotiations. Her redemptive depiction of the state was reinforced when she relocated treaties outside of the law as symbolic elements of national culture. The staging of treaty negotiations became, in her archeology of national becoming, the root of U.S. theater and poetry.

In Rourke's portrayal of the origins of U.S. poetry, for example, Thomas Jefferson was a figurative rhetorician, an assumed knowledgeable orator of "the Indian manners of address" rather than a state official whose campaign to promote indigenous debt was designed to break up tribal alliances.[109] Rourke recognized the charade of benevolent colonial occupation as dependent on narrative fabrication. Yet by reading legal transactions as nationalist gestures, she exculpated nationalism as a central component of crimes of conquest. In Rourke's rendition, the art of exoneration took place through symbolic compensation; U.S. theater emerged when White actors took the stage to rehearse verses recorded in treaties. In the tradition of treaty recitation, Rourke heard "troubled" efforts to "obliterate a wrong by handsome tributes."[110] Despite the attempt to dissociate the nation from its speculative grounding, Rourke imagined in culture what she had learned from the market. As with the underlying belief that speculative economies could expand economic benefits to all shareholders, there remained in her appeal to nationalism an optimistic supposition that speculative national culture might universally result in democratic equality. Culture became, in this regard, a necessary legal formation for reestablishing the authority of the colonizing state.

In reinforcing the legal norms of the colonial contract, national-popular culture participated in a broader context of New Deal transformation whereby the project to "Americanize" indigenous people symbolically reconfirmed U.S. nationalism's universalist conceits. In practice, the Indian New Deal forced indigenous children into boarding schools as part of a campaign to redistribute tribal land into private ownership. Joel Pfister has shown that campaigns to educate Native American children in the knowledge and comportment of liberal individualism were intended to break up tribal autonomy. To achieve dispossession as if it were desired by the dispossessed, a major component of boarding school curriculum encouraged indigenous children to voluntarily identify freedom and autonomy with the U.S. nation-state. This educational policy signified the efforts of the settler state to exercise its sovereignty through culturally orchestrated subvoluntary enclosure. Ascriptive Americanization was a means to disclaim the state's absorption of indigenous geography into its own landscape of freedom by rendering existing indigenous formations obsolete. As it intersected with the legal stage, Rourke's progressive construction of national culture as a movement from primitivism to civilization took form as a colonizing denial of Native personhood.

Like Rourke's reading of the law, indigenous education balanced on a poetic externalizing of harm through a surreptitious internalization of indigenous compliance with ongoing conquest. In both cases, the art of nationalist incorporation reiterated dispossession as nationalist policy as if it were an emancipatory request. For example, well into the twentieth century "Enfranchisement Day" was when Indian boarding schools celebrated the Dawes Severalty Act of 1887, which divided communal land into individual allotments and released "surplus" property onto the open market. Indigenous students whose daily training was designed to prepare them as service and wage workers were taught to revere tribal breakdown and their futures as exploitable labor as a promise of upward mobility.[111]

Under circumstances different from those that gave rise to the plantation blues, but with similar effect, colonial state cultural and educational power supplanted indigenous people's already existing rights to full personhood. A legal treaty was a form of tribal recognition through which Indians' self-determination was collectively recognized through rights to tribal self-governance. New Deal cultural incorporation circumscribed sovereign tribes' autonomous identities with a racializing rearticulation. No longer treated as members of independent tribal nations, all indigenous children were racially marked via educational practice as part of a singular Indian population. Mark Rifkin argues that this form of racial production enabled the nation-state to rule Native territory as if its colonization had been obvious and consensual.[112] Like the counter-epistemological interjections of jazz performers, indigenous people in the 1930s adapted old forms and changing circumstances into pan-Indian resistance rhythms. Transformative dance was one way to make money while pushing against White expectations in order to claim tribal life and autonomy in and against the odds. For example, the invention of fancy dancing, a modern dance form from the 1930s that made its way from Wild West spectacles and Omaha dance to Powwow competitive circuits, responds to the conscripting circumstances of settler colonialism with pan-indigenous dance epistemology.

Sherman Alexie captures the ongoing power of the fancy dance as a counter-colonial negotiation in the film *The Business of Fancydancing*. In the tension between two central characters—one who leaves the reservation for a White education and the other who remains and struggles with questions of tribal authenticity—the film registers the origins of fancy dancing in the contradictory expectations of 1930s White audiences. Forced educational policy was grounded in an imperative to assimilate into White cultural and political-economic norms.[113] Simultaneously, Wild West shows built their success by selling the idea of indigenous authenticity through employment of native actors who were paid to play themselves as static figures tied to nature through traditions.[114] Both ends of this schism fixed the meaning of indigenous life as existing out of time: either stuck in a past destined to disappear or predestined for civilization in a White nationalist future. Fancy dancing occupied the impasse, staking its claim on the present through the strategic synchronicity of fast-moving feet and drum beats. The form claimed space through a present-tense living tradition and sensory overabundance. Dancers often perform leaps and splits along with familiar steps, calling energetic attention to the fast pace necessary to negotiate change. They adorn themselves with bright ribbons and dress that takes up space. Drummers take over the aural senses, bringing total corporeal attention to the action of now.[115]

Alexie's film elegantly illustrates fancy dancing as a medium through which transgressive identities emerge in the friction between nationalist lies and people's claims on time and space.[116] Myths of tribal authenticity and educational erasure are shattered in the poetry, sweat, and psychic violence of the dance. The steps carry new forms of claiming life by inhabiting freedom through movement.

Nationalist promises of "not yet" freedom, on the other hand, limit the terrain of freedom to the horizon of the nation-state. The cultural imaginary and legal minstrelsy of the New Deal era rescripted present-tense claims on self-determination, recognition, and creatively enacted life as atavistic signs of a lingering past to be shed in the interest of national unity. It is understandable that the social and economic uncertainty of the 1930s and early 1940s would cause scholars and artists like Rourke to desire a recovery of the assuaging optimism of nationalist progress. However, the racializing effect of temporal deferral positioned people whose legal gains were usurped by cultural games to absorb the costs of corporate expansion. The lived status of denied personhood during the early twentieth century fed artificial corporate persons' hunger for increased rates of profitable return. The economic use value of the nationalist project that Rourke's research exemplified was a system of differentiation that increased corporate odds for shareholder returns. On one hand, legal repression and spatial displacement of Black and indigenous personhood created a potential pool of low-waged workers on whom capital could draw to increase production. The art of nationalist incorporation transformed structural inequality into industrial possibility. On another hand, constructing indigenous people as racialized citizens mitigated dissent against colonial occupation, normalizing corporate claims to raw materials and resources.[117] On multiple fronts, nationalist culture worked for corporate expansion as an instrument of economic adaptation. At the center of this transformation, the hopes and personhood of those whose freedom was deemed "not yet" available were subsumed under liberal nationalism's masked pretense of unity.

Sacred Spaces of Structural Adjustment

Erotic Fraternity, Institutional Dispensation,
America and Education

The money changers have fled from their high seats in the temple of our civilization. We may now restore that temple to the ancient truths. The measure of the restoration lies in the extent to which we apply social values more noble than monetary profit.

—FRANKLIN DELANO ROOSEVELT, 1933

If life were not hard, we would not have so much use for poets, the secret of whose power over us lies in the way they provide us consolation when, in a Lear or an Oedipus, they are most tragic. They bring us back to a love of life by a deepened acceptance of men's constant desperate ruin, and, in the face of that, of man's heroic capacity for no less constant renewal.

—F. O. MATTHIESSEN, 1947

There is only one thing for civilized human beings to do when facing such a problem, and that is to learn the facts, to reason out their connection and to plan the future; to know the truth; to arrange it logically and to contrive a better way. . . . We must in the end, produce for the satisfaction of human needs and distribute in accordance with human want. To contend that this cannot be done is to face the Impossible Must.

—W.E.B. DuBois, 1938

The Scene of Exchange

When President Franklin Delano Roosevelt famously counseled the nation to fear nothing but fear itself in his first inaugural address, he spoke with a decisive confidence that the early twentieth-century economic crisis had purged speculation from U.S. society. To vanquish the paralysis of panic, he assured an economically distressed populace that their material hardships were only temporary challenges because "the rulers of the exchange of mankind's goods [had] failed, through their own incompetence, [had] admitted their failure, and . . . the practices of the unscrupulous money changers [stood] indicted in the court of public opinion, rejected by the hearts and minds of men."[1] He insisted that the public assessment of economic greed would be permanent, declaring, "There must be an end to speculation with other people's money."[2]

The counter-exclusive categorization of regular people and speculators in Roosevelt's oration reproduced the long-standing U.S. cultural tradition of spatializing the United States as an island of virtue against a corrupt sea of capitalist tyranny. In Roosevelt's formulation, economic collapse had pushed the wave of capitalist encroachment away from the nation's shores and thus, he reassured his audience, the "unjustified terror" marking the "dark hour of our national life" was over. Recovery would come, he proclaimed, because "nature still offers her bounty."[3] Roosevelt's Depression-era reiteration of U.S. nationalism's foundational dualism collapsed spatial promise into a militant "American spirit of the pioneer."[4] He grounded the possibility of democratic renewal, not just in the landscape but in the characteristic virtues he advised U.S. citizens to internalize to secure the nation's "true destiny."[5] In antagonistic response to the crisis of the Great Depression, he defined U.S. virtue through a warrior ethos when he conscripted U.S. citizens as a "great army of our people dedicated to a disciplined attack upon our common problems."[6] He framed the nation's common enemy as a "generation of self-seekers" whom he held solely responsible for the economic collapse. Declaring war on economic greed, he rhetorically stripped speculators of U.S. identity, framing the "foolish optimism" of speculative economies as counter-exclusive to U.S. ideals.[7]

Roosevelt's presidential incantation of national myth in 1933 set the stage for an unprecedented use of state capacity for economic readjustment. Interestingly, the ideals he articulated as the basis for democratic renewal—"national unity," "moral values," and "performance of duty"—emerged in his speech less as materialist concerns than as spiritually and historically transcendent features of the American people. In fact, early in his delivery Roosevelt dismissed a litany of national difficulties—tax hikes, pay drops, monetary collapse, frozen exchange markets, foreclosures, mass unemployment—as secondary to the "happiness" that comes from the "thrill of creative effort."[8] He condemned the "falsity of material wealth as the standard of success," projecting "the joy and moral stimulation of work" as the uniting feature of "national life."[9]

Elements of ritual and religiosity in Roosevelt's disclamation of speculators were a central component of an economic recovery premised on racial readjustment. When he spoke of the nation as a temple of civilization, the president located the potential for democratic renewal in ancient moral principles, imaginatively restoring the nation's innocence in the face of speculative catastrophe by appealing to ideals that presumptively preceded the national experiment. His call for "restoration" of "noble" social values rested on a fraternal obligation to "act and act quickly" in the "warm courage of national unity."[10] In tone and effect, Roosevelt's ritualistic incantation of an American Credo was a world reordering with loose cultural ties to the rites and sacred oratory of fraternal associations. His performance from atop a weak temple of virtue idealized freedom as a potential that springs from hope without restitution, grows from association without dispensation, and matures through moral attachments without historical redemption. The "essential democracy" underlying Roosevelt's recitation of ideals resonated with a much broader fraternal filtering of racial readjustments that came to shape New Deal–era institutions.

In practice, Roosevelt transferred racializing speculative logics into New Deal public policy by promising to restore the nation's "not yet" democratic imaginary. The economic recovery that followed this speech was predicated on cultural promises of universal uplift that in form and function became racializing readjustments. On one hand, New Deal cultural endeavors like the Federal Music Project, the Federal Writing Project, and the Federal Theatre Project incorporated immigrants and African Americans into an idealization of American brotherhood as potentially equal citizens in a progressively expanding democracy. Relatively high employment of African Americans in the Works Progress Administration and the Civilian Conservation Corps suggests a concerted effort to incorporate racialized people's hopes and dreams for better futures into the national project.[11] Yet the small material gains of cultural uplift and temporary relief were overshadowed by a national concentration on moral and abstract legal change as the pathway to racial equality.

Roosevelt's emphasis on virtue and unity made deferral of rights and resources a condition of nationalist belonging. His speech emulated contemporaneous scholarly frameworks that regarded inequality as an outcome of psychological and social prejudices. Whereas Roosevelt individualized economic injustice by pitting the predatory depravity of speculators against the moral integrity of citizens, academics individualized racial inequalities by framing discrimination as the moral pathology of White cultural prejudice. Bolstered by anthropologist Franz Boas's invalidation of the biological thesis of Black inferiority, the sociological consensus following Gunnar Myrdal's analysis in *An American Dilemma* was that racial inequality stemmed from White racism and individual immorality.[12] The political incarnation of this limited New Deal policy placed job discrimination, housing discrimination, and credit redlining beyond the scope of material reform. Isolating discrimination as personal prejudice created conditions that turned the Federal Housing Authority and the Social Security Administration into central forces of racial readjustment and spatial segregation.

The Form of Transfer

Speculative economies are patterned on ritual repetitions. In the grand scale of history, bubbles repeat as booms and busts. Speculative markets are made day to day through ceremonial rituals of exchange. During a speculative purchase, a hope is reiterated as an act of exchange. In the abstract realm of circulation, optimism inheres through unspeakable violence—systematic repetitions of deferral, denial, and exploitation ritually rehearsed as economic sacraments to the gods of investors' expected returns. When bubbles collapse, lost dreams of futurity are rehearsed once more as rationales for recovery and renewal. Given the sacrosanct underpinnings of speculative confidence, it is little wonder that early twentieth-century economic speculation mapped culturally and historically at a conjuncture with the popularity of fraternal associations. Like speculative markets, fraternal societies are structured on interconnected cosmologies. Their rites are often rehearsed in the pageantry of intimate interactions through which interconnected aspirations and expectations are formalized into an idealized system of financial growth.

This chapter investigates economic readjustment in the Great Depression era through the fraternal imagination of two major U.S. thinkers, F. O. Matthiessen and W.E.B. DuBois. In addition to their work creating new institutional formations for academic inquiry, both men wrote prolifically of themselves as historical and national subjects. Through self-narration, each transformed himself into an object of analysis using the autobiographical form to reckon with being a democratic subject in an historical period marked by financial failure. Both men engaged in the retrospective art of disclosure as an intimate public act through which to make sense of the changing terrain of U.S. democracy, creating in the process an historically situated democratic consciousness that arose from the national expression of a particularly feeling self. DuBois explained this use of autobiography in the preface of *Dusk of Dawn*: "I have written then what is meant not to be so much my autobiography as the autobiography of a concept of race, elucidated, magnified and doubtless distorted in the thoughts and deeds which were mine."[13] The subject of history, his framing suggests, inverts the person into a concept that is brought into being by contradictory forces, tendencies, and material conditions.

Similarly, Matthiessen opened his final autobiographical text perplexed by people's anomalous attraction to the promise of U.S. society. He began, "I want to write about some of the things it means to be an American today. That is the chief thing I came to Europe to think about."[14] In the distance between self and other, Matthiessen found a "freedom of interchange" through which his encounter with Europeans and U.S. Americans abroad allowed reflection on promises of democracy that had become alien. The self that emerged from Matthiessen's European journals was a tortured subject of historical destruction who wrote himself back into America using a trope of renewal. This self-construction emulated a longer pattern in Matthiessen's life, a repetition of themes and fraternal ideals that he had drawn on to internalize being a U.S. subject as an intimate aspect of his personal and institutional identity.

The sacred democracy that Matthiessen sought to recover in his travels to Europe was certainly shaped by his attachment to fraternal figurations. Matthiessen was an active lifetime member of Yale's Skull and Bones secret society. DuBois claims he "knew nothing of and cared nothing for fraternities and clubs" while he was a student at Harvard. Yet he is rumored to have been inducted into the Prince Hall Widow's Son Lodge, which, like Skull and Bones, is located in New Haven.[15] As Susan Gilman has extensively argued, whether or not DuBois was an active Freemason, his materialist conception of global historiography was influenced by his affiliation with Masonic historians—namely, Arthur Schomburg, John Bruce, and George W. Crawford. Whether or not DuBois took part in fraternal ritual is inconsequential for assessing how the occult logics of fraternal association informed his construction of himself as a concept. By the same token, although Matthiessen and DuBois were not in direct dialogue with one another, the ritualistic linking of ancient pasts, present crises, and future ideals at the center of each author's self narration suggests their coexistence in a nationalist system of democratic disarrangement—their simultaneous imbrications in a historical situation of temporal disruption that created a challenge and an opportunity to publicly reimagine U.S. democracy as an imperative to act in response to "present startling reality."[16]

Autobiography breaches the boundaries of liberal individualism, disrupting the privacy, property, and sense of self that gives rise to the abstract equality fueling unequal economic relationships. Speculative liberalism assumes at the point of exchange that all parties are equal actors. However, the prolonged condition of "not yet" freedom is a form of dispossession through national belonging that structures all relations around differential arrangements of time and space. The universalisms of liberal democracy tend to transfer rewards upward to inheritors of White privilege and tend to racialize risk through downward flows of deferral and denial.

Both DuBois's and Matthiessen's autobiographies suggest an attempt to control the terms of inscription by writing a self against the impersonal experience of universalism. In the case of Matthiessen, writing the self as a public expression was a means of opening up the universalism of "American" belonging with the hope of restoring the lost promise of a plural democracy. DuBois disrupted the notion of race as a concept in his framing of self as an outcome of racialization. The self he produced in his autobiographical writing exposed particularity as a forced inscription into material conditions that were historically laced with violence, poverty, and material denial. Both authors wrote a life into collective being through strategic attachments to fraternal organizations. And both mobilized the selves they re-created toward claiming institutional spaces they imagined could give rise to new democratic formations.

What follows are two sides of a similar series of transactions through which the cultural rites of speculative nationalism were institutionalized and challenged in the curricula of U.S. universities. In the first instance, the field of American Studies took form through speculative longings and panic via the life of F. O. Matthiessen. The scholar's distraught purchase of "not yet" freedom helps to explain how populist democracy took institutional form as a segregating field of nationalist study. The protective approach to democratic futurity taken by American Studies created a need for separate development of Black Studies, which DuBois initiated in his scholarship and his activism for Black education. For the founders of these critical legacies, democracy—and the universalist promise to eliminate the cruel human calculus of differentiation through which inequalities are lived—was first and foremost at stake. Each saw in education a possibility for expanding the scope of democratic understanding. Both sought to create institutional spaces for the careful study of U.S. society, culture, and identity. Yet the approach to economic adjustment that underlay the democratic hopes of each project diverged in accordance with how each scholar was differentially ensnared in the tripartite structure of speculative democracy. Whereas Matthiessen despondently reinvested his hopes for plural democracy in the anticipatory liberal script of "not yet" freedom, DuBois refused the imperative of assimilation by reframing the historical reality of segregation as groundwork for an inclusive, economically egalitarian democratic commons. For DuBois, Jim Crow segregation exposed the philanthropic structure of "not yet" freedom as contingent on perpetuation, rather than transformation, of the racialist settler state. Whereas Matthiessen imagined the possibility of nationalist recovery and futurity through the specter of death, DuBois proposed building educational infrastructures with "organic connections to the community around" as a "dream . . . worth considering."[17]

Mourning into American Studies

Depression-era longings for romantic recovery of national purity tended toward idealizing a past that had never been. This revisionist impulse was mirrored in F. O. Matthiessen's intimate struggle with psychological depression. While developing the manuscript that would become perhaps the twentieth century's most influential critical contribution to the study of U.S. literature, Matthiessen unexpectedly found himself plagued by insomnia. Fearing that he might buckle under the pressure of becoming "bogged down before" a project with which he felt "less satisfaction and less control," he admitted himself into McLean Hospital for psychiatric evaluation. According to his self-reflections, during his eighteen-day stay he dedicated a considerable amount of time to puzzling over the "incomprehensible state" of being trapped in the "monotony of nervous thoughts about [his] work."[18] By the time that this episode occurred, in late December of 1938, Matthiessen had already produced three substantial and successful scholarly books.[19] He had been promoted to associate professor at Harvard with no indication that full professor would not soon follow. Both public audiences and his "acutest critics" had responded to sections of *American Renaissance* with strong approval.[20] Still, as he found most peculiar having never before experienced depression, loss of sleep, self-doubt, and uncontrollable fear, he became mired in a desperate miasma: "A film of unreality between myself and everything that had seemed most real," which caused him to become "recurrently filled with the desire to kill myself."[21]

Matthiessen's self-sacrificial longings for a secure sense of objective reality dismantled and then rearticulated the artifice of distinguishing personal queer desire, professional aspirations, and political social ideals. His confused and contradictory private framework for comprehending and working through his symptoms bounced between and often inverted public and private registers demarcating little difference between his scholarship and his personal relationships.[22] The author ultimately recomposed himself from his shocking state of melancholia through a series of cross-articulated affects and interwoven desires, an often incoherent identification of feared personal injury that concurrently reacted to the chronic condition of capitalist crisis.[23]

This is to suggest that Matthiessen's queer desire for reorganizing social relationships through intersecting intimate networks was an affective structure shaped in tandem with the emergent capitalist transformation that undergirded his anxiety about the future of the nation. Although he could not fully articulate the injury he saw as imminent, tracking the dynamics of political mourning that informed Matthiessen's fraternal desire to imagine and preserve a sacred retreat from the social crises of capitalism reveals a poignant case study of the intimate desires that shape economic readjustments.

The critical return to a queer political economy by scholars such as Kevin Floyd skillfully emphasizes how conditions of possibility for queer social formations emerge relationally in ongoing negotiations with capitalist transformation. The early twentieth-century accumulation crisis in Fordist capitalism registers in Matthiessen's autobiography as a panicked idealization of the objective relations of productive laborers. Floyd's discussion of the shifting social terrain of early twentieth-century sexual knowledge from the physiology of sexual bodies to a performative partitioning of masculinity is instructive.[24] In Matthiessen's case, capitalist transformation was registered in the author's reclassification of his sexual desires from an early identification as a "sexual invert" into a mature partner in an ideal relationship. In the transition from youthful shame to queer fraternal maturity, Matthiessen inscribed himself as a resolute and resistant interloper against capitalist disorder and imbalance.

Matthiessen resolved his psychological breakdown through logical inversion. In reversing the order of public and private, he staked a claim on a type of imaginative historical rematerialism, a reconceptualization of reality that emerged from his complex desires for his same-sex partner, labor solidarities, fraternal protection, and transhistorical national attachments to dead male writers. Canonization of the literary imagination that followed from Matthiessen's personal and political mourning suggests that queerness operated through him as more than a simple response to changing political economic exteriors. Rather, his affective rearticulation of capitalist relations constituted a desiring abstraction of productive labor relations that remains at the heart of American Studies. Political mourning led Matthiessen to invest his hopes for justice and democracy in a sacred idealization of "reality" that he imagined free of the conflicts of material life. Psychic removal from objective relations became for him a means of restoring national democracy. The inversion of "reality" and "materiality" in Matthiessen's thinking suggests that queerness may operate within capitalist transformation as a central modality of structural adjustment. That is, the act of political mourning generated, in Matthiessen's case, an affective structure of desire for inverting the relationship between the material conditions of production and the fictitious idealizations of fraternal transcendence. The dynamics of the sacred through which he fashioned this inversion and envisioned an escape from capitalist crisis is suggestively resonant of the relational rearticulation of the U.S. economy during the post-Fordist era—an increasing movement toward corporate and financial systems of fictitious capital superimposed on and abstracted from the productive labor force. That is, speculation.

The prose that Matthiessen employed to make sense of his condition stylistically parallels his interpretation of his depression as fully "irrational." It lacks coherent transitions, jarringly slipping between scholarly fear, social anxiety, and domestic preoccupation. The fluid entanglement of multiple concerns in the text is strikingly similar to the chiasmic grafting that runs through much of his professional writing. In a critical parallel to his personal upset, Matthiessen's scholarship often melded social hopes for a sustainable democracy indistinctly with erotic and idealized desires for intimate interpersonal attachments and unity. Unlike the writing that he produced for audiences, however, his self-reflective journal from McLean Hospital displays the tenuous sutures that once held together an "American mind" assured of "being more definite than life."[25] To explain how deeply his self-confidence and his social confidence had been shaken by depression, Matthiessen portrays himself as startled by a recognition that he had "shut off more than [he was] aware."[26] He finds himself "baffled" by his incapacity to put a name to exactly what he had repressed. In his confusion, he describes himself as caught in an "increasingly vicious circle," as immobilized by a fear of becoming colonized by an unidentifiable injury. Retreat from this "nightmare that had to be constantly fought back to keep it from becoming [him]" becomes his chosen strategy for ameliorating the sting of his un-nameable wound.[27]

Ultimately Matthiessen came to terms with his panic by interpreting it as an unreasonable fear about the far-off possibility that his lifelong partner, Russell Cheney, might predecease him. He narrated the thought of life without Russell as a psychic shock caused by the risk of his own unraveling. Given that he understood the nature of his being—his knowledge of the beauty and richness of his life as well as breath itself—through the merging of self and other, he was struck by an ontological insecurity about his ability to exist in the absence of the other. He negotiated this risk by both negating and affirming the fictiveness and the reality of the loss that he perceived as threatening the future. In one instance he articulated the illogic of mourning a loss that had yet to occur: "Why try to settle a situation that does not exist?" Yet he later prefigured a strategy for surviving this illusionary loss: "When you give yourself entirely to love you cannot demand that it last forever."[28]

The extensive archive of personal and published writing that the critic produced during his lifetime overwhelmingly suggests that he measured love for his partner, his research, his nation, and democratic society from a single set of precepts: the organization of human relationships around a deep unity of ideals and shared values forged through intimate engagement with others on a quest for universal understanding. The fluid and often indiscernible overlap of private, scholarly, and social concerns in Matthiessen's confused struggle to narrate his melancholic state resonated with a propensity that not only informed his most renown publication but also ran throughout his private correspondence and personal journals, his involvement with Skull and Bones, his educational experiences as a Rhodes scholar at Oxford, and later his professional role as a professor of American Studies in Harvard's tutorial system. The future panic that struck Matthiessen during the writing of *American Renaissance* was not explicit in the book, but was suggested in the way he hoped to recuperate an idea of U.S. democracy from the destruction of economic rupture with a cognitive inversion of public and intellectual desires for intimacy—and redolently erotic—unity with nineteenth-century authors.

The critical compulsion to identify universal principles as the basis for transhistorical national connections in *American Renaissance* evidences Matthiessen's vigorous scholarly goal of revealing linguistic, generic, and mythical components that could sustain a lasting national literature and art. The homosocial bonds and homoerotic ideals that structured his attachment to the past, however, also transferred his private insecurities into a public forum. Scholarly production thus seems to have become an additional platform on which the scholar continued to work through the future panic that had caught him off guard during the early stages of writing.

The stated intervention of mobilizing art against the corruption of capitalism in *American Renaissance* was delivered through an ideal of national democratic unity that the text presents as an antipodal force against the "ruthless elements in [the nation's] economic life."[29] This critical project reflects a common modernist response to collective loss, enacting the balancing of political hope and social despair that Seth Moglen describes as an attempt to collectively mourn the social injury to democracy caused by economic crisis and industrial expansion. In his retreat to the nation's literary past, Matthiessen hoped to identify and recognize models and forms of association that could restore "man's heroic capacity for no less constant renewal" in order to recuperate "a love of life" for a nation faced with "constant desperate ruin."[30] The evocation of lost objects and lost causes in this sentiment of ruin provided a basis for political hope as it beckoned members of the nation to identify with and reinforce the parts of themselves that were lost and the inspiration they were denied when they were injured by social forces. Collective recognition and development of explanatory mechanisms for understanding loss, Moglen argues, enable social groups to locate an imaginative home in which to envision future possibilities for social justice. Failure to mourn, or the incapacity to reckon with, recognize, and explain what has been lost, on the other hand, often generates political despair and displaced anger.[31] This can take the form of an internalized melancholia—as it did for Matthiessen the person—or it can become externally destructive when groups cannot locate who is to be held accountable for their losses, what exactly they have lost as a consequence of social reorganization, or how structural transformations have contributed to their experiences of injury.

The state of melancholia that compelled Matthiessen's desire to bring new life to lost democratic ideals was not simply confounded by his inability to name a loss; more disruptively, much like the imagined future death of an intimate other, it balanced on mourning a situation that did not yet exist—the loss of a fraternal unity and universal equality from a cross-class solidarity that he imagined was doomed to failure by capitalist crisis before it could ever materialize.

Preemptive panic impinges on the critic's sense of the logical and the rational because loss does not provide an adequate explanation for the continuity of social inequality under an ideal that the author desires as "real." This condition is structured by the necessity of working through a trauma marked by the near impossibility of distinguishing the conditions of social inequality constituting the antecedent of loss from conditions that presumably extend from a perceptible and novel present injury. The longing for a predictable, manageable, and stable social order depends on constantly fighting against the unpredictable insecurity and transformative disorder that is both a symptom of capital's stratifying effects and a condition of any radical recognition and struggle to overturn continuous and ongoing inequalities. Matthiessen's future panic, in this regard, positioned him to "settle a situation that does not exist" with a promise of recuperating an object—a figuration of lost but never realized democratic ideals. Consequently, working through his anxiety required him to relinquish his attachments to loss with an openness to the unknown and the unpredictable possibilities that necessarily come with leveling social hierarchies. Or he could endow loss with a *sense* of reality that might provide occasion for collective mourning and subsequent hope. Matthiessen opted for the latter. In the absence of a social foundation for politically mourning an imagined loss, the author substituted his personal recollections of trauma as a central mechanism for working through the nationalist injury caused by capitalist transitions.

As a young scholar, Matthiessen developed affiliations and cognitive mechanisms of rearticulation to work through the stigma and social exclusion that he felt as a sexual "invert." In his later depression, this deeply personal early struggle informed his political mourning. It gave him a strategy for transcending trauma that he reframed as a nationalist incapacity to overcome the damage of capital and recover the "ideals" of U.S. democracy.

Matthiessen's writing about his depression suggests that the decussation of social-political hope and private injury initially failed to alleviate his social anxieties. Further, the act of substitution threatened to create additional damage as it revitalized the trauma of his sexual shame, forcing him to relive the doubt and despair that he had experienced during the original trauma as if it were a symptom of professional doubt. In his reflections, he questioned his credibility as a scholar and expressed shame that he might only be "an enthusiast trying to be a critic."[32] Then, in a seemingly incongruous response, he narrated overcoming his anxieties about his present work and place in society by facing his fears of losing his sexual partner. As I discuss in greater detail later, the collapse of scholarly and domestic concerns that Matthiessen experienced during the writing of *American Renaissance* reignited—as a doubt about the democratic capacity of a capitalist nation—the experience of sexual insecurity that he had earlier seemed to resolve using a social interpretation of Hellenic ideals during his fellowship at Oxford. When faced with what he perceived as the ensuing loss of these ideals during his later time at McLean, he reverted to the specter of sexual inequality. To alleviate his panic about the nation's democratic future, he substituted his love of his partner as the source of his anxiety, but he also responded to his depression with a protective retreat that paralleled his early response to his feelings of sexual shame. Like the way he described the social alienation he experienced as a young homosexual man, he narrated himself as becoming abstracted from social life, of being overcome by a feeling of separation from his research and his ability to contribute to society. In the book that took form after his depression, *American Renaissance*, the fraternal friendships from his college days at Yale that had helped him overcome his sexual insecurity, recurred in the intellectual effort to unleash higher truths for national regeneration with an intimate relationship to form.

As Giles Gunn argues, Matthiessen's disillusionment with the social and economic forces that promoted "reckless individualism" at the expense of ethical obligations to others and spiritual ideals compelled him to engage deeply with the politics of literary form, in what he saw as a cooperative exercise in democratic production.[33] Although Matthiessen has been criticized variously for using his scholarship as an escape from political commitments, any fair treatment of his work must recognize that he saw concentrated contemplation of philosophical ideals as a form of, if not a model for, political engagement.[34] Gunn rightly argues that Matthiessen thought that "showing how the liberating energies of mid-nineteenth century American literature were expressed within the exigencies and complications of form" would provide his twentieth-century readers with usable historical insights.[35] His approach undoubtedly later shaped New Critical methodologies that drew on limited and exclusionary ideas about the nation's past to endorse Cold War consensus. However, it is important to remember that for Matthiessen close study of literary form *constituted* an engagement in democratic politics. It appeared to identify a source of collective social injury—capitalist chaos and crisis—and sought to mobilize new political possibilities with a memory of the past that he hoped might reinforce universal ideals for a classless democracy. What he found most useful in the canon he resurrected was neither evasion nor celebration of the violent social and economic conditions of nineteenth-century history; rather, he gained insights into living through chaos from the tactics used by writers of the past to confront the tragedies of their own era. He aimed to repossess the psychic structures of social desire that made it possible for authors to hold the idea of democracy against the "rising forces of exploitation" and the "full emergence of the acquisitive spirit."[36] He understood this recovery effort *as* participating in a broader political struggle of the Cultural Front by offering his research as an urgent call to protect the nation with the energy of the reform movements of the 1840s. He imagined that this might invigorate the Popular Front as it struggled against the growing devastation of economic exploitation and the rise of global fascism.

In a demonstration of solidarity with artists and labor activists, *American Renaissance* reveres the "mariners, renegades, and castaways" of Melville's floating factory, and pays homage to "countless fellow-workers, past and present," with a memory of emancipatory success against the corruptions of nineteenth-century capitalism.[37] The book opens in a spirit of comradeship: "The true function of scholarship as of society is not to stake out claims on which others might not trespass, but to provide a community of knowledge in which others may share."[38] Its ambition to "recover" democratic possibilities through critical intimacy, however, emerges from a form of mourning that can quickly become dangerous. In particular, the concept of inversion—the modern medicalized assertion of the congenital origins of homosexuality—that filled the scholar with sexual anxiety during his studies at Oxford—remained the organizing logic through which he envisioned protecting an ideal of cross-class egalitarian democracy as he wrote his influential manuscript. What seems to be a radical resignification of alterity as the basis for an inclusionary society takes a destructive turn. The multiple grafts in his narrative framework for understanding injury make it impossible for him to locate and identify what is causing his ontological insecurity and who is responsible. This results in a protective retreat into intimate sameness that, when repeated in a new context, becomes an exclusionary lesson in symbolic affiliation. The tactics of psychic retreat he developed from reading the Greeks as a young scholar gave him a powerful resource for working through his sexual anxiety and also ignited his desire to generate models for social tolerance, sympathy, and understanding. The "America" that Matthiessen discovered and attempted to protect in nineteenth-century literature by drawing on similar strategies and logics, however, was an illusionary construction of sacred spaces that ultimately regulates and protects against the very stratified and devalued populations hardest hit by capitalism.

Greek Love: Erotic Recovery

Matthiessen's training in the Oxford tutorial system gave him an intimate education in speculative optimism. In the absence of a lived history of democracy to recover, his engagement with the Greeks prepared him to deal with crisis by investing his hope in philosophical ideals. On graduating from Yale, Matthiessen moved to Oxford on a Rhodes Scholarship, staying from October 1923 to August 1925. Well before his arrival, nineteenth-century university reformers had revamped Oxford's curriculum around a Socratic system of tutorial exchange that emphasized close engagement with Hellenic texts. The university's earlier focus on Latin recitations of classical republican literature had served to educate an infantry for the British Empire with a warrior ethos premised on deference to external authority.

By the mid-nineteenth century, however, liberal reformers such as Benjamin Jowett began to refashion the curriculum on a Greek model, advocating forms of knowledge, individual creativity, and social diversity that could mediate "the effects of laissez-faire capitalism and . . . the approach of mass democracy."[39] Like other liberal thinkers, Jowett saw the university as a key institution in England's national and imperial growth. He asserted that national regeneration (and imperial projects) required abandoning the curricular focus on staid recitation and memorization of Latin grammar, which he saw as contributing to stagnation, and replacing it with critical dialogues that he imagined would foster adaptable intellectual perspectives for a society undergoing transformation.[40] To this end, Jowett read Platonic texts with his students to arrive at transcendental truths and democratic principles.

What Jowett did not foresee was that some of his students would draw on the tutorials and the reformed Greats curriculum to script homosexuality as "the purest model of Victorian liberalism itself."[41] Linda Dowling has shown that, for a brief moment during the late nineteenth century, Greek studies at Oxford opened up a transitory discursive space for philosophically circulating a "homosexual code" that expressed same-sex desire as a transcendental example of liberal values. For Oxford undergraduates like John Addington Symonds and Walter Pater in particular, the Socratic Eros of the tutorial system and the treatment of same-sex desire in Plato's *Symposium* and *Phaedrus* proved that the most elevated means of regenerating the virtuous ideals and values of the nation were contingent on male homoerotic love. For example, *Symposium* 209 was understood as inextricably linking Socratic Eros to corporal expression:

> Above all when [he who in youth is inspired by wisdom and virtue] finds a beautiful and noble and talented soul, he embraces the two in one person, and to such a one he is full of speech about virtue and the nature and pursuits of a good man; and he tries to educate him; and by touching the beautiful and consorting with him he gives birth to and propagates that which he had conceived long before, both when with him and through recollecting him when apart, and together with him he tends that which was brought forth; and they are married by a far nearer tie and have a closer friendship than those who beget mortal children.[42]

Jowett's classes infused the engagement of young students and mature scholars in the Oxford tutorials with an erotic affect when they read such passages as elevating male sexual exchange as the highest means for socially reproducing beauty and truth. The sexual energy of the reformed system certainly informed the movement among Uranian poets to apprehend the complexities of "heavenly love" from the 1880s to the 1930s. Although these poets often claimed sexual innocence through their assertions that the poetic pursuit of spiritual ideals transcended embodied experience, Dowling argues that the Uranians invited even those who opposed homoerotic expression into intimate discursive contact with male Eros.[43]

Matthiessen arrived at Oxford thirty years after the trials of Oscar Wilde. By then, the erotic vocabulary that had radically linked a notion of higher sodomy to "spiritual procreancy" had been subsumed in the scientific discourse of sexual abnormality. Matthiessen's early letters to Russell Cheney, whom he had met on his return passage to Oxford following the summer break of 1924, shows that, prior to his graduate studies, he had internalized the repression of sexual normativity, which caused him profound and prolonged sexual shame.

As if pulling directly from the psychic anxiety of his youthful social disgrace, an unpublished and undated account that Matthiessen had filed among his letters from 1925 accentuates the memory of panic in his first nervous attempts to disclose his sexual leanings to Cheney. Signs of his fear of the possibly unbearable social stigma at the moment of revelation added narrative tension to his account. Matthiessen recalled a titillating progression toward disclosure that was at pains to overcome the socially shaped self-judgment impeding his attempt to "drag out the skeleton of his twisted psychology . . . gulping for courage and the right opportunity without success."[44] Despite his best efforts to maintain a casual delivery, when he finally mustered the "nerve" to confess, he did so with a "queer and remote" assurance that his aberrant impulses had been previously resolved: "I *was* sexually inverted. Of course, I've controlled it since [my italics]."[45] As his letters immediately following his introduction to Cheney demonstrate, this will to repress conflicted with his contradictory attachment to his social desire to contribute to the development of a vibrant democracy and the sexual desires that marked him as a "pariah" for "the unforgivable sin of being different from the great sum of mankind."[46] The category of purity became a benchmark of his self-assessments, a principle that he claimed he had "never experienced . . . since [he] went to boarding school when [he] was twelve. Stories, abuse, and *the rest* [italics mine]."[47] Here purity stood in for an object of loss constituting sexual contact as a trauma in which the locus of grievance was an aspect of a defective self. The impossible return to a fictive antecedent state of wholesomeness, Matthiessen's reflections seemed to suggest, produced a prolonged inner turmoil about his inability to control the "ferment when [he] was alone, the seeking eye when [he] was in a city" that plagued him with sexual desires into which he occasionally "slipt back."[48]

Meeting Cheney drew him once again into a "sex battle" between his pure and fulfilling feelings of deep attachment and his sexual urges, which he understood as threatening and needing to be "controlled." To maintain confidence that he had successfully mastered his sexual desires, in the days following his disclosure to Cheney he narrated his passion as a literary form that did not depend on sexual release. Having been "stirred" into "a new vibration of life in which there is so much poetry," Matthiessen assured his potential lover that "there is no room for anything else."[49] In this response to internalized injury, the burdens of the body were transformed into tractable measures of interpersonal mastery via shared idealization. In his letter, Matthiessen proclaimed that the poetry of the couple's love could empower them to practice "temperance in sex" based on their knowledge that, despite the "natural and healthy" arousal that often accentuated their thoughts of one another, "other contact would tarnish the harmony" of their connection.[50]

Soon after returning to Oxford, however, having sensed the residual sexual energy of the Greeks curriculum, Matthiessen dramatically reoriented his feelings of injury. Writing to friends back home about his budding relationship, he declared, "Externally Oxford is just the same as it was last year. Internally it is altogether different."[51] In his letters to Cheney, Matthiessen increasingly drew on a Greek ideal of homoerotic unity by reframing social convention as a threat to the fullness of freedom that he now articulated as originating in erotic expression. Within a month of connecting with Cheney, his apologies for experiencing sexual desire in his letters were transformed into an exuberant philosophical treatment of his lust as an emblem of an intimate ideal that mimicked the affect of the *Symposium*. When the younger scholar recollected his bond to the older man from a distance, he envisioned the closeness of their friendship as a unity erected on virtue and beauty:

> I thought I realized it all that last night together; but first the intellect sees, and then when it has created its imaginative symbolism it gives the whole man something to live by. I saw very clearly that night and called it a marriage. . . . Marriage! What a strange word to be applied to two men! Can't you hear the hell-hounds of society baying in full pursuit behind us? But that's just the point. We are beyond society. We've said thank you very much, and stepped outside and closed the door. . . . And so we have a marriage that was never seen on land or sea . . . a marriage that demands nothing and gives everything. It does not limit the affections of the two partners *it gives* their scope greater radiance and depth. . . . Its bonds indeed form the service that is perfect freedom.[52]

Latent reference to the Greeks became for Matthiessen a cognitive framework for overcoming sexual shame. It led him toward a philosophical exceptionalism whereby he came to understand the possibility of an ideal society that had yet to be lived through a promise of perfect freedom. Homosocial bonds constituted for him the highest ideal of the equality of sameness. In its nascent formation, this exceptionalist romance offered the young scholar private compensation for a sexual anxiety that he had only recently come to articulate as caused by a social injury:

Well, when you have admitted that you are sexually inverted, what are you going to do about it? The law and public opinion are clear enough on this point. But law and public opinion represent the majority who do not either understand, or even know about the question. There cannot be laws made for a small fraction of the minority. But does this mean that the small minority must resolutely shut themselves out of the most beautiful expression of life, when if they love they cannot possibly do harm to anyone except themselves, and in point of fact, as we know they actually find a new fullness and balance to life? If you and I know that our love is the richest and purest and most sacred thing imaginable, if it strengthens and develops us as characters, if it gives us the assurance and sense of completion that enable us to give our very best to our work, our friends, why should we not embrace it fully?[53]

The protective retreat from social injustice that Matthiessen envisioned inhabiting with Cheney created a private refuge for working through the social trauma he associated with being "sexual inverted." This emergency measure, however, became the foundation for a general philosophy. As he extended it into other areas of his life, this philosophy often caused him to invert his understanding of the material and the ideal in his overarching comprehension of reality. In his early effort to sustain the narrative fantasy of social escape, Matthiessen staked his relationship in the dangerous territory of exceptionalist melodrama, where he envisioned spiritual regeneration distantly removed from historical precedent: "Of course this life of ours is entirely new—neither of us know of a parallel case. We stand in the middle of uncharted, uninhabited country. That there have been other unions like ours is obvious, but we are unable to draw on their experience. We must create everything for ourselves."[54] The philosophical cartographers that he most relied on to remake reality through the reflection of an ideal were the generation of students who had eroticized Oxford's Greeks curriculum.

Returning to Havelock Ellis's "Impressions and Comments," for example, Matthiessen reflected on the idea that immorality is the name of a social convention describing individual impulses that do not conform to a "given time and place."[55] He then embraced this category as an exit from current norms, imagining himself generatively occupying the territory of immorality with Cheney, where he claimed to find a utopia of dreams that bequeathed to them "an earthly paradise."[56] In this instance, his desire to fully occupy a poetic realm protected from the impurities of social regulation made the ideal figuration of virtuous union that he found in language more real to him than the material world that was the impetus for his retreat.

The interpretation of Whitman that Matthiessen derived from John Addington Symonds worked harmoniously with this inversion; at the same time, it more suggestively centered physical erotic expression as the ideal that he envisioned would become the basis for liberal democratic regeneration.[57] In

Symonds's reading of the poet, Whitman was a modern Plato; Symonds argued that "no man in the modern world has expressed so strong a conviction that 'manly attachment,' 'athletic love,' 'the higher towering of comrades,' is . . . a virtue upon which society will have to lay its firm foundations, and a passion equal in permanence, superior in spirituality, to the sexual affection."[58] The generative spirit of free and fearless intellect that Symonds found in Whitman neither condemned nor insisted on embodied sexual exchange, "leaving its private details to the moral sense and special inclination of the individuals concerned."[59] Matthiessen's experience of "living" Whitman through his "affectionate, compassionate" love of Cheney, however, drew from Symonds an ideal of unity that did not sacrifice embodiment as a factor of whole being.[60] At the same time that the latent erotic energy of the Greeks curriculum validated Matthiessen's private sexual desires, it also transformed his sexual shame into an encompassing philosophy that he saw extending from intimate exchange into all aspects of life. The Whitman that he found in Symonds—a philosophical idealist, scholar, and sexually explorative democratic citizen—suggested to Matthiessen a flexible synthesis from which he developed a holistic ideal for sublime being: "Blend[ing] together the mind, body, and soul so that they are joined in a mighty symphony. The mind and soul give an idealization and exaltation to the body; and the body in turn gives an intuitive, impalpable channel of expression to the soul and mind."[61] In his self-understanding, this translated as a near total fusion of his love of Cheney, his love of knowledge, his love of teaching, and his love of nation.

Love—a philosophical proposition cobbled together from a combination of Christian faith, Socratic Eros, fraternal bonds, and nationalist longing—came to function in Matthiessen's writing as a projection of desire through interpersonal intimacy. Through all-encompassing "love," he imagined it possible to achieve an idealized future of social stability and unity. The emphasis on pursuing truth through an honest engagement with even the most minute details of human experience that he derived from Edward Carpenter's discussion of Uranianism provided Matthiessen with a disciplinary framework for making the fulfillment of private desire an ethical obligation for social improvement: "Life is fluid, so do not build rigid laws. But try to discover what your deepest nature is, and live up to it."[62] To this end, intimacy and confession often worked synonymously as a means to "discover" the "details that made life vivid."[63] Talking about sex thus became as important to him as acting on it, both as a foundation for producing intimate connections and as a discursive mechanism for reconstituting reality in his figuration of an ideal.

Matthiessen asked Cheney to disclose "all the sordid details of [his] sex business" so that they could understand one another through "clear scientific analysis," warning at a later time that "any little detail that is slurred over and left unsaid makes a tiny crack in the foundation and our union is not the perfect masterpiece."[64] The notion of social removal that enabled this intimate revelation was for Matthiessen a protective retreat from which to imagine coming "pretty close to being virtue."[65] Yet he conducted these intimate exchanges with a social purpose by drawing on Carpenter's framework for holistic becoming: "Realization of life is a great harmony of elements."[66] Through this lens, he configured his sacred pursuit of private desire as a "divine gift" that he would later share as a living commitment to "a spirit of development" because he imagined that the intimacy forged in private life was a pathway for rebuilding society in accordance with the ideal.[67]

Not surprisingly, much like liberal reformers of the nineteenth century, Matthiessen envisioned as a model for national uplift the intimate engagement—and latently erotic attachments—of scholars to text and students to tutors at the Oxford tutorials. Following his first meeting with his tutor after returning to Oxford, he wrote to Cheney: "Stimulated at having heard [himself] talk."[68] Youthful self-absorption aside, the letter expressed an excitement over intellectual work that collapsed with lust in a newfound celebration of his intimate private life. It remains unclear whether this excitement related to hearing from Cheney or from the tutorial exchange. Both possibilities are suggested in the corporeal stimulation Matthiessen recalled experiencing: his "heart was too full—[his] hands shook, [he] couldn't sit still."[69] This energy translated into his drive to forge an intimate relationship with his objects of research, becoming the primary characteristic of his scholarly objective: "I want to know a few things, a few great figures so well that I can feel them *throbbing as a part of me.* I don't want to be a professor of English, but a student of the Human spirit . . . with a far more intimate sense."[70]

Before meeting Cheney, Matthiessen had felt an ethical imperative to access in his teaching and research the love and social connections that he could not experience through "sexual love."[71] Later, however, the idealization of the erotic that helped him overcome his sexual anxiety positioned him to reframe his sense of the tutorial exchange not as an inadequate compensatory outlet for navigating a personal deficiency but as a necessary social practice for spiritual regeneration. Sexual fulfillment in his private life, he believed, enhanced his understanding of reality in ways that would augment his professional contributions: "Mind, body, and soul . . . are convenient labels to give harmony of elements which compose a man. To me the dominating force of my life is love . . . that is the whole basis of my faith, of my desire to teach, of my happiness."[72]

Matthiessen's association of his teaching with virtue and love throughout his career suggests that his advocacy of the tutorial system and his chairmanship of Harvard's Board of Tutors in history and literature from 1931 to 1948 were not simply services he performed for professional advancement. More politically intended, they were likely an expression of his desire to create and protect institutional spaces where he assumed the intimate pursuit of higher ideals would result in unified goals for democratic procreation. Although this framework was compatible with his understanding of democracy as a union forged by egalitarian pursuits of virtue and truth, when he made this desire for protective retreat from the murky complexities of material life his standard for social fulfillment, he was faced with the impossible dilemma of imagining democracy at a distance from social and political life.

His rendition of life in Skull and Bones bridged the contradiction for Matthiessen. The experience of overcoming private sexual shame led him to reconsider his relationship to the fraternal body that had previously reinforced his ideas about his sexuality as aberrant. He reconciled fraternal conflict by renarrating his associations as enabling him to make private injury a basis for collective association. Greek love and fraternal regulation collapsed in his recollections of the secret society's "real" rituals. When Matthiessen filtered his memory of the group through his desire for social fulfillment, he celebrated secret association, routine group confession, and the nepotistic dissemination of intergenerational privilege as evidence of a total freedom to explore collective transcendence through a solidarity secured by contractual silence. Where Greek love provided Matthiessen a philosophical framework for erotic veneration, Skull and Bones gave him an experiential fiction that taught him how to inhabit his desires in a world that existed beyond social constraints. "We are blest," he told Cheney. "Ours is a B-n-s [bones] marriage quite apart from the barbarian world. In fact, it's a world that doesn't exist."[73]

Fraternal Intimacy: Managed Democracy

Matthiessen's "bones" marriage was defined by a hierarchical unity that replicated the anticipatory becoming of speculative nationalism's "not yet" freedom. It was not by chance that Matthiessen "found" Cheney on his return journey to Europe during the early autumn of 1924.[74] Earlier that summer, members of Matthiessen's Bones cohort "had gotten ahold of [Cheney] in the 'T' [tomb]" and suggested that he get to know their clubmate on their shared voyage to Europe.[75] It is no surprise that Matthiessen's closest friends overlapped with Cheney's— and no doubt many other powerful and influential alumni of the secret order— at the Tomb, the name of the temple at 324 High Street in New Haven where the group holds its meetings and reunions.[76] Becoming a "bonesman" was a family tradition for both Matthiessen (1923) and Cheney (1904). Cheney's father was initiated with his cousin Howell in 1892, and his brother Philip joined in 1901. Ward Cheney (1922), a close cousin, certainly would have been among the cohort of "close friends" who initiated Matthiessen into Skull and Bones in 1923.[77] Matthiessen also had an uncle, George Pratt, who joined in 1857. The club's standard practice of cloaking its existence in public secrecy has obscured the fact that Skull and Bones was the fundamental fulcrum that united Matthiessen's personal, professional, intellectual, and political philosophy of harmonious love.

When Matthiessen committed suicide in 1950, he left three items on the dresser of his hotel room: the keys to his apartment; a letter of instruction for the distribution of his property, including an apology for his actions; and his Skull and Bones ring.[78] When he met Cheney, he proudly wore his club badge as "a token that [the club's] Goddess gave [him] when [he] became Sir Little

Devil, Knight of Utopia, the symbol that she considered [him] worthy to live a life of Truth."[79] From the outset, the couple's relationship was indivisible from the imagined utopia of fraternal knighthood. Until Cheney's death in 1945, the two referred to one another using monikers bequeathed to them by Skull and Bones. Matthiessen's "physique, small and foursquare" plausibly made him the shortest of the initiates who were ritually measured for anointment in 1923, which earned him the symbolic name "little Devil." According to Alexandra Robbins, all initiates are called "little Devils" prior to becoming knights, but it becomes a permanent nickname for the shortest member of each cohort.[80] The name also assigned Matthiessen the status of perpetual child in anticipation of a maturity made impossible by the infantilizing nomenclature, thus imposing on him a permanent intergenerational deference at the bottom of the society's hierarchical structure.

From the perspective of his subordinate position in an association proclaiming itself egalitarian, Matthiessen's later efforts to offer his research in solidarity with industrial workers begins to look less like a cross-class misapprehension than an act of identification with the secondary status of mid-nineteenth-century working men in a hierarchically organized democracy. Working men, of course, also participated in fraternities to mediate their tenuous status in the nation's changing democracy. Dana Nelson has argued that the fraternities, purity movements, and professional societies that exponentially grew in the United States at the historical conjuncture of universal White male suffrage propped up the nation's class structure by reconfiguring the meaning of equality. White men who had yet to materialize the official equality of enfranchisement, Nelson contends, found through fraternal membership an abstract equality by reconstituting themselves as brothers.[81] Fraternal practices invited men whose daily lives were structured by the competition and inequality of the capitalist economy to be semipublicly recognized through ritualized sameness. Like other fraternal organizations, Skull and Bones, which was founded in 1832, offered elite White men a highly regulated social arena where they could enact themselves as equal individuals in a collective community at an abstract remove from market competition and social tensions.

In Skull and Bones, the illusion of equality balances on an elaborate death lore, which is compounded by a physical location in a "Tomb," where members imagine inhabiting an afterlife where difference is equalized. A rumored display of skulls that make even "kings" indiscernible from "pawns" symbolically instills the meeting place with an air of equality, reminding knights that despite their status on earth everybody leaves the living world in exactly the same way, through death.[82] The fraternity's elite and exclusive membership of White male seniors for whom Yale is often a family legacy brings the exclusionary conditions of this fictional equality into stark relief. When nineteenth-century fraternities beckoned to the norms of universal citizenship as the basis of collective organization, they often determined women and people of color too particular for incorporation. Fraternal rituals, Nelson demonstrates, taught men "to love their Others, but only in the most symbolic, denatured, purified form—the symbolically pure mother, the symbolically noble Red Man, the symbolically mystic 'primitive.'"[83] Because members were trained to identify with a standard of social mobility, which reinforced their own inferior status, symbolic gestures ameliorated the inequality by "allowing men to experience the 'traumatic pleasure' of their social power . . . as their own 'innocent' victimization."[84] In this vein, initiations requiring ritual submission to the authority of predecessors taught members of fraternities to think of social belonging as a right to be earned through rituals that were generationally passed down. The precondition for attaining the fraternal and/or social power to manage others was identification with the notions of progress through which internal hierarchies were reproduced. Homosexuality, in this framework, suggested for many a threatening sameness with the potential to radically upset the managerial structure.[85] The homophobia of many fraternities helped to maintain internal hierarchies by retaining individual difference within the group as the modality for constituting authority over others.

Matthiessen was ambivalent about "the life of Truth" that he proudly embraced as a member of Skull and Bones. He claimed to wear his badge as a sign that he had accepted Truth as an ideal, with the caveat that it did not "mean that [his] ideals as a whole [were those of the fraternity]. . . . It simply meant that [he] accept[ed] Truth for a standard."[86] His allegiance to the club left Matthiessen struggling with the homophobia upholding stratified sameness. He filtered his sexual shame through the fraternity as a site of regulating against deviance: "Oh, the B-n-s . . . gave me the love of god alright and that was enough to keep me straight."[87] Indeed, the disclosure of the "twisted psychology that [he] had given to the Cl-b in the T [Club in the Tomb]," which he had disclosed as part of the mandatory recitation of his "Life History" in front of the group, made his private shame the locus for proving himself willing to capitulate to the group's model of human improvement and social unity.[88] He narrated overcoming his sexual desires as submitting completely to the group's ideals and aid.

Matthiessen's vow of Truth filled him with anxiety when he took up his "B-n-s marriage" with Cheney because his internalization of confession as the sign of an honest life made him believe that divulging his desires was "the basis of complete G.B. [Great Bonesman] freedom."[89] Yet, he feared that his revelation would register as his failure to "escape all [his] old passionate weakness [through fraternal] love" and appear as a rejection of the group's principles and support.[90] His early exchanges with Cheney were overwhelmed by a feeling of future doubt in a prolonged conversation about whether they should ever tell the "outside" world about their "uncharted" union. Risking the possibility that he would be severed from the society, Matthiessen put his faith in the public sexual contract that members sealed when they ritually told their sexual histories to the goddess of "Connubial Bliss."[91] To muster the confidence that it ultimately took for him to first write to his clubmate Mitch Davenport about Cheney, Matthiessen folded his relationship into a memory of this rite: "What I am now experiencing is what I have deeply known only once before—and that vicariously in the C.B. [Connubial Bliss confessional] of my cl-bmate X-T. That night over the fire in 324 I heard a story of beauty and truth. And now that story is my own."[92] By drawing on the ritual sexual confession with which the group established trust, Matthiessen optimistically invested in a form of sharing that he hoped would reinforce his bonds of brotherhood around the "necessity and beauty" of love.[93] When his bet paid off, he professed to Cheney that "our union is fully known to another, and understood." Excitedly, Matthiessen took in the affirmation with a retrospective confidence around which he renarrated his status in the fraternity: "I knew my club would understand, and this bears me out."[94] Through his disclosure, he established a revisionist faith in the "firm rock foundation in 324" and restored a trust that "in the T [members] give [them]selves completely, mind complete and soul."[95] This secured his attachment to a "brotherhood" that he reactively argued was "built to stay."[96] Yet to ensure the future stability of a fiction that emerged from folding the group's imagined past into his projection of a higher unity, he increasingly remapped the society's regulatory homosociality as a homoerotic discursive responsibility to live up to the fraternity's reputed democratic ideals.

First, he relocated Truth from his repressive submission to the group's abstract ideals to a vow to live honestly in pursuit of his individual desires: "I wrote to my M-g-g [Magog, the member of his cohort presumed to have the most sexual experience] all right a vivid flashing letter (that's another thing; you've given me a new keenness to my relationship with my Cl-b. I tell them what I mean now. I'm no longer pompous, self-righteous and dull)."[97] This revised framework later emboldened him to become increasingly sexually explicit in his narrations to the group: "But it being the B-n-s, and the truth of a L.H. [Life History] lying in the truth of its details, I did not neglect to add that we had full sexual expression—very often."[98] Then he made his confession of homoerotic desire the basis of collective group regeneration: "It is my job to tell them. And I do it radiantly, joyfully. It's their job to understand."[99] In this regard, he shifted the onus for group cohesion from his own duty to overcome perceived sexual digression to the fraternity's collective obligation to live up to its own standards of honesty and trust. In the rebuke in which he first openly discussed his relationship to his entire cohort, Matthiessen marked as a risk to the fraternity's future the men's failure to "make enough effort to say what [they] mean in those scattered times [they] are together." In marking himself as an authority poised to avert such a crisis, he imaginatively secured the future of the club in the image of his own desires for protected spaces where "tolerance, sympathy, and understanding" were foundations for building social cohesion around a shared quest for universal Truth.[100] In grafting the Bones world onto the idealization of intimacy that he had adapted from the Greeks, he temporarily worked through his experience of sexual trauma. He drew on the fraternity, as a semipublic body that confirmed his social acceptability, to reconcile his erotic desires with his desires to contribute to society. He also, however, reaffirmed his understanding of reality as existing beyond lived relations. He did this by cognitively relocating the secret activities of his fraternal participation from a memory that he had experienced in material life to an abstract ideal that he imagined transcended the historical.

Matthiessen's melancholia over a decade later notably heightened when he broached the anticipatory desire of this paradigm. The antidemocratic back-lashes following the economic crisis of the 1930s seem to have acutely disrupted his unspoken hope that beauty and Truth might one day return to the nation as democratic fruition; he could neither avoid nor name the social limits of his intimate philosophy but simply questioned "the self-knowledge which I have believed to be my sureness in making my life an unregreted [sic] one, shut off more than I am aware, has it left nine-tenths of the iceberg hidden?"[101] This failure of confidence took form as political mourning, a loss of desire for pro-ducing ideals that he now imagined he could no longer help materialize: "At one point in [therapy] I broke into tears, and said that I loved life, that I had felt myself in contact with so many sides of American society and believed there was so much work to be done, absorbing it, helping to direct it intelligently."[102]

This stated objective to dedicate his work to building a vibrant and just cross-class democracy was certainly not an empty gesture for Matthiessen. As a student and later as a professor, he sought connection with the working class by teaching English to immigrants at the New Haven Hungarian Club and, throughout the 1930s, by offering literature courses at Boston's Samuel Adams School of Social Studies. His interactions with workers led him to ques-tion his own class status and challenge the objective relations of class division. He recalled in some of his last writing, "I had felt in the natural and hearty comradeship of these men a quality that I was just beginning to suspect might be bleached out of middle-class college graduates. *It was a kind of comradeship I wanted never to lose* [my italics]."[103] Much earlier in his life he had narrated meeting Cheney at a crossroads. He expressed a fear that following his desire might cause him to lose such cross-class connections: "All my high-sounding principles told me to stay down with the proletariat. All my impulses told me to go above."[104] Later this fear erupted as loss in the social panic that moved him to tears in his frenetic struggle to make sense of depression. In the hazy confusion of overlapping anxieties, his articulated future fear of losing Cheney—now his lifelong partner—clouded this past doubt about joining Cheney on the upper deck. The tension between fraternal ideals and working-class solidarity reso-nated in Matthiessen's melancholia as an anxiety over his tenuous configura-tions of the real and ideal—a homoerotic longing that became a desire for the rebirth of the nation.

Sacred Retreat

In his melancholic state, Matthiessen's insecurity about his lost ties to demo-cratic politics manifested subtly as a fear that "living Whitman" erotically in his private life had not carried over to national identity. The Whitman of expectant desire who expressed for Matthiessen and Cheney a richness of life accessed in the deferred state of anticipation, in verses such as "My love, was / on his way coming—O then I was happy! / O then each breath tasted sweeter, and all that day food nourished me more, and the beautiful day passed well," was a "touch-stone" of Matthiessen's intimate life.[105] In his state of depression, he feared that he had become disassociated from Whitman. Matthiessen's anxiety revealed constant anticipation as unsustainable. The work of cutting through and giving shape to beauty and truth that Whitman carried out in the labor history "Song of the Broad Axe" offered Matthiessen a challenge: if he "couldn't swing this book for some reason," he might take up a different axe "as a teacher, as a vital member participating in shaping life."[106] In the depths of Matthiessen's trauma, Whitman called forth an internal "torture" that made it difficult for him "to see the shapes and colors of the world, to feel the values of society or any mean-ing of good."[107] Whitman became a site of cathexis between the social and the imaginative such that loss was aligned with a failure of vision and a panic over fraternal democracy's failure to arrive. Struck by fears about capitalist corrup-tion, the litany of shapes that Whitman celebrated as arising from the collective efforts of a diverse society—"The Main shapes arise! / Shapes of Democracy total, result of centuries, / Shapes ever projecting other shapes"—became for Matthiessen cause for panic, a loss of vision and a failure to see any "shapes" clearly.[108] *American Renaissance* mediates this anxiety through homosocial union with dead writers of the nineteenth century. It transposes Matthiessen's erotic ideals and fraternal desires into his feelings for national democracy. It subtly resolves his ontological insecurity through intimate engagement with textual details as the foundation for a narrative arc of democratic becoming. It appeals to an ostensible collective commitment to universal truths among writ-ers of the past in continuity with the staging of twentieth-century desire as an enduring quality of U.S. democracy.

The Whitman that Matthiessen found and loved in Symonds's read-ing of the "Calumus" poems did not appear in *American Renaissance*, but he remained in the erotic legacy that shaped Matthiessen's struggle to discover the nation's "timeless" ideals.[109] Deflecting Matthiessen's future panic about the nation, the text reacts against twentieth-century scholars whom Matthiessen saw as having lost their moral compass when overly focused on the particular-ity of history. He thus attempted to retain structures for intimate exchange and spiritual reproduction that he imagined could regenerate a second American Renaissance. To carry the "still undiminished resources" of the nation's imagi-native past into the timeless perpetuity of a future that he hoped to solidify, Matthiessen reverted to a fraternal model of intimate association—now intel-lectually forged with writers of the past—to bring the utopian promise of Greek ideals into the heart of the nation's being.[110]

Matthiessen introduced Emerson as the source of democratic rebirth through an obscurely erotic, colorful metaphor: "the cow from which the rest drew their milk."[111] This pastoral reference absorbs Emerson into an agrarian ideal, rendering him a solitary individual grazing in the pastures of an uninhabited country. The birth scene intimately reflects Matthiessen's own sense of living in "uncharted" democratic territory through his love for Cheney.[112] If Emerson was the source of U.S. literature, the intellectual dynamic that made him fertile was his relationship to Plato: *American Renaissance* opens with "The representative man [Emerson] most revered was Plato, for Plato had been able to bridge the gap between the two poles of thought, to reconcile fact and abstraction, the many and the One, society and solitude."[113] This foundational vision of unity emerges precisely from a transhistorical Socratic encounter that strongly reflects the *Symposium*. It gives "birth to and propagates [a democracy] conceived long before" through the intimate dialogue of an older philosopher and a young exemplar of a virtuous nation.[114] The ideal of transcendence enters Matthiessen's reading of Hawthorne, whom he revered for his ability to account for material circumstances and to overcome the burdens of history, through an "imagination [that] could surge up in rebirth."[115]

The restructuring of time that this reading suggests parallels Matthiessen's personal effort to attach his sense of reality to an imagined retreat from material life. It also inverts the historical with a claim to a timeless eternity. Historical time, as Matthiessen's rendition of Thoreau suggests, is marred by human fallibility and unfulfilled political aspirations. Tragedy structures history as the inevitable failure to arrive at personal and social ideals.[116] History hurt the authors of the Renaissance, Matthiessen implies, because, in knowing about the injustices that plagued their present, they were not always able to overcome inequalities:[117] "Hawthorne knew that he lived both in time and out of it, that the process of man's history was a deep interaction between eternity and time, an incessant eruption of eternity into time. And he knew the tragic nature of such conflict. In spite of the capacity of man's soul to share immediately in eternal life, his finite and limited nature made it inevitable that nothing perfect could be realized in time."[118] Establishing a basis for transhistorical attachment to a national grievance, Matthiessen points to history itself as a trauma that, in the case of the nineteenth century, inspired collective mourning. He imagines that this feeling of loss created a fleeting example of philosophical transcendence, a period of promise when imaginary ideals actively helped the nation to restore hope in the face of crisis.

In myth, allegory, and symbolism, Matthiessen found "the hidden strivings of the human spirit" that he believed had been lost to capitalism.[119] The dark struggles and tragic confrontations in the mythic representations of Melville, for example, were for him a timeless democracy of equality and brotherhood: "[Melville] gave full expression to [the] abundance of [his age], to its energetic *desire to master history by repossessing all the resources of the hidden past in a timeless and heroic present.* But he did not avoid the darkness in that past, the perpetual suffering in the heart of man, the broken arc of his career which inevitably ends in death [my italics]."[120] Although historical pessimism seems to predetermine the impossibility of democracy in historical time, in this reading Matthiessen imparts to Melville his desire to retreat into the psychic structures of a democratic ideal through heroic memory of a mythic encounter with the past.

This rendition of national rebirth aligns with Matthiessen's fraternal experience because it depends first and foremost on the death of the material world. The Skull and Bones preoccupation with the historical inevitability of death is reflected in Matthiessen's forlorn bond to affective spaces where hope emerged from ritual retreat. Literary escape into a timeless occult preserves democracy as a sacred space of intimate transhistorical attachment to "exterminat[ing] a specifically debased, sinful, unmanly, and dirtied self."[121] *American Renaissance* reads as an initiation ritual, inviting readers into intimate engagement with literary symbolism, allegory, and myth. It also authoritatively schools readers in textual analysis and a democratic consciousness that is contingent on submission to the ideals of five national patriarchs.

Similar to the rhetorical turn that he took when reproaching his clubmates for their failure to live up to a set of retrospectively imposed desired ideals, Matthiessen's literary "national recovery" dangerously managed a "crisis" with a repressive expectation that self-actualized freedom would submit to social regulation. Such mourning carried tangible social risk. The layers of substitution and inversion that constituted and confounded Matthiessen's experience of personal grieving often caused him to misdiagnose the nature and source of the nation's democratic limits. As a consequence, *American Renaissance*'s implied admonishment of the twentieth-century nation for having lost sight of its ideals often led him to miss the "real" in favor of his erotic idealizations.

A long excerpt from Louis Sullivan in the "Methods and Scope" section of *American Renaissance* lays out the stakes of the bond Matthiessen hoped to proleptically restore with the working class. He intended his book to connect to the proletariat: "True scholarship is of the highest usefulness because it implies the possession and application of the highest type of thought, imagination, and sympathy . . . for the good and enlightenment of all the people, not for the pampering of a class."[122] Yet his hope that his book would help heal the psychic and social wounds of class inequality was belied elsewhere by his propensity to submit workers to an external set of literary conventions that he mapped onto lived social encounters. Although he had limited contact with working people, Matthiessen often desired proximity to them: "It isn't a question of duty, but of happiness. I am uneasy when there are any more barriers than necessary between me and the laboring men."[123]

When Matthiessen came into contact with actual workingmen, however, he reinforced his own class privilege by objectifying difference through representation of masculine virility. During a spring vacation in 1925, he wrote to Cheney: "Going into the cathedral this morning we passed a workman—husky, broad-shouldered, 40, the perfect Chaucerian yeoman. . . . He caught my eye—both as a magnificently built feller, and as fitting in so perfectly to the type of a Fourteenth Century work man."[124] Matthiessen became physically aroused when he was approached and addressed by the worker: "As he went on I deliberately let my elbow rub against his belly. . . . He probably didn't even notice it, and it thrilled me: not only with sex, but with friendliness."[125] In yet another inversion, a brush with materiality seems to have confirmed for Matthiessen that the realm of the imagination might have actually been real. Like his affective attachment to his immigrant students, his perception shrouded the worker in an aesthetic demeanor, idealizing him at the cost of engaging him as an equal in the kind of honest exchange that he celebrated as the cornerstone of Truth and social unity. It is not surprising that a scholar who was well versed in English writing and particularly fond of figures like Symonds and Carpenter reflected the kind of homoerotic objectification of proletarians that Eve Kosofsky Sedgwick argues is a predominant theme of English literature.[126] On one hand, Matthiessen expected workers would behave in accordance with a set of timeless representations of abstract virility if they were to be recognized as workers. On another hand, the fraternal framework that became his model for the nation balanced on an expectation that workers would internalize an ideal of abstract individualism to prove their allegiance to democratic norms. Although they were meant to incorporate workers into the rites of democracy, these regulatory imperatives to abstraction absorbed difference only so long as it came with no "Life History" of its own.

At the moment of crisis, Matthiessen found himself pulled into a memory of preemergent cross-class democratic relations, staking a claim on the "real" as a transcendent spirit of social unity accessed through desire for an abstract idealization. This inverted restructuring enacted a subjective transformation that neatly aligned with the breakdown of a labor movement that was losing its sway in the transformation of the Fordist economy. When Matthiessen did attempt to reclaim his limited ties to the working class after his depression, by heading the citizen action committee against deporting International Longshore Workers Union leader Harry Bridges and joining the Massachusetts branch of the Civil Liberties Union, *and* through an intimate relationship with the details of form in the writing of *American Renaissance*, his affective desire for a sacred ideal aligned less with resistance to capitalist disparities than with the readjustment of social relations under the corporate restructuring of labor within a speculative economy.[127]

In the melancholic longing for a not yet experienced loss and a not yet recognizable social injury, Matthiessen's subjective undoing collapsed into the structural crisis of the productive economy and the breakdown of national meaning. Mourning took form as social restructuring—offering a homoerotic fraternal idealization as the modality through which to recover a never realized democracy as a gatekeeper for "not yet" freedom. Chiasmic crossings reconstructed social confidence through a reflection of personal—often erotically inflected—desire. Anticipatory inversions appeared in *American Renaissance* as latent outcroppings of imagined losses of democratic association with groups as diverse as nineteenth-century writers and early twentieth-century critics, homosexual lovers and working-class movements, Hellenic figures and U.S. fraternal societies. *American Renaissance* gave birth to a perverse form of historical materialism, reworking reality to cooperate with social longing in a dematerialized scripting of the nation through desire.

Matthiessen's attachment to homosocial and homoerotic idealizations also plagued him with assumptions about gender, causing him to see women's inequality as a consequence of their intellectual failures. Three years after publishing *American Renaissance*, he returned to the Samuel Adams School to teach a course on the democratic value of nineteenth-century literature. He left after only one year, seemingly because of his severe disappointment over students who did not fit his ideas about workers. In a memorial essay, Paul Sweezy writes, "He hoped that he would have a chance to teach real workers and was somewhat disappointed when most of the students turned out to be stenographers and salesclerks."[128] Matthiessen's physical retreat from the classroom seems to suggest that having been caught up in an erotic idealization of the industrial working class, he was unable to adequately respond to the structural adjustments of U.S. capitalism during the 1930s. He not only failed to recognize how corporatization had created a professional middle class that relied on a gendered and racialized clerical- and service-sector economy; he also failed to see how the class expectations that he envisioned as a national ideal performed in accordance with the emergent managerial logics of this transformation.[129]

Certainly his ideas about gender seem to have been largely shaped by his overvaluation of homosociality. When ruminating on the promise of Greek love and Bones marriage as a young man, for example, Matthiessen openly exposed what he saw as women's inherent difference: "The reward we reap [from a Bones marriage] is a complete understanding that 'passeth the love of women.' At least that of most women. There are a few of them—if I may judge from my Cl-bmates CBs [Connubial Bliss confessionals] who are capable of the Experience of Truth. Whereas we have perfect Truth as well as love and life abundant."[130] Similarly, his impressions of women at the Samuel Adams School were marred by a vision that he adapted directly from the "d—d mob of scribbling women," Hawthorne found so vexing, writers who knew the inner workings of American life so intimately that he imagined their allegiance to the nation had to be monitored and controlled.

Where he did critically allow for women's contribution to the nation, in his book on Sarah Orne Jewett, for example, he exercised this control by questioning women's intellectual capacity. He credited Jewett with having style but said she lacked substance: "Without style Sarah Jewett's material would be too slight to attract a second glance."[131] He suggestively saw the value of her work as a foil for nativism. In Jewett, Matthiessen identified fears of industrial encroachment that put women on the front lines of nationalist racism. Her regional descriptions took place precisely where he took up his own private residence in a bucolic retreat with Cheney.[132] He deflected the segregating realities of his institutional ideals onto her as a political stance: "People do not know what they lose when they make away with the reserve, the separateness, the sanctity of the front yard of their grandmothers. . . . More things than one may come in without being asked; we Americans had better build more fences than take any away."[133] What he envisioned as a radical inversion of capitalist inequality, a sacred preservation of ideals of truth and unity, mobilized the erotic toward capitalist restructuring. The intersecting frameworks that he variously deployed led him dangerously into sacred spaces where he could take comfort in an abstract ideal of class equality that simultaneously rearticulated lived disparity as a symptom of failed homoerotic intimacy.[134]

Matthiessen's sacred fraternal imaginary in this manifestation constituted the national subject through a series of affective longings for intimate affiliations and backroom retreats for protected negotiations. This psychic spatial formation reflected less a revolutionary retreat from capital's chaos than a model of social adjustment that worked harmoniously with the reproduction of speculative nationalism. Like the transition in the economy he disavowed, Matthiessen's psychic investment in abstract anticipatory values mapped a future of exclusion to absorb disappointment.

On the Periphery of Imagined Recovery

The abstract appeal undergirding Matthiessen's hope that American Studies could create an arena for escaping the harshness of history resonates with a recurring theme in W.E.B. DuBois's autobiographical writing. Across his texts and speeches, DuBois represented himself as in conflict with social scientific standards of scholarly objectivity removed from the "hot reality of real life."[135] Activist social science was for DuBois an intellectual political project of developing theory in the context of action. Activist knowledge production, he argued, could not simply take form "by intuition and emotion, without seeking in the midst of action, the ordered knowledge [generated by] research and tireless observation."[136] On this basis, DuBois critiqued universalism in both general and personal terms.

In his early work, DuBois disparaged "car-window" sociology because he saw university social science as predicated on the internal authority of disciplinary gatekeepers whose views of the world were shaped at a distance from the social experiences of the subjects they purported to explain.[137] Chandan Reddy analyzes DuBois's intervention as a disruptive demonstration of resistance to incorporative violence. Disciplinary removal from social life legitimates the process whereby subjects who have been excluded from framing universal norms and values are ascribed with meanings and expectations that are not of their own making. Progressive universalism enacts a politics of race through denial of actions, meanings, and qualities that exceed the authoritative truths of universalisms. The force of legibility conscripts alternative meanings and values into mandatory liberal assimilation.[138] And, as DuBois repeatedly insisted, White scholars' investment in racial uplift was fundamentally capricious and contingent.

DuBois implicated his early self as willing prey of the imbalanced scholarly authority of racial progressivism. In various instances, he recalled optimistically experimenting with the higher truths of scientific study only to be disordered and dislodged by the harsh realities of racism: "Had it not been for the race problem early thrust upon me and enveloping me, I should have probably been an unquestioning worshipper at the shrine of the social order and economic development into which I was born."[139] In repeatedly framing his materialist historiography in collision with the violent outcomes of universal boundaries, DuBois pointed to the higher "truth" of universal aspiration as a psychosocial weapon of exclusionary racial formation. It is the ideal of liberalism that becomes a justificatory apparatus in the actual practices of racialization. The imagined and expectant optimism of racial progressivism serves a dual legitimating function for speculative nationalism. First, it confirms through the delayed justice of "not yet" freedom the borders, security, and common causes of a suppositiously bounteous national democracy. Second, the promise of an ideal becomes a means of legitimating the violence that is necessary for turning fictions into reality. DuBois witnessed "truth" as lynching, murder, and starvation; the repeated outcomes of racial reactions he narrated as outcomes of economic readjustments.

It is no small thing that DuBois's scholarly idealism broke along lines of social order and economic development. Confronted with a past that repeatedly erupted in new elaborations as present concerns, he narrated himself late in his career as having been tricked into complicity with universalist denials: "I regarded it as axiomatic that the world wanted to learn the truth and if the truth was sought with even approximate accuracy and painstaking devotion, the world would gladly support the effort. This was, of course, but a young man's idealism, not by any means false, but also never universally true."[140] In the disruption is a necessary refusal of both truth and fiction, a holding of human difference that creates an impasse from which emerges revolutionary consciousness. DuBois's revolutionary proposition that somebody must try to make historical facts clear was rooted in economic booms and crisis recovery. The "fact" he most clarified was that the progress of U.S. American optimism balanced on the backs and dreams of the "Negro" working class—a category imperial in scope.

This dynamic, of course, is the organizing theme of *Black Reconstruction in America*. Interestingly, however, DuBois later said that the Reconstruction era was less critical to Black subordination than the boom years of the late nineteenth and early twentieth centuries: "The age of triumph for Big Business, for Industry, consolidated and organized on a world-wide scale, and run by White capital with colored labor."[141] Telling a materialist history of this and other worldwide speculative movements challenged DuBois's scientific sensibility. On observing race riots, he wrote, "Facts, in social science, I realized were elusive things: emotions, loves, hates, were facts; and they were facts in the souls and minds of the scientific student, as well as the persons studied. . . . There was so much of decisive truth missing that any story I told would be woefully incomplete."[142] DuBois's extensive autobiographical writing, and the way he episodically repeated and reframed the same story, refrains, and ideas in different contexts, was, from this perspective, a method of materialist historiography through which to more fully engage how the elusive facts of the soul intervene in and are shaped by world historical economic transformation. Through this form, he called attention to the ways that people caught in racializing economic equations necessarily can and do consistently intervene with life-affirming struggles to reshape historical odds.

To this effect, DuBois framed his investment in sociology as taking shape in speculative circumstances. He wrote of his work during the boom years: "My work assumed . . . a certain tingling of risk; what the 'Captain of Industry' of that day was experiencing in 'kick' from money changing, railway consolidation and corporation floating, I was, in what appeared to be on a larger scale, essaying in the relations of men of daily life."[143] DuBois spoke in an economic language that revealed the contingency of exploitation on the repression and compliance of racialized people. It also implicates knowledge production as a medium of exchange within speculative relationships. DuBois defined his approach to sociology as "the attempt to measure the element of Chance in human conduct"—an effort, that is, to identify where and when opportunities arise for disrupting the grand narratives of racialized capitalism.[144]

DuBois wrote of his experience during the Depression: "The economic boom and depression in the United States were necessarily for all Americans a time of heart searching and intellectual stock-taking. I was nervous and restless; in addition to all my activities, I ranged the country from North to South. . . . I had to be part of the revolution through which the world was going and to feel in my own soul the scars of its battle. Still racial injustice prevailed."[145] In *Black Reconstruction in America*, he argued that 9 million enslaved people developed a revolutionary consciousness out the revolutionary acts that logically resulted from being caught in the cross hairs of a civil war in which neither camp regarded their interests. Like these slaves who freed themselves in the struggle against human depravity, he narrated his own coming into revolutionary consciousness as the logical result of asymmetries of power through which White nationalists accumulate authority and institutional spaces *and* assume control of the resources and life chances available to others.

The declarative "still" that gave DuBois pause was both predictive and imperative. It pointed intertextually to the way he regarded race as a register of the social consequences of unbridled optimism. Optimism revealed itself as the capriciousness of Whiteness in DuBois's rendition of the early twentieth-century boom. While industry flourished, he noted, Black culture, art, and *The Crisis* slowly folded. His focus on racialized suffering as part of the boom called attention to the fundamental economic and political restructuring that takes place prior to crises. Periods of growth are in part constituted through racial readjustments. The race-based experience of cutbacks and repression foreshadows as well the broader economic crisis.

In retrospective explanation of the work he took up in Philadelphia conducting a social study of "the Negro problem," DuBois wrote, "The world was thinking wrong about race, because it did not know. The ultimate evil was stupidity. The cure for it was knowledge based on scientific investigation."[146] Staking a claim on materially grounded empirical study of social systems, DuBois inverted accusations of Black pathology as symptoms of White power. The degraded place of Black people in the city, he demonstrated, was the outcome of a long historical development. Scientific study, which meant for him a materialist investigation of the historical forces in relation to which the facts of society are produced, stands as a revolutionary act in his autobiography. By mapping the truth of race as a historical development, he aimed to break the nation of its dependence on repression by exposing race as a concept designed for the protection of power and wealth.

Elsewhere and often, despite consistent struggle against incredible odds, DuBois repeated, "What was true in 1910 was still true in 1940 and will be true in 1970."[147] This prophecy was also a revolutionary command. It was couched in the text by the collective struggles of "Negroes joined with Negroes [who] co-operated with Negroes in order to fight the extension of . . . segregation and to move toward better conditions."[148] Activist historiography in this framing became a call to arms, to use shared struggle as a counter-force against racialized futurity. Black education, a grounded investigation of how and why U.S. Americans create, ritually repeat, and perpetually reinvent the vocabularies of race to fit changing economic terrains, was an activist intention to produce emancipatory rupture.

The crux of DuBois's autobiography, emphasized as self-remembrance, is his schooling in the ways that race is perpetually reminted to sustain economic booms and recoveries. He situates his years at Fisk and Harvard within a speculative cultural imaginary: "Wealth was God. Everywhere men sought wealth and especially in America there was extravagant living; everywhere the poor planned to be rich and the rich planned to be richer; everywhere wider, bigger, higher, better things were set down as inevitable."[149] Simultaneously, "Science was becoming religion" within the academy, a phrase that in proximity to the deification of wealth points to impenetrable disciplinary narratives as a corruption of science whereby facts and reason fall victim to predetermined expectations.[150] In contrast, he inscribes himself as coming into political consciousness against the fantasies of White optimism. His was a sensory education. He looked out windows and saw segregation. He felt "scars upon [his] soul" in response to the "recurrent horror during [his] college days" of "seventeen hundred Negroes [who] were lynched."[151] He heard "sorrow songs sung with primitive beauty and grandeur."[152] And in the call and struggle he challenged the fictions of White universalism with a materialist focus on the racializing conditions that hold up the illusions of speculative power and privilege, again and again and again.

Textual repetition mirrors how speculative history episodically doubles into itself. DuBois repeated the scene at Harvard as the backdrop of his first years teaching. When he returned to the profession in the midst of the Depression, he wrote an historiography of postslavery reconstruction, a warning and call to fight Jim Crow segregation in the early twentieth century. The boom of the twenties became during the 1940s a call to divest from institutional promises and privileges that were contingent on delayed racial incorporation. Through repetition, the revolutionary imperative of DuBois's sensory science revealed itself as a rallying call against assimilative prescriptions for racial uplift that transformed Black dreams into White wealth. Based on the historical materialist recognition that there is no winning in an institutional and economic system that parasitically depends on keeping down Blackness, DuBois wrote off the fight against segregation with a radical proposal for education. Divestment from speculative nationalism's racializing returns, he suggested, required breaking from uplift progressivism and the "not yet" freedom of industrial education, which was funded precariously by White philanthropy. Thus his proposals for Black education imaginatively translocated the possibility for plural democracy beyond the exclusionary fraternity of the existing nation-state.

Transhistorical Democratic Fraternity Redux

Although the existing historical record is inconclusive about whether or not DuBois was ever officially a Prince Hall Mason, his approach to history and to cooperative social transformation was certainly built in association with the brotherhood. Susan Gilman tracks these connections in great detail, noting in particular DuBois's participation in the Black history project led by Arthur Schomburg and John Bruce, both of whom were noted Prince Hall initiates. In Gilman's synthesis, the Masonic influence resonates in DuBois's capacious approach to historical evidence.[153] The evidentiary basis of his work moves from empirical study to mystical proposition, from occult collectivism to refused local knowledge, from unconscious experience to transhistorical revolutionary inference. The opening of *Darkwater* crystallizes Masonic thought as a commitment to cooperatively building inclusive, lived social democracy. As Charles H. Wesley has argued, DuBois's "Credo" replicates in tone and form George Crawford's rendition of the Prince Hall credo.[154] Like the Prince Hall doctrine, DuBois's rendition is premised on Black Nationalist politics. For Prince Hall Masons, Black nationalism was a "door of benevolence, securely tiled against the unworthy, but open wide to men of good rapport, whether Ayran [sic] or Hottentots."[155] In his 1896 version of the Credo, DuBois rendered the Mason's "corporate adventure in universal brotherhood" an effect of historical circumstances that positioned all people "black and brown and white" to engage their souls around "the possibility of infinite development" in opposition to those "who spit in the faces of the fallen, strike them that cannot strike again, believe the worst and work to prove it."[156] His framing mirrored the Masonic articulation of humanity as "potentially God's other self," and it prefigured the type of joint sacrifice that Roosevelt called for thirty years later in the context of the Great Depression.

Unlike the New Deal's racial compromises, however, for DuBois race figured as a point of pride from which to "scorn injustice to other selves." Race was a foundation from which to transform structures that propagated class division, to eradicate militarism, and to bring about material changes that would allow "Liberty" to all beings: "The space to stretch their arms and their souls, the right to breathe and the right to vote, the freedom to choose their friends, enjoy the sunshine, and ride on the railroads, uncursed by color; thinking, dreaming, working as they will in a kingdom of beauty and love."[157] Tellingly indicative of the Credo's inclusionary intention, Wesley says, Black people often hung it in their homes and schools assigned children to commit it to memory.

When George Crawford persuaded Tuskegee to award DuBois an honorary degree in 1930, DuBois revisited the spirit and themes of his Credo in his speech, "Education and Work." His call for educational transformation beckoned silently to the material roles that Black fraternal societies had assumed in response to Black people's economic exclusion. As he noted in a 1906 study of Black economic cooperation, fraternal societies figured heavily in feeding both the bodies and the souls of Black people: "They furnish past times from the monotony of work, a field for ambition and intrigue, a chance for parade, and insurance against misfortune."[158] In 1897, he estimated that 70 percent of Black adults living in Philadelphia's seventh ward were members of fraternal, mutual benefit, or other insurance societies.[159] His appeal in 1930 to "take some definite and intelligent part in the production and goods and in the furnishing of human services and in the democratic distribution of income so as to build civilization, encourage initiative, reward effort, and support life" extended the insurance and mutual aid functions of Black fraternities into general social cooperation.[160]

The economic depression weighed heavily in DuBois's speech as a demand for counter–social revolution: "We are on the threshold of an economic expansion such as the world never saw before."[161] Drawing from the lessons of history, he stated, "The transition period between slavery and freedom is a dangerous and critical one."[162] In this context, he called attention to the failures of gradual uplift and deferred rights. The experiment in industrial education had integrated Black workers into economic relations in service to capital at the expense of failed uplift: "The Negro college, its teachers, students and graduates, have not yet comprehended the age in which they live: the tremendous organization of industry, capital and credit which today form as a superorganization dominating and ruling the universe, subordinating to its ends government, democracy,

religion, education and social philosophy."[163] In discussing industrial education, he implied that "the merciless mechanism which enslaves us," was the
promise of "well-being" that inscribed Black workers into labor on subordinating terms.[164] Students were educated to assume liberal dreams and optimism
without the material basis for fulfillment: "We are graduating young men and
women with an intense and overwhelming appetite for wealth and no reason-
able way of gratifying it, no philosophy for counteracting it."[165] Cooperative fraternity in this context became for DuBois a means to dismantle and replace the
predatory elements of the existing economy.

To this end, DuBois transmuted abstract fraternal ideals into practical
principles for social transformation. He delineated the "Ideal of Poverty" as a
mechanism for material redistribution: It "is in direct antithesis of the present
American ideal of Wealth [that] no person should have an income which he does
not personally need; nor wield a power solely for his own whim."[166] In combination with the ideal of work worth doing and knowledge, his focus on material
dispensation highlighted sacrifice as a collective obligation to deal with the situation in which Black life had become "embodied Dissatisfaction"; to "increase
abiding satisfaction for the mass of our people, and for all people, someone must
sacrifice something of his own happiness. This is a duty only to those who recognize it as a duty. The larger the number ready to sacrifice, the smaller the total
sacrifice necessary."[167] The "real and definite surrender of personal ease and satisfaction" registered in the speech as a initiation into the occult possibility of a
collective democracy.[168] DuBois both reassured and rebuked the graduates: "But
with the death of your happiness may easily come increased happiness and satisfaction and fulfillment for other people—strangers, unborn babes, uncreated
worlds. If this is not sufficient incentive, never try it—remain hogs."[169]

This was a call for a fundamental divestment of the hopes and promises
of White liberal nationalism. DuBois later recognized the challenge it posed:
"American Negroes have always feared with perfect fear their eventual expulsion from America. . . . There is no place where they can go today and not be
subject to worse caste and greater disabilities from the dominant White impe-
rialistic world than they suffer here today."[170]

In an unpublished study of the effect of the New Deal on Black people between 1933 and 1936, DuBois painted a grim picture of the promise of
recovery. First he found that the work available to Black workers was inadequate
to their "gifts and training" and that their income insufficiently "support[ed]
healthy families according to the standards of modern culture."[171] Second, the
New Deal reorganization of the economy gave Black workers little protection
from substandard wages, treatment as disposable labor, and educational disenfranchisement. The solution to deferred racial justice, he argued, could not be
located in the "development of upper classes who seek to exploit workers" nor in
"individual genius."[172] That is, DuBois saw as racializing readjustments both the
speculative recovery logic that sought to reignite the economy through incor-

poration of exploited people into formerly denied opportunities and the type of cultural separation into a set of exclusive ideals like those Matthiessen desired.

His analysis thus inverted the fear marking Roosevelt's introduction to the New Deal. When the president declared, "We have nothing to fear but fear itself," he assuaged public panic with a paternalistic promise to deliver the nation back to an era of prosperity. When DuBois discussed Black people's fear of divesting from White society, he cautioned against buying into the presidential decree. Instead he mitigated doubt by forging transhistorical solidarity between those who continued to suffer under the New Deal and those who had suffered under slavery. He wrote of the circumstances preceding the revolutionary chance of Reconstruction in *Black Reconstruction in America* as defined by the fact that the only legal protection and information available to enslaved people was held by slave masters. Under constrained conditions, available to enslaved peoples' capacity to engage in political action was mediated by their dependence on the slave owners' world.[173] In drawing a rhetorical comparison between plantations and the nation-state's promise of recovery, DuBois implicated his own era as one pregnant with not yet recognized revolutionary potential. To ignite this potential, he reiterated a fraternal credo.

DuBois had contracted with Alain Locke for the American Association for Adult Education to publish his analysis of the New Deal's false promise of Black racial uplift. When it was rejected for publication, DuBois reissued his "Basic American Negro Creed" in the conclusion to his 1944 autobiography, where he called for racial planning in jobs, education, and health; common and cooperative ownership of industry; and the use of taxes to equalize wealth in order to achieve material equality as the basis for a living plural democracy. He repeated the ultimate purpose of cooperative racial movements as "the abolition of all racial distinctions."[174] Incorporative violence and White liberal philanthropy stood in his analysis as roadblocks to democracy. The challenge in this regard was where to plant roots for a free democratic society:

> The difficulty was to know how, without revolution, violence, and dislocation of human civilization, the wrong could be righted and human culture started again upon its upward path. One thing, at any rate was clear to me in my particular problem, and that was that a continued agitation which had for its object simply free entrance into the present economy of the world, that looked at political rights as an end in itself rather than as a method of reorganizing the state; and that expected civil rights and legal judgment to re-establish freedom on a broader firmer basis, was not so much wrong as short-sighted; that the democracy which we had been asking for in political life must sooner or later replace the tyranny which now dominated industrial life.[175]

The answer he proposed was institutional transformation and a dramatic rethinking of the end goals of Black education.

Democratic Translocation

The Masonic impulse was the backdrop of DuBois's "Evolving Program for Negro Freedom." In 1944 he explained his agenda as combining scientific inquiry with organized Black action, "*in close cooperation, to secure the survival of the Negro race, until the cultural development of America and the world is willing to recognize Negro freedom* [italics in original]."[176] The deferral expressed in the "until" of this plan was less temporal than imaginatively spatial. Against the exploitation, discrimination, cultural biases, and material exclusions hidden in the gift of nationalist inclusion, DuBois proposed that Black education become a site for living toward actually existing human freedom.

According to Susan Searls Giroux, DuBois regarded education as one of the few nonviolent sites from which to plan and enact a democracy that was predicated on fulfilling unmet human needs. Giroux foregrounds DuBois's understanding of the violent disappointment that accompanies failed promises of recovery: "People feel cheated and they burn with resentment."[177] In a talk delivered at Fisk University on the occasion of his fiftieth anniversary of graduation, DuBois proclaimed,

> There is only one thing for civilized human beings to do when faced with such a problem. That is to learn the facts, to reason out their connection and to plan the future; to know the truth; to arrange it logically and to contrive a better way. In some way, as all intelligent men acknowledge, we must in the end, produce for the satisfaction of human needs and distribute in accordance with human want. To contend that this cannot be done is to face the Impossible Must. The blind cry of reaction on the one hand, which says that we cannot have a planned economy, and therefore, must not try; and the cry of blood which says that only by force can selfishness be curbed are equally wrong. . . . The reformation of the world is beginning with agony of soul and strain of muscle.[178]

In his "Evolving Program," DuBois called attention to the limits that educational asset stripping places on life-enhancing uses of learning. Public schools were developed and funded according to the ideal that shared learning "is the best and surest path to democracy."[179] Yet under the cultural influence of social segregation, funding for schools was systematically diverted away from democracy for private purposes. Thus DuBois identified a need for building alternative infrastructures out of the conditions created by oppression. To do this, he reframed segregation not as a choice or a political goal but as an historical situation that created a chance for Black thinkers to engage in radical world remaking. Segregation was an historical fact, DuBois argued, that would not be amplified and further entrenched by sustaining and constructing separate institutional spaces for liberatory Black education. Rather, he argued, the economic conditions under which the Black struggle was waged demanded a carefully thought out economic agenda predicated on careful negotiating of segregation as means to establish a baseline for freedom. By this he meant "*full economic, political and social equality with American citizens, in thought, expression and action, with no discrimination based on race and color* [italics in the original]."[180] Creating freedom out of segregated spaces, he said, "did not establish a new segregation; it did not advocate for segregation as the final solution of the race problem; exactly the contrary; but it did face the facts and faced them with thoughtfully mapped effort."[181] For it was only beyond the logics of speculative liberalism that the fullness of life could be treated with dignity.

In the Fisk speech, DuBois advanced an educational curriculum in resistance to instrumentalist learning. His plan entailed teaching "youth what the world is and what it means" and leaving until after graduation "the technique of earning a living in any way one can and wishes."[182] Elsewhere he proclaimed, "Education that trains men simply for earning a living is not education"; rather, he saw it as a means of claiming life against the odds. Life, as DuBois defined it, was living up to the Credo's potential to recreate democracy from the ground up: "Life is the fullest, most complete enjoyment of the possibilities of human existence. It is the development and broadening of the feelings and emotions, through sound and color, line and form. . . . Here roots the rise of the Joy of Living . . . the ever widening realms of thought, in increasing circles of apprehended and interpreted Truth."[183]

In contradistinction to the retreat into death by scholars like Matthiessen, DuBois anticipated early on that plural democracy in the New Deal would not come freely. It would have to be taken, he argued at Tuskegee, through organized collective action. Adopting the cooperation of the occult, he said, "We are going to force ourselves in by organized far-seeing effort—by outthinking and outflanking the owners of the world today who are too drunk with their own arrogance and power successfully to oppose us, if we think we can learn and do."[184] Elsewhere DuBois harkened back to the life-affirming act of institutional creation as contributing to the unfulfilled promise of Radical Reconstruction. During that era, he said, educators "came not to keep the Negroes in their place, but to raise them out of the defilement of the places where slavery had swallowed them. The colleges they founded were social settlements. . . . In actual formal content their curriculum was doubtless old-fashioned, but in educational power it was supreme, for it was the contact of living souls."[185] Fraternal promise erupts in the mysticism of the soul, calling for a plural democracy that begins from the needs and freedom dreams of disinherited people whose cooperation opens the world to realizing democracy, not through "lifting the lowly, but [through] the unchaining of the awakened mighty."[186]

PART III
COLLECTIVITIES

We are now living in the product of corporations' masquerade of legal personhood. Advanced financialization is an effect of Fourteenth Amendment theft. Corporate personhood has emboldened companies to reorganize the economy around categories of financing, risk, debt, and leverage. Codification of corporate persons' rights to buy governance through the "free speech" of unlimited campaign contributions under *Citizens United v. Federal Election Commission* (2010) is only one aspect of the contemporary condition whereby capital works with the state to orient all production and the entirety of social life around financial profit making. This phase of speculative normalization is organized through the conquest of power by financial ideologues, but it also penetrates social institutions. Social goods like education, health care, and long-term security have been remade into personal investments. In effect, financialized capitalism is exercised through states via new expectations of conduct that call on individuals to meet human needs by marketing themselves as autonomous enterprises.

The worldwide rationality of financialization enjoins all people to inhabit a speculative persona. It calls on workers, neighbors, and nations to vie with one another in generalized competition. Mainstreamed securitization results in a culture of heightened distrust. Surveillance and audits focus attention on safety and efficiency. Heightened monitoring reassures corporations, shareholders, and the public that economic and social risks are under control. The financial world has repackaged political, economic, and social equations to conjure into being a nation-state that is designed to secure society for market interests. The financial universe inverts national democracy and the common good. Financial power now governs by proxy, orchestrating nationalism to conscript subjects into the idioms and meanings of economic instrumentalism in a vision of human action and relationships shaped only by a web of market-based exchanges. Extreme financialized capital is the result of decades of deregulation enabled by the corporate conquest of democratic infrastructures. Economically, the normalization of speculation as the foundation of the twenty-first-century global economy has produced severe polarization between the rich and the poor. Socially, the financial takeover of governance takes form through the individualization of social relations at the expense of collective solidarities.

The chapters in this section call attention to financialized capitalism's masked dependence on race as a conduit for social individualization. Postracial multiculturalism and economic bubbles and crises go hand in hand because the logic of liberal individuation conditions people to think about race and gender as obligations to overcome structural inequality through individual market negotiation. Under extreme financialization, the speculative social contract of "not yet" freedom makes national participation a contingency of individualization. Disenfranchised citizens are positioned to prove their personal worth by demonstrating their rational participation in market competition. When state resources disappear, the neoliberal world reorder declares that the citizen must invest in the failure to keep the economy afloat. In the case of the early twenty-first-century housing bubble, the conscriptive imperative to consume entailed a life-compromising reordering of race, space, and power to absorb the surplus optimism of Wall Street speculators. Conscripting people who were opportunistically dispossessed into nationalism as citizen-debtors created both the necessary preconditions for economic expansion and a release valve for crisis recovery when the bubble collapsed.

The global financial meltdown of 2008 made it apparent that racial differentiation is no longer fully sufficient for absorbing higher volumes of risk and injustice. In the post–Civil Rights context, what first appears to make what Lauren Berlant terms "crisis ordinariness" seem unique is that populations who generally take the privileges and protections of nationalism for granted have been burdened with circumstances of debt and deferral.[1] The general promise of nationalist prosperity is now a form of psychic cruelty. Prolonged decades of mutually constitutive economic, social, environmental, and global crises have produced a cognitive rupture. Socialized risk is not new. It is a manifestation of the unresolved injustices of genocidal violence, dispossession, enslavement, and villainy that have returned from the past as cumulative consequences of speculative nationalism. Although the effects of the 2008 collapse have been global in scale, there is a great deal to be learned from the U.S. context about capital's dependence on the nation-state form for speculative renewal and regeneration. The example of the United States is not universal. However, because of its determining role in the global economy, it serves as an important example of the frantic cultural and political measures that financialized states employ to incorporate virtually everything into speculative promises of "not yet" freedom. Now is the time for people who are interested in fundamental antiracist social change to invest in a different form of collective optimism.

Speculative nationalism is predicated on trust. I have argued in this book that the power of the nationalist promise of "not yet" freedom is that it binds an ever expanding pool of potential investors into the endless stream of necessary buyers that speculators depend on to hedge their bets. From the perspective of those whose freedom dreams are appropriated and rearticulated into alignment with nationalist visions, accepting the bargain of liberal incorporation requires trust in the nation to fulfill its promises to "official" citizens at whatever cost to others. Trust is a hierarchically organized reciprocal relationship of expectation. In exchange for the citizen's loyalty, the nation promises security. The situation of trust is tenuous because it is always oriented toward the future. Through trust, citizens abandon autonomy for self-protection with the expectation that the nation-state will take control and behave in their interest. Trust relationships are preconditioned by commonsense assumptions of fairness, honesty, and benevolence. Yet a trust is a legally binding inscription into a relationship of apprehension. It is precisely the sense of distrust that formalized binds attempt to control that encourages people to fear their neighbors and place their faith in the protective promises of the securitized security state. In this regard, trust-based optimism limits the field of possibilities for future action into legally enforceable obligations.

Like legal trust, the optimism of speculative nationalism is an exertion of will. Nationalist promises of "not yet" freedom construct emancipation as an individual achievement that is realized in the contradiction of time binding citizens to unspoken exertions of patrimonial obligation. Chapter 5 explores the public and financial anxiety that optimistic trust entails through the lens of the U.S. housing crisis. To establish trust, speculative nationalism persistently absorbs and rearticulates collectively generated freedom dreams into promises of liberal individualism to be sealed through distanced identification with consumptive citizen ideals. When revolutionary collective movements call for radical equality, they often build their demands not just from an optimism of a binding trust but from the insights gained from lived solidarities. Collectively lived freedom entails more than what is imaginable in submission to liberal state authority.

People who claim life in and against the odds tend to build optimism on hope rather than trust. One of the reasons that festivals like the one that is the topic of Chapter 6 are so important for understanding justice is that they help to shake nationalism out of commonsense assumptions. When people take to the streets on May Day in Minneapolis's Powderhorn Park each year, they *enact* freedom through the play of poetry and puppetry, affirming life by loosening attachments to everyday norms. Collectivities come into being through the art and hope of making do. When May Day performers explored the theme of "life as we know it now" in the 2012 festival, they shared radical propositions with antiracist world-remaking potential. Life-affirming freedom means coming to terms with our inevitable dependence on others. When we think of human life as interdependent rather than independent, we act not out of the supremacy of sympathy but from the necessity of solidarity. We act because we are. We act because an injury to a part hurts the whole. Differentiating logics do not hold up in life-affirming justice. There is no such thing as a subhuman life, only values, institutions, and actions that designate life as dispensable. The radical proposition that justice requires something akin to love does not mean that love always gets it right. In fact, vulnerability is the condition of quite often getting it wrong.

What makes this risk different from speculative risk is timing. The immediacy of life-affirming action depends on "making do with what we have."[2] This is very different from paying dues after drawing on credit to buy what we do not yet have. Making do is not settling for scraps; rather, it is an act of cobbling life-affirming relationships into being by refusing injustice and deferral. Optimism garnered through acts of making do emerges from conjoined efforts to make sense of circumstances that are not of our own design, using whatever materials and opportunities are currently on hand to nurture and cultivate freedom in the present. First, making do works against external impositions of speculative optimism. The hope for freedom in making do circulates from existing ideas and resources that people have at their immediate disposal. In practical circumstances, hope often looks like recycling, repurposing, and rethinking need, survival, desire, and freedom as interrelated to material and ecological environments. As a cognitive disposition, making do may mean rescinding attachments to autonomous authorship and political worship in favor of the common genius of collective activity. In the doing, hope manifests. My action is my hope. Hopeful actions express themselves as personal insights, through sharing others' struggles, and in the daily collaborations people depend on to get by. To risk through hope in collective desire is to seize an opportunity to live toward freedom now.

Imagine hope—not later but manifestly—as the glue of social life. Where does this take us? This type of question too often leads back to the future. Speculative nationalism connects everyone it touches in systems of violence and power that perpetually return us to scenes of injustice. When the past erupts into new waves of crisis, the ruptures in collective consciousness and institutional function call on those interested in fundamental social change and justice to honor and build on refused struggles for freedom. The way people are conditioned to want predictability so often refuses to reckon with this call to imagine freedom now.

The immediate in life-affirming collective figurations is not a temporality of stasis, suspension, or impasse. It is transformative, changing, unpredictable, and never the same because making do is a transformative action. To make do requires the generative reworking of contexts and capacities in ways that nourish and change existing institutions, structures, and relations. Making do is a proclivity that extends beyond sustainability. Making do is not living with it; it is *making* something out of the messy contradictions, confusions, and, yes, even desires and delights that differentially entangle humans in complicated webs of power and privilege. Collectivity means that every action is always tied to other actions. I act because we act. I act because I must. I must because we hope. The call of life-affirming collective envision-acting is to draw on a capacious storehouse of action as a repository of possibilities with which to make do and, hopefully, make freedom anew.

Home Ownership Hope and the Sellout of the State

Predatory Nationalism, Racialized Risk,
Life under Terms of Last Resort

In the archetypal case, at the top of the market, everyone has turned into a
believer and is fully committed, leaving no unconverted skeptics left to buy from
the first new seller. That was, in essence, what happened in 2008.
—ALAN GREENSPAN, 2013

Move that bus!!!
—*EXTREME MAKEOVER HOME EDITION*, 2012

How you gonna tell somebody to move / When they can NAME the last 100
generations / of kin that farmed that particular plot of the goddesses' green soil
/ Fertilized with the bones and blood / Of they own people for so long / It may
as well be forever? / How you gon tear down a whole neighborhood / In a town
fulla homeless people?
—*SPIRIT HOUSE*, 2013

The Scene of Exchange

The story of racialized risk in the U.S. mortgage market has come to define the historical mythography of financialization. In familiar refrains
of racialized deflection, the immediate response to the 2008 meltdown
appeared as an export-import trade in the category of "toxic mortgages." The
explanatory specter of borrower contagion spread through a signifying spiral of
financial, political, social, and cultural exchanges that ended up blaming racialized subprime mortgage holders for contaminating the entire global economy.
Now, however, after a half-decade of deflated dreams and diminished denials,
a strange ideological inversion has left even the architects of financialization
rehearsing subtle Marxian analyses of "accumulation by dispossession."[1] Former Federal Reserve chairman Alan Greenspan, for example, has staked his
recovery of neoclassical (non)regulatory models on dismissing the bubble as
pure speculation.[2] Early on he conceded: "The big demand was not so much on
the part of the borrowers as it was on the part of the suppliers who were giv-

ing loans which most people couldn't afford,"[3] and he argues implicitly that in order to fuel speculators' insatiable appetite for fictitious capital, opportunities for exploitation had to be created.

The world of financial abstraction effaces the racializing contours of fiscal practice. But the racialization of risk remains evident in the historical geography of "not yet" freedom that returned once again during the foreclosure crisis. Financialization of U.S. home ownership—the bundling, repackaging, and speculative exchange of unaffordable predatory loans as securities—depended on the incorporative violence of nationalist fantasy. Shadow banking emerged from the shadows of decades of social dispossession. In the era of privatization, the nation framed home ownership as the most viable path to economic stability and social prosperity.[4] Subprime loans were the raw material for a global conveyor belt of investment products. Private loans were melded into mortgage-backed securities (MBSs), purchased from lenders and grouped with other loans secured by borrowers' promises of future repayment. Investors responded to the risk of default and foreclosure not as a warning but as an opportunity to produce even more volatile securities. Financialized mortgage debt institutionalized preexisting racialized class hierarchies.[5] The process of primitive accumulative within the mortgage economy depended on convincing those on the margins of the economy to believe in the freedom of American home ownership. Expanded credit opportunities in turn inflated the price of houses, which led to the invention of more and more ways to gamble on leveraged risk. Credit default swaps (CDSs), for example, made it possible for investors to bet on aggregate future payments even it they had not directly invested in the underlying security.[6]

Feeding speculative hunger for steady yield depended on creating a stream of fees and investment returns across the financial industry.[7] To do so, mortgage lenders looked to people who were already dispossessed by decades of state privatization and spatially concentrated social asset stripping.[8] Speculation in this context was predicated on the production of new conditions for dispossession. Discriminatory incorporation into American home ownership inscribed preexisting racialized inequality in financial circuits as opportunities for expropriation. The outcome of preying on the hopes and struggles of people whose limited opportunities had been structured by long legacies of inequality were lost homes, lost wealth, lost health, and lost opportunities.

To be clear, the economic, social, cultural, and political costs of the early twenty-first-century housing bubble have yet to be fully tallied and understood. What is known is that people whose ancestors were cornered historically by speculators have been disproportionately positioned to absorb the costs of the housing crisis. Between 2007 and 2102, 12.5 million homes went into foreclosure.[9] For people in any situation, the numbers are grave. For groups that face a twenty-seven-year high in unemployment (16.2 percent of African Americans and 12.9 percent of Latinos compared with 9 percent of whites) and who are disproportionately challenged by conditions of poverty (24.6 percent of African

Americans and 23.2 percent of Latinos compared with 8.6 percent of whites), the numbers are catastrophic.[10] Between 2007 and 2009, 2.5 million home foreclosures were completed, and African Americans and Latinos experienced them at higher rates.[11] Early in the collapse, economists estimated direct losses from subprime mortgages among people of color to be $164 to $213 billion.[12] Now, when accounting for spillover losses related to property devaluation in neighborhoods with high rates of foreclosure, minority neighborhoods face losses of $1.1 trillion in home equity. Add to this the strains on local governments caused by lost taxes and increased costs associated with vacated properties.[13] Foreclosures are bad for health, as has been documented in higher rates of depression and suicide attempts in highly foreclosed neighborhoods and in general self-economic rationing of access to medical care.[14]

Mortgage predation was also gendered. During the 1990s, only one in fifteen women were independent home owners; during the early years of the bubble, they were one in five. During the upswing of the housing bubble, women were 32 percent more likely to receive subprime loans than men and 41 percent more likely to receive high-cost loans (interest rates above 9 percent). In 2006, although women held only 30 percent of U.S. mortgages, they carried 38.8 percent of the nation's subprime loans. Even when measuring in the same income bracket, women were 46 percent more likely to be sold predatory subprime loans. Some studies have found that Latina women were 177 percent more likely than white men with similar incomes to receive subprime loans whereas African American women were 256 percent more likely to be predatory targets.[15]

Lopsided racialized and gendered impacts were predetermined in the ways that Wall Street repackaged injuries of social exclusion as financial opportunities to charge higher fees and interest rates.[16] Fraud and deception were contributing factors, but the necessary conditions for recreating race and gender as conduits for future dispossession were rooted in the culture of speculative nationalism as the uneven organization of time, space, and power created by centuries of deferred and delayed democratic freedom. In its most pernicious form, twenty-first-century speculative nationalism transformed the tentative freedom of minority inclusion into affective highs for traders at a distance. In the abstraction, investors cast "nets" under wagers by betting on the payment of mortgages and by speculating on low-income home owners' likely misfortunes.

The Form of Transfer

A housing bubble is a contradictory image. A house is an object weighted and embedded in physical geography. A bubble is the inflationary result of investors riding the high of exploded prices. For people who have been systematically displaced, uprooted, and distanced by repeated episodes of speculative fury in the United States, investment in a house signifies heavily as the desire for stability, rootedness, relationships, and neighborhood. The image of a bubble connotes a fantastical formulation that floats those basic needs beyond the normal reach of many. People who live with the legacy of "not yet" freedom do not enter markets with good timing (when prices are low), with historical advantage (access to resources and markets), or with privileged purchasing power (capital, savings, favorable loans, and fair credit). Desperation and destitution were foreshadowed in the housing bubble from the moment speculators saw historical disadvantage as an opportunity to prey on the "credit risks" of the economically marginalized.

Mortgage predation was an effect of the neoliberal sublime, an attenuated aesthetic experience leveraged by reverence for the greatness of market fundamentalism. The huge credit expansion was an effort to create predictability in a world of uncertainty, a neoliberal effort to conquer the fundamental uncertainty of the economic universe's sublime and unreachable will. Decades of democratic regression into free-marketeers' economism pushed the U.S. populace onto a cultural cliff with no safety net. During this period, many people were left hanging with limited resources to feed their hopes for life affirmation. Wages stagnated. Jobs and benefits disappeared. Basic infrastructures for long-term security, health, and education were privatized and constricted. The middle class absorbed lost wages and opportunities through credit expansion.[17] Many drew on their homes as sources of income.[18] People living on the margins of "not yet" freedom were brought into the fold through the drama of deregulation.[19] After state usury laws were dismantled in the 1980s, creditors used the language of reparation to create new conditions for disenfranchisement. Lenders "democratized" credit to fold the poor into neoliberal freedom for higher prices. Credit expansion layered what Marx called "secondary forms of exploitation" onto already existing low wages, leaving people working as much to pay debts as to survive. The tethers of credit scoring empowered financial institutions to extend credit "to a broader spectrum of consumers" using variances in creditworthiness to pass competitive market costs "through to borrowers."[20]

Value in this inverse economic equation was produced through financial speculation, risk management, and the circulation of money, all of which were contingent on an ever expanding pool of buyers to complete the double sale of an optimistic exchange. Hoping to buy low and sell high, speculators anchored their optimism in peoples' unmet needs for shelter and stability. Risk scoring in this context was a calculated endeavor to repackage systematic deferrals of access and resources into diversified pools of potential payments. Securitization balanced on a system of valuation in which a single home owner's capacity for repayment was less of a focus than a collective debt. Mortgage brokers fed the fire with predation and occasional fraud. Loans were bundled into complicated securities. Tranches were sliced for geographic diversity. A financial product intimately enmeshed the risks of buyers who were segregated spatially into a single exchangeable abstraction. Moreover, obscure and deceptive securities ratings made the racial signifier of subprime mortgages into a sign of oppressed people's continued victimization.[21]

For poor people who were and were not targets of high-rate loans, subprime mortgages demarcated another episode of negotiation through which collectivities of dispossessed people exercised new strategies for sustenance, healing, and freedom. When organized around the hopes of collective support and sustenance, claims on housing were often claims on healing. Buying into nationalist ideologies of home ownership equality, on the other hand, took trust in a system that was contingent on imbalances. In the context of wage stagnation, diminished opportunities, and state privatization, home ownership for many became a buffer against poverty and discriminatory backlash.[22] Credit expansion to people living in low-credit-score neighborhoods reorganized social problems into individual debts, in effect replacing welfare with "debtfare."[23] A "high-risk" loan was a social construction that reflected stigmatization of poor people, racial/ethnic minorities, and women. But it was also a marker of cumulative histories of dispossession and injustice that buried the fact that the housing crisis ran much deeper than subprime loans.

From the perspective of counter-geographies of race, space, power, and history, the American Dream of owning a home is haunted by much more than access to property. *Spirit House*, a choreopoem commissioned by the Greater New Orleans Fair Housing Action Center in 2013 maps the U.S. housing economy as a system built on the perpetual uprooting of racialized people excluded from opportunities to buy into nationalist formations of progress. Like a housing bubble, a spirit house is an ethereal illustration of a dematerialized relationship to physical structures. But whereas a bubble floats speculators' ambitions to release material houses into abstraction by turning buyers' vulnerabilities into opportunities for exchange, a spirit gestures to a soulful intention to make the immaterial refuse of history knowable through collective research and memory.

The outcome of the *Spirit House Project* was a multimedia staged performance exploring how people inhabit, relate to, find, and make a home between layered histories of housing exclusion. It began with community-focused storytelling among women, families, and sexually non-normative youth in collaboration with Junebug Productions. With the research support of the Women's Health and Justice Initiative, the production highlighted policies and practices of housing discrimination extending from New Deal–era redlining to the reverse redlining of the neoliberal subprime mortgage market. With multimedia visual backdrops calling forth legacies of manifest destiny, enslavement, environmental degradation, and the cross-cultural solidarities that erupt in the cross hairs, performers uncovered minority home ownership as a ritual recitation of oppressive repetition and resistance.

The nationalist spirit of housing opportunity is a steady stream of creation and destruction. Public housing where communities are formed become future lives abandoned by destruction. "Slum removal" becomes "urban renewal." Then, as with the state-made Katrina crisis of dispossession by "blight," it becomes an excuse for white gentrification. And houses where lives and neighborhoods were made across generations are subject to bank foreclosure and state repossession. The subprime mortgage market pivoted on economic, political, and mainstream cultural circulation of houses as the American Dream. In the capitalist circuit of cultural flow, grounded struggles for freedom from suffering were transformed into marketplace freedoms to exploit future buyers. As with any object that is exchanged in a tripartite speculative transaction, *Spirit House* shows that houses and homes also shelter resistant potential within them.

The Neoliberal Sublime

The balance between margin bets and household debts is a record of historical inequality. In the twenty-first-century housing bubble, the ledger of injustice that speculators called risk was carried in the numbers of credit expansion. A credit rating is a cultural production. Equations are the stage on which inherited injuries are performed as numerical differentiation between the worthy and unworthy. Credit contracts mediate risk on a precipice of sublimated cognition. The numbers with which lenders wrote risk in the housing bubble were narrative strategies of selective history.[24] Abstract quantification brought a sense of market fairness into the present at the expense of reckoning with historically produced inequalities.

The constellation of panic and pleasure that defines the twenty-first-century abstraction of the "market" registers both fear and enticement. The fraternal order of financial capital is conditioned by horror and awe—the euphoria of profit and fear of collapse.[25] Credit maintains *Homo economicus*'s conceit of autogenesis in the face of the abyss of risk. Neoclassical displacement of nature into the invisible hand of the deregulated marketplace is sublime mythology. Every credit negotiation demands reverence for acquisitive possession. Credit scoring offers borrowers and lenders a figurative means of living vicariously in the pleasure of (false) knowledge that they are protected from ruin and destruction by a deferred future. Credit sustains a fiction of economic mastery that is determined through submissive obedience to economic laws. The imaginary compensation of credit transforms the terror of human vulnerability into approving acquiescence to asymmetrical transactions.[26] Mastery in the sublime, a dark drive to dominate, is assumed at a distance through the production of race.

Economists will argue that the statistical formulation of creditworthiness is color-blind, that it uses impartial categories to measure the likelihood of a debtors' repayment.[27] Neoliberal rationality makes credit an operative technology for imagining justice in alignment with markets. The numerical "objectivity" of a credit history is a statistical formulation that supplants narrative construction. Credit risk is an expression of cultural tropes—personal responsibility, market equality, property, and nationalist belonging—organized to preemptively punish inheritors of injustice for being denied resources. Yet when lenders loosen the system of ranking and oversight to entice new buyers into the market, they act on a pretense of transcendence.

The racializing effect of subprime home loans exposes the sensory alienation from material conditions written into contractual terms and rates. Differences in credit scores often document historical patterns of discrimination. Racialized spatial segregation is reconfigured as the temporal delay of an individual's history in the abstraction of a credit score. White spatial reorganization marks low-credit-score areas as areas of racialized concentration.[28] White suburbanization is a spatial effect of the way in which middle-class aspirations in the twentieth century were organized through privileged educational, job, and housing markets.[29] Even when the scoring abstractions indicated lower risk, racialized borrowers in these areas were disproportionately sold subprime loans. Speculators' zeal for higher-rate borrowers folded preexisting racisms into financial circuits in tandem with the biases of loan brokers.[30] Financial conceits of leveling risk through differential credit broadened access to the American Dream but only on terms of uneven payment that registered "risk" as individual negligence.

Financial securities markets banked on inscriptive violence, investing in racialized injustice to procure higher-cost loans. Legacies of racial and gender inequality were the conditional backbone of the stock market bubble.[31] Securitization spread racialized risk resulting from betting on the hardships and histories of segregation and exclusion in the entire financial economy. Only 9 percent of home mortgages in 2002 were subprime. By 2006, 25 percent were subprime or Alt-A products, which were expressly created in the 1990s for limited use among buyers with low credit scores, questionable credit histories, or, in the case of Alt-A loans, incomplete income and asset verification. In 2002, U.S. mortgages were at a fifty-year low, suggesting that without the demand by financial investors, home owners would have had relatively good odds for low-cost fixed-rate loans.[32] But strategic expansion of credit to low-credit-score neighborhoods filled the market with products that prefigured future borrower dispossession. Adjustable rates, balloon payments, interest-only loans, and no income verification made repayment contingent on housing price inflation.[33]

Financial "innovation" reversed the order of speculative anticipation by allowing brokers and traders to skim off the top up front through high fees and insurance derivatives that emboldened investors to bet on foreclosures.[34] Credit default swaps were designed in the 1990s by J.P. Morgan to exchange risk without transferring ownership of underlying securities.[35] They were racialized in the early 2000s, when deregulation allowed multiple investors to simultaneously speculate on risk and hedge their bets by netting their investments. Investors concurrently purchased securities that would pay off when mortgages were repaid and reverse contracts that paid out like insurance when homes went into foreclosure.[36] This entailed an historical shift in U.S. racial formation whereby inclusion in rather than exclusion from the American Dream became the cultural-economic technology through which racial inequality was deepened and spread.

The travesty of it all is not that white people ended up in a 99 percent where many saw for the first time how racial discrimination has been experienced by others. Rather, the racial legacies of speculative nationalism deepened cumulative injuries into new instabilities. Neighborhoods where subprime lending was largely concentrated did not fall one house at time. They collapsed in waves: as houses became vacant, squatters occupied empty spaces, crimes increased, fires sparked, and businesses closed.[37] Mortgage securitization caused tremendous insecurity in devalued neighborhoods, adding new problems to preexisting vulnerabilities: homelessness, lost jobs, lost education, incarceration, and working to pay debts rather than to sustain life. Predatory lenders did not act alone.

Predatory Patriotism

U.S. nationalism is implicated in housing predation in state redirection of public policy. During the late twentieth century state infrastructures to support human survival were replaced by policies to promote purchasing housing as private investments. The Personal Responsibility and Work Opportunity Act remade welfare into workfare, turning unskilled low-paid labor into the "not yet" freedom of future independence. The Quality Housing and Work Responsibility Act of 1998 ended public housing. With state-subsidized shelter limited to beds locked up in iron cages, poor people turned to the private rental market for shelter. "The only place where people from miles around can get three hots and a cot, aside from that damn Angola prison," *Spirit House*'s Mama Celeste says, is in a private home.[38] Even before rental prices skyrocketed in relation to economic and environmental disasters, state policy replaced social support and nationalist participation with "asset-based welfare."[39]

In 1995 Clinton proposed a National Homeownership Strategy to help poor people with down payments and closing costs so that they could become "partners in the American Dream." Like the 1933 Home Owners Loan Corporation, Clinton's proposal was presented as an emergency measure to distribute loans to millions of people. The difference during the Clinton era was that the intended targets for new borrowing were people excluded from housing by redlining and restrictive housing covenants created by past government subsidies.[40] Clinton invoked the spirit of the New Deal and the GI Bill in his proposal, but rather than distribute direct government loans as those laws did for white people, he called for financial innovation in the private mortgage economy to allow lenders to stretch the limits of risk in loan products.[41] The public-private partnership Clinton envisioned registered home ownership as a tool to "make people believe that they can have some permanence and stability in their lives even as they deal with all the changing forces that are out there in this global economy."[42] As with his welfare policy, Clinton predicated this stability on two-parent families who demonstrated economic responsibility through private consumption. In this instance, he framed poor citizens' personal responsibility as taking on risky credit to purchase a house.

George W. Bush's American Dream Down-Payment Initiative of 2003 focused directly on subsidizing down payments, closing costs, and construction costs for minority home ownership.[43] This was largely a symbolic gesture with material incentive to fold low-income people into the housing market.[44] Bush promoted possessive patriotism as a responsibility to confidently trust a market that was purportedly made secure by the initiative's oversight of affordability, predatory lending, and loan transparency.[45] During the New Deal, many immigrants took advantage of subsidies out of a desire for freedom from rent and risks of eviction. The promise of freedom often came at the expense of school, food, shoes, and health care.[46] Selling a similar promise as an aspect of neoliberal responsibility in the context of housing inflation was patriotic predation. Presidential endorsements of home ownership as a highest national priority enabled the mortgage market to cash in on histories of deferral by charging minority home owners higher prices.

The Work of Culture in the Age of Mortgage Expansion

The distracting gaze of neoliberal reality also staged home ownership as the last vestige of freedom under the hollowed-out neoliberal nation-state. Reality television did not create the housing bubble. It did, however, mediate and moderate the political-economic transition toward advanced financialization with normative scripts of consumer nationalism. The "not yet" freedom of sweat equity stages the American Dream of home ownership as a bootstrap project of self-selected deferral. The hard work of improving shelter today, the promise goes, will become future savings protected as home equity. New Deal–era do-it-yourself magazines framed sweat equity as the path to middle-class prosperity. Do-it-yourself television during the early twenty-first century pushed the margins of nationalist uplift toward spending on housing improvements beyond the means of average people. During the early years of the housing bubble, even programs like PBS's *This Old House*, which began in 1979 as a modest instructional program for property restoration, ensnared spectators into a fantasy realm of overindulgent million-dollar renovations.[47] The spread of reality lifestyle programs from public television into cable and network broadcasting reflects a political-economic shift toward low-budget programming in corporate media. But it is also a form of speculative culture. Like economic speculation, which removes profit from "real" productive economies, speculative culture invites viewers to imagine that scripted representations of consumptive investment are normatively "real."

Reality television kept pace with speculative inflation as a nationalist pedagogy in subjective transformation. The launch of ABC's *Extreme Makeover: Home Edition* in 2003 was emblematic of this transition. The program is premised on a patronizing narrative of middle-class uplift waged through the impossibility of people's access to wealth. Against a soundtrack of U.S. patriotism, "expert" renovators remove "deserving" families facing economic hardship from their homes and lives, and within a week reconstruct their houses and identities. In addition to overhauling, if not fully replacing "unsalvageable" homes, the program stages a process of neoliberal subjection, reacting to abject economic scarcity with disciplinary imperatives to engage in high-stakes consumption. In each episode, the cast constructs, narrates, and imposes meaningful attachments to family and consumption on errant home owners, at once promoting sponsors like Sears and Disney and reconstituting hetero-familial intimacy as the cultural formation that secures property values. In textualizing sorted-out cities and underresourced neighborhoods as spectacles of individual deficiency, the program invites viewers to identify with "not yet" freedom through the individualist lens of personal responsibility.

By sentimentalizing poverty, *Extreme Makeover: Home Edition* interpellates middle-class spectators as a neomissionary liberal democratic crowd. Filling in for the sellout of state services, each episode invites privileged people to become sanctimoniously benevolent as participants in rebuilding. The show also encourages viewers to act as moral executors, judging who among the dispossessed is worthy of housing salvation. It rewards audiences for charity and shrewdness with membership in the middle-class multitude. Through this inclusion, spectators garner indirect recognition for participating in ostensibly benevolent reconstruction of the lives of the needy family.

The big reveal is enacted through shouting in unison "Move that bus!!!" a refrain that disturbingly carries an undercurrent of the racial politics of home ownership used by the financialized state to supplant the Civil Rights tradition. Freedom riding, bus boycotts, and busing children for school integration made buses a central symbol of antiracist struggle. Antibusing activism kept suburbs segregated. Highway subsidies came at the expense of efficient public transport systems that poor people relied on. Buses remain sites of struggle through which race is perpetually remade.[48] The euphoric chant, "Move that bus" wills away collective struggle, replacing it with corporate-sponsored individuated optimism for privatized housing wealth.

Cable versions of home equity television efface housing inequality with multicultural entrepreneurialism. The strategy of direct marketing to different interest groups shows up on cable as an incorporation of individuals with diverse backgrounds as "everyday people" who fit the commercial requirements necessary to make home ownership the gold standard of citizenship.[49] Programs like DIY Network's *Sweat Equity* (2006), HGTV's *Curb Appeal* (1999), HGTV's *Hidden Potential* (2006), and countless others routinely display non-White, gay, and lesbian couples as relatively mundane.[50] Emphasis on sweat equity and successful normativity, however, displaces criticality around housing disparity with instructions on turning home ownership into profit. Programs like TLC's *Trading Spaces* (2000), HGTV's *Rate My Space* (2008), and DIY Network's *Turf Wars* (2009) train viewers in market competition by framing renovation as a "friendly" game to literally outdo the neighbors.

There is an element of sublime awe and horror in this kind of realty television. On the sedentary side of the television screen, viewers can vicariously experience the "delightful horror" of disappointed home owners when the

consumer mold is disjointed from the home owners' tastes or, more profoundly, when the investment fails. Just a year into the housing bubble, programs
like *Flip This House* (A& E, 2003), *Flip That House* (TLC, 2005), *Flipping Out*
(Bravo, 2007), *Property Ladder* (TLC, 2004), *The Real Estate Pros* (TLC, 2007),
Million Dollar Listing (Bravo, 2006), and others went all in to promote speculation as a path to middle-class prosperity. By refurbishing sweat equity as a disciplinary device, these programs represented risk as individual failures. Even
after the crash of 2008, HGTV's *Real Estate Intervention* (2009) represented
"expert" flippers as a remedy for the personal failures and ignorance of people
who got caught with unsellable houses at the tail end of the bubble.[51]

The contradictory relationship of expert points of view and affectively
democratizing culture in mediated and scripted reality resonates with the feelings of estrangement that Walter Benjamin associated with the technological
reproduction of art. To witness film, he suggested, is to become somewhat of
an expert in it. This is in part a result of the distance that the camera creates
between the audience and the actor. Film demarcates a perceptual transformation that disallows actors from responding to the demands of an immediate
audience, consequently detaching it from identification with the actor. Viewers
are thus aligned with the perspective of the camera, and, once removed from
the performance, they are positioned as critics. Technology creates a new form
of proximity through shots and angles that show depths across the surface and
expand perceptive capacities beyond the human eye. It also democratizes life
in its capacity to transform virtually anyone into a screen image. The imposing
role of the camera, however, also prescribes meaning through cuts and sensory
manipulation with the potential to exploit.

Benjamin was wary of "illusion-promoting spectacles and dubious specula-
tions" that opened audiences up to consumerist exploitation.[52] He saw the shift
in perception that film created for modern audiences as indicative of the social
transformation of industrial capital. The universalizing tendency of film, its
ability to satiate the desires of the masses for closeness, and its suggestion that
exclusivity could be overcome through reproduction emancipated art from tradition with a form that penetrates deep into its object. As the camera cuts into
that which it represents, it encourages a perception of reality that is premised on
emotional distance. Cinematic infiltration creates a distracted proximity from
which the emotional enjoyment of audiences is fused to the external orientation of the camera. Benjamin registered perceptive distraction as a mechanical
anesthetic to absorb through enjoyment the shock of workplace exploitation
under industrial repetition.

Reality television, much like film in the period of modern industrialization,
registers the era of financialization through another perceptual transformation.
The work of television in the age of mortgage expansion is to penetrate both
vision and voice as repetition of privatized subjectivities. The camera's gaze is
coupled in this medium with circulated scripts that "real" people repeat across
programs and episodes. Generic expectations fix real people to an acceptable

set of reactions, intercepting familiar and familiarizing "reality" with pre-figured consumptive desires. In the spectator distance of the televisual cut, viewers receive anesthetic relief from the daily shocks of a flexible labor econo-my and systemic vulnerability. The script expropriates self-generated response from consumers by calling on them to speak in compliance with the likes and dislikes of current trends. The disciplinary pressure on actual consumers is to recuperate this deflated agency by purchasing objects that reflect their "own" taste, to prove themselves worthy citizens in a context that makes consumption contingent on credit. And in the equation, a mortgage becomes the promise on which citizenship is waged.

Housing Freedom against the Odds

Speculative investment depends on cognitive and cultural maps that preserve and prolong racialized and gendered inequalities of the past for future profits. Houses can and do resist because people inhabit them against individuation and hetero-familial norms. "I don't owe this city nothin' and my property aint blighted," Mama Celeste poetically declares in *Spirit House*. "I ask what does the city owe me? How can I be reimbursed for the bend of my back and the sweat of my brow in service to my community and this city!"[53] *Spirit House* undermines speculative cartographies by claiming rights to space as home by virtue of conjunctive dislocations. Memories are carried in the elements of air, fire, water, and earth, with water recalling "When our ancestors came to this land, mostly by boat either willingly, or enslaved, or washed up on the shore, a rift in the fabric of time opened up, as those who came from afar made the home that we all now share."[54] The play occupies that rift in time by looking at how justice is made through interdependence. It registers freedom in collec-tive struggles to meet human needs for shelter and connection. When Mama Celeste calls out the state as impinging on peoples' capacity to love and survive, she refuses the conditional freedom of nationalist belonging and exposes trust in illegitimate laws as a scheme that empowers the nation-state to collude with capital in human displacement.

Spirit House is a collective reckoning with the racializing fabrications that speculative nationalism uses to uproot lives. At the center of the narrative, a house that has been held for generations by free people of color is at risk of repossession because of back taxes. The play is situated in a fissure of "hard times" in the shadow of gentrification following Hurricane Katrina and under a wave of national subprime housing foreclosures. The house is located in peo-ple's hopes for justice and salvation in "destroyed and disrupted neighborhoods [that] were centers of the African American community" in the city of New Orleans.[55] The performance puts on trial policies that deprive communities of space and connection "for the convenience of the wealthy."[56] In so doing, it wrestles with contradictions of possessing a house as a form of property, but also recognizes that individual ownership is a survival tactic for beating the odds of the removal strategies that remain standard practice in an illegitimate settler-state.

Spirit House is a battle cry against housing policies that exclude, evict, and erase opportunities for poor people of color to reside in sanitary and safe conditions. It is also rooted in differentially displaced peoples' traditions of sharing "survival secrets, recipes, songs, prayers and hopes" across groups. Midway through the performance, the players, carrying on the legacy and breaking the heaviness of cumulative burdens, erupt into a chant written by Big Chief Brian Harrison Nelson of the Guardians of the Flame. "Let's go get 'em" is a spirit call by Mardi Gras Indians to revolt against discriminatory landlords and lenders who are the contemporary gatekeepers of freedom. The chant beckons to the elements to "pray . . . on the bayou" and calls on the audience to place hope in shared struggle: "All we got is us."[57] This is the spirit that is suggested in the tentative freedom made and held within the walls of *Spirit House*.

Mama Celeste narrates the house as an inheritance of freedom: "This house go back to 1809. My mama made sure to tell me, Celeste, your people were free people of color and as long as you own this property, you and your children will be free people too."[58] She tells of the steady pressure to sell the house and her refusal because of her obligation to pass on the stories and legacies of freedom that it symbolizes. Her claims on the house reveal that freedom is a dream that cannot be sold and a promise that cannot be deferred. Rather, in cultivating life the house reveals that freedom must be constantly remade and claimed through memory, adaptation, and mutual support. The right to reside is not the owners' alone but belongs to all who enter.

In a reading of the play in April 2013, the Dryades Theater was staged as the house with the audience seated in its different rooms. Performers sat, cooked, laughed, and screamed alongside spectators such that everybody became an occupant. The performance inhabited fissures in time to broaden collectivity across space and difference in defiance of nationalist individuation. The production opened with Mama Celeste directly addressing the audience and the elements, encouraging viewers to call out the names of their own ancestors, to invite spirits back "home" in a new context. In the fullness of dwelling alongside friends, performers, unknown others, and ancestors, freedom takes place as a healing process, a sharing of stories and struggles that begins with desublimation of injuries inflicted across and within power, to work through racializing and gendered divisions.

The characters who live in the house are people susceptible to dispossession by housing discrimination.[59] The newest arrivals are a single mother and her son; she has lost her apartment for late rent and suffers her landlord's sexual advances. The exclusionary effects of hetero-familial nationalist norms play out in the struggles of a transgender young person who is vulnerable to homelessness and violence and discrimination against lesbian partners repeatedly shut out of the rental market because of their sexual orientation. Joe, an elderly African American man, has been a renter in the house the longest. His relentless effort to repair the house's aging plumbing is a reminder of the blocks, anger, and lingering injustice that the house carries in the bowels of its spirit.

Spirit House is an archive of insubordinate memories that refuse to be forgotten. A multimedia backdrop brings conflict and violence to the forefront at the same time that Mama Celeste offers the house as a safe space for building intentional communities. Conflicts between occupants, who become a nontraditional family out of proximity and need, register how social injuries often reveal themselves through intimate violence. Healing wounds is a transformational process. It is about hearing the chant that "enough is enough" as a deadly serious call to end the predatory power of speculative nationalism to enter into the spirit and appropriate freedom. There is no waiting when "we slide into time our feet / dancing with the ancestors / our brows sweaty with freedom."[60]

Keeping up the spirit of freedom in the house requires remaking culture, coming up with new ideas, figuring out new relationships, placing collective responsibility above personal responsibility, and nurturing values of mutual support over material possession. Characters claim freedom under terms of last resort by hoping that collective sustenance will meet unfulfilled needs. In reversing the temporal trajectory of future optimism, the house is constructed as a site of radical becoming. People claim life against the odds through knowledge of the past and present hope. *Spirit House* makes this possible by conjoining grounded structure with soul as confirmation that all who enter have a right to existence: "My life and my love are mine to own / My future is mine to create and own / As my gift from the universe."[61]

The visions and practices of people whose futures have been traded to create speculative opportunities for later dispossession demonstrate the experiential wisdom that comes from negotiating systemic racism and sexism. "The understanding is," Mama Celeste explains, "that as long as our ancestor's skin color was the so-called cause of their oppression, we black, brown, yellow, and red-skinned survivors of the great trouble will stand in solidarity. That's why we won't bow down. Ya'll young people need to keep up your faith and keep on 'til you get the house that is going to support you."[62] In the unknown future of transformational politics, a house does not signal individual property. It is a story of ongoing struggle from which people attain life-affirming consciousness. The unwavering spirit of this house suggests that the only thing that is too big to fail in the aftermath of the subprime crisis is people's collective capacity to imagine and will freedom into existence on terms that meet everybody's needs for justice and survival.

Revelry in the Multicultural Finance State

Urban Abandonment, Identity Adjustment,
May Day the Powderhorn Way

I am so frustrated about this. I just see it as another taskforce, another report, another reporting mechanism. I get these reports every single week from the police department, where in my neighborhood sixty shots are fired every single week and the rest of the city it's ten. What are we doing about that? When are we going to spend some time on that? This is so frustrating to me. I'm just really angry.
                                                                —BARBARA JOHNSON, 2014

We regard this fight as a battle in a great war—the war between predatory capital and exploited labor. The war between the classes. The hour has now struck when we are to be put to a new test. Local 574 has shown the world that it has a body of courageous fighters. . . . The world admits that we can fight. Now the question arises: Can we stick? And our answer must be: We'll bow our necks and stick it out it if it takes all summer.
                                                                —JAMES P. CANNON, 1934

Thank you, Powderhorn Park for receiving our festival for 40 years! Thank you to those who marched with the MPLS Truckers' Strike 80 years ago! Thanks to ALL who come together to build a healthy world!
                              —IN THE HEART OF THE BEAST PUPPET AND
                                        MASK THEATRE AND FRIENDS, 2014

The Scene of Exchange

People in Minneapolis's Powderhorn neighborhood take their trash seriously. They know that you cannot build a democracy by throwing the dreams and desires of entire populations away. Every spring they clean out garages, dig through trash piles, and appeal to local businesses for excess waste. In the common well of Minneapolis's refuse they locate tools they can use to fill the streets with diverse expressions of freedom and association. With the treasures they find—cardboard, newspapers, rubber tubes, plastic bottles, paint, fabric swatches, tin cans, and random objects relegated disposable in a capitalist society run as usual—they project their dreams into an array of puppets. On

May Day, neighbors, friends, and others come together to stage an eclectic vision of a democratic world dreamed and enacted through collective artistry.
When they carry and embody their shared and individual dreams through the
city in the form of puppets at the annual parade and festival, they invite others
into a delightful mess of possibilities, demonstrating how collectivities unearth
democracy and freedom when they create art together.

In the wake of the Vietnam War, the Powderhorn Puppet Theatre initiated this annual ritual as a community offering to an audience of about one
hundred people. They filled streets with puppetry and poetry to practice communal regeneration, bringing people together around a common joy of giving
life to inanimate objects. Ever since, every year, the renamed In the Heart of
the Beast Puppet and Mask Theatre (HOBT) has invited community members
to dig into their pockets, participation, and imagination and conjure a world of
nonviolent radical planetary equity into collective being.[1] Today members of
the now working-class, racially varied, queer, immigrant, poor, middle-class,
artistic community continue to draw on the labor and environmental roots of
May Day with hundreds of puppets while tens of thousands of spectators and
participants gather in the streets.[2]

At the fortieth annual May Day Festival on May 4, 2014, the neighborhood
celebrated the eightieth anniversary of the Minneapolis truckers' strike of 1934,
demonstrating solidarity with the mass demonstrations that turned Minneapolis
into a union town. The 1934 strike is recognized as a watershed moment in U.S.
labor history because it incited general strikes across the nation and led to passage of the National Labor Relations Act of 1935. On the local level, the strike was
meaningful because its organizers broadened the scope of of labor resistance into
a vision of social democracy. The truckers organized themselves on an industrial
basis rather than as an isolated craft. Their holistic view of labor emphasized the
exploitation of truckers as just one symptom of general class warfare: "We see
the issue between capital and labor as an unceasing struggle between the class
of exploited workers and exploiting parasites. . . . The exploiters are organized to
grind us down into the dust. We must organize our class to fight back."[3] Rejecting any possibility for labor-management deals and partnerships, Local 574 built
solidarity with all types of workers, filling the streets alongside many different
local unions. They had the support of farmers, who fed their families throughout the strike. They honored and recognized the reproductive and paid work of
women as "indispensable" to the strike's success.[4] They showed the world that
social unions create transformative power when they set aside the self-interest of
the trade for the common good of working-class democracy.

Forty years later, the Powderhorn puppeteers carried the truckers' struggle
forward when they chose the theme of "Wonder" at May Day to explore "the
obvious yet mysterious connection of all things."[5] In the contemporary context, artists extended the struggle for food, sustenance, and general well-being
that the truckers had demanded from employers, banks, and politicians into a
general call for economic justice and environmental sustainability. Noting the

lethal toxicity that profit motives introduce into daily life, performers called on observers to open all of their senses, to register small connections between even the tiniest organism and ecological balance. They also called attention to trans-spatial interconnections, noting how the movement of immigrants and animals across artificial borders continues to result in state-sanctioned death. In the search for alternatives to powerful "isms"—racism, classism, sexism, and so forth—the parade explored alternative energies, generating "soul-ar power" as an antidote to environmental racism—a power to protect the human spirit and living environments. The actors' intricate dance of interconnection directly responded to structural inequalities and called for a careful reckoning with ongoing historical hardships.

Three days after the fortieth annual May Day, a minor outburst by Minneapolis City Council president Barbara Johnson demonstrated how circumstances of inequality in the city tend to trap people in crisis logics. At a general council meeting, Johnson expressed frustration over spatially concentrated, visible violence in Minneapolis. In response to a presentation about the city's commitment to a "Racial Equity Action Plan," she demanded that city workers spend less time studying disproportionate racial impacts and more solving immediate "critical issues" of public safety. Johnson's remarks highlighted how race, space, and power were mapped in the city, such that police reports of gunshots, narcotics, music, alcohol, loud fighting, "nuisance properties," and the like, were more likely to be filed in wards like hers in North Minneapolis than in other, Whiter areas of the city.

In the post–financial crisis land of 10,000 lakes and Fortune 500s, Minneapolis is a divided city. The Twin Cities outpaced other Midwestern cities like Chicago and Detroit in general economic recovery.[6] The Brookings Institution placed Minneapolis in the top third of U.S. cities for successful recovery. More than 10,000 jobs were lost following the financial collapse, but by 2013, in addition to regaining 10,000 jobs, the city had added 5,000 more. Venture capital seems to be a major driver of projected economic growth.[7] Anticipated economic recovery through more intellectual and professional labor will likely increase disparities and displacement in Minneapolis just as it has in San Francisco, New Orleans, and New York. While city officials and businesses are banking on an elite cadre of professional labor, people are suffering from an uneven recovery that maps along racial lines. Predatory lending and foreclosure expanded a racial gap that has given Minnesota the worst proportional record of home ownership among people of color in the country.[8] Black people are over three times more likely than White people to be unemployed in Minnesota, which leads all fifty states in educational and criminal justice disparities based on race.[9] When viewed from the perspective of spatially concentrated racial disparity, Johnson's concern about public safety resonates as a panicked police-state solution to crimes of dispossession. Her urgency sublimates how racially spatialized "crime" expresses limited life chances caused by lack of jobs, shelter, opportunities, and justice in parts of the city.

In the ethos of May Day, Civil Rights director Velma Korbel generously responded with a long historical perspective to temper Johnson's panic. The subprime crisis and recovery have exacerbated racial inequalities that have been accumulating for hundreds of years. Cities like Minneapolis demonstrate that the solutions people come up with to solve patterns of injustice often become racializing injustices that they will have to solve in the future. After eighty years and forty festivals of people's engagement in democratic struggle, the post-crisis opportunity of 2014 is not one to waste.

The Form of Transfer

"Waste is not 'waste' until you waste it."[10] This is the history of the United States declared as an axiom. Using only six short words, the declaration—which was presented at the 2012 May Day festival—manages to pile centuries of social struggle, the theoretical challenges of interpretative dissonance, and overlapping systems of value into a few rolls of the tongue. It weaves multiple temporalities into an intricate representation of ongoing transformation. The statement's evasive subject/object—waste—enacts a process of constant change metamorphosing in meaning each time it occurs. At first the term appears to articulate a clear and apparent object. The letters—*w, a, s, t,* and *e*—are linguistic containers that, when placed in precise proximity, come to signify useless, rejected, and disposed-of material. The "not" preceding the term's second enunciation thrusts the concept into a tautological trap. The adverb exacts an impossible achievement. It enables something's becoming despite imposing a structure of negation that makes a becoming unattainable. The transition from noun to verb in the third iteration transforms the word from object into action. "Waste" is a peculiar verb because it, too, balances on a principle of contradiction. The action of wasting is the action of inaction. As it appears in the phrase, the act of not doing is a kind of doing that performs an undoing. Waste becomes an accusation in this third formation. The offense of wasting is also a crime of contradiction. The liability of failing to act is premised on an indictment that not to do a thing is to produce destruction, generate decay, and create failed opportunities.

The shifting significations in the statement "Waste is not 'waste' until you waste it" instill it with an insurrectionary invitation. The circulation of waste also results in a revolutionary recalibration of time. The call to change the present balances the potential of the future on the seeming impossibility of changing the past. As the term *waste* cycles through the intervals of the sentence, it becomes a clock with which to contemplate conditions of constantly changing sameness. Meanings change even as the form of the word remains constant. The word is a configuration of five signs extracted from a much larger alphanumeric system. It is a combination of letters that effect meaning precisely by not changing their spatial organization to make up the term. The *w* must appear first, always removed to the left of the *s* by the presence of the *a*. The consistent, persistent, and indistinguishable symbolic sameness of the word itself suggests a reconstruction of time's expected operation. What was remains the same; *w a s* cannot change if the form is to remain comprehensible. Yet what was becomes something else as the past folds in on itself. *w a s t e* can never be what it was. When waste returns from the past, it creates a playful platform for a politics of the possible.

The tempo of the sentence carries the collective work of world remaking through whimsical contradictions and temporal convergences. The phrase keeps time in rhythm with spatial geography. We can see an attention to location in the *it* that completes the sentence. This final articulation of *waste* has shed its original form, taking shape as a culminating repercussion of previous repetitions. The pronoun demarcates the perimeter of the sentence, but it also points to content that the phrase cannot contain. The referent to *it*—the prior location of *waste* to which the pronoun points—is there but undetectable. *It* points to some place, but *where* cannot be fully comprehended. Is *it* the knowledge suggested by the conceptual coherence that fleetingly appears in the first articulation of *waste*? Is *it* the challenge of interpretation caused by the second emergence that presses us to question how knowledge congeals? The pronoun presumes that *it* is a thing, but might the momentum of repetition make it also a movement? Grammatically, *it* indicates singularity, yet the ambiguity of overlapping significations makes the pronoun multiple. Just like *you*, *it* is open to a limitless scope of grammatical abstraction. In this iteration, *you* are the actors hailed by the sentence's call to rethink what it might mean to collaboratively build new knowledge from waste. The preposition *until* suggests that the failure to do so might mean losing the potential of what *it* could become. Whatever *it* is—personal, local, national, international, global, or something else all together—*it* is greater than you. The simple axiom encapsulates how people in Powderhorn bring worlds into being by constructing puppets from waste. It suggests that quite a lot can be done with very little material.

The revelers who convene in Powderhorn each spring know that waste is an indispensable resource for social imagination. Powderhorn is a place where demographic shifts, spatial reorganization, resilience, and adaptation are permanent features of the urban landscape. Circumstances of constantly changing sameness have given people with attachments, affinities, and alliances to the neighborhood a firsthand education in dissonant value systems. When they rematerialize trash into puppets, they undermine how *waste* has been used as a unit of measure to justify patterns of genocidal dispossession, racialized disenfranchisement, and exploitative conditions of unfulfilled need. Performers entice audiences into disorderly intersections where they share lessons they have learned in daily negotiation with imbalanced power and freedom. Their art makes clear that common sense is not the only sense. Indeed, when commonsense is predicated on curing cravings for democratic community with the compensation of consumption, commonsense makes no sense at all, especially for people living on few cents a day. Improvising from the refuse makes new sense out of these multiple senses.

May Day is a place for creating connections, for building new modes of freedom out of networks that relegate some lives refusable. It is a place where capitalist value is flipped on its head in favor of collective engagement in life-affirming action. It is a time for trying out tactics for justice and freedom and for learning to speak in multiple registers.[11] The festival and parade are a public pedagogy in collaborative reinvention staged through the art of contradiction. Waste is not "waste" when it reclaims the streets as a community springboard for jumping into the messes of our conflicts and connections. Waste is not "waste" when it is crafted into puppets who playfully orchestrate difficult discussions. Waste is not "waste" when it materially proves that, even when all hope seems lost, all resources seem depleted, and all chances have been thrown out, there may be joy beneath the rubble. Waste is not "waste" when it becomes the common resource for a cultural poesies that carries people through the "painful process of renewal."[12]

The proposition "Waste is not 'waste' until you waste it" is a deadly serious imperative for the political present. In a conscientious treatment of the painful work that social renewal entails, Powderhorn poet Louis Alemayehu asked his neighbors at the 2012 May Day festival to contemplate the following: "For the earth to live, America must die, all nations must die." The poet's assertion was neither lament nor aggressive anti-Americanism. Rather, it was a statement of his philosophical faith in the power of ordinary people to build a new freedom from the "sanctuary" of "compassionate action"—the action of "robust[ly] singing in a deep democracy beyond what we know." Alemayehu's differentiation of knowledge and action challenges us to think toward justice through study of the past. His verse suggests that not knowing is not equivalent to never having been. It beckons to a freedom recorded not in words and documents but in the rhythms of a verse that can only be sensed through ongoing struggles that keep on singing. The deep democracy beyond our knowledge may have been lived even if we can no longer hear the sound of its recurring beats.

Race, Place, and Structural Adjustment

Life as it has been lived in Powderhorn is and is not like life in other U.S. multiethnic urban neighborhoods that faced the intertwined fates of regeneration and degeneration during the liberal multicultural period. Minneapolis in the 1980s harbored a proud progressive history of farm and labor alliances,[13] cross-class cooperation,[14] and institutional support for extending New Deal social safety nets into a Civil Rights agenda. Following World War II, Keynesian economic philosophy was instrumental in job and real estate desegregation for Minneapolis's relatively small African American population.[15] The underlying logic of Roosevelt's national proposal for a Fair Employment Practices Committee rested on the Keynesian theory that access to jobs was imperative for securing economic expansion through the creation of new consumers.[16] Minnesotans did not directly experience the close ties between the rise of the welfare state and the expansion of the warfare economy. Yet warfare production fueled their primary economies of mining and agriculture with increased steel manufacturing and available federal Farm Credit System loans. In the postwar period, the space that distanced Minnesota's economic stability from its allegiance to warfare production made it seem as if the rise of the welfare state was a measure of government accountability to the historical left's continued struggle for equality of opportunity. Investment in the nation-state, it likely appeared, gradually led to universally fulfilled freedoms. Desegregation, in this view, could be read as the natural outcome of collective farmer, labor, and popular activism to extend social securities to excluded groups.[17]

Minnesota experienced the sting of the nationwide transfer of resources and power from public goods to speculative finance in the 1980s. Between 1981 and 1987, land values dropped 50 percent in rural areas. The farm crisis was exacerbated when the debts that were generously distributed in the 1970s came due in a context of overproduction. People owed more than their assets were worth.[18] New technologies alongside reductions in steel manufacturing beginning in the 1980s made the jobs of more than 10,000 people in the state's northern iron ranges obsolete.[19] Structural changes also caused the reorganization and deindustrialization of meat packing and other industries, subjecting residents of southern Minnesota to cutbacks on union gains and revived efforts by industries to break labor solidarities. Workers demanded equitable pay and treatment in small resistances and actions, such as the nationally visible strike of the Austin Hormel plant. Industries, on the other hand, demonstrated their commitment to profits over people by cutting wages, condoning dangerous working conditions, hiring younger workers at less pay, and disregarding seniority contracts.[20]

In Minneapolis, labor, civil rights, feminist, gay and lesbian, and antiwar movements and communities made it seem that the racial stratification that had produced devastating inequality in other cities had been avoided through institutionalized social justice policies and practices.[21] Urban activists expressed solidarity with rural crisis. Outside groups of feminists, peace activists, and minority groups, for example, publicized and materially supported strikers at Austin Hormel.[22] Minneapolis in the 1980s was a primary hub connecting reservations and regions through the American Indian Movement.[23] The city hired academic feminists Catherine Mackinnon and Andrea Dworkin to draft an antipornography civil rights ordinance in 1983. Although the mayor vetoed the ordinance twice, that it was considered speaks to city planners' attention to community concerns for women's safety.

Minneapolis's progressive veneer of multicultural diversity belies a contradictory past. The strong activist tradition in the state supports an enduring commitment to the ideals of democratic freedom. Yet many of these movements have ended up inadvertently affirming the divisive imperatives of speculative citizenship. National identification is a powerful force in Minnesota because it is a state that defines itself around generations of workers and immigrants who fought their way into opportunities and recognition. White liberal confidence in future freedom, however, is often tinged with nativist sentiments that mask how economic structures continue to racialize injustice and inequality. Jim Lee's study of multiculturalism during the urban crises of the 1980s elucidates how nationalist diversity worked in tandem with the state's alignment with finance, insurance, and real estate markets to deepen structural racisms. The "not yet" freedom of multicultural inclusion invited a select few racialized people into representational equality at the expense of many. Lee argues that bourgeois nationalism often used multicultural facades to legitimize policies that stripped assets from poor and racialized neighborhoods. Multiculturalism set standards for urban triage, articulating a baseline for "who would thrive, who would die, and who would remain the walking wounded" of stripped and sorted-out American cities.[24] Symbolic inclusion of diverse people empowered officials wielding economic and political power to wage a war of words against social "waste," condemning working and nonworking poor people as undeserving of social resources.[25] As in most cities, the logic of personal responsibility played out in Minneapolis as spatially concentrated urban abandonment. Its effects were compounded by the subprime crisis, but its origins run deep in the land.

Land

Social spaces like Powderhorn Park are repositories of cultural memory and historical struggle. In the 1970s and 1980s, celebrations of diversity in Minneapolis masked changes in the city's racial geography. The Powderhorn Park neighborhood was particularly susceptible to racial disparity during this period of multicultural economic adjustment. As in most U.S. cities, nonnormative populations in Minneapolis found themselves pushed to the city's economic and physical margins.[26] This small area on the east side was all at once the location of one of the city's earliest Black communities; a site for feminist, environmental, and queer organizing; and—pointing back to its origins as a working-class immigrant community—home to an emerging White middle class.[27]

Civic planners of the late nineteenth century designed Powderhorn Park to represent a national ideal of free democratic association through which a universal public could be imagined in the presence of social difference. The creation of public parks in 1880s Minneapolis called on culture to mediate the contradictions and conflicts created by the industrial convergence of European immigrants, Black migrants, and working women. Public parks in this context worked to contain social difference in culture, maintaining the idea of sameness in the political state. In the nineteenth century, public space was imperative for the social management of severe market inequalities. The idea of universal equality in park spaces suggested a future freedom that could be universally attained through political membership and political and civil rights.[28] However, for the marginal groups on the city's outskirts, identification with this illusionary future required that they put aside their own and others' histories. Because doing so depended on misreading social inequality as harmonious multiplicity and internalizing structural inequalities as individual differences, at the same time that public parks offered a means for envisioning democratic unity, they also preserved and contained long legacies of racialized injustice, beginning with the fact that the land had been held by an intertribal confederacy well before the city was imagined.

Powderhorn Lake was once a swamp. In 1865 the area that is now a sixty-five-acre urban park was donated to the city of Minneapolis (which had been incorporated in 1856). A local farmer offered his unusable farmland to the city in hopes that it might later become an urban refuge.[29] When the city stretched its boundaries southeast in the 1880s, the blocks around the unusable wetland rapidly emerged as one of the largest residential neighborhoods, housing the city's European immigrant working class.[30] To accommodate a housing shortage, early planners proposed filling in and building up the entire area. In 1880, however, the land was secured as a future park by the Minneapolis Board of Park Commissioners as a way to attract "a class of residents who [would be] glad to avail themselves of the opportunity [an attractive city] affords them to display their own taste in the creation of homes in keeping with the surroundings."[31] Despite the neighborhood's expressed urgent need of more single- and double-occupancy housing for working people, city developers proposed a plan for raising property values.[32] People needed houses for use, but city developers optimistically planned for a housing economy predicated on financial equity and exchange. Planners used the Minneapolis park system as a way to align the needs of the poor with the aspirations of the rich. They used the park as evidence of guaranteed security and stable property values and, in so doing, made private property ownership a precondition for social freedom. This economically bound form of freedom invariably sees entitlements to home owners as public goods and misreads the pressing needs of aggrieved groups' as private interest. It puts an onus on communities with limited resources to pursue freedom and equality through market participation.[33]

Liberal promises of "not yet" freedom have been instrumental historically in uniting antagonistic social groups in Minneapolis. Minnesota maintained the highest rate of "foreign-born" residents in the United States well into the late nineteenth century. Even in the early twentieth-century context of exclusionary immigration policies that constructed U.S. citizenship around gradual incorporation into Whiteness, ethnic tensions simmered among European immigrants.[34] People who worked together did not live together. People who lived together did not pray together.[35] Middle-class reformers committed to policies of "Americanization" often pegged immigrants as perpetrators of labor unrest. In Minnesota, however, when coupled with nationalist promises of middle-class reform, solidarities forged in class struggle ameliorated deeply held ethnic tensions. Even in the aftermath of the truckers' strike of 1934,

ethnic assimilation into White property ownership undermined the collectivity that defined the movement. Working people's access to home ownership
deradicalized democracy because it encouraged workers to identify with self-
interest over and above the common good.

Charles Rumford Walker's foundational study of the 1934 strike revealed
that, even as workers in Minneapolis felt a deep class consciousness, many
identified with the ideals of middle-class nationalism.[36] Walker documents
daily attitudes in Minneapolis two years after the strike, finding that nearly
all of the strikers bought into liberal promises of classless equality. Noting that
at least two-thirds of the city's population spent leisure time in public parks in
1937, Walker reveals a dramatic shift in collective culture. Workers who had
previously been engaged in militant class struggle imagined themselves in alliance with the managerial ethos of a "common" middle class.[37] The social transformation that Walker studies replicated the exclusionary democratic equality
of nineteenth-century universal White male suffrage.[38] In retrospect, strikers
justified their involvement in violent protest as necessary for protecting masculinist notions of the family wage.[39] Their attachment to the male-breadwinner
ideal reinforced nationalist narratives of democratic progress such that the proclaimed centrality of women as equal members of the working class during the
strike was denied by the achievement of male access to freedom.[40] Moreover,
as Lizabeth Cohen argues, masculine protection of the family wage squan-
dered the militancy, talents, and leadership potential of an entire generation
of women workers. The "not yet" freedom that working men assumed hinged
on property relationships to public space. The filter of shared democratic space
protected a veneer of "radical" gains while upholding market inequalities
around racial and gender difference. It is fitting that parks like Powderhorn
serve as sites for registering such ruptures and continuities in working-class
consciousness. They produce a sense of classless equality even as they provide
respite from persisting tensions.

Like parks, movie theaters in the early twentieth century supported the
fantasy production of liberal inclusion. According to Walker, the majority of
workers following the strike attended films regularly, film was a primary topic of discussion from country clubs to union picnics, and people talked about
film as part of the "common" culture of Minneapolis. Of course, 1930s movies
were replete with narrative promises of democratic assimilation that supported
and produced people's impressions of universal middle-class cultural norms.[41]
Theaters themselves are interesting for where they were geographically placed
and also for how they were internally arranged. For example, in 1937 the New
Avalon reopened on the commercial strip of Lake Street in the Powderhorn
neighborhood. Promotional ads in the *East Lake Street Shopper* celebrated the
theater as an elevating institution equally available for the "supreme happiness"
of all members of the community. It was a "work of art," but would not stratify
audiences according to class: "All seats in the auditorium will face the screen
in such a manner as to make each seat equal with each other." In addition, the

advertisement presented the opening as evidence of the middle-class sensibility of the neighborhood: "Pictures will be selected with great care showing at no time anything that will be embarrassing to women or children."[42] The promotion thus constructed democracy through consumer equality, projecting a moral fiction of Powderhorn as becoming a color-blind society.[43]

Although Powderhorn's African American residents in the roughly eighty blocks of the neighborhood rapidly rose to more than four thousand between 1940 and 1960, their stability and prosperity were dramatically challenged in the late 1950s by the development of Highway 35 West, which sliced through the Black neighborhood, breaking up community and limiting existing resources. There is little evidence to suggest any collective protest, cross-class concern, or neighborly opposition to this construction. Instead, in the 1970s and 1980s other groups in the neighborhood interpreted the dispersed effects of racist urban planning as evidence of personal conflict. They perceived the problems caused by urban abandonment as the discrete crimes of a few individuals whose "offense" to private interests was the fact that their lives and existence were read by the middle class as signs of urban "blight."

The environment did resist. When highway construction lowered the water table, Powderhorn Lake dried into a mud hole.[44] Environmental and economical instability caused by urban redevelopment contributed to lowered property values. Although the lake was restored, by 1970 many of the grandiose houses that had earlier evidenced urban progress for a Whitening middle class were selling for less than $15,000. According to a 1965 community improvement report, nearly 10,000 established residents had left the neighborhood between 1950 and 1960. The racial return on developmental progress was concentrated multiracial urban poverty. The report euphemistically blamed people with problems for being problems, explaining poverty as the result of the neighborhood's failure "to share completely in the city's growing prosperity" and its "rapid increase of a long-established but relatively small ethnic [Black] group."[45] The city treated urban "waste" by manufacturing intergroup antagonisms.

At the same time that it fragmented Powderhorn's Black community, the development of highways for suburban commuters allowed city planners to abandon older neighborhoods. This abandonment brought pornography to the New Avalon Theater. By 1957, the theater that laborers experienced as evidence of their inclusion in national equality converted its "family-friendly" screenings to nudist and highbrow foreign films. The owners hoped to increase profits by double-billing these risqué films with Hollywood features. As property values plummeted in the 1970s and 1980s, the New Avalon became one of the most popular hard-core theaters in Minneapolis.[46]

Areas where pornography is tolerated or encouraged can attract creative non-normative populations and social relations.[47] They can also produce conflicts over space by groups unable to move away from one another. Feminist protesters demanded that the state protect their rights to a nonviolent environment. They insisted that the theater be closed on the grounds that the social blight it created directly impinged on their civil rights to private protection. An unnamed protester claimed, "It seems that as neighbors we are being raped by [adults-only businesses]. Their presence makes us fear their expansion each time a local business falters, undermines our neighborhood's image and property values, insults us as we pass by, and discourages people from patronizing shops."[48] This attachment to civil equality made it impossible for feminists to challenge poverty-generating social structures of state racism. In May of 1982, more than 150 feminists and home owners aligned themselves with the Police Department's vice squad in confronting "irate citizens and homosexuals" who were proclaiming that the regulation of Adults Only establishments was sexual harassment.[49] Feminists and others invested in ideas of personal and property protection at the expense of association and accountability.[50] The model of social justice they drew on made shared space the contested terrain of diametrically opposed private rights. In the market logic of citizenship, women's justice can only come when queer justice is deferred; Black freedom is available only as much as immigrant rights are constricted, and so forth and so on, down a long chain of deferrals.[51]

In a context of decreasing resources and increasing social and domestic tensions, Minneapolis's active feminist movement had legitimate concerns about women's safety. Yet these concerns blinded antiporn activists to the value of transgressive uses of normative and non-normative spaces. Moreover, they did not register the antidemocratic impulses underlying their appeals to police. In the economic restructuring of the 1970s, when you fought with the law, the law won. Many others in the neighborhood were aware of this fact. They knew that asking for exclusions in one context often legitimated injustices in another. They began an anticensorship campaign to protect the neighborhood from private interests. According to spokesperson Ronald Mahler, "When any special-interest group tries to capture PPNA [Powderhorn Park Neighborhood Association], the very purpose of PPNA is subverted."[52] In the violent context of increased domestic police forces and covert military action internationally, many in Powderhorn were rightfully wary of allowing state authority to control neighborhood activities.

Nevertheless, the antiporn movement was successful in pressuring porn businesses out of the neighborhood, without considering how this might have created new problems for other neighborhoods. Pornography, like capital, in the 1980s was certainly mobile. Similarly, the antiporn pro-property movement won its bid for safety, but its activists were not aware of the ways that discourses about safety could be used to eradicate spaces that foster interclass association. In his discussion of New York's Times Square redevelopment project, Samuel Delaney argues that the destruction of porn theaters in the city took away some of the last scarce locations where people who were stratified by class and market relations could come together around shared vices. Feminists' desires for safety were legitimate and genuine. Yet their movement for "civil rights" further served the regulatory use of White racial and heterosexual norms for policing queerness and racial difference.[53] This appeal to market citizenship in a neighborhood that was increasingly defined by non-normative categories during the 1980s left many aching for alternatives. Closing the New Avalon limited possibilities for one form of transgressive and erotic cross-class association, but the misfortunes of the sexual economy created opportunities for another form.

In 1988, HOBT moved into the Avalon. By then, it had dreamt fifteen years of May Day celebration into being. Now, the democratic pretenses of 1930s commercial culture promotions of the space were transformed into social realities for democratic art and organizing. HOBT founders envisioned their work as preserving the refusable pasts of the community. They knew that the past was something they could not let go. Their hope was that the theater would keep "alive a host of images and stories, of possible and potential human relationships, kept like seeds of ancient plants against the time when the monoculture comes crashing down, and we need to turn to the old fruits again."[54] However, the event they chose for sharing these seeds comes with contradictions of its own.

May Day is one of the most radical traditions in the United States, but it has also served as a conservative ritual for upholding the economic inequalities of speculative nationalism. I have argued that the structural adjustments culminating in the 1970s and 1980s fostered normative appeals to private property ownership and white heteronormativity in the Powderhorn neighborhood. I have also shown that multiculturalism rests on color-blind discourses that enable structural negligence. These points suggest that, even though Powderhorn's initial May Day was expressly opposed to U.S. militarism, criticized capitalist exploitation, and spoke to multicultural differences, its struggles for abstract equality took form in a context of regulatory democratic inclusion in a national system of property protection. Like park space of the nineteenth century, the freedom of collectivity that May Day created tends to offer temporary relief and imagined unities that cover a generalized condition of social exploitation and competition. Thus, like social space, it is always dangerously at risk of restoring and preserving the social and economic inequalities it aims to challenge. This problem is compounded by the diverse histories of May Day that residents of Powderhorn invariably sift through when they pinpoint May 1 on their calendars as an annual day of dissent.

May Day Many Ways

May Day in the United States has many histories, but each one includes elements that delimit race and sexuality for a market economy. In the United States, May Day has been used for colonial appropriation, revolutionary association, patriotic celebration, radical labor transformation, and multicultural communication. In general we associate it with memories of radical labor activism or with sexually excessive festivals of misrule that enable temporary disruptions of bourgeois norms. Although we are aware that the return to normal following carnivalesque festivals reinforces cultural norms, we do not usually think of May Day as a conservative tradition. In North America it points to a long legacy of cultural management that draws on the traditions of misrule for market preservation. The conservative roots of May Day are always in tension with the radical possibilities that the day suggests. May Day is not only a contested site of cultural negotiation; it is also one of the oldest borrowed traditions used in the United States to foster the racial and sexual norms of market citizenship.

As I discuss in Chapter 1, Thomas Morton drew on the traditions of May Day in 1627 to foster working and trade relationships between indigenous people and proletarian workers. He attempted to create intimacy between Indians, who had the knowledge and resources that could make colonial expropriation more efficient, and European workers, who were charged with the labor of material extraction. When he documented this event, Morton combined Christian and Druid iconography with Greek and Roman mythologies.[55] From the stories that he wove together, he manufactured mythologies of erotic renewal. With these intimacies, he imagined the infinite possibility for labor regeneration. He hoped that the private attachments that European men had to indigenous women would lead to increased profits from primitive accumulation. Morton's was a strategy for efficiency and profit making. The private connections he fostered offered workers who were obligated to extract the raw materials for global production direct access to Indians with knowledge about where to locate and how to obtain these resources.

Morton turned the maypole into a commercial site around which differentiated working and erotic bodies were defined through exchange. Indentured servants worked on contract, but imagined their freedom. Native men traded and negotiated with colonists to retain political autonomy. Finally, Morton invoked and likely provoked indigenous women into sexual exchange to guarantee market stability on the plantation. Fertility and family were good for settlement and production. In addition to the crime of trading weapons with Native people, Morton was penalized for sexual transgression. Richard Slotkin suggests that the name "Mare-Mount" marked the plantation with the specter of sodomy.[56] Furthering this transgression, the sexual exchanges that solidified commerce at Ma-re Mount took place in a context where men and women dressed like animals as they frolicked and seduced one another.[57] Morton, of course, was arrested and exiled for the intimacies and negotiations that he managed and manipulated. Although this "Lord of Misrule" was punished for his "licentiousness" and "profane life," the tradition he introduced to the colonies was later reclaimed for revolutionary purposes.[58]

The May Day revels of the Schuykill Fishing Company, a Pennsylvania fraternal club of the eighteenth century, invoked traditions of misrule to celebrate native inheritance and the coming of spring. Members prepared for new fishing and hunting seasons by spinning tales about "their" imagined Delaware leader. As the story went, King Tammany had once ruled the hunting grounds that these White men "rightfully" inherited. In his honor, they named their May Day "King Tammany Day" and danced around the maypole in Indian costumes.[59] During the Revolutionary War, these bonded brothers easily reinvented their revels for patriotic purposes. Indeed, the Tammany Society (established in 1789) turned the colonial world on its head by building White male privilege through indigenous appropriation, dispossession, and exclusion. Society members dressed as Indians and celebrated an Indian past as a way of imagining themselves "Native Americans." This display and identification made it possible for White men to see themselves as the rightful inheritors of the North American continent because it relegated indigenous people to the past. As Philip Deloria has argued, red-face appropriation established a means for White patriots to imagine themselves in a free republic premised on the "essential" American character that they stole (and rescripted) from indigenous people. They obfuscated indigenous struggles and histories and inverted the terms of rightful occupancy. The racial project of this May Day included reframing acquisitive colonialism as an inherent right to White property ownership. The fraternity "Americanized" its ritual when it ordained Tammany the "Saint of America" under the motto "This is my right; I will defend it."[60] Revolutions waged in the interests of the few are well positioned to become central forces in the oppression of the many. Following the war, the Tammany Society became one of the most influential and exclusive political forces of the nineteenth century.[61]

Given these early deployments of May Day to encourage cultural identifications with property, power, and privilege, it is no wonder that the small town of Burlington, Wisconsin, considered May 1 an appropriate day for celebrating patriotic antagonism during the McCarthy era. By the second half of the twentieth century, cultural unity in the United States had taken shape against the imagined threat of international communism, making democracy and capitalism synonymous.[62] This was the case for the people of Burlington in 1954, when they converted the anticapitalist history of May Day into an anticommunist platform for U.S. patriotism and community unity.

In a town populated by fewer than 10,000 residents, Burlington's May Day attracted an audience of over 30,000 spectators with its anticommunist propaganda.[63] "May Day, U.S. Way" celebrated patriotism and the abstract freedoms of the Bill of Rights with commercial pride. Burlington framed its May Day as a counter-force to political fantasies about communist invasion, celebrating local businesses with more than sixty-one floats to emphasize "the positive side of the American way of life."[64] The town celebrated "political freedoms" by investing in local businesses, parading anticommunist propaganda, and inviting Senators Joseph McCarthy and Alexander Wiley to deliver gatekeeping nationalist polemics. The local bank displayed the city's land grant for property, local businesses compared prices of U.S. commodities to the cost of communist goods, and the local drugstore proudly displayed a banner ordering, "Be thankful we do not have socialized medicine."[65] The dairy float declared, "We're glad we live in the U.S.A where the Gov't can't take our pony away."[66] In tune with anticommunist Cold War nationalism, the protective freedom in this event contradictorily made social antagonism and competitive private interest imperatives for divisive democratic engagement.

Like the rest of the nation, people in this small town had lived through decades of speculative economic chaos. Given their experience of a bust-fueled depression and warfare relief, it is understandable that many found the social stability promised through affective identification with local commerce appealing. As James Lee argues, the "communist menace" made this stability possible. The specter of external military threat legitimated the warfare economy. Increased military production, in turn, laid a foundation for individuals to get ahead because their chances of doing so improved. In periods of market growth, it makes sense that people associate their universal happiness with market promises of progress. This identification is enticing precisely because it suggests that commercial activity guarantees social security. The speculative logic of patriotic freedom not only paints a picture in which everybody has the right to keep a "pony" but also projects a promise in which boundless profits make it possible for anyone to imagine they too will some day own a "pony."

When the fantastical futurity of speculative nationalism collapses, however, noncapitalist forms of emancipation become imaginable and necessary. Peter Linebaugh writes that in Chicago's Haymarket of 1886 "horses were part of the working class" and not objects for private accumulation.[67] Horses carried tons of hay and vegetables to Chicago and other markets. The labor they performed as part of the proletariat came in the form of transportation. Those who celebrate May Day in remembrance of the self-activity and collective resistance of nineteenth-century workers do not see owning a horse as a sign of freedom. They know that when market growth falters, promises of stability often degenerate, turning life—like horses and neighbors—into objects to be disputed in an open marketplace.

When elites pursue endless profits based on the exploitation of workers, animals, and the environment, it becomes difficult for the poor to identify with abstract promises of equality. When workers refuse to dream according to the market ambitions of the wealthy, their emancipation depends on their own imaginations. Booms and busts during the late nineteenth century produced waves of unemployment and worsened working conditions. Industrial unions were the outcome of workers' self-activity and willingness to dream against the odds of capitalist intentions. In his renowned history of labor's May Day, Philip Foner explains that this day off allowed for springtime May festivals that gave seasonal workers in construction trade unions an opportunity to persuade employers to sign union contracts. By 1867 Chicago workers were calling general strikes on May 1 in their fight for an eight-hour workday. By May 1, 1886, the labor movement's general strikes had appeared in most industrial cities and included immigrant and common laborers from across a wide range of European origins and industrial occupations.

Working-class solidarity sustained working-class culture. Workers associating during leisure time provoked anxiety among state authorities.[68] On May 3,
1886, Chicago police fired into a crowd of 6,000 workers protesting a lockout
by the McCormick Harvester Plant, killing four. The next day, a smaller crowd
of 3,000 gathered in Haymarket Square to strategize resistance to police violence. When the crowd had dwindled to less than 200, 180 armed police officers
militantly invaded the square. Seven officers were killed when they attempted
to break up the peaceful protest. Eight anarchists, many of whom had not even
been involved in the incident, were taken into custody to serve as examples in
a state campaign to suppress resistance by generalized fear. Four were executed
by court decision, and one took his own life before the state could have it.[69]

The authorities claimed this history for themselves, raising a statue of a
police officer in Haymarket Square.[70] James Green argues that the police and
legal violence at Haymarket put an end to campaigns for an eight-hour workday, creating a turning point for labor radicalism. However, internationally
workers and others continue to reclaim and celebrate the histories of rebellion,
self-activity, and direct resistance to exploitation and inequality as they gather
and remember on May Day. Peter Linebaugh tracks the international growth of
May Day movements, for example, Cuba in 1890, Mexico in 1913; the Socialist
International Congress joined the campaign for an eight-hour workday in 1890,
and France, Italy, and Spain all had their May Days. German workers stalled
business operations on May Day 1917, and on May Day 1925 New York garment
workers sang the "Internationale" in the Metropolitan Opera House ("May
Day with Heart"). Given the framework for spreading the resistant memory
internationally that May Day created, it is no wonder that the Cultural Front
claimed the day as a radical marker.

Michael Denning documents May Day traditions as powerful cultural symbols for international Cultural Front solidarity. He rightly reads them for how
they symbolically register the "commitment and disenchantment, of solidarity
and separation" at the core of the multiethnic international solidarities of the
period.[71] The international movement that Denning traces through the symbolic
activities of May Day certainly engaged in well-intended efforts to overturn
social and economic power through direct confrontation with class and race
violence. Yet the legacies of May Day that he salutes for their proletarian solidarity may not be adequate for understanding the heteronormative reproduction of racial inequality that market citizenship produces. Like other versions
of this tradition, the Cultural Front's symbolic engagement with the traditions
of May Day are conditioned by market constructions of race and sexuality.

When it comes to perceiving possibilities for social change, metaphors
can be just as powerful as marches. The Lincoln Republic, Denning argues,
labored with the intention of "birthing . . . a new American culture, a second
American Renaissance."[72] This and similar labor metaphors used by the proletarian Cultural Front conditioned the movement's symbolic attachment to
May Day with an ideology that normalized men as workers and viewed women

primarily as the reproducers of the nation. This heteronormative grounding invested its emancipation in the market logics of national culture. It also committed any new "American culture" to the racist underpinnings of national market society. Roderick Ferguson has shown that from the 1930s onward, American constructions of the normative bourgeois family authorized racial and gendered exclusions from the legal and social life of the nation; public policy and social analysis made aberrant Black sexuality the refusable backdrop for White nationalist becoming. Consequently, Black sexuality, cultural practices, and family compositions have been persistently racialized as "pathologically nonheteronormative" exceptions "not yet" disciplined for nationalist freedom.[73] In the process, the culture of unity normalized White masculine productivity by appealing to White women's bodies as the lifeblood of American racial inequality.

Against these odds, the ideal of socially transformative working people's solidarity can be moving and appealing. It makes sense that actors in Powderhorn, and even the primarily Latino and Latin American workers who used Powderhorn Park as the scene for their May 1, 2006, strikes to protect undocumented workers, would appeal to the international labor history of May Day. Memories of collective resistance and global empowerment provided historical armor to these recent May Days.[74] Resistant memories exponentially multiply the self-activity of the present with the human agency of the past. Yet American May Day celebrations tend to reproduce racialized and normative nationalism in both its conservative *and* radical articulations. All histories leading up to Powderhorn's May Day celebrations point back to contexts of social and cultural violence and inequality.

When people in Powderhorn sift through the waste of refusable pasts each May, they do so through a form that is fraught with contradictions in a context of racialized urban abandonment and privilege. When they claim the park as theirs, they do so on top of a system of private property protection that makes social antagonism the center of community. When they engage the roots of May Day, they inherit normative impulses that have been perniciously leveraged against people of color, women, immigrants, and queers. Given these contradictions, when they ask for social justice and imagine lived democracy, the hopes they pursue are always in danger of devolving into deferrals for people without time to wait. The past they look to is a reminder that universal inclusion without representation (nationalism), representation without material change (multiculturalism), material change without self-determination (paternalism), self-determination without collective accountability (neoliberalism), collective accountability without global perspective (provincialism), and global perspective without local attachments (abstract universalism) carry big risks.

Negotiating this terrain is not always easy, but it is something people in Powderhorn treat as urgent. The poetic response is not a reactionary impulse to fix deeply embedded problems with one-dimensional short-term solutions, such as solving policing crises with more resources for "safety." It is about using art to open the imagination to freedoms that have yet to be known. Making puppets takes all of the senses. The smell of clay and papier-mâché combines with the gentle sounds of tools and trash moving across workroom floors. Hundreds of hands mold objects into visions, and the sweet taste of mindfully coordinated collectivity brings the past into contact with the fierce urgency of now. The process works against the odds of racializing returns by working through historical injuries that cumulatively hurt.

The Time Is Now

Faced with recurring nationalist nightmares of racism, materialism, and militarism, the thirty-second annual May Day parade in 2006 declared, "The Time Is Now" to shift away from a thing-oriented society to a life-sustaining society.[75] From three decades of working together, members of the neighborhood had learned that creating a just future requires that they "speak the truth of [their] past. Bring shame and regret into light and acknowledge the choices that have led to our present."[76] They gravely struggled to understand the relationship of the past to the present, yet dreamed a future to carry justice forward and plan a future built on equity. On giant placards they asked the community, "Can we afford" endless war, overconsumption, and gutted public infrastructures? They dreamed for cities like New Orleans, calling out governance for the human-made disaster of Hurricane Katrina and honoring the power of refused people to work in solidarity through mourning and hope.[77] They recognized Powderhorn as another place where public officials and institutions are not adequately answerable to racialized poor people. They called on the spirit of the Declaration of Independence to "alter or to abolish" a government that sells people out by privatizing natural resources, housing, food, education, and health care. With danced, mourned, prayed, and played present action, they directly challenged speculative longings for national progress, instead creating and demanding freedom right here, right now.

May Day the Powderhorn way is about bringing new worlds into being out of the refuse of the old. Puppets are constructed out of free, inexpensive, and readily available resources.[78] HOBT technical director Duane Tougas estimates that nearly 90 percent of the parade is built using only clay, cardboard, newspaper, foam, plywood, and rubber bicycle tires.[79] The puppets are imagined in collaborative conversations between community consensus and individual interpretation. Each spring community members go to the theater, check in with their neighbors, and brainstorm a general theme. With the aid and guidance of theater artists and artistic director Sandy Spieler, May Day comes to life through weeks of public workshops and voluntary participation. The theater opens its doors freely, inviting the neighborhood to turn their dreams into art and expression. People build cities out of cardboard boxes. They claim space using wood, foam, and rubber tires for stilts that make them taller. They build puppets using mud and papier-mâché, feeling with their hands the pains, joys, trepidations, and connections that they visually parade on puppet visages. They transform trash into a movement of memory, bringing to life objects that might otherwise be relegated to landfills.[80] In the process of remembering together, they reconstruct social relationships that speculative nationalism forces apart. The stories people tell at Powderhorn's May Day thus emerge from centuries of confusion created by capitalism. Because these stories are imagined in the context of contradiction, they are neither clean nor without compromise.

The play with waste on May Day is a visual reminder that struggles over meaning are always struggles over resources. When refused people are incorporated into legitimating narratives, they are willingly and often unwillingly positioned to "connect with and ratify the present" according to the norms and expectations of liberal nationalism.[81] When it comes to tradition, Raymond Williams says, stories are often the most powerful resource that subordinated people have for challenging hegemony. The nationalism of "not yet" freedom is a form of inscriptive violence that is designed to align the freedom dreams of unruly resistance into preexisting economic hierarchies. Promises of future freedom are designed to hold people in waiting with the requirement that they refuse their visions for other forms of freedom.

Because they live in a world of constantly changing convergences of power and privilege, access and denial, people in Powderhorn do not move on. They think forward by looking backward. They do not remember nostalgically, but rather recall urgently to better understand the "actively shaping force" of tradition.[82] They watch for the way their dreams are appropriated as bastardized expressions of national virtue. They make do with the resources they have at their disposal: tradition, puppets, state grants, NGO contributions, and commercial advertisements. This may seem a counterintuitive way to think about justice, a recipe for co-optation by conservative forces. It may even seem as if the event is complicit in speculative nationalism or too eager to embrace multicultural diversity uncritically. Refusing traditional strategies of direct resistance, however, makes it possible for May Day to meet people, who may or may not be invested in struggles for justice, where they are. The festival offers participants new categories and associations for changing the logics through which power lives and acts. New ways of knowing empower people to imagine how to reshape the "obvious," to disrupt the "common sense" of deferral, and to see difference, memory, and uncomfortable associations as productive tensions for remaking the world.

Puppets are subversive, according to Peter Schumann, "because the meaning of everything is so ordained and in collaboration with the general sense of everything, and they, being only puppets, are not obliged in this sense and instead take delight in the opposite sense."[83] The confusion created by forms that are logically innocuous but intellectually disruptive carries the potential to change injurious nationalist frameworks as much as it does to change the lives of the oppressed. When narratives are unsettled in this way, even elites, who otherwise command authority, come face to face with the nightmares their privilege creates—socially, environmentally, spiritually, and economically. Their story is also conditioned by refuse. When the people in Powderhorn invite others to join them in this tradition, their subversion sneaks beneath a playful radar.

The delights and affective joys of puppetry do not remain in the park. Seeds of justice carried in the form likely marinate in the memories of participants and viewers. In his discussion of police and state discomfort with puppets at antiglobalization movements, David Graeber addresses how puppetry inverts state claims on safety and protection When states designate as a threat "hundreds of activists in fairy suits tickling police with feather dusters, or padded with so many inflatable inner tubes and rubber cushions they seem to roll along like the Michelin man over barricades, incapable of damaging anyone else but also pretty much impervious to police batons," the violence of state repression becomes playfully visible.[84] Police efforts to criminalize puppets of the caliber made popular as a form of protest by the Bread and Puppet Theater in Vermont, HOBT, activists in antiglobalization movements, and political convention objectors end up making state authority look ridiculous.[85] At the April 15, 2000, rally protesting the IMF and the World Bank in Washington, DC, for example, police declared a fire hazard to shut down a warehouse where activists were building puppets. Claiming that the workspace was being used to manufacture weapons, police rounded up 600 marchers. At the 2000 Republican National Convention in Philadelphia, police, with no legitimate excuse for interfering with peaceful protestors, locked up a warehouse, incarcerating the puppets being made inside and creating an excuse to arrest 75 puppet makers on charges that they were making weapons. Puppets were subsequently banned from George W. Bush's presidential inauguration in Washington, DC.[86] In 2003, the city of Miami proposed a ordinance that would ban puppets from the Free Trade Areas of the Americas summit.[87] There is something silly about arresting puppets. It makes identification with state authority look absurd. Puppets make it necessary to rethink safety and protection around lives and meanings that state securitization refuses. From scraps and debris, people in Powderhorn create hundreds of shaking heads that mourn the past, laugh in the present, and refuse to accept a life of deferral.[88] Puppets make waiting one more day for freedom seem disturbing and absurd.

Persons

Because puppets call on people to rethink norms and attachments, they change social demographics. Immigration since the 1990s has shifted the racial and ethnic composition of the Powderhorn Park neighborhood. Census data in 1990 figured 70 percent of people in Powderhorn as White. The neighborhood became majority minority, according to census data from 2000, when White residency fell to 42 percent. In the aftermath of the housing bubble, the neighborhood became 52 percent White. For a relatively small population of around

8,500 people in a relatively White state, Powderhorn is a self-reported ethnically mixed neighborhood: 26 percent Hispanic, 13 percent Black, and 4 percent Native American.[89] Although smaller in number, the rising percentages of Somali and Cambodian refugees in the area contribute to its global heterogeneity. Many new immigrants in Minneapolis claim to identify more with global than with U.S. culture, report no desire to assimilate into U.S. society and politics, and inhabit the city as temporary residents waiting to return home.[90] As evidenced by flourishing Latino businesses along Lake Street and by Minneapolis's version of the 2006 Day without Immigrants protest in Powderhorn Park, others justifiably claim rights to inhabit and contribute to the city where they live and work.[91] Although it cannot be determined whether the changes in May Day that have temporally corresponded to recent demographic shifts are causal or coincidental, it is certain that the constellation of local change and global flows of capital and humans bring people together in ways that call into question social imperatives of national identification.

In the landscape of overlapping economic, political, racial, environmental, and cognitive crises that have brought diverse people into unforeseen contact in the era of globalization, the imperative that recent arrivals and targets of state-sanctioned discrimination catch up with the purported progress of U.S. nationalism cannot cohere. The idea that liberal nationalism is the absolute exemplar of freedom and development, and that others must race to make up for lost time, is shattered by the experiential knowledge that people exchange. Even as the U.S. nation-state mobilized a global war against a nonstate abstraction to pressure the world to believe that its version of democracy was the only one possible, people's creation of new subjectivities out of unpredictable contacts and transformative forms suggests that other freedoms are both possible and essential. The creative process that HOBT adopts to create May Day each year requires participants to work through preexisting power and privilege. Although tradition suggests a certain repetition of ideas and practices, direct democratic production invites adaptation and reimagination over and above inscriptive imperatives to relinquish difference. In this context, people are not asked to set aside their freedom dreams in favor of a single nationalist vision. Rather, the May Day parade is open to any person or group who wants to be represented. Any group with a message, delivered peacefully, is welcome to join the Free Speech section, which follows the HOBT-produced parade.[92]

The creative process that gives shape to the parade each year is not always easy and is often imperfect, but it is a conscientious mode for critically questioning who "we" are and "where" we are every year. In three public forums preceding the event, community members are invited to air their concerns and hopes in a collaborative forum to establish the annual theme. In response to the first meeting, artists and community members draw up proposals subject to consensus-based direct decision making at the second meeting. Here, rather than vote all or nothing on a single proposal, community members engage in open dialogue where proposals are reworked to a point of general acceptability, if not full agreement. At a third meeting, artists create storyboards to present a theme for the parade. Community members can work on a particular section where they can produce their own interpretation of a general concept, work on various segments, or merely listen or offer commentary.

Public meetings are followed by a month of free public workshops in which all are welcome to construct or collaborate on the year's theme. The opportunities for autonomous expression combined with the free distribution of shared resources result in poly-vocal free expression.[93] Although it is imagined collectively, the parade often unfolds unpredictably. People come to May Day for different reasons: some to celebrate the world that is, others to remember worlds that were, and still others to imagine worlds that could become. The unlikely and likely contacts and associations that emerge in cross-class collaborations and open-ended festivity do not cohere in narrative synthesis. In asking people to imagine and work together, HOBT urges them to think about what it might mean to live together in just and equitable social relationships. The motley convergence of stories and dreams erupts as an overabundance of possibilities of freedom around an orderly chaos of living democracy.

But May Day is also difficult and traumatic because it is staged on the hard work of turning time on its head. The 2006 parade, for example, focused on "Speaking the Truth" of the past as it shapes the present. In it participants grappled with the skeletal remains of deferred justice to prisoners, immigrants, and free thinkers. Much as on the Mexican *Día de los Muertos*, as skeletons move into the future they honor lives that are leveraged and lost under speculative nationalism. In the context of militant patriotism following the World Trade Center attacks, the parade entered "the Haze" to issue a bold reflection on the "role the United States plays in perpetuating institutionalized misery in the world."[94] It also disrupted the time clock of capitalist futurity with sluggish drones reciting the refrains of repression: "Time is money, money is time." In taking people into the wounds of speculative nationalism, the parade puts on display their deep and intimate entanglement in structural violence and calls for collective accountability to bring about justice in the request to "Let Your Heart Break."

Part of the struggle and process of healing is figuring out how to ethically inhabit space. In 1987 the parade adopted wisdom from Chief Seattle's speech to think through how "we all may be family after all." In the early 1990s, the festival focused on the implications of living in the entrails of settler colonialism with the parade themes "Return to Turtle Island" (1991) and "I Am Another Yourself."(1992) Engagement with indigenous history and knowledge systems also ties the event to antiglobalization resistance and environmental justice movements. Giant turtle puppets in 2002 and 2007, for example, pointed to the deaths of hundreds of thousands of sea turtles caused by the World Trade Organization's override of nation-based regulations to protect endangered species.[95]

When they call into question the roots of the nation, celebrants must tread lightly on the way that the nation-state has been an important, albeit imperfect, resource for demanding justice and historical transformation for antiracist freedom struggles. Taken from Martin Luther King's 1967 address to the Southern Christian Leadership Conference, "Where Do We Go from Here?" the theme of May Day 2005 clearly did not abandon the struggles and gains of former movements for justice but rather asked for a collective reckoning with the failures of the past in the context of new social formations and daily associations. Picking up on the global undercurrents of Dr. King's demands for structural transformation, Powderhorn engaged in a poetic assessment of the unfulfilled democracy of the past to strategize a politics for the global injustices of the present. As volunteers in this and subsequent years followed up on the structural critique of private ownership of public resources such as water, food, and books which was an emerging consideration of the SCLC's late Civil Rights agenda, they, like King, proposed a dramatic reconsideration of social freedom through cultural relationship rather than solely as a practice of public policy.

In addressing global responsibility for equitable sharing of resources, open expression of insubordinate histories that converge in the park space overwhelm divisions fostered by the market state and state violence. For example, the emphasis on global rather than individual injustice has required an accounting of human loss from multiple locations in the community's return to the formative antiwar convictions of May Day. At a time when the patriotic media silenced and nationalized the travesty of war, in 2005 May Day volunteers spent weeks hand-painting the names of the war dead regardless of national borders. As the banners they produced trailed for blocks, tens of thousands of spectators were humbled by symbols of the weight of war. In the overwhelming presence of names representative of the racial demographic of Powderhorn, residents ruminated on their shared sorrows, finding human affinities in defiance of a market state that promotes human antagonisms. Here the history of U.S. racial oppression and imperialism in the Middle East were figured as common causes, making justice a global concern rather than an outcome of nationalist political victory. In Powderhorn Park, this dramatic evidence of a racialized war within the ranks of the U.S. military as well as within the identities of its victims created cause for a radical reassessment of the nation-state as the guarantor of democratic equality. As depicted in the cover image, the nation-state was stripped to the bone and dismantled, positioning spectators to assess their responsibilities to others and their participation in perpetuating inequality.

Local poet Louis Alemayehu, in a poem he wrote for the 2012 festival, called this intersubjective attachment the "blessed curse" in which "I am because you are." The chronic crises defining the twenty-first century create renewed urgency for directing critical capacities toward contradictory ideas about freedom, equality, and justice that constitute capitalism's cultural contract with the U.S. nation-state. The challenge to think about democracy by thinking about life as inscribed in a global web of interdependence encourages ethical assessment of the violence that liberal individualism and inscriptive nationalism endorse against the self and others. Like James Scott, Alemayehu registers a curse as a "loving prayer," an indication of subtle resistance that burdens people with an obligation to alter the fate of destiny.[96] A curse is a form of speech that recognizes, recharts, and remythologizes reality by laying asymmetrical power bare.[97] A curse is a portal into dehumanizing social relations. A curse testifies to ongoing life, to the continuing being of people who persist despite conditions of subordination. A curse is a claim to the life and dignity of the oppressed. A curse points to the injustices that lead the subjected to seek revenge. A curse also demands reparation with a vision of retribution. If successful, a curse transports perpetrators of oppression into the liminal space where they can no longer exercise their power to coerce. A curse is thus a philosophical aperture into the universal susceptibility of social contracts to become violent acts of "wasting" life. When life is held ransom for continued existence, no future is ever secure. A curse declares that anyone might become the next one whose life is relegated nonexistent. When Alemayehu calls the curse that connects all people a blessing, he proposes a radical conception of human equality. The proposition that every life is worthy means that there are no legitimate grounds—either national or economic—for "wasting" life. In the collective reckoning with such propositions, May Day claims Powderhorn Park as sacred ground.

The symbolic action of imagining the death of the nation-state in Powderhorn rescripts the park as a scene of refused possibility rather than a site for regulating private property and market individualism. But it is also a preamble to a conversation about justice, inequality, and the cumulative consequences of capitalist crises. Alternative possibilities emerge from reimagining political desires for detachment (e.g., freedom *from* injustice, emancipation *from* enslavement) as devotions to building freedom through attachments (e.g., freedom *to* thrive, social value *as* justice). As they remember the injustices of the past in their current relationships, Powderhornians are under no illusion that they have solved racial injustice, but as more of the neighborhood's new and long-term residents actively engage and respond to the hurts of history on May Day, what they suggest is that a redefinition of our attachment to space is certainly worth imagining. Part of this reimagining takes place through listening for the ways that people targeted in the cross hairs of racialized capitalism somehow still resist and beat the odds. In 2015, Powderhorn stood in solidarity with Black Lives Matter with a thematic reminder: "And Still We Rise." The parade exposed the "Elephant in the Room" as a culture of White privilege that has systemically profited through the repression and deferral of Black freedom and power. The struggle of making do is not just about fixing streets and fighting "crime." It is about transforming streets with bold expressions of recognition, reparation, and redemption. The 2015 parade did this with visions of alternatives to policing and imagining safe communities premised on freedom and health and sustained by systems that are established on "cooperative abundance."[98] Participatory collectivities remake space by fundamentally rethinking concepts of the public and safety around the lives, needs, and dignity of all human beings. It takes a long historical commitment to working through cumulative injuries to build a new society out of the refuse of the old. It is not easy work. Yet the odds are in favor of transformative justice so long as May Day and acts like it happen again next year and more.

Notes

INTRODUCTION

1. The U.S. housing crash resulted in an estimated loss of over $6 trillion in household wealth. Of this total, United for a Fair Economy estimates White American asset loss at 7 percent, Latino American asset loss at 43 percent, and African American asset loss at 27 percent. Risk is felt more by African Americans and Latinos not only because people of color are disproportionately targeted for predatory home loans but also because they are the hardest hit by job losses in a recession. According to the *Wall Street Journal*, for example, between June 2009 and November 2010, 557,000 African Americans and 292,000 Latinos experienced recession-related job loss (see "Job Gap Widens in Uneven Recovery," *Wall Street Journal*, November 11, 2013, available at http://online.wsj.com/article/SB10001424052748703946504575470001733933356 .html#articleTabs%3Dinteractive, accessed July 6, 2014. The speculative tendency of other socially destructive investment markets is undergirded by remarkable parallels to the euphoria that drove up home prices. Ruth Wilson Gilmore's analysis of the massive post-1970s build-up of the U.S. prison regime as a spatial outlet for surplus financial capital, land, labor, and state capacity points to the speculative inducement to invest in incarceration. The euphoric sentiment of financial gain driving a tough-on-crime society is that prisons can always be filled. The outcome is a severely imbalanced carceral system in which 2.4 million people are denied freedom in America's cages. Adam Gopnik claims that there are currently more African American and Latino men contained in the unfreedom of the various arms of the correctional system than were held in slavery in 1850. Speculation in health care is seen in Elizabeth Rosenthal's investigative journalism on price gouging and new entrants in the hospital marketplace in the post–Affordable Care Act economy. Health care speculation also racializes risk. According to United for a Fair Economy, prior to the passage of the Patient Protection and Affordable Care Act, 29 percent of African Americans and 19 percent of Latinos were uninsured, as compared to 11 percent of White Americans. Thus African Americans and Latinos had the most

to gain from the act. However, twenty-five states, primarily in southern regions where poverty is disproportionately racialized, refused to expand Medicaid programs under the act, which does not cover undocumented immigrants. It is likely that if the bubble effect of hospital closures and skyrocketing prices collapses, African Americans and Latinos will be disproportionately subject to unaffordable medical costs. Mark Naison sees a similar trend in the charter school movement. As is evident in the city of New Orleans, school privatization has become a backdoor tactic for dismantling teachers unions through the use of temporary Teach for America nonprofessional volunteers. Not only does this movement destabilize the unions that have been the historical anchor of the Black middle class in the U.S. South; it is fueled by an investment fever related to available federal funding. The charter school funding stream, which is often based on high-stakes test scores, has resulted in a system of broad racialized discrimination in which historically underresourced schools are again stripped of self-determination by the "innovative" interventions of for-profit charter schools. Research shows that charter schools not only do not outperform public schools with comparable student populations but also systematically discriminate against English learners and special-needs students; systematically expel students with low test performance; and engage in abusive disci- plinary practices and strict enforcement of behavioral codes to procure profitable test scores. See Gilmore, *Golden Gulag* (Berkeley: University of California Press, 2007); and Gopnik, "The Caging of America," *New Yorker*, January 30, 2012. Also see Rosenthal's series in the *New York Times*: "The Health Care Waiting Game," July 6, 2014; "The Price of Prevention," July 3, 2014; "Medicine's Top Earners Are Not the M.D.s," May 18, 2014; "Cost Is the Greatest Taboo in U.S. Health Care," April 27, 2014; "When Health Costs Harm Your Credit," March 9, 2014; and "Patients' Costs Skyrocket; and Specialists' Incomes Soar," January 18, 2014. See also United for a Fair Economy, *State of the Dream 2014: Healthcare for Whom?* available at http://FairEconomy.org, accessed July 30, 2014; and Naison, "Why Charter School Scandals Resemble the Subprime Mortgage Crisis," *With a Brooklyn Accent*, April 9, 2015, available at http://withabrooklynaccent.blogspot .com, accessed July 30, 2014.

2. Initiated on July 8, 2013, the sixty-day strike led to one death and resulted in the California Department of Corrections and Rehabilitation agreeing to hold public hear- ings. The Short Corridor Collective at Pelican Bay issued the following demands: (1) end group punishment and administrative abuse; (2) abolish debriefing policies and modify active/inactive gang status criteria; (3) comply with U.S. Commission on Safety and Abuse guidelines on ending long-term solitary confinement; (4) provide adequate food and nutrition; (5) provide programming and privileges for indefinite solitary housing unit inmates. See http://prisonerhungerstrikesolidarity.wordpress.com/, accessed July 8, 2014.

3. The African American movement to clean up bank-abandoned homes is informed by a long history of segregation and urban abandonment. In the racial politics of neighborhood instability, bank-pursued evictions resonate as community defilement because vacant properties in distressed communities tend toward survivalist strate- gies (squatting, illicit economies, territorial confrontations) that spread interpersonal harm. See Laura Gottesdiener, "The Great Eviction: Black America and the Toll of the Foreclosure Crisis," *Mother Jones*, August 1, 2013.

4. Idle No More began in Canada in December 2012. It is a grassroots call for a peaceful revolution built on the principles of mutual respect and coexistence between indigenous and nonindigenous people, with the express goal of honoring indigenous sov- ereignty and protecting land and water. The movement is made up of a network of indig- enous communities in a struggle to protect and honor indigenous treaties, hold national

governments accountable to the U.N. Declaration of the Rights of Indigenous People to resist development in their territories, and to forge an active resistance to gender-based violence against indigenous women. See Idle No More, *Turn the Tables: Self-Determination Not Termination*, August 19, 2014, available at http://www.idlenomore.ca, accessed August 24, 2014; and Amanda Morris, "Twenty-First Century Debt Collectors," *Women's Studies Quarterly* 42, no. 1–2 (2014): 242–256.

5. Jordan Flaherty, *Floodlines: Community and Resistance from Katrina to the Jena Six* (Chicago: Haymarket, 2010).

6. Heidi Hoechst, "Epidemiology of Entrepreneurialism: Reflections on the Social Innovation Industrial Complex" (paper presented at the Annual Meeting of the American Studies Association, Washington, DC, November 2013).

7. Costas Lapivitsas rightfully differentiates extreme financialization—the expansion of the financial sector's capacity to profit from the trade of financial assets and complex financial instruments—from speculation. Although somewhat of a porous distinction, financialization serves a systemic purpose: to infuse the economy with the means to support the productive sector. Speculation, conversely, is a zero-sum form of exchange in which the procurement of profits serves no relevant purpose for productive growth. The ready slippage between financialization and speculation in the twenty-first century results from the financial sector's steady success in placing near total regulatory control in the hands of financiers. Thus the financial industry has been self-empowered to expand financial profits with little to no accountability to any public or productive body. Expanded ability to profit from financial assets begets a system of financial extrapolation in which expectant climates of risk with no risk (i.e., the invention of financial netting) create the conditions for crafty predatory financial innovation. Jonathan Levy, among others, argues that, because every commercial transaction entails some aspect of risk and uncertainty, to a degree all profit making is speculative. See Lapivitsas, *Profiting without Profits: How Finance Exploits Us All* (New York: Verso, 2013); and Levy, *Freaks of Fortune: The Emerging World of Capitalism and Risk in America* (Cambridge, MA: Harvard University Press, 2012).

8. Ash Amin and Nigel Thrift, eds., *The Cultural Economy Reader* (Malden, MA: Blackwell, 2004).

9. James Baldwin, "On Being White . . . and Other Lies," in *The Cross of Redemption: Uncollected Writings*, ed. Randall Kenan (New York: Vintage, 2011), 168.

PART I

1. David W. Noble, *Death of a Nation* (Minneapolis: University of Minnesota Press, 2002), 200.

2. Thomas Jefferson to William Ludlow, September 6, 1824, in Merrill D. Peterson, *The Political Writings of Thomas Jefferson* (Charlottesville: University of Virginia Press, 2002), 211.

3. George Lipsitz, *How Racism Takes Place* (Philadelphia: Temple University Press, 2011); and Lipsitz, *The Possessive Investment in Whiteness* (Philadelphia: Temple University Press, 1998).

4. The foreclosure epidemic had yet to reach its halfway mark in 2011 with 2.7 million foreclosed U.S. homes and an additional 3.6 million loans at imminent risk. African American and Latino borrowers, the disproportionate targets of predatory lending, were twice as likely as White home owners to lose properties. See Elvin Wyly, C. S. Ponder, Pierson Nettling, Bosco Ho, Sophie Ellen Fung, Zachary Liebowitz, and Dan Hammel,

"New Racial Meanings of Housing in America," *American Quarterly* 64, no. 3 (2012): 571–604; and Center for Responsible Lending, "Lost Ground, 2011: Disparities in Mortgage Lending and Foreclosure," November 17, 2011, available at www.responsible lending.org, accessed August 23, 2014.

5. With First-World consumption of the cut of a diamond, for example, the force of depth intersects with colonial deprivation and the sale is structurally implicated in a trade that has advanced through warfare.

CHAPTER 1

Epigraphs: Thomas Jefferson, "Address to the Deputies of the Cherokee Upper Towns" (January 9, 1809), in *The Writings of Thomas Jefferson*, ed. Albert Ellery Bergh (Washington, DC: Thomas Jefferson Association, 1905), 16:458; Chief Koychezetel, quoted in Rowena McClinton, ed., *The Moravian Springplace Mission to the Cherokees* (Lincoln: University of Nebraska Press, 2010), 93; and Chief Justice John Marshall, majority opinion, *Johnson v. M'Intosh*, 21 U.S. 543, 5 L. Ed. 681, 8 Wheat. 543 (March 10, 1823).

1. Davis Rich Dewey, *Financial History of the United States* (London: Forgotten Books, 2012 [1903]), 68.

2. The Land Act of 1796 provided for the survey and sale of public land through an auction system. It authorized the sale of one-half of surveyed townships in one-quarter allotments—5,760 acres—to large land companies, with remaining sections—640 acres—to be auctioned at a minimum price of $2 per acre. The plan explicitly aimed to make small plots of land available to farmers and individual property owners and to promote the interests of large speculators. See Songho Ha, *The Rise and Fall of the American System* (London: Pickering and Chato, 2009).

3. "Ordinance for Ascertaining the Mode of Disposing of Lands in the Western Territory," in *Journals of the Continental Congress, 1774–1789*, ed. C. Ford Worthington et al. (Washington, DC, 1904–1937), 29:923.

4. Paul W. Gates discusses Jefferson's 1774 framing of preemptive rights as making any land that a citizen finds vacant subject to allotment. See Gates, *History of Public Land Law Development* (Washington, DC: Public Land Law Review Committee, November 1968).

5. Jerry Mashaw argues that the government extended debt relief because the social prohibition against purchasing a neighbor's land made it such that forfeited properties were virtually unsellable and because debtors blamed the government for creating poor economic conditions with the War of 1812. See Mashaw, *Creating the Administrative Constitution: The Lost One Hundred Years of American Administrative Law* (New Haven, CT: Yale University Press, 2012).

6. Tiya Miles, *Ties That Bind* (Berkeley: University of California Press, 2005).

7. Internal tribal disputes and external tribal differences, however, impeded diplomatic efforts to create a united indigenous front. See Rowena McClinton, ed., *The Moravian Springplace Mission to the Cherokee* (Lincoln: University of Nebraska Press, 2010), 170.

8. Vernon L. Parrington, *Main Currents in American Thought* (New York: Harcourt Brace, 1927); and F. O. Matthiessen, *The American Renaissance* (New York: Oxford University Press, 1941).

9. Larry Reynolds, "Strangely Ajar with the Human Race: Hawthorne, Slavery, and the Question of Moral Responsibility," in *Hawthorne and the Real: Bicentennial Essays*, ed. Millicent Bell (Columbus: Ohio State University Press, 2005). Reynolds provides a detailed

treatment of Hawthorne's ambivalent feelings about slavery and national purification. Teresa Goddu argues that Hawthorne's attachment to a market system that depended on slavery shaped his authorial identity and his romances. See Goddu, "Letters Turned to Gold: Hawthorne, Authorship, and Slavery," *Studies in American Fiction* 29, no. 1 (2001): 49–76. For an argument about the crisis of language Hawthorne experienced because of the Compromise of 1850, see Michael T. Gilmore, "Hawthorne and Politics (Again): Words and Deeds in the 1850s," in *Hawthorne and the Real: Bicentennial Essays*, ed. Millicent Bell (Columbus: Ohio State University Press, 2005). Shelley Streeby's reading of *The House of the Seven Gables* counterposes Hawthorne's novel to sensational working-class fiction, arguing that it was against the backdrop of class conflict that Hawthorne inscribed nationalism as a middle-class fantasy. See Streeby, "Haunted Houses: George Lippard, Nathaniel Hawthorne and Middle-Class America," *Criticisms* 38, no. 1 (1996): 443–472. For a class analysis, see David Anthony, "Class, Culture, and the Trouble with White Skin in Hawthorne's *The House of the Seven Gables*," *Yale Journal of Criticism* 12, no. 2 (1999): 249–268. Michael Gilmore argues that Hawthorne struggled to express a "radical" egalitarian message in negotiating a constrained literary marketplace; see Gilmore, *American Romanticism and the Marketplace* (Chicago: University of Chicago Press, 1988). For an extended study of how market changes/technologies created Hawthorne's popularity and influenced his literary style, see Richard Brodhead's foundational study *The School of Hawthorne* (New York: Oxford University Press, 1986). John Carlos Rowe explores the racial dynamics of Hawthorne's temporality, arguing that his allegories resolve international and transnational conflicts as strangely national "American" presents. In Hawthorne's mode of national destiny, Rowe identifies a type of cultural imperialism in which U.S. ideals are assumed as a model for global replication. See Rowe, "Nathaniel Hawthorne and Transnationality," in *Hawthorne and the Real: Bicentennial Essays*, ed. Millicent Bell (Columbus: Ohio State University Press, 2005), 88–106; also see Rowe, *The New American Studies* (Minneapolis: University of Minnesota Press, 2002).

10. The speculative history of this case all but disappeared until 1991, when Lindsay Robertson followed an archival hunch to a descendant of the last secretary of the land company who had saved hundreds of corporate records. With acute detail, Robertson reveals that the initial purchase of the indigenous land that later became the point of contention in *Johnson v. M'Intosh* was a fraudulent acquisition that Murray made in the hope that the impending revolutionary upset of territorial jurisdiction would later work in his favor. Murray's purchase in 1773 was a gamble that revolutionary forces would defeat Britain. It was made on transactions backed by legal fictions. See Robertson, *Conquest by Law: How the Discovery of America Dispossessed Indigenous People of Their Lands* (Oxford: Oxford University Press, 2005).

11. Daniel M. Friedenberg documents the particular land holdings and corporate stock holdings of figures such as George Washington, Thomas Jefferson, Benjamin Franklin, and Patrick Henry. See Friedenberg, *Life, Liberty and the Pursuit of Land* (Buffalo, NY: Prometheus, 1992).

12. The land under review in the case included both the 1773 purchase and an additional 20,000 square miles the company had purchased directly from the Pinakishaw Indians in 1805.

13. Marshall's decision argued that the colonial doctrine of discovery, in which the first government to encounter had the first right of purchase, was a legal justification for the Trade and Intercourse Act. He added in his *obiter dicta* that possession of discovery gave colonial governments title to the land. In effect, he established U.S. ownership of lands that the nation would have had to pay for otherwise.

14. Quoted in Robertson, *Conquest by Law*, 176.

15. Walter R. Echo-Hawk, *In the Courts of the Conqueror: The 10 Worst Indian Law Cases Ever Decided* (Golden, CO: Fulcrum, 2010).

16. Theda Perdue, *Cherokee Women* (Lincoln: University of Nebraska Press, 1998), 26–27. Michelene Pesantubbee draws on oral tradition and archeological records to conjecture that formal recognition of women's agricultural labor restored values of "balance, restitution, reciprocity and consensus" in the Green Corn Ceremonies of the Choctaw people. She argues that, after almost five hundred years of corn cultivation, French colonization during the seventeenth century caused deterioration of Choctaw harvests. The political-economic shift toward an exchange economy reorganized the Choctaw means of subsistence such that women's relationship to the land and social knowledge faded along with the Choctaw version of Green Corn Ceremonies.

17. Claudio Saunt, *A New Order of Things: Property Power, and the Transformation of the Creek Indian, 1733–1816* (Cambridge: Cambridge University Press, 1999), 43.

18. Kathleen DuVal, *The Native Ground: Indians and Colonists in the Heart of the Continent* (Philadelphia: University of Pennsylvania Press, 2005).

19. Gregory Evans Dowd, *A Spirited Resistance: The North American Struggle for Unity* (Baltimore: Johns Hopkins University Press, 1992), 173.

20. Angie Debo, *The Road to Disappearance: A History of the Creek Indians* (Norman: University of Oklahoma Press, 1941); Theda Perdue, *Nations Remembered: An Oral History of the Five Civilized Tribes, 1865–1907* (Westport, CT: Greenwood, 1980); and Jordan Paper, *Native North American Religious Traditions: Dancing for Life* (Westport, CT: Praeger, 2007).

21. Perdue, *Nations Remembered*, 88.

22. Paper, *Native North American Religious Traditions*, 102. According to Creek scholar Kenneth McIntosh, "Green Corn ceremonial[s] continue to keep Muskogee culture and identity intact despite two centuries of pressures to assimilate," quoted in Paper, *Native North American Religious Traditions*, 104. Living through ancestral land from a distance continues in the present day at sites as diverse as Yuchi settlements in eastern Oklahoma, where the Green Corn Ceremony signals tribal longevity and endurance, and the Mashantucket Pequot's Foxwoods Casino, where it is a point of pan-Indian reference at the Foxwoods museum. For some the tradition remains sacred; for others it has been secularized. Either way, appealing to the corn harvest calls up a gendered epistemology for regenerating life by making delicate cyclical adaptations to environmental and social systems to germinate new growth. The objective of long-term social sustenance for tribal longevity remains a central feature of Green Corn traditions. The ceremony is used in diverse ways to stake claims on indigenous sovereignty through the endurance and adaptability of the sacred land/cultural/socioeconomic epistemologies of colonized people. See Jason Baird Jackson, "The Paradoxical Power of Endangerment: Traditional Native American Dance and Music in Eastern Oklahoma," *World Literature Today* (September–October 2007): 37–41.

23. Peter Temin, *The Jacksonian Economy* (New York: Norton, 1969).

24. Alasdair Roberts, *America's First Great Depression: Economic Crisis and Political Disorder after the Panic of 1837* (Ithaca, NY: Cornell University Press, 2013).

25. Stanley Lebergott documents a White-settler hoarding mentality that developed in the 1840s among settlers who sought to purchase land for future generations. According to his math, monopolist purchases were 5 percent of total land sales. See Lebergott, "The Demand for Land: The United States, 1820–1860," *Journal of Economic History* 45, no. 2 (1985): 181–212.

26. Citizens without access to expendable capital were not always as confident in the profitability of a debt society. The monetary and credit system, one Virginia Congressman feared, encouraged the "few who have money and are inclined to speculate on the distresses of the country to monopolize the property of fellow citizens, and constitute them '*hewers of wood and drawers of water*,'" quoted in Charles Sellers, *The Market Revolution: Jacksonian America 1815–1846* (New York: Oxford University Press, 1994), 105. This is to suggest that citizens knew that credit was often leveraged on the ability of lenders to foreclose properties and on the propensity of investors to exploit labor when they failed to produce the necessary surplus value for meeting credit obligations and profit expectations. When economic need forced workers from land into factories, laborers were often bound to future work in a form of debt peonage created by price discrepancies between what they earned and what they were charged as expenses in company stores. In this climate, confidence was sustained by capital's ability to restructure modes of production and profits in the event that prices fell or changing conditions limited means of payment. That is, if value did not rise to meet desired profits, increased exploitation was the likely method for avoiding losses.

27. Walter Johnson, *Soul by Soul: Life inside the Antebellum Slave Market* (Cambridge, MA: Harvard University Press, 2001); Miles, *Ties That Bind*; and Alexander Saxton, *The Indispensable Enemy* (Berkeley: University of California Press, 1975).

28. Michael Denning, *Culture in the Age of Three Worlds* (New York: Verso, 2004).

29. In his gloss of *New English Canaan*, Jack Dempsey argues that the text likely derived from a long legal brief. See Dempsey, ed., *New English Canaan by Thomas Morton of "Merry Mount"* (New York: Digital Scanning, 2000).

30. Dempsey, *New English Canaan*, 2.

31. Ibid., 113.

32. Ibid., 185.

33. Beth Piatote, "Domestic Trials: Indian Rights and National Belonging in Works by E. Pauline Johnson and John M. Oskison," *American Quarterly* 63, no. 1 (2011): 95–116.

34. My goal in approaching the works of such a canonized and debated author is not to provide a definitive new reading of particular texts; nor am I intervening in ongoing debates regarding the author's particular relationship to the social dynamics of the racism of his era. I do not seek to make a claim for U.S. Cultural Studies on what Gordon Hutner has termed a "critical proprietorship" of Hawthorne—that is, a return to the author that seeks to advance a particular critical stance in a struggle waged over meaning. Robert Levine's contention with Joel Pfister is indicative of the tension around Hawthorne's racism. Levine reads Hawthorne as much more progressive in his thinking on race than many of his contemporaries at the *Democratic Review*. Pfister calls attention to Hawthorne's ideological grounding in middle-class ideals that were premised on racism, sexism, and antisemitism. Yet he is also attentive to the ways that Hawthorne critically chronicled the racial violence of the past as a social theorist. My reading assumes that literary texts implicitly bear traces of the context of production, yet it does not assume that Hawthorne himself was not critical or aware of the problems of his era. See Levine, *Dislocating Race and Nation: Episodes in Nineteenth-Century American Literary Nationalism* (Chapel Hill: University of North Carolina Press, 2008); also see Pfister, "Hawthorne as Cultural Theorist," in *The Cambridge Companion to Nathaniel Hawthorne*, ed. Richard Milliton (Cambridge: Cambridge University Press, 2004), 33–59.

35. Nathaniel Hawthorne, "The May-Pole of Merry Mount," in *Twice-Told Tales*, introduction by Rosemary Mahoney (New York: Random House, 2001), 41.

36. Ibid.

37. David Noble, *Death of a Nation: American Culture and the End of Exceptionalism* (Minneapolis: University of Minnesota Press, 2002).

38. The global reach of U.S. credit was an outcome of the predominance of British mercantilism. Because Britain had limited demand for agricultural products, the United States relied on trade around the world to establish credit for financing imports from British markets. See Sellers, *Market Revolution*, 21. Global exchange was the primary source of U.S. national revenue in the early nineteenth century. Prior to the land boom of the mid-1830s, 90 percent of U.S. revenue was attached to tariffs. See Temin, *Jacksonian Economy*.

39. Hawthorne, "May-Pole of Merry Mount," 39.

40. Ibid., 42.

41. Ibid., 41.

42. Ibid.

43. Mikhael Bakhtin, *Rabelais and His World*, trans. Helene Iswolsky (Bloomington: Indiana University Press, 2009); James Scott, *Domination and the Arts of Resistance: Hidden Transcripts* (New Haven, CT: Yale University Press, 1992); and Peter Stallybrass and Allon White, *The Politics and Poetics of Transgression* (Ithaca, NY: Cornell University Press, 1986).

44. Hawthorne, "May-Pole of Merry Mount," 43, 45.

45. Ibid., 41.

46. Ibid., 48.

47. Gates, *History of Public Land Law Development*, 227–228.

48. Much like contemporary crises, the Panic of 1837 spread systemically beyond the boundaries of the United States. See Jill M. Lepler, *The Many Panics of 1837: People, Politics, and the Creation of a Transatlantic Financial Crisis* (New York: Cambridge University Press, 2013).

49. Jackson had sold 68,750 acres of land on promissory notes, which he used for additional purchases. When the buyer went bankrupt and could not fulfill his debt obligation, Jackson was forced to cover the amount he expected to receive from his other assets. See Robert Remini, *Andrew Jackson* (New York: Harper Perennial, 1999).

50. Sean Willentz, *Rise of American Democracy: Jefferson to Lincoln* (New York: Norton, 2006).

51. The 1824 tariff on cotton was set at 33 percent; the 1828 tariff was 50 percent. See Ha, *Rise and Fall of the American System*, 121.

52. Credit economies always gamble on expectations that commodity prices or additions of productive value will raise prices, that discrepancies in exchange rates will remain imbalanced in favor of profits, and that both creditors and debtors will honor the original terms of their obligations. In the mercantile system of the eighteenth and nineteenth centuries, elitism and pedigree were the basis of trust in credit agreements. Economic opportunities were often reserved for those with preexisting wealth and social ties because merchants depended on acquaintances and affiliations as collateral for debt. With the expansion of the U.S. banking system during the 1820s, confidence fell more heavily to faith in the value of U.S. bank notes. Jackson in particular was infamous for his effort to fix the value of currency to what he imagined was the fixed value of gold and silver. Of course, the value of specie that he thought could back confidence in paper notes was no more given in any natural law than the value of the counterfeit notes that flooded U.S. markets during the early nineteenth century. Money, either "real" or "fake," is more than anything premised on a collective social expectation that abstract values

will be honored. When counterfeit bank notes filled the markets during the nineteenth century, they performed like money so long as they were honored. Every exchange of a bank note, however, was a gamble that the debt it represented in the present would be honored through payment in the future. In the context of speculation, payment in the future depends on producing a surplus value to cover the gaps between what is borrowed, owed, and hoped for in profits. When this hope emerges from an authoritative predilection to secure profits by force—such as through dispossession—economic confidence most often depends on social fictions of racial difference as justification for the force it takes to exact returns, especially when bubbles deflate. See Stephen Mihm, *A Nation of Counterfeiters: Capitalists, Con Men and the Making of the United States* (Cambridge, MA: Harvard University Press, 2007).

53. During the 1830s, the price of cotton doubled: from ten cents per pound in 1826 to 8 cents in 1831; cotton prices rose to 15 cents per pound by 1834, never falling below 14 cents and in many months reaching 17 cents. In comparison, land sales prior to 1835, while defined to a degree by speculation, did not rise above 5 million acres. In the boom of 1835, this number rose to 15 million acres of land sold. See Temin, *Jacksonian Economy*.

54. Alasdair Roberts, "'An Ungovernable Anarchy': The United States' Response to Depression and Default, 1837–1848," *Intereconomics* 45, no. 4 (2010): 197.

55. Songho Ha reports a general population growth in southern states from 115,000 in 1800 to 2.1 million by 1840. Between 1830 and 1840, the population of Alabama doubled while that of Mississippi tripled. See Ha, *Rise and Fall of the American System*. Walter Johnson records the movement of slave sales from the East into the Southwest by decade: 155,000 in the 1820s; 288,000 in the 1830s; 189,000 in the 1840s; and 250,000 in the 1850s. See Johnson, *Soul by Soul*.

56. Hawthorne, "May-Pole of Merry Mount," 43. The concept of counterfeit itself, of course, is intimately tied to the context of speculation. Here indigenous people are conflated with the volatile money markets of the early nineteenth century. See Johnson, *Soul by Soul*, 61.

57. Ibid., 87.

58. Ibid.

59. Hawthorne became fixated on resurrecting the past in the face of undemocratic national expansion. After resigning from his consular post in Liverpool in February 1857, he made himself and his wife two years younger on their applications for Italian passports. In 1854, he wrote to Longfellow that he had "had enough of progress" and wanted to "go back twenty years," quoted in Reynolds, "Strangely Ajar with the Human Race," 37. Twenty years is about what he gave himself when he recuperated the promise of Merry Mount in his novel *The Marble Faun* (1859).

60. Nathaniel Hawthorne, *The Marble Faun: Or the Romance of Monte Beni*, introduction by Richard H. Broadhead (New York: Penguin Classics, 1990), 3.

61. Millicent Bell, "The Marble Faun and the Waste of History," *Southern Review* 35, no. 2 (1999): 354.

62. Hawthorne, *Marble Faun*, 86–87.

63. Blythe Ann Tellefsen argues that Miriam stands as a tragic Mulatta in the novel whose fall represents a White national future for the United States. See Tellefsen, "The Case with My Dear Native Land: Nathaniel Hawthorne's Vision of America in *The Marble Faun*," *Nineteenth Century Literature* 54, no. 4 (2000): 455–479. Augustus Kolich follows the rumor that Miriam's darkness reflects a Jewish ancestry. See Kolich, "Miriam and the Conversion of the Jews in Nathaniel Hawthorne's *The Marble Faun*," *Studies in*

the Novel 33, no. 4 (2001): 430–444. Jenny Franchot argues that anti-Catholicism in the antebellum United States was often invoked to connect Protestantism with progress as a way to divert national attention from conflict over immigrant differences, sectionalism, industrialization, and slavery. Working-class tensions in the mid-nineteenth century were dramatically mollified when different groups joined forces in imperialist projects that garnered their ideological force from nativism and anti-Catholicism. Shared opposition to an imagined external threat transformed internal differences into a common cause. Anti-Catholicism in *The Marble Faun* reaffirmed a social dynamic in the United States whereby immigrants assimilated into existing categories of White nationalism through Protestant identification and imperial participation. Rome thus became the repository of U.S. anxieties about purity, national boundaries, and racist economic practices. Transposing U.S. conflict as European corruption rectified Protestant virtue as the providential guarantee of a progressive future of White middle-class U.S. nationalism. See Franchot, *Roads to Rome: The Antebellum Protestant Encounter with Catholicism* (Berkeley: University of California Press, 1994).

64. Hawthorne, *Marble Faun*, 461.

65. Ibid., 446.

66. Ibid., 462.

67. Ibid.

68. Ibid., iii.

69. Ibid., 4.

70. Ibid., 153.

71. Ibid., 165, 173.

72. Ibid., 174.

73. Ibid., 146.

74. Ibid., 148.

75. Ibid.

76. Ibid., 152.

77. Ibid., 158. In this regard, national history replaces the concept of nature in Kant's formulation of the Sublime. Rather than experience shock or fear regarding the unsettling and overwhelming force of nature, Kant argued for a sensible stance in which the observer recognizes himself at a safe remove from the object as independent and superior. This stance, Susan Buck-Morss argues, depends on an understanding of reason that separates the individual from the senses in order to maintain the illusion of autogenesis and safety from external forces. See Kant, *Critique of Judgment*, trans. Werner Pluhar (New York: Hackett, 1987), 120–121; and Buck-Morss, "Aesthetics and Anesthetics: Walter Benjamin's Artwork Essay Reconsidered," *October* 62 (Autumn 1992): 3–41.

78. Wagner's music is a case in point for Buck-Morss. In producing the sound of human experience, the music encourages listeners to identify with the idea of an individual affective experience to numb against the shock of mechanized life. See Buck-Morss, "Aesthetics and Anesthetics."

79. Buck-Morss accounts for the changes in social representation through the rationalization of the medical profession. The agency of medical authority is put on display to be absorbed and appreciated by an audience who does not identify with the embodiment of the insensate patient, who is made into an object for observation. See Buck-Morss, "Aesthetics and Anesthetics."

80. Duane Champagne, "From First Nations to Self-Government: A Political Legacy of Indigenous Nations in the United States," *American Behavioral Scientist* 51, no. 12 (2008): 1672–1693.

81. Claudio Saunt, "Telling Stories: The Political Uses of Myth and History in the Cherokee and Creek Nations," *Journal of American History* 93, no. 3 (2006): 673–697.

82. Edward Lazarus, *Black Hill / White Justice: The Sioux Nation versus the United States, 1775 to the Present* (Lincoln: University of Nebraska Press, 1991).

83. Fred Moten, *In the Break: The Aesthetics of the Black Radical Tradition* (Minneapolis: University of Minnesota Press, 2003), 1.

84. Audra Simpson, *Mohawk Interruptus: Political Life across the Borders of Settler States* (Durham, NC: Duke University Press, 2014); and Audra Simpson and Andrea Smith, eds., *Theorizing Native Studies* (Durham, NC: Duke University Press, 2014).

85. Andrea Smith, "Dismantling the Master's Tools with the Master's House: Native Feminist Liberation Theologies," *Journal of Feminist Studies in Religion* 22, no. 2 (2006): 85–97.

CHAPTER 2

Epigraphs: Senator Lafayette Foster, *Congressional Globe*, 37th Congress, 2nd Session (1862), 94; Senator John Conness, *Congressional Globe*, 38th Congress, 1st Session (1864), 2300; and Harry, quoted in Ray Allen Billington, ed., *The Journal of Charlotte L. Forten: A Young Black Woman's Reactions to the White World of the Civil War Era* (New York: Norton, 1953), 159.

1. Edward E. Baptist, "Toxic Debt, Liar Loans, and Securitized Human Beings and the Panic of 1837," in *Capitalism Takes Command*, ed. Michael Zakin and Gary Kornblith (Chicago: University of Chicago Press, 2012), 69–92; John Kouwenhoven, *Partners in Banking: An Historical Portrait of a Great Private Bank, Brown Brothers Harriman & Co., 1818–1968* (New York: Doubleday, 1968); and Richard Holcombe Kilbourne Jr., *Debt, Investment, Slaves: Credit Relations in East Feliciana Parish, Louisiana, 1825–1885* (Tuscaloosa: University of Alabama Press, 2014).

2. Baptist, "Toxic Debt," 81.

3. Walter Johnson, *Soul by Soul: Life inside the Antebellum Slave Market* (Cambridge, MA: Harvard University Press, 2001).

4. Edward E. Baptist, *The Half Has Never Been Told: Slavery and the Making of American Capitalism* (New York: Basic Books, 2014); and Walter Johnson, *River of Dark Dreams: Slavery and Empire in the Cotton Kingdom* (Cambridge, MA: Harvard University Press, 2013).

5. Kenneth Pomeranz, *The Great Divergence: China, Europe and the Making of the Modern World Economy* (Princeton, NJ: Princeton University Press, 2000).

6. Kyle Sinisi, *Sacred Debts: State Civil War Claims and American Federalism* (New York: Fordham University Press, 2003).

7. Pomeranz, *Great Divergence*, 278.

8. Willie Lee Rose, *Rehearsal for Reconstruction* (Athens: University of Georgia Press, 1964).

9. At the time of Olmsted's hiring, the paper's name was *The New York Daily Times*, but it was shortened during his tenure as a reporter. To avoid confusion, I have chosen to use *New York Times* consistently to discuss the newspaper that hired Olmsted.

10. Arthur M. Schlesinger Sr., ed., *Cotton Kingdom* (New York: Modern Library Editions, 1984), 4.

11. Ibid.

12. Walter Johnson, "Agency a Ghost Story," in *Slavery's Ghosts*, ed. Richard Follett, Eric Foner, and Walter Johnson (Baltimore: Johns Hopkins University Press, 2011), 28.

13. Clyde Woods's notion of blues epistemology is a way of reading spirituals and ballads on Port Royal Sound as carrying an alternative archive of meaning and understanding that holds the memory and histories of survival. See Woods, *Development Arrested: The Blues and Plantation Power in the Mississippi Delta* (New York: Haymarket, 2000).

14. Ray Allen Billington, ed., *The Journal of Charlotte L. Forten: A Young Black Woman's Reactions to the White World of the Civil War Era* (New York: Norton, 1953), 159.

15. Ibid., 158–159.

16. Cedric Robinson, "Black Detective Fiction and Subject History" (paper presented at the Annual Meeting of the American Studies Association, San Antonio, TX, November 2010).

17. Joyce Hollyday, *On the Heels of Freedom: The American Missionary Association's Bold Campaign to Educate Minds, Open Hearts and Heal the Soul of a Divided Nation* (New York: Crossroad, 2005), 31.

18. Stephanie LeMenager, *Manifest and Other Destinies: Territorial Fictions of the Nineteenth Century U.S.* (Lincoln: University of Nebraska Press, 2008); Alexander Saxton, *The Indispensable Enemy: Labor and the Anti-Chinese Movement in California* (Berkeley: University of California Press, 1975); and Shelley Streeby, *American Sensations: Class, Empire and the Production of Popular Culture* (Berkeley: University of California Press, 2002).

19. In his writings from the South, Olmsted declared, "Labor is the creator of wealth. There can be no honest wealth, no true prosperity without it, and in exact proportion to the economy of labor is the cost of production and the accumulation of profit." Charles E. Beveridge and Charles Capen McLaughlin, eds., *The Papers of Frederick Law Olmsted, Volume II: Slavery and the South, 1852–1857* (Baltimore: Johns Hopkins University Press, 1981), 109.

20. In his introduction to the 1984 reprinting of *The Cotton Kingdom*, Arthur Schlesinger Sr. says that Olmsted's conclusions were widely challenged and proved fallacious by historians and that Olmsted severely underestimated the profitability of slavery throughout the slave economy. Whereas Olmsted was committed to the idea that the slave system led most large slave owners into increased debt, with the majority of their equity in slave properties, Schlesinger and others have shown that slave investments not only produced great returns for investors but also spurred regional growth. Further, with the boom in global demand for cotton, the South's near monopoly on the crop, in tandem with a large-scale system of organized labor with minimal compensation for laborers, was highly profitable for many southern producers.

21. Karl Marx's theory of valorization drew directly from Olmsted's discussion of the rude instruments and brutality of slavery to center industrial capitalism as the purest mode of labor production. See Marx, *Capital, Volume 1: A Critique of Political Economy* (New York: Penguin Classics, 1976), 303–304.

22. Marx, *Capital, Volume 1*, 303.

23. Schlesinger, *Cotton Kingdom*, 102.

24. Beveridge and McLaughlin, *Papers of Frederick Law Olmsted, Volume II*, 100.

25. Schlesinger, *Cotton Kingdom*, 104–105.

26. Ibid.

27. Ibid., 108.

28. Ibid., 107, 108.

29. Ibid., 106.

30. Ibid., 101.

31. Ibid., 109. He envisioned a system in which "the man who cannot command the current rates is the first to be dropped off on a reduction."

32. Ibid., 108.

33. Ibid., 109.

34. Ibid.

35. Beveridge and McLaughlin, *Papers of Frederick Law Olmsted, Volume II*, 251.

36. Johnson, *Soul by Soul*, 25.

37. Kilbourne, *Debt, Investment, Slaves*, 130.

38. Ibid., 137.

39. Johnson, *Soul by Soul*, 29.

40. Schlesinger, *Cotton Kingdom*, 399. It is noteworthy that when Olmsted did document slave sales, it was with an apologetic, dehumanizing attitude regarding enslaved people's indifference to the experience and outcome of the exchange: "There was not a tear or emotion visible in the whole party. Everything seemed to be considered as a matter of course; and the change of owners was possibly looked forward to with . . . indifference" (p. 596).

41. Ibid., 229.

42. Ibid., 250.

43. Ibid.

44. Ibid.

45. Ibid.

46. Ibid., 253.

47. Ibid., 250.

48. For clarity's sake, it must be noted that the reason that the formulation does not ring false is not that enslaved people necessarily act and think under constrained conditions; people certainly do act and resist in ways that were beyond Olmsted's narrative comprehension. Rather, what makes the statement dubious is that Olmsted absorbed into his framework an enslaver's fantasy of omnipotence. This fantasy was the premise for the construction of total subordination that made it possible to imagine mind and actions as gifts from the master. This formulation is symptomatic of the philosophical underpinning of slavery as a form of debt—the social sign of domination whereby the slave comes to owe the master for her or his life, both in the sense of being alive and in the temporal duration thereof.

49. Schlesinger, *Cotton Kingdom*, 250.

50. Ibid., 255.

51. Ibid.

52. Ibid.

53. Ibid.

54. Ibid., 255–256.

55. Ibid., 183.

56. Ibid.

57. Ibid., 190.

58. Edward Baptist, "'Cuffy,' 'Fancy Maids,' and 'One-Eyed Men': Rape, Commodification and the Domestic Slave Trade in the United States," in *The Chattel Principle: Internal Slave Principles in America*, ed. Walter Johnson (New Haven, CT: Yale University Press, 2004), 165–202.

59. Schlesinger, *Cotton Kingdom*, 109.

60. Ibid., 195.

61. Ibid., 258.

62. Ibid., 257.

63. Ibid.

64. Beveridge and McLaughlin, *Papers of Frederick Law Olmsted, Volume II*, 257.

65. Richard Follet, "Legacies of Enslavement: Plantation Identities and the Problem of Freedom," in *Slavery's Ghosts*, ed. Richard Follett, Eric Foner, and Walter Johnson (Baltimore: Johns Hopkins University Press, 2011), 61.

66. Beveridge and McLaughlin, 198.

67. Ibid., 199. Also see Katherine M. Franke, "The Domesticated Liberty of *Lawrence v. Texas*," *Columbia Law Review* 104, no. 5 (2004): 1339–1426.

68. Schlesinger, *Cotton Kingdom*, 199.

69. Ibid.

70. Ibid., 193.

71. Ibid., 258.

72. Calling attention to the way that speculation can result in a geographic class calculus of economic segregation, in 1855, the *Sun* reported "If the opening of the Park raises the actual or speculative values in its vicinity . . . it is certain that the poorer class of citizens will not settle them extensively when homesteads can be obtained cheaper elsewhere," quoted in Roy Rosenzweig and Elizabeth Blackmar, *The Park and the People: A History of Central Park* (Ithaca, NY: Cornell University Press, 1998), 63. John Punnett Peters was a missionary to Seneca Village who depicted residents as a transient and debased lumpen proletariat; quoted in Rosenzweig and Blackmar, *The Park and the People*, 67.

73. Ibid., 62, 67.

74. Ibid., 162.

75. Ibid., 175, 176.

76. The argument that cross-class association in Olmsted's Central Park both obscured and reinforced nineteenth-century social divisions is by now quite familiar in critical works on Olmsted. Alan Trachtenburg's foundational study, *The Incorporation of America: Culture and Society in the Gilded Age* (New York: Hill and Wang, 2007), highlights Olmsted's therapeutic intentions and his emphasis on the "cultivating" potential for purifying the "vile" cultures of labor neighborhoods. Richard Grusin adds an important aesthetic argument to this reading, highlighting the ways in which the social exchanges in Central Park were mediated through "private aesthetic experiences." See Grusin, *Culture, Technology, and the Creation of America's National Parks* (New York: Cambridge University Press, 2004), 44. Stephen Germic argues that idealized "nature" in Central Park was designed to "materialize the nation" by universalizing the category "man" whereby social uplift could incorporate the threatening differences of the "masses" into the national universal in the face of the economic crisis of 1857. See Germic, *American Green: Class, Crisis, and the Deployment of Nature in Central Park, Yosemite, and Yellowstone* (Lanham, MD: Lexington, 2001), 17. Anthony Gronowicz views Central Park as a scene of socialization in which cross-class associations reinforced the economic subservience of newly incorporated workers who aspired to the norms and universals of bourgeois nationalism. See Gronowicz, *Race and Class Politics in New York City before the Civil War* (Boston: Northeastern University Press, 1998).

77. Follett, "Legacies of Enslavement," 56–59.

78. Silvana R. Siddali, *From Property to Person: Slavery and the Confiscation Acts 1861–1862* (Baton Rouge: Louisiana State University Press, 2005).

79. Hollyday, *On the Heels of Freedom*, 28.

80. Charles E. Beveridge and David Schulyer, *The Papers of Frederick Law Olmsted, Volume III: Creating Central Park, 1857–1861* (Baltimore: Johns Hopkins University Press, 1983), 282.

81. *Congressional Globe*, 37th Congress, 2nd Session (1862), 941.

82. Ibid., 290.

83. Olmsted actively worked to generate media support for the bill, and it was generally assumed that he would be appointed commissioner of Port Royal contrabands by Secretary Chase. Yet between March 8 and March 13, out of deference to Chase, who had offered him Pierce's position as supervisor under the Treasury Department (in place of the administrative control the bill would create), Olmsted let the bill sleep in the House to contemplate this offer. See "Mr. Foster's Bill," *New York Tribune*, February 17, 1862, 4; and "The Slaves at Port Royal," *New York World*, February 15, 1862, 4. Also see Frederick Law Olmsted to Elbridge G. Spaulding, February 16, 1862, in Beveridge and Schulyer, *Papers of Frederick Law Olmsted, Volume III*, 277; and Olmsted to Manton Marble, February 16, 1862, ibid. Olmsted rejected a proposal from Chase on March 15 presumably out of concern for the limited authority Chase had to support the management structure Olmsted's bill was proposing (Olmsted to Marble, ibid., 288–289). While it is no longer known what personal factors might have contributed to Olmsted's decision to decline Chase's offer on March 13, his appeals to secretary of war Edwin Stanton in a speech delivered on April 13 suggest that Olmsted was concerned with Treasury's ability to fully secure the authority of a cotton commissioner under the current military occupation. To garner full control of labor management on the islands, it appeared to Olmsted, he would require the backing of the secretary of war. See Laura Wood Roper, "Frederick Law Olmsted and the Port Royal Experiment," *Journal of Southern History* 31, no. 3 (1965): 272–284.

84. *Congressional Globe*, 37th Congress, 2nd Session (1862), 297.

85. The freedom that Black people might earn under this management policy was ambivalent. Although Olmsted implied a future of full citizenship, conflicts over land sales and federal government efforts to submit Port Royal lands to open-market competition, rather than offer reduced prices to homesteaders in late 1862 and early 1863, suggest the fallacy of any promises that the government would allow Black people access to land ownership.

86. *Congressional Globe*, 37th Congress, 2nd Session (1862), 961.

87. Ibid., 959.

88. D. A. Wasson, "The Law of Costs," *Atlantic Monthly* 11 (February 1863): 241–251.

89. Billington, *Journal of Charlotte L. Forten*, 150.

90. Ibid., 155.

91. Ibid., 169, 170, 182.

92. Ibid., 149, 152, 160.

93. Ibid., 186.

94. Beveridge and Schulyer, *Papers of Frederick Law Olmsted, Volume III*, 282.

95. Victoria Post Ranney, ed., *The Papers of Frederick Law Olmsted, Volume V: The California Frontier, 1863–1865* (Baltimore: Johns Hopkins University Press, 1990), 134, 140.

96. Ibid.

97. Ibid., 194.

98. Ibid.

99. Ibid., 197.

100. Ibid., 203.

101. Ibid., 198.

102. This strategy was not new to Olmsted. Indeed, he is most famous for his work as codesigner and first supervisor of New York's Central Park. As the overseer of park construction under the direction of city government, he honed his capacities for labor

suppression. Under Olmsted's management, thousands of workers suffering the effects of economic depression in 1857 were temporarily pacified with short-term contracts and decreasing wages in a strategy of wide-scale layoffs followed by mass rehiring during the park's construction. See Rosenzweig and Blackmar, *The Park and the People*.

103. Ranney, *Papers of Frederick Law Olmsted, Volume V*, 189.

104. Quoted in Laura Wood Roper, *FLO: A Biography of Frederick Law Olmsted* (Baltimore: Johns Hopkins University Press, 1973), 253.

105. Ranney, *Papers of Frederick Law Olmsted, Volume V*, 197.

106. Ibid., 214. In his 1857 *A Journey through Texas*, Olmsted clearly demonstrated his preoccupation with places where "boarders and idle soldiers [were] hanging about drinking-places, and where different races mingle on unequal terms." These descriptions suggest that he was wary of the violence he imagined such association fostered. In his account, he attached social turmoil to drunkenness without addressing the underlying tensions over resources suggested by the scenes of desolation and idleness. In the context of similar venues in Mariposa, Olmsted's desire that his workers be separated from "the rest" showed his anxiety over the divisions his management strategy created. See Olmsted, *A Journey through Texas: Or a Saddle-Trip on the Southwestern Frontier*, ed. Witold Rybczynski (Lincoln: University of Nebraska Press, 2004), 159.

107. Ranney, *Papers of Frederick Law Olmsted, Volume V*, 232.

108. Peonage was not beyond Olmsted's imagination. Commenting on the Mexican system in 1857, he wrote that there was nothing "*essentially* unjust" about it. Indeed, he suggested that if "the creditor shall not furnish the peon goods, to a greater amount in value than *one half the wages put to his credit* [italics mine]," the system appeared to be no more unjust than an open market. See Olmsted, *Journey through Texas*, 334, 335.

109. California Governor Frederick F. Low appointed Olmsted manager of the Yosemite Land Grant only one day after accepting it on September 28, 1864. The grant was signed into California law on June 30, 1864, after a legislative recess. The joint approval of the governor and the legislature on April 2, 1866, made the transfer of lands to the state of California official on April 2, 1866. See Alfred Runte, *The Embattled Wilderness* (Lincoln: University of Nebraska Press, 1990).

110. *Congressional Globe*, 38th Congress, 1st Session (1864), 2000.

111. Today, of course, Olmsted's vision is memorialized on the walls of the Yosemite Visitor Center.

112. Henri Lefebvre, *The Production of Space* (Cambridge, MA: Blackwell, 1974), 34.

113. Ranney, *Papers of Frederick Law Olmsted, Volume V*, 502.

114. Ibid., 509.

115. The cultural impulse to construct Yosemite's natural environments as art was not unique to Olmsted. The conflation of nature and art in Yosemite had been a running theme prior to any national-political investment in the area. Thomas Starr King's descriptions of Yosemite published in the *Boston Evening Transcript* between December 1, 1860, and February 9, 1861, highlighted the "cultivating" potential of Yosemite's natural scenery, equating landscape tourism with the "cultured" activities of visiting art museums and attending concerts. Given King's fame as a popular minister as well as the wide circulation of his writing, John F. Sears has argued that he had a major influence on the establishment of Yosemite as a "sacred" national treasure. See Sears, *Sacred Places: American Tourist Attractions in the Nineteenth Century* (Amherst: University of Massachusetts Press, 1989), 127–128.

116. Grusin, "Reproducing Yosemite," 342.

117. Ibid., 346.

118. Ranney, *Papers of Frederick Law Olmsted, Volume V*, 504.

119. Ibid., 502.

120. Ibid., 508.

121. Ibid., 505.

122. Ibid., 508.

123. Ibid., 506–507.

124. For more on the ecological cultivation of natural resources in precolonial California, see M. Kat Anderson, Michael G. Barbour, and Valerie Whiteworth, "A World of Balance and Plenty: Land, Plants, Animals and Humans in Pre-European California," in *Contested Eden: California Before the Gold Rush*, ed. Ramón Gutiérrez and Richard J. Orsi (Berkeley: University of California Press, 1998), 12–47.

125. Brian Dippie, *The Vanishing American: White Attitudes and U.S. Indian Policy* (Lawrence: University Press of Kansas, 1982).

126. Karl Jocoby, *Crimes against Nature: Squatters, Poachers, and the Hidden History of American Conservation* (Berkeley: University of California Press, 2001).

127. Quoted in Mark David Spence, *Dispossessing the Wilderness: Indian Removal and the Making of National Parks* (New York: Oxford University Press, 1999), 122.

128. Mark David Spence, "Yosemite Indians and the National Park Ideal, 1916–1969," in *Dispossessing the Wilderness: Indian Removal and the Making of National Parks* (New York: Oxford University Press, 1999).

129. *Congressional Globe*, 38th Congress, 1st Session (1864), 2300, 2301.

130. Ibid.

131. David W. Noble, *Death of a Nation* (Minneapolis: University of Minnesota Press, 2002).

132. Steven Hackel, "Land, Labor and Production: The Colonial Economy of Spanish and Mexican California," in *Contested Eden: California Before the Gold Rush*, ed. Ramón Gutiérrez and Richard J. Orsi (Berkeley: University of California Press, 1998); and Rosaura Sanchez, "The Mission as Heterotopia," in *Telling Identities: The Californio Testimonios* (Minneapolis: University of Minnesota Press, 1995).

133. Lafayette Bunnell, *The Discovery of the Yosemite and the Indian War of 1851* (Los Angeles: G. W. Gerlicher, 1911), 17.

134. Rebecca Solnit, *Savage Dreams: A Journey into the Landscape Wars of the American West* (Berkeley: University of California Press, 2000).

135. Walter Benjamin, *Illumination*, ed. Hannah Arendt (New York: Schocken, 1968), 256; and Bunnell, *Discovery of the Yosemite and the Indian War of 1851*, xviii.

136. Hackel, "Land, Labor, and Production," 122.

137. Alfred Runte argues that Yosemite Indians were "decimated" by disease around 1800. By the mid-nineteenth century, he says, a few Ahawahneechee survivors who had joined surrounding tribes returned to the valley they had learned about in the stories of their grandfathers. See Runte, *Yosemite: The Embattled Wilderness* (Lincoln: University of Nebraska Press, 1993).

138. Susan Lee Johnson, *Roaring Camp: The Social World of the California Gold Rush* (New York: Norton, 2000), 186.

139. Bunnell, *Discovery of the Yosemite and the Indian War of 1851*, 7.

140. Ibid., 243.

141. *Congressional Globe*, 38th Congress, 1st Session (1864), 2300.

142. John C. Olmsted to Robert Underwood Johnson, July 28, 1909. In this letter, Olmsted's son confirmed the history Gardner had earlier offered. The quoted claim was delivered as secondhand information from Olmsted's wife. See *Robert Underwood*

Johnson Papers, 1889–1924 (Holdings of the Bancroft Library, University of California, Berkeley, BANC C-B 385, Box 3). Immediately following his appointment as commissioner of the Yosemite board, Olmsted personally contracted the services of Clarence King and J. T. Gardner to survey the land California had been granted. From this survey, Olmsted designed a plan for the construction and administration of the park.

143. Olmsted was identified as a potential commissioner in the letter Israel Ward Raymond addressed to Conness calling for the creation of Yosemite, but with the condition that board members "shall receive no compensation for their services." Public records show that the language of the bill itself came directly from the pens of capitalists. See *U.S. Statutes at Large XIII*, 325.

144. Israel Ward Raymond to Senator Conness. I read this letter from a copy located in the archives of Yosemite National Park, no. 979.447 Y-7. The original document from the Records of the General Land Office Miscellaneous Letters received, G33572, in the National Archives is presently unlocatable.

145. Ibid.

146. Ibid. Conness also reinforced the logic of a two-worlds metaphor in his address to Congress. He reported that U.S. investors had sent a cross section of a giant sequoia "specimen" to the London World's Fair at "the expense of several thousand dollars." The British who saw it, he claimed, "declared it to be a Yankee invention." Drawing from this event, he differentiated Americans from corrupt Europeans, who were incapable of recognizing the timeless freedom offered in U.S. resources. He called on his fellow citizens to preserve Yosemite Valley and the Mariposa Grove of Big Trees "for public use, resort and recreation [as] inalienable for all time" largely to justify the uniqueness of the natural "wonder of the world" therein contained. *Congressional Globe*, 38th Congress, 1st Session (1864), 2300, 2301.

147. Lefebvre, *Production of Space*, 229–291.

148. Stephen Germic argues for the formal differences of classical labor theories of productive value and the production of space that can "achieve value with no application of what we usually regard as labor. Space only needs to have been mapped into the capitalist network for it to have value and be open to exchange." See Germic, *American Green*, 72. Although I can appreciate the distinction between forms of labor to which Germic points, and accept that surveying lands and mapping space may not fit neatly into industrial conceptions of labor, I am hesitant to fully differentiate the physical work of land surveys, and the intellectual work on which the simple "need" of being mapped, depends from other forms of productive processes.

149. William Cronan, *Nature's Metropolis* (New York: Norton, 1991); and David Harvey, *The Enigma of Capital and the Crisis of Capitalism* (London: Oxford University Press, 2011).

150. Israel Ward Raymond to Senator Conness, July 20, 1864, Yosemite Research Library, Yosemite, CA, box 979.447 Y-7.

151. Senator Conness to I. M. Edmund, March 6, 1864, Yosemite Research Library, Yosemite, CA, box 979.447 Y-7, items 3 and 4.

152. Michael O'Malley, *Keeping Watch: A History of American Time* (New York: Viking, 1990).

PART II

1. Julie Ott, *When Wall Street Met Main Street: The Quest for an Investor's Democracy* (Cambridge, MA: Harvard University Press, 2011), 229.

2. Robert Kuttner's advocacy of "managed capitalism" is a prime example. See Kuttner, *The Squandering of America: How the Failure of Our Politics Undermines Our Prosperity* (New York: First Vintage, 2007).

3. Douglass A. Massey, *American Apartheid* (Cambridge, MA: Harvard University Press, 1993); and Jill Quadagno, *The Color of Welfare* (New York: Oxford University Press, 1994).

4. Thomas Shapiro, *The Hidden Cost of Being African American* (New York: Oxford University Press, 2005).

CHAPTER 3

Epigraphs: Justice Hugo Black, dissenting opinion, *Connecticut General Life Ins. Co. v. Johnson*, 303 U.S. 77 (January 31, 1938); Constance Rourke, *The Roots of American Culture* (New York: Harcourt Brace, 1942), 238–250; and Jelly Roll Morton, "Buddy Bertram's Blues #1 / Mamie's Blues," *Library of Congress Recordings*, vol. 4 (1938).

1. S. Douglas Beets, "Critical Events in the Ethics of U.S. Corporation History," *Journal of Business Ethics* 102, no. 2 (2011): 193–219.

2. David Roediger, *Working toward Whiteness* (New York: Basic Books, 2005).

3. Amy Louise Wood, *Lynching and Spectacle: Witnessing Racial Violence in America, 1890–1940* (Durham, NC: University of North Carolina Press, 2011).

4. Michael Denning, *The Cultural Front* (New York: Verso, 1997).

5. Michael Kazin, *The Populist Persuasion: An American History* (Ithaca, NY: Cornell University Press, 1995).

6. Julie Ott, *When Wall Street Met Main Street: The Quest for an Investor's Democracy* (Cambridge, MA: Harvard University Press, 2011), 74.

7. John Mickelthwait and Adrian Wooldridge, *The Company: A Short History of a Revolutionary Idea* (New York: Penguin, 2005), 105.

8. Ott, *When Wall Street Met Main Street*, 197.

9. Ibid., 175.

10. Robert McElvaine, *The Great Depression: America, 1929–1941* (New York: Times Books, 1984), 23–59.

11. Steve Fraser, *Every Man a Speculator: A History of Wall Street in American Life* (New York: HarperCollins, 2005).

12. Steve Fraser, *Wall Street: America's Dream Palace* (New Haven, CT: Yale University Press, 2008), 81.

13. John Kenneth Galbraith, *The Great Crash* (New York: Houghton Mifflin, 1954).

14. Ellen Hodgson Brown, *The Web of Debt* (Baton Rouge, LA: Millennium, 2007), 139–158.

15. Raymond Williams, *Marxism and Literature* (Oxford: Oxford University Press, 1978).

16. Douglass Blackmon, *Slavery by Another Name: The Re-Enslavement of Black Americans from the Civil War to World War II* (New York: Anchor, 2009); Michelle Alexander, *The New Jim Crow: Mass Incarceration in the Age of Colorblindness* (New York: New Press, 2012); and Noralee Frankel, "Breaking the Chains: 1860–1880," in *To Make Our World Anew*, ed. Robin D. G. Kelley and Earl Lewis (New York: Oxford University Press, 2000), 227–280.

17. David Oshinsky writes, "The number of state convicts quadrupled, from 272 in 1874 to 1072 by 1877" under the Mississippi Pig Law largely because punitive fees attached to incarceration often turned small fines into life sentences when convicts could

not pay. See Oshinsky, *"Worse Than Slavery"*: *Parchman Farm and the Ordeal of Jim Crow Justice* (New York: Free Press, 1996), 40–43.

18. W.E.B. DuBois, "The Reconstruction of Freedom," in *The Gift of Black Folk: The Negroes in the Making of America* (New York: AMS Press, 1924), 184–258. Fred Moten's framing of the keyword "Democracy" is a useful rendition of material and ideological tensions in Glen Handler and Bruce Burgett, *Keywords for American Cultural Studies* (New York: New York University Press, 2007), 76–79.

19. Thom Hartmann, *Unequal Protection: How Corporations Became "People" and How You Can Fight Back* (San Francisco: Berrett-Koehler, 2010).

20. The notion of corporate personhood, of course, preceded the passage of the Fourteenth Amendment, appearing in U.S. law during the early nineteenth century in *Dartmouth College v. Woodward* (1819), which determined that corporate charters fell within the terms of private contract. The 1886 *Santa Clara County v. Southern Pacific Railroad* decision, however, extended and entrenched the property rights of corporate persons by configuring corporate bodies as individuals under the Fourteenth Amendment's due process clause.

21. Naomi R. Lamoreaux, "Partnerships, Corporations and the Limits of Contractual Freedom in U.S. History: An Essay in Economics, Law and Culture," in *Constructing Corporate America: History, Politics, Culture*, ed. Kenneth Lipartito and Davis B. Sicilia (New York: Oxford University Press, 2004), 29–65; and Christopher Newfield, "Corporation," in *Keywords in American Cultural Studies* (New York: New York University Press, 2007), 66–71.

22. My reading of conjunctures draws heavily from Stuart Hall, Chas Critcher, Tony Jefferson, John Clarke, and Brian Roberts, *Policing the Crisis: Mugging, the State, and Law and Order* (Hampshire, UK: Palgrave Macmillan, 1978).

23. Rourke's research, especially her approach to regionalism, resonates closely with writers like Lewis Mumford, in *The South in Architecture* (New York: Harcourt Brace, 1941), and Howard Odum, in *Southern Regions of the United States* (Chapel Hill: University of North Carolina Press, 1936). For a longer discussion of the school of regional and aesthetic thinkers with which Rourke was closely associated, see Michael Denning, "Ballads for Americans," in *The Cultural Front* (New York: Verso, 1997), 115–151.

24. Rourke's received reputation and enduring influence as a forerunner of American Cultural Studies merits the recognition that Joan Shelley Rubin has persuasively and effectively given her as an innovative intellectual analyst and interpreter of the aesthetic and social context of expressive culture in the United States. Her sincerity and idealism also merit Alan Trachtenberg's eloquent recognition of her work as a "usable past" worthy of "remembering and honoring . . . especially as it fades from view." See Rubin, *Constance Rourke and American Culture* (Chapel Hill: University of North Carolina Press, 1980); and Trachtenberg, *Lincoln's Smile and Other Enigmas* (New York: Hill and Wang, 2007), xv.

25. Constance Rourke, *The Roots of American Culture* (New York: Harcourt Brace, 1942), 275.

26. Ibid., 28.

27. Ibid., 12.

28. Constance Rourke, *American Humor: A Study of the National Character* (New York: NYRB Classics, 2004 [1931]), 31, 32, 53.

29. Constance Rourke, "The Significance of Sections," *The Nation*, April 17, 1935, 458.

30. Ibid., 296, 294.

31. Michael Denning reads Rourke as a prime example of the transformative intervention of the national-popular in *The Cultural Front*. Rourke was ushered into the publishing world by figures like Louis Mumford and Van Wyck Brooks, who lent their names and reputations to recognized Popular Front organizations. Her work runs parallel to the strain of thinking in *Modern Quarterly* that saw "Americanism" as an alternative to socialism in the struggle against class inequality. Intellectuals of the 1920s generated utopian hopes in aesthetic practices that imagined possibilities for reinvigorating the social and individual capacities for solidarity that they thought had been lost with capitalist transformation. In this regard, Rourke resembled other modernists with ties to the Cultural Front. See Seth Moglen, *Mourning Modernity: Literary Modernism and the Injuries of American Capitalism* (Stanford, CA: Stanford University Press, 2007).

32. Rourke, *Roots of American Culture*, 295.

33. Rubin, *Constance Rourke and American Culture*. Rourke's expansive archive of folk traditions reveals how earnestly and extensively she carried Van Wyck Brooks's call for a "usable past" from 1918 into the 1930s. See Brooks, "On Creating a Usable Past," *The Dial* 64, no. 7 (1918): 337–341. This sense of inferiority was particular to the 1920s and 1930s, prior to U.S. military intervention in World War II. Unlike later folklorists, Rourke did not live to see U.S. involvement in the war. During the late 1930s, she did, however, filter her love of folklore into support for the cultural projects of the New Deal. In 1939, she supported Lewis Mumford's antifascist isolationism with discussion of mass gatherings and protests as evidence of a "popular judgment" that she saw as a "reaffirmation of faith in democracy against international fascism." She did not, however, go as far as scholars like John Kouwenhoven, who read folklore as a sign of U.S. superiority. See Rourke, "In the Time of Hesitation," review of *Men Must Act* by Lewis Mumford, *The Nation*, February 18, 1839, 206.

34. Ibid., 295.

35. Constance Rourke, "Artists on Relief," *New Republic*, July 15, 1936, 287.

36. Rourke was often critical of nostalgic representations of the nation's past that failed to mobilize popular expression for continued artistic "growth." See Rourke, "Art in Our Town," *The Nation*, March 30, 1940, 424–425, or "A Note on Folklore," in *Roots of American Culture*, 238–250. By 1939, Rourke had rejected liberalism based on its attachment to the "genteel tradition" and its moral fear of making judgments about the European slide into fascism. See Rourke, "In the Time of Hesitation," 206. I argue, however, that even though Rourke's radicalism strengthened during the Depression, her often inadvertent celebration of market categories committed her to a form of liberal nationalism that obscured unequal social structures through cultural abstraction.

37. Rourke, "In the Time of Hesitation," 293.

38. Rourke, *American Humor*, 15.

39. Ibid., 15, 16.

40. Ibid., 40.

41. Constance Rourke, *Trumpets of Jubilee* (New York: Harcourt Brace, 1927).

42. Rourke, *American Humor*, 292.

43. This regional approach to popular culture was as much a direct response to the White supremacist conservatism of southern agrarians as it was a challenge to the limited class politics of urban Marxism among Rourke's Popular Front allies. See Twelve Southerners, *I'll Take My Stand: The South and the Agrarian Tradition*, introduction by Louis D. Rubin Jr. (New York: P. Smith, 1951 [1930]); and Granville Hicks, *Granville Hicks in the New Masses*, ed. Jack Alan Robbins (Port Washington, NY: Kennikat, 1974).

44. Rourke, *American Humor*, 86.

45. W.E.B. DuBois, *Black Reconstruction in America 1860–1880* (New York: Meridian, 1935), 186. DuBois describes abolition democracy as the liberal movement to end slavery and incorporate Black workers into a free-labor system based in education, land ownership, and the civil rights of individuals.

46. F. O. Matthiessen's recognition of Rourke points to his indebtedness to her for his own understanding of mid-nineteenth-century literature as organized around a national commitment to democratic ideals See Matthiessen, *American Renaissance* (New York: Oxford University Press, 1941).

47. See Roderick Ferguson, *Aberrations in Black* (Minneapolis: University of Minnesota Press, 2004).

48. Rourke, *American Humor*, 233, 225.

49. Rourke, *Roots of American Culture*, 296. This sentiment is a repetition of a previous formation that also appears in *American Humor*, 225, 236.

50. According to Robert McElvaine, mass industrialism increased worker productivity by 43 percent in the 1920s; the trickle-down to workers was a mere 8 percent wage increase. Out of this speculative climate emerged privileged promises of individual wealth over commitments to social equality. Corporate profits exceeded 65 percent, and 42 percent of aggregate household income was held by a mere 0.1 percent of U.S. homes. See McElvaine, *Great Depression*, 38. In *The Enigma of Capital and the Crisis of Capitalism* (New York: Oxford University Press, 2010), David Harvey calls attention to the ways that capital circulation, the possibility of procuring profits even in the face of real losses, is always in part a speculative activity. Harvey argues that even when the productive activity underlying rising prices is negative, speculative confidence can drive up prices based on information about perceived value and price fluctuations in the future.

51. By using the future earnings of stocks themselves as collateral for stock investments, those with no monetary savings often literally bet all of their assets—homes, land, and life insurance—on hopes that stocks would inflate. See Hodgson Brown, *Web of Debt*.

52. Caitlin Zaloom engages the centralization of commodities markets as it relates to the physical architecture of cities like Chicago. See Zaloom, *Out of the Pits* (Chicago: University of Chicago Press, 2006).

53. Ibid., 72.

54. Ibid.

55. When demand for land surpassed the number of plots that individual Native landholders were willing to sell in the allotment process, Andrew Jackson voided tribal authority, denied Native people government protections guaranteed by treaty, authorized forced militia duty, increased taxes, and held land lotteries to sell tribal holdings. See Michael Paul Rogin, *Fathers and Children* (Piscataway, NJ: Transaction, 1975).

56. Rourke, *American Humor*, 19.

57. Rourke, *Roots of American Culture*, 55.

58. Ibid., 74.

59. Rourke, *American Humor*, 67.

60. Stephanie LeMenager, *Manifest and Other Destinies* (Lincoln: University of Nebraska Press, 2004), 139–188; Patricia Nelson Limerick, *The Legacy of Conquest* (New York: Norton, 1987); Alexander Saxton, *The Rise and Fall of the White Republic* (New York: Verso, 1990); and Walter Johnson, *Soul by Soul: Life inside the Antebellum Slave Market* (Cambridge, MA: Harvard University Press, 1999).

61. John Higham, *Strangers in the Land* (New Brunswick, NJ: Rutgers University Press, 1955); and Jacqueline Goldsby, *A Spectacular Secret: Lynching in American Life and Literature* (Chicago: University of Chicago Press, 2006).

62. The slipperiness of the fluctuating meaning of culture according to context, discipline, and purpose has been well documented. See Raymond Williams, *Culture and Society* (New York: Columbia University Press, 1958); Michael Elliot, *The Concept of Culture* (Minneapolis: University of Minnesota Press, 2002); and Michael Denning, "Work and Culture in American Studies," in *The Futures of American Studies*, ed. Donald Pease and Robyn Wiegman (Durham, NC: Duke University Press, 2002), 419–440. Rourke, of course, was an important forerunner of Cultural Studies.

63. Rourke, *Roots of American Culture*, 49, 50.

64. For example, in *The Roots of American Culture*, Rourke discusses increased public interest in the "appropriation of folk-life" as a folk movement itself that had "invaded" and taken "possession" of Depression-era America. In this essay, she encourages teachers and students to combine forces and "invade uncharted areas" in their "explorations" of folk history. See Rourke, "A Note on Folklore," 242, 243, 249.

65. Rourke, *Roots of American Culture*, 128.

66. Constance Rourke, "Traditions for Young People," in *Roots of American Culture*, 562, 563.

67. Constance Rourke, "Traditions for a Negro Literature," in *Roots of American Culture*, 262.

68. Ibid., 264.

69. Lisa Lowe and David Lloyd, introduction to *The Politics of Culture in the Shadow of Capitalism* (Durham, NC: Duke University Press, 1997).

70. Rourke, *American Humor*, 21.

71. Karl Marx, "On the Jewish Question," in *The Marx-Engels Reader*, ed. Robert C. Tucker (New York: Norton, 1972); George Sanchez, *Becoming Mexican American* (New York: Oxford University Press, 1993); and Philip Deloria, "I Want to Ride in Geronimo's Cadillac," in *Indians in Unexpected Places* (Lawrence: University Press of Kansas, 2004), 136–182.

72. Marx, "On the Jewish Question," 43.

73. Ralph Ellison, "Change the Joke and Slip the Yoke," in *The Collected Essays of Ralph Ellison* (New York: Modern Library, 2003), 100–112.

74. Ibid., 103.

75. The travesty of minstrelsy lies in rendering inequality natural and inevitable, serving White subjects as they create White citizenship. See Nathan Irvin Huggins, *Harlem Renaissance* (New York: Oxford University Press, 1971), 268.

76. The main audiences of minstrel performances in the antebellum era were dislocated urban men living in southern port cities and northern industrial cities such as Chicago and San Francisco. See Michael Rogin, *Black Face, White Noise* (Berkeley: University of California Press, 1996). The dehumanization of Black people on stage made the failure of schools, denials of jobs, mob attacks, Black codes, and the Fugitive Slave Act appear to be logical measures of social control. See Vincent Harding, *There Is a River: The Black Struggle for Freedom in America* (New York: Harcourt Brace, 1981).

77. Ellison, "Change the Joke," 109. Barry Shank's study of racial masquerade in *Juneteenth* provides insight into the complexities Ellison faced when considering whether the emancipatory possibilities of the mask would be able to bring people of color equality in national culture without their falling victim to the oppressive power of Whiteness. See Shank, "Bliss, or Blackface Sentiment," *boundary 2* 30, no. 2 (2003): 47–64. Jonathan

Arac says that Ellison was an active participant in Popular Front culture and was both politically and artistically committed to the emancipatory potential of a plural national character. See Arac, "Toward a Critical Genealogy of the U.S. Discourse of Identity: *Invisible Man* after Fifty Years," *boundary 2* 30, no. 2 (2003): 195–216.

78. Stephen Mihm, *A Nation of Counterfeiters* (Cambridge, MA: Harvard University Press, 2007).

79. Johnson, *Soul by Soul*, 5.

80. Ibid., 7.

81. Ibid., 6.

82. Rourke, *American Humor*, 25.

83. LeMenager, *Manifest and Other Destinies*, 13.

84. Rourke, *American Humor*, 74, 73.

85. Ibid., 86.

86. DuBois, *Gift of Black Folk*, 286, 274.

87. Ibid., 275.

88. Ibid., 274.

89. Early nineteenth-century blackface minstrelsy was performed by White men for White people in the interest of White dominance. See Eric Lott, *Love and Theft* (New York: Oxford University Press, 1993); and Huggins, *Harlem Renaissance*. Rourke is often understood as one of the first theorists of minstrelsy whose archival approach suggested a relationship between minstrelsy and Black freedom without the development of a critical assessment. See, for example, Mikko Tuhkanen, "Of Blackface and Paranoid Knowledge: Richard Wright, Jacques Lacan, and the Ambivalence of Black Minstrelsy," *diacritics* 31, no. 2 (2001): 9–34.

90. In engaging speculation as a racial logic that bridges U.S. culture and economy, I point to and diverge from the division in the field of American Studies between an older generation of Cultural Front scholars, who bemoan the disruption to emancipatory knowledge caused by the new social movements of the 1960s, and post-sixties scholars of critical ethnic studies. See Leo Marx, "On Recovering the 'Ur' Theory of American Studies," *American Literary History* 17, no. 1 (2005): 118–134; and Gene Wise, "'Paradigm Dramas' in American Studies: A Cultural and Institutional History of the Movement," *American Quarterly* 31, no. 3 (1979): 293–337. In response to and defense of alternative visions of the future that do not depend on Whiteness, assimilation, normative sexuality, and imperialism, see George Lipsitz, "Our America," *American Literary History* 17, no. 1 (2005): 135–140; Amy Kaplan, "A Call for a Truce," *American Literary History* 17, no. 1 (2005): 141–147; and Donald Pease and Robyn Wiegman, "Futures," in *The Futures of American Studies*, ed. Donald Pease and Robyn Wiegman (Durham, NC: Duke University Press, 2002), 1–42.

91. Rourke, *American Humor*, 76; and Fred Moten, *In the Break: The Aesthetics of the Black Radical Tradition* (Minneapolis: University of Minnesota Press, 2003), 12.

92. DuBois, *Gift of Black Folk*, 254.

93. Ibid., 309. Rourke does acknowledge that antislavery activists "deeply resented" the minstrel tradition. See Rourke, *American Humor*, 74.

94. DuBois, *Gift of Black Folk*, 276, 286.

95. Saidiya Hartman, *Scenes of Subjection* (New York: Oxford University Press, 1997).

96. Rourke, *American Humor*, 86.

97. Robinson offers the example of Ethiopia as a symbol of liberation that Black performers used to subtly challenge U.S. imperialism and racism. Although such indications of Black independence might go unnoticed by White audiences, for Black audiences they

registered a global history of struggle that validated continued aspirations for freedom. See Cedric Robinson, *Forgeries of Memory and Meaning* (Chapel Hill: University of North Carolina Press, 2007), 159.

98. Jelly Roll Morton, "The Stomping Ground," *Jelly Roll Morton: Library of Congress Recordings (Highlights)* (Nashville, TN: Rounder, 2007 [1938]), disc 1, track 8.

99. Alan Lomax, *Mister Jelly Roll* (Berkeley: University of California Press, 1950), 65, 64.

100. Quoted in Lomax, *Mister Jelly Roll*, 289.

101. Ibid.

102. Clyde Woods, *Development Arrested: Race, Power and the Blues in the Mississippi Delta* (New York: Verso, 1998).

103. Translated in Lomax, *Mister Jelly Roll*, 74.

104. Ibid.

105. Jelly Roll Morton, "Buddy Bertrand's Blues Continued / Mamie's Blues," *Jelly Roll Morton: Library of Congress Recordings (Highlights)* (Nashville, TN: Rounder, 2007 [1938]): disc 7 track 4.

106. Lomax, *Mister Jelly Roll*, 76.

107. Daniel Fishlin, Ajay Heble, and George Lipsitz, *The Fierce Urgency of Now: Improvisation, Rights and the Ethics of Cocreation* (Durham, NC: Duke University Press, 2013).

108. Rourke, *Roots of American Culture*, 72.

109. Ibid., 72. Also see Bernard Sheehan, *Seeds of Extinction: Jeffersonian Philanthropy and the American Indian* (New York: Norton, 1974).

110. Rourke, *Roots of American Culture*, 72, 73.

111. Joel Pfister, *Individuality Incorporated* (Durham, NC: Duke University Press, 2004).

112. Mark Rifkin, "Making Peoples into Populations: The Racial Limits of Tribal Sovereignty," in *Theorizing Native Studies*, ed. Audra Simpson and Andrea Smith (Durham, NC: Duke University Press, 2014), 149–187.

113. *The Business of Fancydancing*, written and directed by Sherman Alexie (Acton, MA: Wellspring, 2002).

114. Jacqueline Shea Murphy, *The People Have Never Stopped Dancing: Native American Modern Dance Histories* (Minneapolis: University of Minnesota, 2007).

115. Ann Marie Shea and Atay Citron, "The Powwow of the Thunderbird American Indian Dancers," *TDR: The Drama Review* 26, no. 2 (1982): 73–88.

116. Rachel Buff, *Immigration and the Political Economy of Home: West Indian Brooklyn and American Indian Minneapolis, 1945–1992* (Berkeley: University of California Press, 2001).

117. Donald Fixico, *The Invasion of Indian Country in the Twentieth Century: American Capitalism and Tribal Natural Resources* (Niwat: University Press of Colorado, 1998).

CHAPTER 4

Epigraphs: Franklin Delano Roosevelt, "Inaugural Address of the President, Washington, D.C., March 4, 1933," available at http://www.archives.gov/education/lessons/fdr-inaugural/, accessed March 23, 2013; F. O. Matthiessen, *From the Heart of Europe* (New York: Oxford University Press, 1948), 50; and W.E.B. DuBois, "The Revelation of Saint Orgne the Damned," in *The Education of Black People*, ed. Herbert Aptheker (New York: Monthly Review Press, 1973), 145.

1. Franklin Delano Roosevelt, "Inaugural Address of the President, Washington, D.C., March 4, 1933," available at http://www.archives.gov/education/lessons/fdr-inaugural/, accessed March 23, 2013.

2. Ibid., 5.

3. Ibid., 2.

4. Ibid., 6.

5. Ibid., 3.

6. Ibid., 7.

7. Ibid., 3.

8. Ibid.

9. Ibid., 3, 9.

10. Ibid., 5.

11. African American employment in Civilian Conservation Corps projects increased from 6 percent in 1935 to 11 percent in 1939. In tandem with other work relief programs, federal incomes nearly equaled incomes from agriculture and domestic service. See Joe William Trotter, "From a Raw Deal to a New Deal," in *To Make the World Anew*, ed. Robin D. G. Kelly and Earl Lewis (New York: Oxford University Press, 2000), 409–444.

12. Gunnar Myrdal, *An American Dilemma: The Negro Problem and Modern Democracy* (New York: Harper, 1944).

13. W.E.B. DuBois, *Dusk of Dawn* (New York: Harcourt Brace, 1940), xxx.

14. F. O. Matthiessen, *From the Heart of Europe* (New York: Oxford University Press, 1948), 3.

15. DuBois, *Dusk of Dawn*, 35; and Charles W. Wesley, *Prince Hall: Life and Legacy* (Washington, DC: United Supreme Council Southern Jurisdiction, Prince Hall Affiliation, 1977), 186–187.

16. W.E.B. DuBois, "My Evolving Program for Negro Freedom," in *What the Negro Wants*, ed. Rayford W. Logan (Chapel Hill: University of North Carolina Press, 1944), 31–70, 57.

17. W.E.B. DuBois, "The Future and Function of the Private Negro College," in *The Education of Black People*, ed. Herbert Aptheker (New York: Monthly Review Press, 1973), 192.

18. F. O. Matthiessen to Russell Cheney, January 4, 1939, letter #1264, F. O. Matthiessen Papers (New Haven, CT: Yale University Beinecke Rare Book and Manuscript Library, UNCAT ZA MS 444, Folder #59, letters: 1938–1940) (hereafter Matthiessen Papers).

19. F. O. Matthiessen, *Sarah Orne Jewett* (Boston: Houghton Mifflin, 1929); *Translation: An Elizabethan Art* (New York: Octagon, 1931); and *The Achievement of T. S. Eliot* (Boston: Houghton Mifflin, 1935).

20. Matthiessen to Cheney, January 4, 1939, letter #1264, Matthiessen Papers.

21. Ibid. Matthiessen's claim about the exceptional nature of his doubt is contradicted by his earlier correspondence with Cheney. In a letter written in 1929, he stated that teaching had lost its luster and that he had lost site of its higher purposes, which he had forged through the "glow" of the form of knowledge and understanding he sought through participation in Skull and Bones and the Elizabethan Club. He described this as a "problem unlike any [he had] ever had before." F. O. Matthiessen to Russell Cheney, November 30, 1929, letter #903, Matthiessen Papers.

22. The particular psychochemical factors that may have contributed to Matthiessen's fragile mental state, or the degree to which his depression reflected a trauma as it was

lived or merely a discursive mode of self-confession that produced the truth it appeared to reveal, are unknown. It would be impertinent to attempt a diagnosis or to suggest a genesis and reason for the despair that led the scholar to seriously contemplate suicide. See Michel Foucault, *The History of Sexuality: Volume 1* (New York: Vintage, 1978). Regarding the chemical aspects of depression, Matthiessen wrote from McLean that he was afraid of becoming dependent on Nembutal for treating his insomnia.

23. Elizabeth Freeman's dialectical articulation of how the concept of "chronic" expresses both pain and pleasure taps into the interworking of the type of desire and dread informing Matthiessen's aspirations to preserve memory as a sacred site for class idealization. See Freeman, "Chronic Thinking" (paper presented in conjunction with "Strategic Ruptures: Feminist Reflections on Crisis Management" series, Cornell University, February 2011).

24. Kevin Floyd, "Disciplined Bodies" and "Performative Masculinity," in *The Reification of Desire* (Minneapolis: University of Minnesota Press, 2009).

25. Matthiessen to Cheney, January 4, 1939, letter #1264, Matthiessen Papers.

26. Ibid.

27. Ibid.

28. Ibid.

29. F. O. Matthiessen, *American Renaissance* (Oxford: Oxford University Press, 1941), 4.

30. Matthiessen, *From the Heart of Europe*, 50.

31. Seth Moglen, *Mourning Modernity* (Stanford, CA: Stanford University Press, 2007); and Judith Butler, *Precarious Life* (New York: Verso, 2006).

32. Matthiessen to Cheney, November 30, 1929, letter #903, Matthiessen Papers.

33. Giles Gunn, *F. O. Matthiessen: The Critical Achievement* (Seattle: University of Washington Press, 1975), 110.

34. William Cain, *F. O. Matthiessen and the Politics of Criticism* (Madison: University of Wisconsin Press, 1988); Jane Tompkins, *Sensational Designs* (New York: Oxford University Press, 1986); Ann Douglass, *The Feminization of American Culture* (New York: Avon, 1977); Nina Baym, "Melodrama of Beset Manhood," *American Quarterly* 33 (Summer 1981): 123–139; Russell Reising *The Unusable Past* (New York: Methuen, 1986); Eric Sundquist, "Slavery, Revolution, and the American Renaissance," in *The American Renaissance Reconsidered*, ed. Walter Benn Michaels and Donald Pease (Baltimore: Johns Hopkins University Press, 1985), 1–33; Jonathan Arac, "F. O. Matthiessen: Authorizing an American Renaissance," in *American Renaissance Reconsidered*, 90–112; Walter Benn Michaels, "Romance and Real Estate," in *American Renaissance Reconsidered*, 156–182; Eric Cheyfitz, "Matthiessen's American Renaissance: Circumscribing the Revolution," *American Quarterly* 41, no. 2 (1989): 341–361; Donald Pease, *Visionary Compacts* (Madison: University of Wisconsin Press, 1987); David W. Noble, *Death of a Nation* (Minneapolis: University of Minnesota Press, 2002); Jay Grossman, *Reconstituting the American Renaissance* (Durham, NC: Duke University Press, 2003); Timothy Powell, *Ruthless Democracy* (Princeton, NJ: Princeton University Press, 2000); Michael Denning, *The Cultural Front* (New York: Verso, 1997); George Lipsitz, *American Studies in a Moment of Danger* (Minneapolis: University of Minnesota Press, 2001); and Henry Abelove, *Deep Gossip* (Minneapolis: University of Minnesota Press, 2003).

35. Gunn, *F. O. Matthiessen*, 71.

36. Matthiessen, *American Renaissance*, ix.

37. Ibid., xx.

38. Ibid.

39. Including J. S. Mill, Matthew Arnold, Benjamin Jowett, and William Gladstone. See Linda Dowling, *Hellenism and Homosexuality in Victorian Oxford* (Ithaca, NY: Cornell University Press, 1994), 31.

40. With the Greats counting for more on civil service exams, many of the plebian elite that were Jowett's students came to occupy important positions throughout the empire.

41. Dowling, *Hellenism and Homosexuality in Victorian Oxford*, 79. A case in point is John Addington Symonds's collaboration with Havelock Ellis on *Sexual Inversion* (London: Wilson and Macmillan, 1897).

42. *Plato, Symposium: The Benjamin Jowett Translation* (New York: Modern Library, 1996), 76.

43. Dowling, *Hellenism and Homosexuality in Victorian Oxford*, 116. Oscar Wilde's homoerotic controversy in 1895 foreclosed this positive valuation of homosexuality in nineteenth-century England.

44. F. O. Matthiessen to Russell Cheney, n.d., unfiled letter, Matthiessen Papers.

45. Ibid.

46. F. O. Matthiessen to Russell Cheney, September 23, 1924, letter #5, Matthiessen Papers.

47. Ibid.

48. F. O. Matthiessen to Russell Cheney, September 7, 1924, letter #1, Matthiessen Papers. The incitement to confession that Foucault theorizes as the disciplinary technology through which the social truth of "unspeakable" sexual behavior becomes normalized by repetition aptly reflects the mechanisms of sexual identification that contributed to Matthiessen's experience of sexual injury. In this same letter, he promises Cheney a draft of a sexual life history that he had previously written in 1924 after having read Havelock Ellis. As his letters here reflect, his self-inscription into the language of sexual inversion fundamentally shaped his anxious self-identification as a deviant sexual subject.

49. Matthiessen to Cheney, September 23, 1924, letter #5, Matthiessen Papers.

50. Ibid.

51. F. O. Matthiessen to Russell Cheney, November 2, 1924, letter #38, Matthiessen Papers.

52. Matthiessen to Cheney, September 23, 1924, letter #5, Matthiessen Papers.

53. F. O. Matthiessen to Russell Cheney, February 7, 1925, letter #76, Matthiessen Papers.

54. F. O. Matthiessen to Russell Cheney, January 29, 1925, letter #68, Matthiessen Papers.

55. F. O. Matthiessen to Russell Cheney, October 16, 1924, letter #22, Matthiessen Papers.

56. Ibid.

57. Michael Cadden, "Engendering F.O.M," in *Engendering Men*, ed. Joseph A. Boone and Michael Cadden (New York: Routledge, 1990), 25–35.

58. John Addington Symonds, *Walt Whitman* (London: John C. Nimmo, 1893), 68.

59. Ibid., 72.

60. F. O. Matthiessen to Russell Cheney, September 21, 1924, letter # 4, Matthiessen Papers. Ellis accounted for Whitman's fervent rejection of the idea that the "Calumus" poems advocated homosexuality in *Sexual Inversion*. See Betsy Erkkila and Jay Grossman, eds., *Breaking the Bounds* (New York: Oxford University Press, 1996).

61. Matthiessen to Cheney, February 7, 1925, letter #76, Matthiessen Papers.

62. Edward Carpenter, *The Intermediate Sex* (London: George Allen, 1908), quoted in F. O. Matthiessen to Russell Cheney, June 18, 1925, letter#153, Matthiessen Papers.

63. F. O. Matthiessen to Russell Cheney, December 1, 1924, letter #63, Matthiessen Papers.

64. F. O. Matthiessen to Russell Cheney, September 7, 1924, letter #2, Matthiessen Papers.

65. Ibid.

66. Ibid.

67. Louis Hyde, ed., *Rat and the Devil: Journal Letters of F. O. Matthiessen and Russell Cheney* (Boston: Alyson, 1978), 47. Matthiessen grappled with whether to embrace the "innocence" of the Uranian poets and remain nonsexual or to take the position of Symonds in tying higher love to sexual acts. See F. O. Matthiessen to Russell Cheney, letters #42, #68, #80, and #93 in particular (and letters #102 and #112), Matthiessen Papers.

68. F. O. Matthiessen to Russell Cheney, October 20, 1924, letter #25, Matthiessen Papers.

69. Hyde, *Rat and the Devil*, 40.

70. F. O. Matthiessen to Russell Cheney, September 2, 1924, letter #8, Matthiessen Papers.

71. F. O. Matthiessen to Russell Cheney, October 16, 1924, letter #22, Matthiessen Papers.

72. F. O. Matthiessen to Russell Cheney, December 1, 1924, letter #63, Matthiessen Papers.

73. F. O. Matthiessen to Russell Cheney, October 15, 1924, letter #20, Matthiessen Papers. Although "barbarian" was the common term used by the fraternity to refer to nonmembers, its racial undertones to differentiate "uncivilized," "savage," and "foreign" extend from prefeudal Europe into the nineteenth-century United States and align the group firmly with the legacies of White supremacy that structure racial capitalism. See Cedric Robinson, *Black Marxism* (Chapel Hill: University of North Carolina Press, 1983).

74. Hyde, *Rat and the Devil*, 17.

75. Matthiessen to Cheney, October 16, 1924, letter #22, Matthiessen Papers. He specifically names "Max and Put."

76. Antony Sutton, *America's Secret Establishment* (Waterville, OR: Trine Day, 2002); Kris Milligan, *Fleshing Out Skull and Bones* (Waterville, OR: Trine Day, 2003); and Alexandra Robbins, *Secrets of the Tomb* (Boston: Back Bay, 2002). Tim Russert publicly "outed" both presidential candidates on *Meet the Press* on February 7, 2004.

77. In keeping with the codes of secrecy, for example, Louis Hyde edited all mention of Skull and Bones from the published collection of the couple's letters and from the descriptive index he provided of their friendships. A cross-reference of Matthiessen's friendships and Skull and Bones membership exposes nearly all of his friends as members of the society. To maintain the secrecy of the fraternity, Hyde encoded fraternal membership in the collected letters with the phrases "close friend" and "Yale classmate." In the archival record, Matthiessen primarily referred to these friends as "cl-bmates."

78. Accounts conflict as to whether the last of these was a ring (Abelove) or a key (Sweezy).

79. F. O. Matthiessen to Russell Cheney, October 29, 1924, letter #32, Matthiessen Papers.

80. Robbins, *Secrets of the Tomb*, 121.

81. Dana Nelson, *National Manhood* (Durham, NC: Duke University Press, 1998).

82. Robbins, *Secrets of the Tomb*, 89; and Milligan, *Fleshing Out Skull and Bones*, 33–36.

83. Nelson, *National Manhood*, 187.

84. Ibid., 188.

85. Ibid., 15.

86. Matthiessen to Cheney, October 3, 1924, letter #32, Matthiessen Papers.

87. F. O. Matthiessen to Russell Cheney, October 3, 1924, letter #11, Matthiessen Papers.

88. According to Robbins, in *Secrets of the Tomb*, all members of the society are forced to confess their entire sexual history. A November 5, 1924, letter recounting a conversation he had with his fellow bonesman Dick Tighe suggests that Matthiessen, having come of age in the homosocial environment of the Hackley Preparatory School, had no short sexual history to tell.

89. F. O. Matthiessen to Russell Cheney, n.d., unfiled letter, folder #1, Matthiessen Papers.

90. F. O. Matthiessen to Russell Cheney, May 6, 1925, letter #129, Matthiessen Papers.

91. The sexual history of an initiate, Robbins suggests in *Secrets of the Tomb*, is the first act of disclosure that new knights perform, 134–137.

92. F. O. Matthiessen to Russell Cheney, September 23, 1924, letter #34, Matthiessen Papers.

93. Matthiessen to Cheney, January 29, 1925, letter #68, Matthiessen Papers.

94. F. O. Matthiessen to Russell Cheney, April 9, 1925, letter #102, Matthiessen Papers.

95. F. O. Matthiessen to Russell Cheney, September 7, 1924, letter #2, Matthiessen Papers.

96. Ibid.

97. F. O. Matthiessen to Russell Cheney, September 24, 1924, letter #6, Matthiessen Papers.

98. Matthiessen to Cheney, April 9, 1925, letter #102, Matthiessen Papers.

99. Matthiessen to Cheney, May 6, 1925, letter #129, Matthiessen Papers.

100. F. O. Matthiessen to Russell Cheney, November 2, 1924, letter #38, Matthiessen Papers.

101. Matthiessen to Cheney, January 4, 1939, letter #1264, Matthiessen Papers.

102. Ibid.

103. Matthiessen, *From the Heart of Europe*, 73.

104. Matthiessen to Cheney, November 2, 1924, letter #38, Matthiessen Papers.

105. F. O. Matthiessen to Russell Cheney, n.d., unfiled letter, folder #1, Matthiessen Papers. This was Matthiessen's transcription of a letter written to him by Cheney dated December 1, 1924.

106. Matthiessen to Cheney, January 4, 1939, letter #1264, Matthiessen Papers. Matthiessen discusses reading this poem in letter #129, dated May 6, 1929: "I have been reading Whitman steadily, I had never read some of his longer poems—'crossing Brooklyn Ferry' 'Song of the Answerer' 'Song of the Broad Axe' etc. Their freshness is supreme."

107. Matthiessen to Cheney, January 4, 1939, letter #1264, Matthiessen Papers.

108. Walt Whitman, *Leaves of Grass: The 1892 Edition* (New York: Bantam, 1983), 158.

109. In *From the Heart of Europe*, Matthiessen recalls the "Calumus" poems as his first introduction to Whitman.

110. Ibid., xv.

111. Matthiessen, *American Renaissance*, xii.

112. Based on his own investigation of the Matthiessen archives, Henry Abelove argues that for Matthiessen democracy and White male homosexuality were often indistinguishable. *American Renaissance* is structured by "the erotic dynamic, the ties, affections, affiliations, that bound together [the] White men, suppositiously equal, suppositiously brothers, who were the privileged subjects of the old republic." See Abelove, *Deep Gossip*, 62–63.

113. Matthiessen, *American Renaissance*, 3.

114. *Plato, Symposium: The Benjamin Jowett Translation*, 76.

115. Ibid., 257.

116. This ideal is, of course, predominant in Emerson's appeal to living above time with nature in "Self-Reliance."

117. Of particular note, his text is concerned with nineteenth-century authors' response to the conditions and crises in value through aesthetic practices; it further side-steps the problems of the historical through a periodization that leaves out discussion of two wars, the war with Mexico and the Civil War.

118. Matthiessen, *American Renaissance*, 652.

119. Ibid., 654.

120. Ibid., 656.

121. Nelson, *National Manhood*, 185.

122. Matthiessen, *American Renaissance*, xv.

123. Ibid., 57.

124. Matthiessen to Cheney, April 18, 1925, letter #112, Matthiessen Papers.

125. Ibid.

126. Eve Kosofsky Sedgewick, *Between Men* (New York: Columbia University Press, 1985).

127. See Hyde, *Rat and the Devil*, 263–283.

128. Matthiessen supported the school until 1947, when it was closed after being placed on the Attorney General's list of subversive organizations. See Paul Sweezy and Leo Huberman, eds., *F. O. Matthiessen, 1902–1950: A Collective Portrait* (New York: Schuman, 1950), 74.

129. Christopher P. Wilson, *White Collar Fictions* (Athens: University of Georgia Press, 1992).

130. F. O. Matthiessen to Russell Cheney, October 15, 1924, letter #20, Matthiessen Papers.

131. Matthiessen, *Sarah Orne Jewett*, 145–146.

132. Jewitt was Matthiessen's cousin and like him had familial and affective ties to Kittery, Maine, where Matthiessen and Cheney shared a house.

133. Matthiessen, *Sarah Orne Jewett*, 31.

134. David Noble has argued that the democracy Matthiessen found in the past provided him "a usable past but only on a personal, not a public, level; the art of the renaissance could save his soul, but not the soul of the nation." See Noble, *Death of a Nation*, 91.

135. W.E.B. DuBois, "My Evolving Program for Negro Freedom," in *What the Negro Wants*, ed. Rayford W. Logan (Chapel Hill: University of North Carolina Press, 1944), 57.

136. Ibid.

137. W.E.B. DuBois, *The Souls of Black Folk* (New York: Dover Thrift Edition), 94.

138. Chandan Reddy, *Freedom with Violence: Race, Sexuality, and the US State* (Durham, NC: Duke University Press, 2011).

139. DuBois, *Dusk of Dawn*, 27.

140. Ibid., 68.

141. DuBois, "My Evolving Program for Negro Freedom," 50.

142. Ibid., 57.

143. Ibid., 58.

144. Ibid., 57.

145. DuBois, *Dusk of Dawn*, 281.

146. Ibid., 58. See W.E.B. DuBois, *The Philadelphia Negro: A Social Study* (Philadelphia: University of Pennsylvania Press, 1996 [1899]).

147. DuBois, *Dusk of Dawn*, 310.

148. Ibid.

149. Ibid., 26–27.

150. Ibid., 26.

151. Ibid., 29.

152. Ibid., 31.

153. Susan Gilman, *Blood Talk: American Race Melodrama and the Culture of the Occult* (Chicago: University of Chicago Press, 2003).

154. Wesley, *Prince Hall*.

155. Ibid. DuBois did speak of universalisms in masculinist terms. For the sake of this chapter, I am temporarily bracketing an extended discussion of his approach to gender, which includes his use of the masculine *he*, *man*, and *his* as gender-neutral terms. Susan Gilman offers a detailed discussion of protofeminism in Black fraternal societies and in DuBois's thinking. His delineation of materialist freedom indicates a sensibility that by all men he meant all humans regardless of gender. See Gilman, *Blood Talk*.

156. W.E.B. DuBois, *Darkwater: Voices from within the Veil* (Mineola, NY: Dover, 1999 [1920]), 1.

157. Ibid., 2.

158. W.E. B. DuBois, *Economic Cooperation among Negroes in America* (New York: Negro University Press, 1907), 96.

159. DuBois, *Philadelphia Negro*, 185–186, 221–227.

160. W.E.B. DuBois, "Education and Work," in *The Education of Black People*, ed. Herbert Aptheker (New York: Monthly Review Press, 1973 [1930]), 103.

161. Ibid., 88.

162. Ibid., 89.

163. Ibid., 91.

164. Ibid., 91–92.

165. Ibid., 93.

166. Ibid., 106.

167. Ibid., 107.

168. Ibid.

169. Ibid., 108.

170. DuBois, *Dusk of Dawn*, 105.

171. Ibid., 319.

172. Ibid., 320.

173. Robinson, *Black Marxism*.

174. Ibid., 320.

175. Ibid., 289.

176. DuBois, "My Evolving Program for Negro Freedom," 70.

177. Susan Searls Giroux, *Between Race and Reason: Violence, Intellectual Responsibility and the University to Come* (Stanford, CA: Stanford University Press, 2010), 233.

178. W.E.B. DuBois, "The Revelation of Saint Orgne the Damned," in *The Education of Black People*, ed. Herbert Aptheker (New York: Monthly Review, 1973 [1938]), 145.

179. DuBois, "My Evolving Program for Negro Freedom," 67.

180. Ibid., 65.

181. DuBois, *Dusk of Dawn*, 305.

182. DuBois, "Revelation of Saint Orgne the Damned," 191.

183. Ibid., 150.

184. DuBois, "Education and Work," 103.

185. DuBois, "Revelation of Saint Orgne the Damned," 182.

186. DuBois, "My Evolving Program for Negro Freedom," 69.

PART III

1. Lauren Berlant, *Cruel Optimism* (Durham, NC: Duke University Press, 2011).

2. In the Heart of the Beast Puppet and Mask Theatre, 38th May Day Celebration program, May 2012.

CHAPTER 5

Epigraphs: Alan Greenspan, "Never Saw It Coming: Why the Financial Crisis Took Economists by Surprise," *Foreign Affairs* (November–December 2013), available at http://www.foreignaffairs.com/articles/140161/alan-greenspan/never-saw-it-coming, accessed December 12, 2013; *Extreme Makeover Home Edition*, ABC Television, 2012; and Geryll Robinson and Lakeesha J. Harris, *Spirit House* (stage production performed by the Cripple Creek Theatre Company, April 19, 2013, Dryades Theater, New Orleans).

1. David Harvey, "The 'New' Imperialism: Accumulation by Dispossession," *Socialist Register* 40 (2004): 63–87.

2. Edmund Andrews, "Greenspan Concedes Error on Regulation," *New York Times*, October 23, 2008, available at http://www.nytimes.com/2008/10/24/business/economy/24panel.html, accessed October 24, 2008.

3. Jon Meacham and Daniel Gross, "The Oracle Reveals All," *Newsweek*, September 24, 2007, 28.

4. Greta R. Krippner, *Capitalizing on Crisis: The Political Origins of the Rise of Finance* (Cambridge, MA: Harvard University Press, 2011).

5. James Heintz and Radhika Balakrishnan, "Debt, Power, and Crisis: Social Stratification and the Inequitable Governance of Financial Markets," *American Quarterly* 64, no. 3 (2012): 387–409.

6. A CDS allows banks and finance companies to remove credit risks from their balance sheets by selling it in private contracts to any willing investor who holds more than $10 million in assets. See Michael Greenberger, "The Role of Derivatives in the Financial Crisis" (testimony before the Financial Crisis Inquiry Commission Hearing, Wednesday June 30, 2010, Dirksen Senate Office Building, Washington, DC); and Gillian Tett, *Fool's Gold* (New York: Free Press, 2010).

7. Daniel Immergluck, *Foreclosed* (Ithaca, NY: Cornell University Press, 2009); Atif Mian and Amir Sufi, *House of Debt* (Chicago: University of Chicago, 2014); and Nouriel Roubini and Stephen Mihm, *Crisis Economics* (New York: Penguin, 2010).

8. In her comments on unfair lending practices before the U.S commission on Civil Rights in 2009, Lisa Rice testified that investors were often explicit in their desires for exotic mortgage portfolios with subprime loans because they were known to yield higher returns. See U.S. Commission on Civil Rights, "Civil Rights and the Mortgage Crisis" (Washington, DC, September 2009), available at www.usccr.gov/pubs/CRMORTGAGE09509.pdf, accessed February 12, 2010.

9. "2013 Update: The Spillover Effects of Foreclosures," available at responsiblelending.org, accessed August 19, 2013.

10. Ajamu Dillahunt, Brian Miller, Mike Prokosch, Jeannette Huezo, and Dedrick Muhammad, *State of the Dream 2010 DRAINED: Jobless and Foreclosed in Communities of Color* (Boston: United for a Fair Economy, 2010).

11. Although most foreclosures have been White-owned properties (estimated 56 percent), 8 percent of African American and Latino owners were foreclosed compared with 4.5 percent of Whites. See Debbie Gruenstein Bocian, Wei Li, and Keith S. Ernst, "Foreclosures by Race and Ethnicity: The Demographics of a Crisis, CRL Research Report," June 18, 2010, available at responsiblelending.org, accessed December 10, 2010.

12. Estimates suggest that African American borrowers will lose between $72 and $93 billion and Latino borrowers will lose between $76 and $98 billion for the same period. See Amaad Rivera, Brenda Cotto-Escalera, Anisha Desai, Jeannette Huezo, and Dedrick Muhammad, *State of the Dream 2008 Foreclosed* (Boston: United for a Fair Economy, 2008).

13. "2013 Update."

14. "Foreclosures Are Killing Us," *New York Times*, October 3, 2011, A21.

15. Allen J. Fishbein and Patrick Woodall, *Women Are Prime Targets for Subprime Lending: Women Are Disproportionately Represented in High-Cost Mortgage Market* (Washington, DC: Consumer Federation of America, 2006); and Amy Castro Baker, "Eroding the Wealth of Women: Gender and the Subprime Foreclosure Crisis," *Social Service Review* 88, no. 1 (2014): 59–91.

16. As indicated by employees of Enron who laughed at the prospect of blacking out California despite the harm it might cause, profiting from the misery of others is something investors often no longer make an effort to conceal. See Bethany McClean and Peter Elkind, *The Smartest Guys in the Room: The Amazing Rise and Scandalous Fall of Enron* (New York: Portfolio Trade, 2004). In 2003 the Defense Advanced Research Projects Agency went so far as to propose a futures market in terrorism that would allow investors to place bets on the odds that death and violence would erupt in different parts of the world. See Steve Fraser, *Every Man a Speculator* (New York: Harper Perennial, 2006).

17. The household debt ratio peaked in 2008 at 100 percent of GDP. See Atif Mian and Amir Sufi, "The Credit Expansion," in *House of Debt* (Chicago: Chicago University Press, 2014); Nouriel Rubini and Steven Mihm, *Crisis Economics* (New York: Penguin, 2010); and Carmen M. Reinhardt and Kenneth S. Rogdoff, *This Time It's Different* (Princeton, NJ: Princeton University Press, 2009).

18. Regarding 2006 mortgage-backed securities, three-fifths of loans were "cash out" refinances on existing mortgages. The average price of loans was around $223,000, and 90 percent of them were 2/28 adjustable rate mortgages. See John Cassidy, *How Markets Fail: The Logic of Economic Calamities* (New York: Farrar, Straus and Giroux, 2010), 260.

19. The Depository Institutions Deregulation and Monetary Control Act (1980) allowed banks and savings and loans to set fees at their discretion. The Transaction Parity Act of 1982 paved the way for variable-interest rates and balloon payments. The

Secondary Mortgage Market Enhancement Act (1984) allowed investment banks to buy, pool, and sell mortgages. The Interstate Banking and Branching Act (1994) allowed banks to operate across state lines. The Commodities Futures Modernization Act (2000) enabled sales of over-the-counter derivatives with little oversight. The Bankruptcy Abuse Prevention and Consumer Protection Act (2005) shifted terms for filing individual bankruptcy in favor of lenders.

20. "Remarks by Chairman Alan Greenspan" (delivered at the Federal Reserve System's Fourth Annual Community Affairs Research Conference, Washington DC, April 2005), available at http://www.federalreserve.gov/BOARDDOCS/Speeches/2005/20050408/default.htm, accessed May 9, 2015.

21. Paula Chakravartty and Denise Ferreira da Silva, "Accumulation, Dispossession, and Debt," *American Quarterly* 64, no. 3 (2012): 361–385.

22. Jacob Hacker, "The Middle Class at Risk," in *Broke: How Debt Bankrupts the Middle Class*, ed. Katherine Porter (Stanford, CA: Stanford University Press, 2012), 218–234; and Thomas Shapiro, *The Hidden Cost of Being African American* (New York: Oxford University Press, 2005).

23. Susanne Soderberg, "The U.S. Debtfare State and the Credit Care Industry: Forging Spaces of Dispossession," *Antipode* 45, no. 2 (2013): 493–512.

24. Michel-Rolph Trouillet, *Silencing the Past* (Boston: Beacon, 1997).

25. Edmund Burke's classical differentiation between the beautiful and the sublime is instructive for understanding how the aesthetics of the sublime are propped up by masculinist notions of human superiority. See Burke, "Philosophical Inquiry into the Origin of Our Ideas of the Sublime and the Beautiful," in *Burke's Writings and Speeches*, vol. 1 (London: John C. Nimmo, 1906).

26. Terry Eagleton's discussion of Edmund Burke is useful for teasing out the relationship between desires for social stability and the structural force of fantasy and discrimination. See Eagleton, *The Ideology of the Aesthetic* (Malden, MA: Blackwell, 1990).

27. G. A. Reynolds, "Credit Scoring and Other Factors Related to the Granting and Pricing of Loans," in *Civil Rights and the Mortgage Crisis* (Washington, DC: U.S. Commission on Civil Rights, September 2009).

28. George Lipsitz, *The Possessive Investment in Whiteness* (Philadelphia: Temple University Press, 1998); and Lipsitz, *How Racism Takes Place* (Philadelphia: Temple University Press, 2011).

29. Elvin Wyly, C. S. Ponder, Pierson Nettling, Bosco Ho, Sophie Ellen Fung, Zacharay Liebowitz, and Dan Hammel, "New Racial Meanings of Housing in America," *American Quarterly* 64, no. 3 (2012): 571–604.

30. In 2005, Freddie Mac reported that one in five home owners who had received subprime loans could have qualified for prime-rate loans. See Mike Hudson and E. Scott Reckard, "More Homeowners with Good Credit Getting Stuck with Higher Rate Loans," *Los Angeles Times*, October 24, 2005.

31. The Pew Hispanic Center reports that 44.9 percent of Hispanic borrowers and 52. 5 percent of African American borrowers took out subprime mortgages in the bubble economy, compared with only 17.5 percent of White borrowers. According to the National Fair Housing Alliance, the majority of this subprime lending took place in economically isolated and racially segregated neighborhoods. As Lisa Rice testified to the U.S. Commission on Civil Rights in 2009, even after accounting for differences in "creditworthiness," people of color were 30 percent more likely to have been recipients of subprime loans during the crisis. In tests conducted by the National Fair Housing Alliance in which African American borrowers always entered negotiations with higher

credit scores than comparable White applicants, African Americans were up to 66 percent more likely to be treated disparately in the lending process.

32. Dean Baker, *Plunder and Blunder: The Rise and Fall of the Bubble Economy* (San Francisco: Berrett-Koehler, 2011).

33. Up to 80 percent of subprime loans included prepayment penalties (at an average cost of $2.3 billion a year for borrowers). Five- to seven-year balloon payments often required refinance or forfeiture when loans matured. Negative amortization on interest-only loans often left borrowers owing more than a house was worth. Shared-appreciation mortgages relinquished a portion of the home's future value in exchange for lower interest rates. No-interest no-asset loans encouraged borrowers to "lie" about income and assets and were a better predictor of default than credit score. See Howard Karger, "The Homeownership Myth," *Dollars and Sense*, no. 270 (2007), and Amy Gluckman, "The New World of Home Loans," *Dollars and* Sense, no. 270 (2007), both available at http://www.dollarsandsense.org/archives/2007/0507homeownership.html, accessed November 13, 2010.

34. In his testimony before the House Committee on Financial Services on April 20, 2010, William Black discussed how mortgage brokers, bankers, and stockbrokers were paid not for the *quality* of loans they bundled into securities but for the *volume* of loans they accumulated, bundled, and sold down a long chain of speculative exchange. His testimony concisely explained that this practice increased risk and caused the Lehman bankruptcy.

35. On the surface, a CDS seems to allow banks and finance companies to remove credit risks from their balance sheets by selling it in private contracts to any willing investor who holds more than $10 million in assets. The CDS market was imagined and popularized by brokers at J.P. Morgan in the mid-1990s as a way for private parties to exchange the risk of credit investments without requiring a transfer in ownership of the underlying credit. In the world of banking, CDSs developed into both highly profitable investment products and a way for banks to free up capital for increased lending by shifting the risk of their credit obligations to outside investors. Although banks held on to the original loans, the "insurance-like" properties of a CDS meant that, in the case of default, investors would be obliged to cover the losses. See Tett, *Fool's Gold*; and Greenberger, "Role of Derivatives in the Financial Crisis."

36. An estimated three-quarters of CDS contracts in the bubble economy were "naked," meaning that a high volume of investors took out multiple CDS contracts on a single bond that exponentially spread risk among gamblers with no ownership stake in the credit on which they bet, and produced opportunities for investors to short the market by making a logical bet on the likelihood that mortgage-backed securities would default.

37. Douglas S. Massey and Nancy A. Denton, *American Apartheid* (Cambridge, MA: Harvard University Press, 1998).

38. Geryll Robinson and Lakeesha J. Harris, *Spirit House* (stage production performed by the Cripple Creek Theatre Company, April 19, 2013, Dryades Theater, New Orleans).

39. F. Allon, "Speculation on Everyday Life: The Cultural Economy of the Quotidian," *Journal of Communication Inquiry* 34, no. 4 (2010): 366–381.

40. Prior to the passage of the Civil Rights Act of 1965, 98 percent of the 10 million homes that were purchased using loans backed by the FHA were awarded to White buyers. See Kai Wright, "The Assault on the Black Middle Class," *American Prospect Special Report: The Credit Crisis and Working America* 20, no. 6 (2009): A7; and David Roediger,

"A New Deal, An Industrial Union, and a White House," in *Working toward Whiteness* (New York: Basic Books, 2006).

41. The plan was to expand national home ownership from 64 to 67.5 percent. See U.S. Department of Housing and Urban Development (HUD), *National Homeownership Strategy: Partners in the American Dream* (Washington, DC: HUD, May 1995).

42. Bill Clinton, "Remarks on the National Homeownership Strategy," June 5, 1995, available at http://www.presidency.ucsb.edu/ws/index.php?pid=51448, accessed July 1, 2011.

43. Bush's initiative aimed to increase minority home ownership by 5.5 million before 2010 through government subsidies for down payments and closing costs and rehabilitation assistance for low-income buyers. The underlying assumption of both the Clinton and Bush administrations was a trickle-down belief that home ownership would increase consumer markets by creating new construction jobs and renewed consumer demand for large commodity purchases. Both of these neoliberal formations balanced on the residual affects of a Keynesian consumer society while they promoted state deregulation. See Lizabeth Cohen, *A Consumer's Republic: The Politics of Mass Consumption in Postwar America* (New York: Vintage, 2003).

44. Much like Clinton's strategy, the promise of federal assistance in this subsidy was largely a symbolic gesture. With the median national home price in 2003 averaging around $191,300 (and steadily rising), the cap of $10,000, or 6 percent of the purchase price, that ADDI grants offered still required potential home owners to accumulate substantial capital or credit to enter the market. See U.S. Census Bureau, "Median and Average Sale Prices of New Homes Sold in the United States," available at http://www.census.gov/const/uspricemon.pdf, accessed June 14, 2011.

45. George W. Bush, "Remarks on Signing the American Dream Downpayment Act," December 16, 2003, available at, http://www.presidency.ucsb.edu/ws/index.php?pid=64935, accessed July 1, 2011.

46. David Roediger, "A Vast Amount of Coercion," in *Working toward Whiteness* (New York: Basic Books, 2006).

47. The first season of *This Old House* in 1979 focused on keeping costs low in the renovation of older homes during a real estate crunch. The total cost to renovate the Victorian home that was the 1979 season's project was $30,000. See Francis Stors, "This Old House: An Oral History," *Boston Magazine*, February 2009, available at http://www.bostonmagazine.com/articles/this_old_house/, accessed June 12, 2010. In comparison, during the early stages of the U.S. housing bubble in 2001, *This Old House* focused on renovating a colonial revival in Manchester, Massachusetts, at a cost of $1.5 million. See "The Manchester Project," *This Old House*, available at http://www.thisoldhouse.com/toh/tv/house-project/overview/0,,213533,00.html, accessed June 12, 2010.

48. George Lipsitz, "Learning from Los Angeles: Another One Rides the Bus," *American Quarterly* 56, no. 3 (2004): 511–529.

49. Shawn Shimpach, "Realty Reality: HGTV and the Subprime Crisis," *American Quarterly* 64, no. 3 (2012): 515–542.

50. Anna Everett, "Trading Private and Public Space@HGTV and TLC: On New Genre Formations in Transformation TV," *Journal of Visual Culture* 3, no. 2 (2004): 157–181.

51. In this regard, the televisual form abstractly enacts the type of social accounting that Miranda Joseph argues is the organizing disciplinary construction of neoliberal "entrepreneurial" subjectivity. Beneath the judgment expressed by the spectator's script is a matrix of interconnected financial, managerial, legal, statistical, and social

accounting norms through which normative expectations of personal responsibility are reinforced and mass-distributed. See Joseph, *Debt to Society: Accounting for Life under Capitalism* (Minneapolis: University of Minnesota Press, 2015).

52. Walter Benjamin, "The Work of Art in the Age of Mechanical Reproduction," in *Illuminations*, ed. Hannah Arendt (New York: Harcourt, 1968), 232.

53. Robinson and Harris, *Spirit House*.

54. Ibid.

55. Ibid.

56. Ibid.

57. Ibid.

58. Ibid.

59. Fair Housing tests show that racial discrimination excludes African Americans who are qualified by all objective measures from zip codes correlated with higher life expectancy, school opportunities, and long-term life benefits 47 percent of the time. See Greater New Orleans Housing Action Center, "Where Opportunity Knocks the Doors Are Locked," November 2014, available at www.gnofairhousing.org, accessed November 15, 2014.

60. Ibid.

61. Ibid.

62. Ibid.

CHAPTER 6

Epigraphs: Barbara Johnson, comments to the Minneapolis City Council Committee of the Whole Meeting, May 7, 2014, available at http://www.youtube.com/watch?v=lliKdPo9rrc&index=111&list=PLcNuebgSUruBwfFHKPC6QOuHosXodOMSH; James P. Cannon, " . . . If It Takes All Summer," *Daily Strike Bulletin* (Minneapolis), July 29, 1934, available at http://www.marxists.org/archive/cannon/works/1934/mpls02.htm, accessed June 14, 2014; and In the Heart of the Beast Theatre and Friends, 40th May Day Celebration program, May 2014.

1. The first parade was originally imagined in collaboration between the Powderhorn Puppet Theatre (later HOBT), the Almond Tree Household, the New American Movement, and the Street Artist's Guild. See Colleen Sheehy, *Theatre of Wonder: Twenty-Five Years in the Heart of the Beast* (Minneapolis: University of Minnesota Press, 1999), 104.

2. In a public call for more community action volunteers, the Powderhorn Park Neighborhood Association defined the neighborhood in 2002: "We're artists, we're renters, we're workers, we're businesses, we're homeowners, we're families & children, we're community builders . . . we're old, young, single, married, Hispanic, African, Asian, Native, European, gay, straight, on a budget, doing well, writers, contractors, teachers, students, gardeners, entrepreneurs, block clubs, athletes, musicians, optimists, curmudgeons, merchants, actors, volunteers, environmentalists, anglers, backyard mechanics, computer technicians, activists, builders . . . " See In the Heart of the Beast Theatre and Friends, 28th May Day Celebration program, May 2002.

3. James P. Cannon, "The Secret of Local 574," *Daily Strike Bulletin* (Minneapolis), August 18, 1934, available at http://www.marxists.org/archive/cannon/works/1934/mpls07.htm, accessed August 14, 2014.

4. Ibid.

5. Sandy Spieler, "Wonder? Wonder!" In the Heart of the Beast Theatre and Friends, 40th May Day Celebration program, May 2014.

6. Adam Belz, "Twin Cities Economic Recovery Leads Midwest," *Star Tribune*, February 22, 2013, available at http://www.startribune.com/business/192626441.html, accessed March 30, 2013.

7. Michelle Bruch, "Minneapolis' Great Recession Rebound," *Southwest Journal*, November 7, 2013, available at http://www.southwestjournal.com/news/news/minneapo lis-great-recession-rebound, accessed August 30, 2014.

8. Alejandra Matos, "Housing Recovery in Minnesota Leaves Minorities Behind," *StarTribune*, May 9, 2013, available at http://www.startribune.com/local/206703811.html, accessed August 30, 2014.

9. *Unemployment Disparity in Minnesota, Report of the Minnesota Advisory Committee to the U.S. Commission on Civil Rights*, December 2013, available at http://www.usccr.gov/pubs/MNSAC_Unemployment_Final_3.pdf, accessed August 30, 2014; and Jonathan Rose, *Disparity Analysis: A Review of Disparities between White Minnesotans and Other Racial Groups* (St. Paul: Council on Black Minnesotans, 2013), available at http://mn.gov/cobm/pdf/COBM%20-%202013%20Research%20Report%20 on%20Disparities.pdf, accessed August 30, 2014.

10. In the Heart of the Beast Puppet and Mask Theatre, 38th May Day Celebration program, May 2013.

11. Peter Stallybrass and Allon White, *The Politics and Poetics of Transgression* (Ithaca, NY: Cornell University Press, 1986).

12. Louis Alemeyehu, "See the World," poem recited at the 2012 May Day Celebration, Powderhorn Park, Minneapolis, May 13, 2012.

13. During the 1930s, Minnesota was marked by interethnic social and religious antagonisms and conflicting interests between farmers and workers. Nevertheless, Floyd Bjornsterne Olsen, a former radical longshoreman, was elected as the first Farmer-Labor governor in 1931. See Jennifer A. Delton, *Making Minnesota Liberal: Civil Rights and the Transformation of the Democratic Party* (Minneapolis: University of Minnesota Press, 2002), 2–3.

14. Lifelong activist Nellie Stone Johnson connects Minnesota's cooperative movement to the Nonpartisan League, a collective farmers' movement committed to state socialism. See Stone Johnson, *Nellie Stone Johnson: The Life of an Activist*, ed. David Brauer (St. Paul: Ruminator, 2001), 37.

15. Five years prior to Minneapolis's adoption of a Fair Employment Practices Committee to monitor and ban employment discrimination, the Black population of Minneapolis in 1940 was only 4,646 (0.9 percent). Black migration to the state between 1940 and 1950 raised the Black population to merely 1.2 percent of 1 percent (14,022). Delton, *Making Minnesota Liberal*, 61.

16. Ibid., 45.

17. *Nellie Stone Johnson*. In contrast, the economic boom created by warfare production in California between 1950 and 1970 doubled that state's population. During this period, over 100,000 African Americans migrated to West Coast cities in search of job opportunities. When production slowed and government support was suspended, urban Blacks and Latinos were hit hardest by doubled rates of state unemployment. The extreme poverty caused by uneven reforms led many in cities like Los Angeles, Detroit, and Baltimore to revolt and oppose severe inequalities, job losses, and increased state violence. See Ruth Wilson Gilmore, *Golden Gulag: Prisons, Surplus, Crisis, and Opposition in Globalizing California* (Berkeley: University of California Press, 2007), 35–39. The new financial economy of the 1970s and 1980s normalized finance capital, professional "proprietary traders," hedge funds, high-interest lenders, legal and illegal

manipulation of corporate records, mergers, takeovers, and inflated stocks and bonds. See Edward Chancellor, *Devil Take the Hindmost: A History of Financial Speculation* (New York: Farrar, Straus and Giroux, 1999), 192–232. James Kyung-Jin Lee assesses how the new economy created massive class divisions as it produced tremendous wealth for people who barely worked and pulled social protections and fair wages away from those who did. See Lee, *Urban Triage: Race and the Fictions of Multiculturalism* (Minneapolis: University Minnesota Press, 2004). Claire Jean Kim discusses New York's adjustment to the new economy as producing a series of racialized misfortunes that became the fortunes of new immigrants. See Kim, *Bitter Fruit: The Politics of Black-Korean Conflict in New York City* (New Haven, CT: Yale University Press, 2000).

18. David L. Nass, "The Rural Experience," in *Minnesota in a Century of Change: The State and Its People since 1900*, ed. Clifford E. Clark Jr. (St. Paul: Minnesota Historical Society Press, 1989), 149–150.

19. Arnold R. Alanen, "Years of Change on the Iron Range," in *Minnesota in a Century of Change: The State and Its People since 1900*, ed. Clifford E. Clark Jr. (St. Paul: Minnesota Historical Society Press, 1989), 155–194.

20. Peter Rachleff, "Turning Points in the Labor Movement: Three Key Conflicts," in *Minnesota in a Century of Change: The State and Its People since 1900*, ed. Clifford E. Clark Jr. (St. Paul: Minnesota Historical Society Press, 1989), 195–222.

21. Wing Young Huie's photography and conversations with people on Lake Street reveal racial tensions, police profiling, poverty, homophobia, abuse, drug use, prostitution, and the like, as common themes. See Huie, *Lake Street USA* (St. Paul: Ruminator, 2001).

22. Rachcleff, "Turning Points in the Labor Movement," 215.

23. Paul Chaat Smith and Robert Allen Warrior, *Like a Hurricane: The Indian Movement from Alcatraz to Wounded Knee* (New York: New Press, 1996). Rachel Buff offers an important study of pan-Indian identity and Powwow and their relationship to AIM in Minneapolis in *Immigration and the Political Economy of Home: West Indian Brooklyn and American Indian Minneapolis 1945–1992* (Berkeley: University of California Press, 2001).

24. Lee, *Urban Triage*, xxvii.

25. Jill Quadagno, *The Color of Welfare: How Racism Undermined the War on Poverty* (New York: Oxford University Press, 1994); and Ruth Sidel, *Women and Children Last: The Plight of Poor Women in Affluent America* (New York: Penguin, 1986).

26. Neighborhood poet Roy McBride testifies to the conditions of social abandonment and community ingenuity in his poem "Another Typical Powderhorn Day": "So beautiful. / So full of dismay. / . . . In the zone. / Where we call home. / Drug cartels, the Mafia and CIA / Throw the bones. / Free enterprise zones. / The poor are with us everyday. / Poor us. Let us pray. / Another typical Powderhorn day. / The moon is full. / And so are we. / So full of hope. / So full of ennui. / Acts of kindness. / Acts of blindness. / Taste the divine. / Taste the decline. / Sink in all the way / To another typical Powderhorn day." See "Loss, Grief, Renewal," in *Solid Ground*, ed. Powderhorn Writers Festival (Spring 1999), 17.

27. *Powderhorn Community Analysis and Action Recommendations*, Publication no. 156 Community Improvement Series no. 12 (Spring 1965).

28. According to Jane Jacobs, "Parks are volatile places." She considers park spaces socially useful only inasmuch as they are used. See Jacobs, *The Life and Death of Great American Cities* (New York: Random House, 1961), 89.

29. Received knowledge in the neighborhood suggests a longer history of Native American removal and land appropriation. Although historical records attesting to this

are not readily available, popular stories in the neighborhood claim Powderhorn Park as the site of the ancient Sun Dance. See Sheehy, *Theatre of Wonder*, 49. Public records of the late nineteenth century document the land as a farm settlement and dairy.

30. The swamp was deepened and the surrounding marshland filled in 1904 to create a lake. Seasonal changes in water levels created strong smells and unsanitary conditions. The space itself refused to submit to property values. It took the park board ten years to suppress the lake's odiferous resistance.

31. Theodore Wirth, "Minneapolis Park System 1883–1944: Retrospective Glimpses of the Board of Park Commissioners of Minneapolis, Minnesota" (presentation to the Annual Meeting of the Minneapolis Board of Park Commissioners, July 1945).

32. Although pushed strongly by the city, the plan to construct a public park out of the swamp was widely opposed by private residents and developers. See John Akre, "Turning a Swamp into a Park," *The Horn* 8, no. 7 (1989): 9.

33. George Lipsitz, *The Possessive Investment in Whiteness: How People Profit from Identity Politics* (Philadelphia: Temple University Press, 1998); and Thomas Shapiro, *The Hidden Cost of Being African American: How Wealth Perpetuates Inequality* (New York: Oxford University Press, 2004).

34. David Roediger, *Working toward Whiteness: Race and the Making of the American Working Class* (New York: Verso, 1999).

35. April Schultz argues that religion, prohibition, and public schools often perpetuated ethnic tension. She has studied the social tensions of "Americanization" in this period in relationship to middle-class reformers and the association of immigrant groups with radical labor strikes in *Ethnicity on Parade: Inventing the Norwegian American through Celebration* (Amherst: University of Massachusetts Press, 1994).

36. According to Charles Rumford Walker, "Minneapolis, like nearly every American city, claims the life of the middle class as its norm." See Walker, *American City: A Rank and File History of Minneapolis* (Minneapolis: University of Minnesota Press, 1937), 228.

37. Lizabeth Cohen argues that the union movements of the 1930s were less committed to the expansion of democracy than they were to the idea of moral capitalism. She finds that this commitment continued to center the idea of private property in social life, calling on the state and unions to oversee the equitable distribution of wealth. See Cohen, *Making a New Deal: Industrial Workers in Chicago, 1919–1939* (New York: Cambridge University Press, 1990).

38. Eric Foner, *Free Soil, Free Labor, Free Men: The Ideology of the Republican Party before the Civil War* (New York: Oxford University Press, 1995).

39. Elizabeth Faue's analysis of 1930s labor in Minnesota elucidates the connection between mostly male militancy and the gendering of private life in *Community of Suffering and Struggle: Women, Men, and the Labor Movement in Minneapolis, 1915–1945* (Chapel Hill: University of North Carolina Press, 1991).

40. When organized through the family home, "not yet" freedom often balances on a symptomatic throwback to patriarchal laws of coverture.

41. See Sarah Berry's discussion of Rita Cansino's transformation into Rita Hayworth in *Screen Style* (Minneapolis: University of Minnesota Press, 2000).

42. The film billed for the New Avalon's reopening was *Fifty Roads to Town* starring Don Ameche and Ann Sothern. The basic plot follows a man who hides in order not to testify in his friend's divorce.

43. Claire Jean Kim identifies color-blind discourse as the dominant mode of racism in the post-1965 period. The production of middle-class norms through color-blind

discourse evidenced at the opening of the New Avalon celebrated newly formed ethnic solidarities by avoiding discussion of Black migrants who had moved to the neighborhood as early as the 1920s. Color-blind inclusion masked how the development of the park itself disproportionately affected one of the three largest Black communities in Minneapolis, the one located in the Powderhorn Park neighborhood. Powderhorn also shares a fluid boundary with the Phillips neighborhood. Phillips is popularly seen as home to the largest urban Indian community in Minnesota. See *Powderhorn Community Analysis and Action Recommendations*, 12.

44. In the Heart of the Beast Theatre and Friends, 33rd May Day Celebration program, May 2007, 16.

45. *Powderhorn Community Analysis and Action Recommendations*, 14.

46. "Avalon Facts," *The Horn* 7, no. 10 (1988): 2. Kevin Mumford's analysis of progressive-era vice districts and reform movements highlights the profoundly racialized geography of urban sex zones. Historically, the breakup of centralized sex districts often led to the dispersal of commercialized sex, alcohol and drug use, and gambling to less regulated, largely African American neighborhoods, where residents did not control the use value of their area. See Mumford, *Interzones: Black/White Sex Districts in Chicago and New York in the Early Twentieth Century* (New York: Columbia University Press, 1997).

47. Samuel R. Delany argues that the casual contacts and non-normative forms of social exchange in vice districts can be instrumental for breaking down divisions in a stratified society. See Delaney, *Times Square Red, Times Square Blue* (New York: New York University Press, 1999).

48. This position was honored by the Minneapolis City Council, which had hired Andrea Dworkin and Catherine MacKinnon to write an amendment to the city's Civil Rights Ordinance that claimed porn to be a form of sex discrimination and a violation of civil rights. See *The Horn* 1, no. 3 (1982): 3.

49. Ibid., 1.

50. Ibid. The way in which these arguments hinged on presenting queerness as external to the neighborhood engages in a middle-class moral fantasy that erases the history of gays, lesbians, and queers from it. In March 1984, the movement organized a Neighborhood Pornography Task Force to educate the public about the violence of porn and encourage enforcement of restrictions on the industry and the development of "legitimate" businesses. Founders of the task force drew on materials from a course taught by Catherine MacKinnon and Andrea Dworkin at the University of Minnesota and pointed to the centrality of the two feminists regarding local policy.

51. It is hard to determine the size and history of the queer population of this specific neighborhood. Two events point to an apparent gay and lesbian population since the early 1980s. On November 20, 1980, the date of Reagan's election to the White House, Karen Clark, a Powderhorn resident who had campaigned as a radical lesbian feminist socialist, was elected state representative. In 1988 the Twin Cities Annual Gay and Lesbian Pride parade began to be held in Powderhorn Park. From 1977 to 1985 it had been held in Loring Park. Records that may have existed from the years 1986 and 1987 were not available in the Minnesota Historical Society's collection, where this information was gathered.

52. *The Horn* 4, no. 4 (1985): 2.

53. Roderick Ferguson, *Aberrations in Black* (Minneapolis: University of Minnesota Press, 2004).

54. Sheehy, *Theatre of Wonder*, 25.

55. Jack Dempsey, "Reading the Revels: The Riddle of May Day in New English Canaan," *Early American Literature* 34, no. 3 (1999): 283–312; and Raven Grimassi, *Beltane: Springtime Rituals, Lore and Celebration* (St. Paul: Llewellyn, 2001).

56. "Merrymount" was the spelling that the Plymouth colonists adopted because it highlighted the revelry at the site. Richard Slotkin argues that "Marry-mount" was likely closer to Morton's intention for the name because Merry Mount was to be a metaphorical and literal site of marriage between the old and the new world, Native Americans and Europeans. "Mary-mount" connected the pagan ritual to the Christian virgin mother, and "Mare-mount" may have called out the image of sodomy that, according to Slotkin, caused anxiety in Morton's New England neighbors. See Richard Slotkin, *Regeneration through Violence* (Norman: University of Oklahoma Press, 1973).

57. Ibid., 61.

58. William Bradford, *Of Plymouth Plantation 1620–1647* (New York: Modern Library, 1981).

Morton gained prominence at Merry Mount by instigating insurrection against a deputy who was left in charge at Mount Wollaston. Promising indentured servants positions of social equality on the plantation, he created a system that contradicted the master-servant relations that were at the core of much of Massachusetts's social structure. For more on Merry Mount, see Michael Zuckerman, "Pilgrims in the Wilderness: Community, Modernity, and the Maypole at Merry Mount," *New England Quarterly* 50, no. 2 (1977): 255–277; Jack Dempsey, ed., *New English Canaan by Thomas Morton of "Merrymount"* (Scituate, MA: Digital Scanning, 2000); Edmund S. Morgan, "The Puritans and Sex," *New England Quarterly* 15, no. 4 (1943): 591–607; Neal Salisbury, *Manitou and Providence: Indians, Europeans, and the Making of New England, 1500–1643* (New York: Oxford University Press); Alden T. Vaughan, *The Puritan Tradition in America 1620–1730* (Lebanon, NH: University Press of New England, 1997); and John D'Emilio and Estelle Freedman, *Intimate Matters: A History of Sexuality in America* (New York: Harper and Row, 1988).

59. Philip Deloria, *Playing Indian* (New Haven, CT: Yale University Press, 1998), 13–14.

60. Quoted in ibid., 14.

61. Rufus Home, "The Story of Tammany," *Harper's Magazine* (April 1872); Edwin Patrick Kilroe, *Saint Tammany and the Origin of the Tammany or Columbian Order in the City of New York* (Ph.D. diss., Columbia University, 1923); and Francis Von A. Cabeen, "The Society of the Sons of Saint Tammany of Philadelphia," *Pennsylvania Magazine of History and Biography* 26, no. 3 (1902), 335–347.

62. David Noble, *The End of American History* (Minneapolis: University of Minnesota Press, 1985).

63. "May Day, U.S. Way" (Burlington, WI: Bulletin Publishing, 1954).

64. Ibid., 2.

65. Ibid., 6.

66. Ibid., 14.

67. "A Strike, a Boycott, a Holiday, a Refusal: May Day with Heart," *CounterPunch*, April 29–30, 2006.

68. Martin Duberman, *Haymarket: A Novel* (New York: Seven Stories, 2003).

69. Philip Sheldon Foner, *May Day: A Short History of the International Workers' Holiday, 1886–1986* (New York: International, 1986); James Green, *Death in the Haymarket: A Story of Chicago, The First Labor Movement and the Bombing That Divided*

America (New York: Pantheon, 2006); and David Roediger and Franklin Rosemont, *Haymarket Scrapbook* (Chicago: C. H. Kerr, 1986).

70. William Adelman, *Haymarket Revisited: A Tour Guide of Labor History Sites and Ethnic Neighborhoods Associated with the Haymarket Affair* (Chicago: Illinois Labor History Society, 1976).

71. Michael Denning, *The Cultural Front* (New York: Verso, 1997), 55.

72. Ibid., xvii.

73. Roderick Ferguson, "Nightmares of the Heteronormative: *Go Tell it on the Mountain* versus *An American Dilemma*," *Cultural Values* 4, no. 4 (2000): 419–444, 422.

74. Shelley Streeby tracks a discourse around Haymarket memories that ties its continuing struggles to end "slavery" from the Civil War to the Mexican Revolution. See Streeby, "Labor, Memory, and the Boundaries of Print Culture: From Haymarket to the Mexican Revolution," *American Literary History* 19, no. 2 (2007): 406–433.

75. Martin Luther King Jr., "Beyond Vietnam: A Time to Break Silence" (speech delivered at the Riverside Church, New York, April 4, 1967).

76. 32nd May Day Celebration program, May 2006, 6.

77. The theater sponsored water drives and rebuilding efforts. Clyde Woods discusses the long history of southern apartheid, Bourbon rule, and social abandonment in the Mississippi River Delta. While the benevolent efforts by volunteers certainly stemmed from concern and generous efforts to help, Woods highlights the importance of centering Black communities in decision making so that rebuilding enables reform of the social hierarchies and inequalities in the South. The racial dynamics of the state of emergency that many saw as temporary and environmental Woods reveals as centuries old and social. See Woods, *Development Arrested: From the Plantation Era to the Katrina Crises in the Mississippi Delta* (New York: Verso, 1998).

78. Material costs for puppets were only $3,000 out of a total event budget of $126,435 for 2014. See 40th May Day Celebration program, May 2014, 14.

79. *May Day Parade and Festival*, directed by Sandy Spieler for In the Heart of the Beast Puppet and Mask Theatre (Minneapolis: Blue Mood Productions, 1999).

80. Ibid. As Tougas discusses the materials used for the May Day production, he holds a ragged piece of cloth, pauses, and escapes the culturally prescribed terms of documentary interviewing. During the interview, he is distracted, looking deeply toward the potential uses of a piece of cloth. He holds it to the camera and explains the donation of really nice muslin.

81. Raymond Williams, *Marxism and Literature* (Oxford: Oxford University Press, 1977), 116.

82. Ibid.

83. Quoted in John Bell, *Puppets, Masks, and Performing Objects* (Cambridge, MA: MIT Press, 2001).

84. David Graeber, *Fragments of an Anarchist Anthropology* (Chicago: Prickly Paradigm, 2004), 84.

85. HOBT founder David O'Fallon worked with Sam Schumann's Bread and Puppet Theater before cofounding the Powderhorn Puppet theater in the basement of Walker Methodist Church, a central location for many of Powderhorn's activist traditions. The church has been a meeting place for the community to work for "peace, fight for justice, speak against racism, [and] defend the poor." It has hosted readings by the Powderhorn Writer's Festival and planning sessions for community activists and artists; also, it has housed Salvadoran refugees. In its early years, the Powderhorn Puppet Theatre worked closely with At the Foot of the Mountain, a theater that Jill Dolan documents as "one

of the oldest American cultural feminist theatre ensembles." See Dolan, *The Feminist Spectator as Critic* (Ann Arbor: University of Michigan Research Press, 1988), 8. Other theaters and artist organizations that collaborate with HOBT include the Almond Tree Household, The New American Movement, the Mixed Blood Theater, Alive and Truckin' Theatre, Orréa Mime Troupe, Circle of the Witch, the Palace, The Illusion Theater, The Street Artists Guild, and, more recently, Intermedia Arts and CreArte. The artistic gene-alogy that HOBT inherits from Bread and Puppet is also various. David Bell explains: "Our parades reflect those we've seen, studied or been part of: the massive, semi-chaotic Carnival parades of Basel, Switzerland; the intimate street buffoonery of the Catalan theater group Els Comediants; the straightforward determination of twentieth-century political street demonstrations; the boisterous music of New Orleans street bands; the turbulent serenity of Catholic processions of saints and relics; the pots-and-pans 'rough music' of street parades going back to the Middle Ages; the dances of lion and dragon puppets in Chinese New Year street celebrations; the modernist parades designed by Russian revolutionary artists in the 1920s; and the home-made color of patriotic sum-mer parades in Vermont villages and cities." See Bell, "Louder Than Traffic: Bread and Puppet Parades," in *Radical Street Performance: An International Anthology*, ed. Jan Cohen-Cruz (London: Routledge, 1998), 272.

86. Puppet arrests were covered in many independent news sites that are no longer active. David Graeber documents police actions against puppetry in "On the Phenomenology of Giant Puppets," *Autonomous University*, available at http://autono mousuniversity.org/sites/default/files/Graeber_puppets.pdf, accessed March 14, 2013.

87. Brendan Koermer, "Can Miami Ban Giant Puppets?" *Slate*, November 12, 2003, available at http://www.slate.com/articles/news_and_politics/explainer/2003/11/can_miami_really_ban_giant_puppets.html, accessed August 10, 2014.

88. Ella Shohat and Robert Stamm argue about the aesthetics of garbage, "As those whose history has been destroyed and misrepresented, as those whose very history has been dispersed and diasporized rather than lovingly memorialized and as those whose history has often been told, danced and sung rather than written, oppressed people have been obliged to recreate history out of scraps and remnants and debris." See Shohat and Stamm, "Narrativizing Visual Culture: Towards a Polycentric Aesthetics," in *The Visual Culture Reader*, 2nd ed., ed. Nicholas Mirzoeff (London: Routledge, 1998), 52.

89. "Powderhorn Park Neighborhood," *Minnesota Compass*, available at http://www.mncompass.org/profiles/neighborhoods/minneapolis/powderhorn-park, accessed June 14, 2014.

90. Wilder Research Group, "Speaking for Themselves: A Survey of Hispanic, Hmong, Russian, and Somali Immigrants in Minneapolis–Saint Paul," November 2000, available at http://www.wilder.org/Wilder-Research/Publications/Studies/Speaking%20for%20Themselves/Speaking%20for%20Themselves%20-%20A%20Survey%20of%20Hispanic,%20Hmong,%20Russian,%20and%20Somali%20Immigrants%20in%20Minneapolis-Saint%20Paul.pdf, accessed August 20, 2007; and Arjun Appaduarai, *Fear of Small Numbers: An Essay on the Geography of Anger* (Durham, NC: Duke University Press, 2006).

91. Sara Schweid, "Rally Stresses Immigrants' Value," *Minnesota Daily*, May 2, 2006.

92. 40th May Day Celebration program, May 2014, 17.

93. One of the methods that allows for shared resources is the use of postconsumer waste as primary materials for creating puppets. Most of the materials used in the event are recycled from homes or donated by local businesses.

94. 28th May Day Celebration program, May 2002, 6.

95. The Endangered Species Act requires that U.S. shrimp fishermen and all importers use turtle exclusion devises to protect sea turtles. When the World Trade Organization voted against turtle protection measures in 1998, protestors were rightly outraged by the organization's capacity to dismantle any legal and environmental gains attained politically through appeals to discrete governments. The turtle became a central symbol for the ways that neoliberalism values the short-term gains of economic profits over the long-range aspirations of global habitability.

96. James Scott, *Domination and the Arts of Resistance: Hidden Transcripts* (New Haven, CT: Yale University Press, 1990).

97. Avery Gordon, "The Prisoner's Curse," in *Toward a Sociology of the Trace*, ed. Herman Grey and Macaren Gomez-Barris (Minneapolis: University of Minnesota Press, 2010), 17–56.

98. 41st May Day Celebration Program (May 2015), 3.

Index

Heidi Hoechst is an activist, scholar, and educator working in the United States labor movement.